Race, Space, and Riots in Chicago, New York, and Los Angeles

Race, Space, and Riots
in Chicago, New York, and Los Angeles

Janet L. Abu-Lughod

OXFORD
UNIVERSITY PRESS

2007

OXFORD
UNIVERSITY PRESS

Oxford University Press, Inc., publishes works that further
Oxford University's objective of excellence
in research, scholarship, and education.

Oxford   New York
Auckland   Cape Town   Dar es Salaam   Hong Kong   Karachi
Kuala Lumpur   Madrid   Melbourne   Mexico City   Nairobi
New Delhi   Shanghai   Taipei   Toronto

With offices in
Argentina   Austria   Brazil   Chile   Czech Republic   France   Greece
Guatemala   Hungary   Italy   Japan   Poland   Portugal   Singapore
South Korea   Switzerland   Thailand   Turkey   Ukraine   Vietnam

Copyright © 2007 by Oxford University Press, Inc.

Published by Oxford University Press, Inc.
198 Madison Avenue, New York, New York 10016

www.oup.com

Oxford is a registered trademark of Oxford University Press

Library of Congress Cataloging-in-Publication Data
Abu-Lughod, Janet L.
Race, space, and riots in Chicago, New York, and Los Angeles /
by Janet L. Abu-Lughod.
     p.   cm.
Includes bibliographical references and index.
ISBN 978-0-19-532875-2
1. Race riots—United States—History—20th century.   2. African Americans—
Social conditions—20th century.   3. United States—Race relations.   I. Title.
HV6477.A38 2007
305.896′073—dc22   2006102002

9 8 7 6 5 4 3 2 1

Printed in the United States of America
on acid-free paper

Remembering

my mother's tolerance for difference;

my husband's commitment to social justice

*A*ny researcher who has spent long years writing a book is always ambivalent when it is done: happy to see it published but disappointed that its results must be engraved in stone (now digitized)—just as the processes of research and writing have led to a new level of understanding. In an ideal world, perhaps attainable in hyperspace, writers could revise continuously, integrating their new insights and interpretations, asking and answering new questions, in endless iterations and revisions. But that utopia would actually be a nightmare for both writers and readers.

Instead, this book revisits some of the historical questions I posed in my too lengthy and ambitious comparative study of New York, Chicago, and Los Angeles as global cities within four hundred years of America's evolving economic, political, spatial, and demographic patterns and the role of the U. S. in the world system. This book is a sequel. It explores the "race question" in greater detail by comparing the types of major race riots each city experienced in the twentieth century, placing these events in the context of their histories but also incorporating insights that have continued to mature since the first book appeared in 1999.

In this book I ask in more systematic fashion why the racial and ethnic relations in the three cities have been so different—despite being based in the shared racist premises of American society—and to what extent these differences can be explained by the historical, geographic/spatial, and political characteristics of the cities themselves. There are many fruitful ways these questions might be approached, and I encourage other scholars to pursue them. My strategy, however, has been to focus on race riots as "disasters" (following the example of Kai Erickson), that is, as moments in historical time when the veneers of civility and the illusions of continuity are shattered, whether from natural or human social causes (or from both, as in New Orleans). Such events often lay bare fissures in the taken-for-granted social structure, thus revealing agonizing conflicts and pain. Eventually, some healing takes place, as the skin grows back over the wounds, albeit leaving scars over a changed structure. For Americans, the World Trade Center disaster is the most dramatic recent case of human origin, in response to which we are witnessing only the first stages of aftershock and widening repercussions.

Disasters, by their nature, take place in "abnormal time," the experience bracketed in memory by sudden beginnings and more drawn-out endings. Race riots clearly take place in "abnormal" time. But it would be a terrible mistake to either overinterpret their violence as symptoms of unbridgeable difference or to dismiss them as "uncaused" emotional responses.

In this book I use these events as ways to understand more deeply what Gunnar Myrdal and his associates called an "American dilemma." Although I have tried to reconstruct the order of events and to describe how the levels of violence developed over time and spread in space, I have also sought to avoid sensationalism, the almost hysterical approach that journalistic accounts exploit to dramatize race riots as "crimes." I have intentionally not included photographs.

Rather, I am particularly interested in tracing the various ways that the actors engaged in or observing these struggles interpret them, and particularly how the "forces of law and order" (the police and key municipal officials) respond to the events. In short, my approach views riots as a revealing instance of "social structure in action," when the behaviors of each of the parties to the conflict not only act, react, and adjust to the situational crisis itself but are also guided by local precedents for handling them.

A word of caution is needed. My analysis depends largely on data drawn from existing case studies of the six major riots selected for closer study. This has inevitably resulted in a certain unevenness of treatment. The richest sources deal with the 1919 Chicago riot and with the 1965 and 1992 Los Angeles riots. At least two good studies exist that describe the New York riots of 1935 and 1943, but a definitive study of the 1964 New York riot has yet to be written. Lacking that, my analysis of New York's political system and its demographic changes has benefited from the twenty years I have spent living in and studying that city since 1987. To my despair, no synthetic account of the Chicago riot of 1968 yet exists, and I have therefore had to construct one from archival data and public reports. Fortunately, these sources could be supplemented by my 25 years of living in and studying Chicago and by my own observations during the riot itself.

This book, defective as it may be, is the first to compare major riots in the three cities. I hope that it will encourage others to flesh out the missing accounts and to revise and correct the errors for which I must take full responsibility.

Acknowledgments

Obviously, in the course of the decades in which I have been trying to understand cities and more specifically to research and write this book, I have accumulated too many debts to teachers, fellow scholars, friends and students (not mutually exclusive), to critical and constructive readers, to libraries, granting institutions, and supportive universities to even begin to enumerate them. They know who they are, and I bow to acknowledge them. However, I want particularly to single out the anonymous reviewers for the Press who called my attention to additional sources, to Michael J. Rosenfeld, Amanda Seligman, and Michael Flamm who read individual chapters and/or provided useful primary documents, and to Jeffrey Morenoff, Willlam Bowen, and Donna Genzmer for making available original computer-generated maps.

My chief debts, however, are to the authors of books and articles I have absorbed and pondered ever since, as a high school student growing up in Newark, New Jersey, I wrote my senior thesis on the "Negro Novel" more than sixty years ago. That was my first attempt to make sense out of what I call the "American disease" of racial oppression, against which I have marched and protested, although this is the first time I dare to add my published voice to the vast dialogue on race relations in the United States. Truly, we all stand on the shoulders of giants: many of their names can be found hidden in the endnotes.

There is, however, my special debt to the Harry Frank Guggenheim Foundation, which, even as my book on *New York, Chicago, Los Angeles: America's Global Cities* was on its long road to publication at the University of Minnesota Press, awarded me a research grant in 1997–98 to begin a project tentatively titled "Race/Ethnicity, Space, and Political Culture: A Comparative Study of Collective Violence in New York, Chicago, and Los Angeles." It is with embarrassment that I realize that a decade has elapsed since then, but I hope they will accept this belated fruit from the seed they helped to plant.

At Oxford University Press, I have been blessed. I am grateful to editor James Cook for shepherding the manuscript through the complex intellectual, technical, and bureaucratic processes that publishing now entails, but even more, for his patience and, indeed, indulgence, as he allayed my anxieties and reassured me that publication schedules would be met. Copy editor Martha Ramsey called my attention to inconsistencies I needed to fix or missing information I needed to provide. But I am most indebted to production editor Robert Milks whose contributions are evident at every stage; it was his incredibly dedicated hands and mind that literally guided the black box details of converting computer files into an actual book.

I am awed by their hard work and their efforts to attain perfection. The residual errors are all my own.

Contents

Illustrations

Race, Space, and Riots in Chicago, New York, and Los Angeles

An Overview of Race Riots in Chicago, New York, and Los Angeles

Almost half a century has now elapsed since the 1960s when African American neighborhoods in more than 300 cities experienced civil disorders or ghetto uprisings.[1] Most of these were relatively minor and short-lived, but a number of them, particularly in America's largest northern cities, were far more serious, lasting days, resulting in hundreds of injuries and dozens of deaths, and involving massive destruction and looting. These rebellions were ruthlessly suppressed by local police forces, often assisted by military reinforcements.

Many white Americans reacted with shock and fear to this "inexplicable" (to them) expression of pent-up anger. And since much of the destruction took place within predominantly black segregated neighborhoods, they asked *not why African Americans were confined to "ghettos" but why "they" were burning down their own communities.* In their fear, many whites approved the promise of protection by agents of their governments, local, state, and federal (presumed to maintain a monopoly over legitimate force), expecting them to put down what they interpreted as "outlaw" behavior, whether they were called riots, insurrections, rebellions, or revolts. Some, in their more rational moments, questioned why these outbursts were happening, especially when progress on civil rights seemed finally to be occurring.

Toward the end of July 1967, after that month's particularly bloody riots in Newark and Detroit (but only a few years into what would turn out to be a decade-long series of uprisings), President Lyndon Johnson addressed the nation, exhorting it to

> attack...the conditions that breed despair and violence...ignorance, discrimination, slums, poverty, disease, not enough jobs...not because we are frightened by conflict, but because we are fired by conscience.... [T]here is simply no other way to achieve a decent and orderly society in America.

He followed this by announcing the appointment of a National Advisory Commission on Civil Disorders, to be headed by such high-profile politicians as the governor of Illinois, Otto Kerner, as chair, and John Lindsay, the mayor of New York, as vice chair, who were to lead an 11-person commission of inquiry. The commission, in turn, was to be supported by advisory panels on various topics and assisted by a professional staff that, at its peak, included some seventy researchers.

Seven months later (on March 1, 1968), the commission released the complete text of its report (more than 600 pages in length, arranged in 17 chapters). It came to be known as the Kerner Report.[2] Hailed as a definitive inquiry into America's troubled race relations, the report was characterized by a single sentence on the opening page that was to become its most widely quoted passage, despite the historical amnesia it revealed: "This is our basic conclusion: *Our nation is moving toward two societies, one black, one white—separate and unequal.*"[3] Given such tunnel vision, it should not be surprising that the inquiry and its recommendations yielded so few new insights. The tunnel vision was also implicit in the narrow mandate given to the commission. It was charged with answering three questions. What happened (in the recent riots)? Why did "it" happen? And what can be done to prevent "it" from happening again?

The report not only failed to answer the first two questions coherently but came out with recommendations that not only recycled earlier "solutions" but called for an ambitious expansion of the existing programs in Johnson's "War on Poverty," at a cost estimated so high that it was unlikely to be funded, especially in competition with the war in Vietnam.

The first three chapters were intended to answer Johnson's first question: "What happened?"[4] Despite their bulk (almost one-third of the total volume) and apparent "scientific method," the main analysis was focused on narrating

23 case studies of minor as well as major outbreaks of violence that occurred in the summer of 1967, accompanied by background data and charts plotting the daily levels of activity. More detailed "profiles" were constructed for 10 of them. Beyond classifying them by their degree of violence, the authors concluded, not surprisingly, that generalizations were difficult to come by—to say the least, a disappointing result.

The authors' decision to confine their study only to civil disorders occurring in the summer of 1967 meant that the report basically ignored serious riots in America's three largest cities. The authors did not address the uprisings in 1964 and 1965 in New York and Los Angeles that preceded the summer of 1967 and, naturally, could not include the deadly Chicago riot of 1968, which took place only one month after their document was submitted and published. (The third chapter in this section, only two pages in length, was appended by the commission itself and reported that they had found no evidence of a conspiracy.)

The next five chapters addressed the second question: "Why did it happen?" After acknowledging the longstanding but evolving history of strife-torn black-white relations, the authors diagnosed the same underlying causes of black disaffection that Johnson had already enumerated in his address to the nation, adding to them "culture," crime, merchant exploitation, and lack of political representation. They identified and ranked African Americans' expressed grievances on specific matters while insufficiently recognizing that powerlessness and frustrated alienation from the system of white dominance underlay all of them.

The final eight chapters recommended solutions. Chapters 10–15 focused narrowly on mechanics: ways to improve local community responses to civil unrest and police–community relations; to develop better techniques to control crowds and handle mass arrests; to devise better ways to compensate owners for riot losses; and finally, to encourage better and less sensational media coverage. Chapter 16 considered three alternative policy choices for the future: (1) continuing present policies, which the authors predicted would be likely lead to greater polarization and riots; (2) vastly expanding expenditures for and the efficacy of "enrichment" programs "to make a dramatic, visible impact on life in the urban Negro ghetto"—a task they judged so enormous in scope that it probably could not be achieved in time to prevent further riots *without much fuller incorporation of Negroes into power, which might risk even greater separation of the races*;[5] and (3) the authors' preferred alternative: fuller integration of Negroes in housing, education, and jobs, accompanied by "enrichment" programs designed to reduce existing inequalities between the races.

The lengthy final chapter singled out unemployment and underemployment as items of highest priority, noting that these were "among the most persistent and serious grievances of our disadvantaged minorities" and that "the pervasive effect of these conditions...is inextricably linked to the problem of civil disorder."[6] They proposed a comprehensive national manpower policy to create one million new jobs for minorities in the public sector over the next three years and an equal number in the private sector, although what it would cost and who would pay for it remained unspecified. Ignoring the ongoing disinvestments in cities and their growing fiscal difficulties, the authors made the logical but unrealistic observation that

> in the public sector a substantial number of such jobs can be pro-
> vided quickly, *particularly by government at the local level,* where there
> are vast unmet needs in education, health, recreation, public safety, sanita-
> tion, and other municipal services.... Creation of jobs for the hard-
> core unemployed will require substantial payments to both public and
> private employers to offset the extra costs of supportive services and
> training.[7]

Furthermore, to motivate recruitment, these jobs must not be "dead-end" but must offer opportunities for advancement along "a clearly defined 'job ladder' with step increases in both pay and responsibility." Needless to add, "arbitrary barriers to employment and promotion must be eliminated."[8]

A second priority was to substantially expand and improve public educa-tional opportunities for minority students to prepare them for jobs, not only by encouraging school desegregation but by substantially increasing federal funding to improve ghetto schools, modernize facilities, reduce overcrowding, reform curricula, and recruit more skilled and motivated teachers. The wish list extended from early preschool to college tuition supports, and from charter schools to year-round remedial enrollment.[9]

Welfare and housing were the final foci of the report's recommendations, and these would have not only been the costliest but the ones least likely to be adopted and funded. Recognizing the inequities in and the cumbersome task of administering the welfare system, the commission not only recommended mod-est reforms but, in a breathtaking leap, seemed to embrace a "National System of Income Supplementation" to guarantee every American a "minimum standard of decent living," regardless of any rules of eligibility except need. The authors admitted that "such a broad system ... would involve substantially greater federal expenditures than anything now contemplated." Equally unrealistic were their recommendations to "solve" the problems of slum housing, concentrated in center-city ghettos, by replacing and/or adding some 600,000 low- and moderate-income housing units "next year, and 6 million units over the next five years" (preferably enforcing open occupancy rules and building public housing in scattered sites outside the segregated ghettos, etc.).

The estimated costs of such programs were not only astronomical and unrealistic but also ill adapted to either the ideological or fiscal constraints imposed by weak and unsympathetic local governments and by a Congress struggling to fund the increasingly unpopular war in Vietnam. As Johnson reflected in his post-presidential memoir, "I will never understand how the commission expected me to get...Congress to appropriate an additional $30 billion for the same programs that it was demanding I cut by $6 billion. This would have required a miracle."[10]

The psychologist Kenneth Clark, testifying in the early stages of the commission's hearings, had warned members of this disjuncture between the ambitious recommendations of blue-ribbon commissions of inquiry and the money and the political commitment to change realities on the ground. He sardonically described his experiences of reading earlier riot reports (on Chicago in 1919, Harlem in 1935, and Watts in 1965), as "a kind of Alice in Wonderland—with the same moving picture re-shown over and over again, the same analysis, the same recommendations, and the same inaction."[11] Unhappily, the outcome was as Clark feared. Like many previous recommendations for reform, these, too, would go unfunded until concern receded, along with the violence, lapsing into (not so benign) neglect until the problem resurfaced a generation later.

POST-MORTEMS

Between 1967 and the beginning of the 1970s, the number of ghetto uprisings doubled, as conditions continued to deteriorate. In their wake, literally hundreds of post-mortem studies were produced and dozens of critiques of the Kerner Report appeared, alleging, *inter alia,* that findings had been censored and dissident views of more radical staff members suppressed. These joined the large body of literature by scholars who had already produced important works dealing with the long history of contentious race relations and numerous case studies of preceding riots.

Is there something more to be said? Yes. At least, this is my reason for writing this book that compares six major race riots that took place in the three largest American metropolitan centers over the course of the twentieth century. In this book I attempt a methodological approach that differs from previous riot studies, asks somewhat different questions of the data, and seeks a more nuanced understanding of variations in the spatial and historical contexts of race conflicts and their possible resolutions. By concentrating in detail on only six major race-related riots/revolts, which represent distinctive types and took place within different spatially organized patterns of segregation, I hope to achieve three ends:,

First, I hope to illustrate the changing conditions of urban race relations over time, as these have been affected by internal and international patterns of migration, wars and wartime production demands for labor, legal changes governing housing segregation, and the civil rights movement.

Second, I hope to explain variations in riots in the three largest metropolitan regions by examining differences in their demographic compositions, the spatial distributions of racial and ethnic groups within each city, and the degree and patterns of racial segregation in their unique physical settings.[12]

Third, I hope to demonstrate differences in the ways relevant city government regimes have responded to sequential outbreaks—ways that reflect the distinctive power structures of each city and the prior "social learning" relevant to race relations that evolved in each place.

IN DEFENSE OF THE METHOD OF CONTROLLED COMPARISONS

How do these methods and aims differ from the large body of existing studies on race riots? Prior investigations into racially charged collective violence have been either large-scale, often quantitative, studies of a variety of specific "eruptions" that occurred in numerous places at crucial moments in time or fine-grained case studies of single explosive events.

Large-scale quantified comparisons, although valuable for generating causal hypotheses, cannot take into account the historic antecedents and evolved spatial patterns of individual cities and thus offer too little context for understanding individual events. They also offer few prescriptions for policies that might yield greater urban peace. Even the techniques of event history that have recently been applied specifically to urban race riots of the twentieth century, while specifying more explicit and thus relevant hypotheses, cannot be tested in detail without greater contextual information.[13]

Unlike these positivist efforts to isolate and quantify the causes (or rather, the correlates) of race riots, my goal is neither to identify multiple causes nor to measure their relative importance. I assume that these underlying "causes" of racial strife are fairly universal and known, although their exact manifestations have varied by region and period. Nor am I interested in graphing the high and low cycles of race-related explosions, although such variations need to be explained, and indeed provide the historical context for understanding specific riots.

On the other hand, studies that focus on individual riots tend to be so thick with description that they fall short on analysis or, what is worse, tempt one to gloss uncritically from the single case to unspecified others. Their authors run the risk of becoming so immersed in the momentary discrete occurrence that they slight the changing historical and spatial contexts in which successive riots occur. These detailed case studies are, of course, indispensable because they not only offer "raw material" for subsequent generalizing analysis but also capture temporal and spatial sequences that help us unravel underlying processes. This literature is often extremely rich. However, its focused agenda often forces authors to bracket the "events," extracting them from historical developments and continuities in the cities where they occur. (The best of them are distinguished by careful attention to these matters.)[14]

Detailed middle-range studies (what might be called controlled comparisons) are conspicuously absent from the literature on race riots. This book seeks to fill that void. Aiming between too many cases and too few, it focuses selectively on a limited set of comparative cases over time, benefiting from both the hypotheses suggested in the large-scale comparisons and the details available in the individual case studies. This strategy, made possible by my prior comparative histories of New York, Chicago, and Los Angeles, opens the possibility of asking different questions in new ways.[15]

My aim, as a historically grounded student of cities, is to tease out the temporal and spatial configurations or forms that particular race riots have taken at particular times and in specific places, and to account for differences in the ways their local governments have characteristically dealt with them. To do this, I look closely at how these cities were formed and grew, how and by whom they were populated, the systems of class and caste that were shaped by their economic base and its transformation over time, and, most important, the distinctive local political cultures in each city, produced over time not only by their institutional arrangements of governance but by their past experiences in dealing with racial and ethnic tensions.

Any detailed comparison of six race riots in three cities between 1919 and 1992, ambitious as it is, cannot fully explain their occurrence, nor can it offer easy prescriptions for avoiding their recurrence. My more modest goal is to provide a deeper understanding of racial/ethnic relations in contemporary American cities and, through attention to economic, political, and spatial processes of exclusion and marginalization of African Americans, to suggest some paths to achieving greater empowerment, progress, and peace for the excluded and the most vulnerable. By paying particular attention to the historic context within which such "explosions" have occurred and the increasing importance of globally generated factors in the economies and demographics of major American cities in recent times, I hope with this study to contribute to an eventual amelioration of the persisting racial tensions that, despite changes in their manifestations, have been a blot on American democratic ideals from the start.

Perhaps an analysis of what went "wrong" or "right" in the past may help to avert future policy failures and destructive outbursts of violence that seem to recur as the generation that experienced them gives way to one for whom memories are dim or only secondhand and distorted. After a period of relative quiet, America may now be on the verge of a new generational cycle.[16] This may be an opportune time to reevaluate past explosions. Before proceeding, however, we need to better define the terms and assumptions central to our analysis.

DEFINING RACE AND RIOTS

The issue of race remains at the center of the social structure and latent conscience of the United States. Many white Americans assuage or suppress their guilt about the institution of slavery and its enduring effects, arguing that they and their ancestors were not directly responsible, since they arrived after the Civil War and the passage of the Fourteenth Amendment.[17] This seems an inadequate excuse, because even if today's racially privileged citizens were not directly responsible for the root causes of racial inequalities, they have often participated in perpetuating the disabilities that African Americans have suffered as a group and, at the minimum, still benefit from the advantages they enjoy as a favored unmarked group of alleged "whites."

Whether or not one participated in the "original sins" of conquest and slavery, one cannot escape their consequences. The subjugation and virtual elimination of the indigenous population that occupied the land before Europeans arrived, and the enslaving of a second people forcibly imported from Africa to do the new country's dirty work, remain as much a heritage of American culture as the democracy it has sought to nurture. It should, therefore, not be surprising to find that lingering animosities between whites and blacks especially have created ongoing tensions in the American system, subject to periodic explosions that reveal fissures and conflicts that seem to intensify polarization and defy healing. That is not to deny that the moving frontier resolves some issues while sparking others, or that tensions may temporarily subside when general prosperity mutes competition for resources.

Social science literature has reflected the cycles of real-world racial tensions and violence, at times concentrating on the issue of what was originally called race relations and at other times according it something like benign neglect. Often, preoccupation with race moves inversely with concerns over immigration (dubbed ethnicity), with both being affected not only by changing demographic ratios but also by perceptions of the relative degrees of activism/victimization. The mass media tend to follow a similar pattern of alternating attention and neglect, rousing themselves during the widespread ghetto rebellions of the 1960s and 1990s and lapsing into lethargy in the apparent lull between storms.

I admit that I have great difficulty not putting the term *race* between quotation marks. There are, of course, no unambiguous genetic markers that could distinguish between "whites" and "blacks" in populations that have coexisted for centuries, divided for a long time by formal legal status but not by human genetic exchanges.[18] It is also true that, in the variegated and fragmented social scene of "hyphenated" Americans, many immigrant groups from Europe, such as the Irish, Jews, and Italians, were originally defined as belonging to "inferior races," only to eventually be reclassified in ways that broke through the caste-like lines separating whites from everyone else. Long excluded immigrants from Asia—including Japanese, Chinese, Koreans, and darker peoples from the Indian subcontinent[19]—have only recently been able to translate their social capital into the "whiteness" side of the divide. And, of course, immigrants from the Spanish-speaking Americas, bewildered by the taken-for-granted racial categories of the United States, have largely ignored the census choices by routinely identifying themselves as "other." It is still too early to predict whether the recent migrants from Mexico, against whom there has been race-like hostility, will follow the trajectory of assimilation in the way that rejected European immigrants did, becoming "white."[20]

It is thus patently true that race is socially constructed[21] and its boundaries fluid in almost every case—except for the ambiguously located "color line"[22] in America between blacks and everyone else, which has proven only slightly permeable, through individual passing or exceptional achievement. The only reasonable explanation lies in the stigma of slavery, the belated lifting of legalized caste-like apartheid, and its residual persistence in de facto residential, job, and institutional segregation.[23]

I have a similar reluctance to use the term *race riot* and am also tempted to put it between quotation marks. I have retained it because it has an apparently clear reference in the literature to interracial violence, whether initiated by collectivities of whites against blacks or by collectivities of blacks against whites. Historically, the former types prevailed and were designed to discipline and punish potential insubordination. When the latter became more common, alternate terms, such as "rebellions" or "uprisings," have been suggested. Undisciplined actions by whites in authority against blacks are sometimes called "police riots."

There have been numerous attempts to define *riot*. The broadest of these, based on legal precedents, is "any group of twelve or more people attempting to assert their will immediately through the use of force outside the normal bounds of law."[24] This does not seem very useful, even if a subcategory of race-related riots is distinguished. Far more useful is the definition suggested by David Halle and Kevin Rafter in their chapter that compares recent riots in New York and Los Angeles:

> [A] riot...involves at least one group publicly, and with little or no attempt at concealment, illegally assaulting at least one other group or illegally attacking or invading property...in ways that suggest that the authorities have lost control. In order to constitute a riot...the attacks...need to reach a certain threshold of intensity.... Once they have reached that threshold, riots can be further classified by their level of gravity.[25]

The authors go on to distinguish between megariots, those of greatest intensity, and less serious but still major riots, depending on "how long the riot lasts, how many people are killed or injured, the number of arrests, the amount of property damage, and the riot's geographic spread." They suggest that megariots meet at least three of the following levels of intensity: they last longer than two days; more than 10 people are killed; more than 500 are injured; more than 1,000 are arrested; more than 500 stores or other buildings suffer damage; and the rioting spreads "beyond two adjoining neighborhoods unless the neighborhood is very large."[26]

By these criteria, all six of the race riots I compare in this book qualify as either megariots or (almost) major riots. But I add to their criteria that a race riot must pit two or more groups against one another on the basis of putative racial/ ethnic identities and, because we are particularly interested in political culture and institutions in given regimes, must primarily fall within a single governmental/administrative jurisdiction whose leaders react to them.[27]

THE CASES SELECTED

In Chicago

1. *The white-on-black race riot of 1919* that served, whether intentionally or as a byproduct, to "ingather" the small and relatively decentralized black population of the city within the so-called black belt on the South Side, in what Drake and Cayton would later designate as *Black Metropolis.*[28]

2. *The black (and separate Latino) West Side ghetto revolts that occurred in the late 1960s* and especially the massive one triggered by the assassination of Martin Luther King, Jr., in April 1968, during which the West Side "Second Ghetto" was

allowed to burn out of control.[29] It was the culmination of Chicago's "border wars" and was closely associated with the failure of King's campaign for open housing in that part of the city.

Both Chicago riots were spatially confined and locally mounted, because participants moved largely on foot and the objectives were not only to express rage but to gain or maintain control over local space. This was true in 1919, when the chief battleground was on the South Side, at the so-called dead-line of Wentworth Avenue, and in 1968 when the westward march of the Second Ghetto met the retreating battle lines of white resistance.

In New York

3. *The African American uprisings in Harlem in 1935 and again in 1943,* caused by longstanding grievances over the lack of jobs and public services, poor-quality and overpriced housing, and police oppression. In both cases, these endemic tensions erupted briefly, triggered by specific acts (or rumors) of police brutality. They were similar events, albeit of increasing seriousness, and were met with similar responses from the city government. The number of fatalities rose from one to six, and there were more arrests, looting, and damage, and yet each lasted little more than a day. In response to both rebellions, Harlem was simply cordoned off temporarily from the rest of the city until order was restored, in part by the grant of specific concessions relevant to the demands.

4. *The Harlem/Bedford-Stuyvesant uprising of 1964,* one of the first significant riots in the sequence of widespread protests that occurred in hundreds of other American cities in the mid- to late 1960s. And yet its toll was remarkably low. Although sporadic rioting lasted for six days, spread to two separate locations, and involved considerable looting and some arson, only one person was killed (in addition to the shooting death **caused** by a policeman that set off the riots), only about 150 were injured, and the number of arrestees did not exceed 550. Property damage, however, was considerable.

Given the density of New York City and its dependence on mass transit, major outbreaks have been largely confined to specific neighborhoods. In general, the police have been able to isolate and indeed cordon off zones of hostilities by the simple expedient of closing specific subway stations. The ethnic diversity of New York's black population and its multiple sites of concentration have made it difficult for minority groups to mount broad concerted actions but also have made it difficult for the police to subdue them completely. Furthermore, protests in New York, especially in recent years, have tended to be more goal directed, revolving around such major issues as school segregation/community control and specific charges of police misbehavior.

In Los Angeles

5. *The Watts riot of 1965*, largely initiated by African Americans and targeting Jewish-owned commercial establishments within this former "suburb" (annexed to Los Angeles in 1926), which, due to an influx of African American migrants during World War II, had changed from a mixed area of whites, Mexicans, and blacks to an almost exclusively black community. The term "Watts" is inaccurate, however. Although the "spark" (the DUI arrest of an African American) occurred just outside Watts, it quickly spread to arson and looting over a zone of 46.5 square miles that the police cordoned off (and then deserted).[30] The riot resulted in 34 deaths.

6. *The 1992 South Central riot*, a wide-ranging revolt of poor Latinos and African Americans against not only Korean-owned shops in the neighborhood but also more "upscale" targets outside South Central. The name "South Central" is erroneous, since the core zone in which the riot erupted, and which was most affected, was almost identical to that of 1965. It was even more deadly.

Three things had basically changed in the interim. By 1992, the "outside" shopkeepers were Korean rather than Jewish. Second, the residents of the curfew zone were almost evenly divided between poor African Americans and poor Latinos, many of the latter undocumented. A third difference was the use of cars in 1992 to reach upscale commercial areas outside the cordoned-off area, facilitated by more "democratic" automobile ownership and the existence of the Harbor Freeway connecting South Central to downtown. This made the South Central riot one of the first "drive-in," or rather "drive-out," riots. It is a type likely to be repeated in other cities, especially those where dependence on the automobile is as great as in Los Angeles.

SPACE/TIME: THE ORGANIZATIONAL MATRIX FOR THE BOOK

By employing the strategy of controlled comparisons, I hope to make a significant contribution to our understanding of the evolving nature of racial/class/and cultural cleavages in the United States. Because the three cities differ in terms of their spatial forms of segregation, their political cultures, and their legal and police practices, such comparisons may allow us to move beyond simple generalizations to a deeper understanding of how space, racial politics, and police practices interact with generic underlying grievances to move race relations ahead or backward.

If space is one key to understanding such changes, time is of course the second. No city's experiences are independent of larger historical trends, even though they may be played out in ways that are relatively unique to place. That is why I have selected the two most serious events in each city, one earlier and one later. Given the greater age of New York, I have gone back farther to include precursors; Los Angeles' ascent to major metropolis accounts for the selection of a later period.

In this chapter, I review the temporal cycles of population movements and interracial relations, chiefly as they have affected coexistence and conflict in the three cities. In chapters 2 and 3, I take up the case of Chicago, one of the country's most segregated metropolitan regions, developing a theory of one strategy to achieve "racial peace," namely, the attempted separation of two combatants through a system of metropolis-wide apartheid on a vast spatial scale. This black-white dyad has been modified in recent decades by the addition of other minorities, but, unlike Los Angeles, these have not yet begun to play a significant intermediary role in Chicago.

Chapters 4 and 5 look more closely at the five boroughs of New York City, which contain approximately the same number of inhabitants as the Chicago metropolitan region. Here, ethnoracial diversity and a multiplicity of noncontiguous race-specific zones mediate against simple bifurcations or the unfettered exercise of "white" dominance. Many of the repertoires for intercommunal conflict seem first to have been honed in New York City and applied later in other cities. Paradoxically, the fact that racial protests in the city have often achieved concessions has tended to "contain" violence by offering alternative means of bargaining, but without the long and sophisticated capacity of African Americans in New York to organize politically, such an outcome would have been inconceivable.[31]

Chapters 6 and 7 examine the county of Los Angeles.[32] I ask how the existence of two quite different major "minorities"—African Americans and Latinos (chiefly Mexicans and Central Americans)—creates an unstable situation of *tertius gaudens* (divide and conquer), in which coalitions are potentially as likely as zero-sum games. Unhappily, the 1965 and 1992 riots seem to persist in a time warp: the uprisings did not achieve their ends but cycled back to equivalent levels of powerlessness, albeit with added players. What will the future hold, now that Latinos are becoming the majority?

Chapter 8 draws these themes together, comparing the relative success each city has had in resolving the tensions that lead to riots. These differences are related to each place's unique history and governmental structure and the political culture it has evolved through social learning. I also examine recent trends in the three cities, focusing especially on policies designed to achieve greater control over offensive/provocative police behavior. Finally, I look at the prospects for achieving social justice in the face of current trends in mass incarceration and displacement of minorities, and the potential conflicts between blacks and Latinos in declining economies. Within each group, as in American society in general, class cleavages are becoming greater. Although the fortunate from among historically oppressed minorities are achieving embourgeoisement and a greater political voice, they are increasingly isolated from the pains of alienation and protest they have left behind. Deeper, common, and more intractable causes persist, however, that inhere in American racism. Although some improvements can be acknowledged, much remains to be done. Our society is undergoing fundamental shifts, whose outcomes can never be fully predicted.

THE GENERAL HISTORICAL CONTEXT FOR THE SIX CASES

Highly volatile race riots have erupted periodically in the United States ever since the Civil War.[33] At least three successive types can be distinguished.[34] The earliest and most persistent forms involved attacks on blacks by whites (as civilians or as police) and were especially conspicuous in the Reconstruction period after the Civil War. Although most of these occurred in the South in the form of lynchings, the North was not immune.[35]

In the opening years of the twentieth century, interracial violence in cities outside the Deep South typically took the form not of lynchings of individual victims but of more collective and impersonal attacks by white "mobs" on small colonies of resident blacks. Thus, for example, in 1900, an altercation between Irish and blacks in New York City's Tenderloin district led to a minor riot. And between 1906 and 1908, a number of northern U.S. cities experienced outbreaks of violence against their tiny black settlements, including in such unlikely places as Springfield, Ohio (in 1906), and Springfield, Illinois (1908). These seem to have been motivated chiefly by scapegoating. It was at this time that the black community began its organizational response. It is not without significance that in 1909 the NAACP became the first organization of African Americans with national ambitions, followed shortly by various local branches of the Urban League.[36]

These outbreaks of local interracial violence coincided with a recession in the Western world and with new forms of labor strife, not necessarily related to racial animosities, since blacks were still essentially excluded from industrial employment.[37] In New York and Chicago, Jewish and Italian immigrants in the garment trade were beginning to use wildcat strikes and other still primitive labor union actions to disrupt production and gain more humane working conditions, but the beneficiaries of their protests were white.[38]

World War I

Recessions and wars have often exacerbated racial tensions. This was certainly the case during and immediately after World War I, when a clustering of race riots in towns and cities of the South, North, and West occurred between 1917 and 1919, extending even to 1921. These included East St. Louis in 1917, Washington, D.C., and Chicago in 1919, and Tulsa, Oklahoma, in 1921. Arthur Waskow lists 15 of these in the year 1919 alone.[39] In all these cases, white attacks on blacks initiated the hostilities.

Joseph Boskin sees these riots primarily as a consequence of job competition, although the situation was far more complex. It is true that wartime demands for labor had drawn African American males (and their families) into northern industrial centers, but conscription had also enrolled them in the armed forces. In both settings, segregation increased—in residential quarters, to which an increasing number of recent migrants were confined, and in the army, where they served in segregated brigades.

The effects on whites and blacks were opposite and on a collision course once the war ended. Demobilization plus an economic downturn in 1919 meant that white workers sought to return to their jobs in a contracting domestic economy, if necessary replacing black workers, at the same time that displaced or demobilized blacks, having sacrificed for their country, assumed they would share in its rewards for service. The two clashed head-on in, *inter alia*, the Chicago race riot of 1919, which was so devastating that it induced one of the first serious inquiries on a local level to diagnose causes, record particulars of the events, and suggest policies for the amelioration of tensions. This riot occurred in a wider context of union organizing and strikes for better working conditions, but is most noteworthy because blacks, for virtually the first time, fought back with firearms. This was not unexpected, since many had served in the military.

The 1919 race riot in Chicago may have been prototypically related to jobs, but it was also about space—both residential and recreational. And turf battles were as likely to occur when jobs were abundant as when they were scarce. In the early period after World War I, whites responded to the recent increase in black populations of large northern cities by trying to confine it to limited quarters and, in later years, to consolidate opposition to black expansion outside those areas, tightening the noose of racial segregation via racially restrictive covenants.

The Interwar Period

Although throughout the 1930s and 1940s NAACP lawyers repeatedly went to court to challenge these agreements (that ran with ownership deeds) not to rent or sell to Negroes, such covenants operated most effectively with respect to owner-occupied dwellings; they were far less effective with respect to large rental buildings, especially those operated by absentee owners. This may be why restrictive covenants were more typical of Chicago and Los Angeles than New York.[40] Furthermore, they were supplemented by direct action designed to instill fear in those defined as "invaders." A bomb and/or a fire was as good as a court, and indeed, after racially restrictive covenants were finally declared unenforceable in a Supreme Court case in 1948 (brought from Los Angeles), attacks by "neighbors" were the "court of last resort," for example, in the Chicago suburb of Cicero in 1951.

The contrast between Chicago and New York during this period is striking. In Chicago, the initiative remained with whites, and the primary focus was on competition for space, although competition for jobs was a subtext. In New York in the 1930s, the black community was more likely to take the initiative, and its goals were primarily economic. Although the explanation for this contrast is complex, it was due, at least in part, to differences in the composition and organization of the black communities in the two cities. New York's black community was proportionately smaller than Chicago's, its origins were more geographically diverse and urban, and it was far better organized for political action. In Harlem, which had changed from largely Jewish and Italian to predominantly African American occupancy during the 1920s, community organization and political leadership were routinely strong. Indeed, many of the techniques in the protest repertoire that would later be used in the civil rights movement were already being perfected in New York.

In 1935, in the depths of the depression, for example, a one-day Harlem riot had been preceded by an organized boycott of white-owned stores ("Don't Buy Where You Can't Work")[41] and by rent strikes against white slumlords. These organized activities might have continued without violence but for a triggering incident. The white owner of one of the picketed stores accused a black teenager of shoplifting and held him until the police arrived. A rumor spread throughout the already mobilized community that the boy had died at the hands of a white policeman. Although this rumor was soon revealed to be false, feelings were so tense that it set off organized marches as well as spontaneous looting of shops along the major thoroughfare.

Rioting, albeit combined with astute political organization, achieved results that boycott alone had failed to do. After the day-long outburst, during which affected subway stops were closed and the area cordoned off, Mayor Fiorello La Guardia sent in immediate relief supplies and then hastily announced a new public housing project for Harlem. Other aids to the community were to follow, even though the report of the Mayor's Commission, assigned to investigate the causes and to make recommendations, was never officially adopted or released.[42]

World War II

In the period of high demand for labor during World War II, African Americans were once again drawn from the rural South to industrial cities (this time also including Los Angeles), only to be met with hostile white reactions as they attempted to infringe on white working-class residential and recreational zones. It should not surprise us, then, that the year 1943 was particularly marked by interracial/interethnic tensions. There were conflicts in many cities, including Mobile, Detroit, Chicago, New York, and Los Angeles. But it would be a mistake to attribute them to the same causes or to prematurely classify them as "race riots." Their differences illuminate much about the special forms of conflict characteristic of each city and the unique ways these conflicts were resolved.

The most serious of these altercations was, of course, the large-scale and prolonged battle between blacks and whites that erupted on a hot Sunday at Belle Island Park in Detroit in 1943 and spread to many border areas of that segregated city. I call it an anachronistic event because it was perhaps the last large-scale "turf riot" between whites and blacks of the type that had wracked Chicago in 1919.[43]

Nevertheless, more limited turf battles continued to plague Chicago up to the major riot of 1968. These were, however, on a smaller scale, often involving public housing projects. The year 1943 saw one of these minor, short-lived altercations over housing in Chicago. Federally subsidized public housing projects were already under construction in numerous cities when the United States entered the war. Opposition from "neighbors" to the locations of such subsidized housing had been deflected by promises that new residents would be drawn from the immediate neighborhood and that, therefore, the projects would not alter the racial composition of the area. However, in the wartime emergency, many of these projects were adapted to house war workers. One such project was located on the north side of Chicago in a largely Sicilian area. When black war workers, assigned to a minority of units, attempted to move in, they were blocked by local residents—a phenomenon common to Chicago's border wars.

The dispute was resolved, but fear of something equivalent to the Detroit riot was on the minds of Chicago's decision-makers, who noted obvious parallels to their 1919 riot that had been triggered in Jackson Park. To head off such a repetition, the mayor's office established a Race (later Human) Relations Committee, which was charged with defusing racial tensions, primarily in the area of housing.[44] Despite their efforts, Chicago's "border wars" would continue throughout the 1950s and 1960s on the south and west sides. And, typically for Chicago, the 1968 riot, which was concentrated on the West Side, was a competition not over jobs but over turf—as well as a demand for "respect."

The Los Angeles case was deviant indeed, and I question whether the 1943 outbreak of conflict between white sailors and Mexican youths should be included in any list of urban race riots. (It would not be until 1965 that a race riot *in strictu sensi* would erupt in that city.) The so-called zoot-suit riot of 1943 was, rather, an undisciplined rebellion of sailors drawn from many parts of the country who were stationed in a single base in Los Angeles. Bands of out-of-control sailors, resentful of Mexican youths who were perceived to be immune from the draft, invaded Mexican areas of the city, in some cases stripping young males of their zoot suits and beating them.[45] It was, more properly speaking, a riot that *happened in* Los Angeles but was *not of* Los Angeles, except insofar as Mexicans constituted a growing minority of the city's residents and would become the objects and subjects of later racial/ethnic conflict in the early 1970s.

During World War II, the size of the African American population in Los Angeles doubled, from about 75,000 in 1940 to 150,000 by war's end, due to the demand for war-related industrial labor. This intensified housing segregation in areas such as Watts/South Central but did not yet result in serious overt black/white hostilities. It was not until 1965, when the African American population in Los Angeles had risen to 650,000, that their exclusion from the housing and labor markets would yield the city's "first" major race riot, more properly termed a "ghetto uprising."

As usual, New York's African American community was ahead of other places in its repertoire of actions—in its economic goals, coupled with demands for respect and power, and in its relative success in achieving them. The 1943 Harlem riot presaged a newer set of battles for equality in the economic sphere and for more courteous treatment by the police. Together with the less destructive riot of 1935, it signaled the beginning of a second generation of northern urban race riots: the ghetto revolts that would become more widespread throughout the country from the mid-1960s on. The immediate *casus belli* was a fight between a black serviceman and a white policeman outside one of Harlem's fanciest hotels over the police officer's harassment of a woman. The serviceman pushed the officer, who shot at him as he escaped. As in 1935, the false rumor of his death was enough to trigger a riot. The deeper issue was, of course, the discrepancy between fighting for one's country and being treated disrespectfully, but there were ongoing economic grievances as well.

The Harlem revolts of 1935 and 1943 had established a pattern of localized property destruction and theft within the ghetto—one that presaged patterns of internal destruction, the targeting of "white" business, and the looting that would become familiar scenarios in the 1960s. But in both instances, the responses from city government officials were quick and decisive. In both cases, the uprisings were controlled by a police strategy of cordoning off the involved territory—a strategy only possible when segregation already existed. With police at the peripheries and subway stations closed, the only outlets for anger were *within* the zone of segregation.

As had happened in 1935, the riot resulted in real gains for the black community, which distinguishes New York's riots from those of Chicago. After the 1943 protest, New York passed its own Fair Employment Act, a goal that had been forcefully advocated by leaders in the well-organized African American community. The city also passed rent control laws, making it the last city in the country to impose rent controls.[46] New York blacks, therefore, had developed political know how, even if they still had little representation on the city council (called the Board of Aldermen) and virtually none yet on the powerful Board of Appropriations. Furthermore, their leaders had developed many non-riot mechanisms for protest, including demonstrations, marches, and boycotts. Because these actions bore some fruit, they continue periodically to this day.

Unlike Chicago in 1919, the riots did not immediately increase segregation but, in fact, led to the growth of "satellite Harlems." Especially in the post–World War II period, these mixed settlements proliferated in many parts of the five boroughs. In addition to the expansion of a "Second Ghetto" in Bedford-Stuyvesant, other parts of the outer boroughs, such as the South Bronx, experienced in-migrations of African Americans, in part because of the scattering of public housing projects.[47] This diffused or at least differentiated several zones of riot potential.

The Civil Rights Movement of the 1950s

Although African American activism did not cease, in the 1950s its primary focus shifted to the South and to the courts. During the late 1940s and early 1950s, the civil rights movement was spearheaded largely by lawyers of the NAACP who gained stunning successes in *Shelley v. Kraemer* (outlawing enforcement of racial restrictive covenants in 1948) and *Brown v. Board of Education* (overturning the principle of "separate but equal" schools in 1954). The *Brown* decision's call for desegregation would become a central issue of growing and geographically widening tensions, although at first its major focus remained on the South, which had maintained de jure separate schools. The de facto segregation of students in public schools in northern cities was of secondary significance in the early days of the civil rights movement, although opposition to busing and support for neighborhood schools would eventually tear northern cities apart.

In those early years, the grassroots organizing of the civil rights movement developed most rapidly in the South (albeit supported by northerners) and became more church-based, codified in the very name of Southern Christian Leadership Council (SCLC), organized in 1957. The SCLC sought to invalidate Jim Crow laws and to remove the "legal" barriers to voter registration—both of which were considered "southern" issues. The bus boycotts and the lunch counter sit-ins that occurred in the South resonated less among urban blacks in the North, where obvious Jim Crow affronts—such as legalized separate places on public conveyances, separately labeled drinking fountains and restrooms, and the like—were scarcely issues.[48] Nor were poll taxes and blatant denial of voting registration rights salient in the North, where black voters may have been manipulated but were often prized by urban "machines."

The passage of the 1957 Civil Rights Act, simultaneous with the organization of SCLC and the appointment of Ella Baker as the organization's "assistant" executive director, meant that gaining the franchise for black voters became an increasingly important focus, especially in the South, where poll tax and other requirements had disenfranchised African Americans in many districts where they otherwise would easily have constituted the majority.[49] Here, again, this campaign was somewhat less salient, though no less important, in northern cities, where "getting out the vote" and preventing arbitrary denials of eligibility took priority.

The first steps toward building a broader, more national coalition were evident in the 1963 March on Washington, designed to commemorate the one-hundredth anniversary of the Emancipation Proclamation. It marked a true "change of focus," expanding the civil rights movement beyond its heavily southern leadership, exercised largely through black churches, and its preoccupation with Jim Crow laws and practices. Alliances were formed with northern-based (and often more secular) organizations that were traditionally preoccupied with more bread-and-butter issues: employment opportunities, equal access to housing, and improvements in the quality of educational institutions. While some of these "northern" organizations were longstanding and gradualist, such as the NAACP branches, others, like the interracial Congress on Racial Equality (CORE) and, later, the more militant Black Panthers, employed more confrontational strategies.

This expansion in organizational coordination drew greater attention to the salient demands of black populations in northern ghettos. De facto residential segregation and unadvertised discrimination in jobs (despite the New York Fair Employment Practices law enacted during the war) were central to this constituency, as were inadequately funded and inferior, "informally segregated" schools tied causally to poverty. The subtle bars to service in selected public places and expensive restaurants that existed in northern cities would not be much affected by lunch counter sit-ins in the South. Ending police brutality was also seen as a prime goal in the North. Whereas police mistreatment in the South was seen as a by-product of larger forms of white oppression, in New York, Chicago, and Los Angeles it was a central issue.

Ending discrimination in housing was not universally perceived as among those primary goals, in either the North or the South. In northern cities, some of the stakes in keeping ghettos tightly circumscribed were reduced, once the housing shortage that had accumulated during World War II was finally being met by massive housing developments on open land. But where that open land was located in any particular metropolitan region had a decided effect on political responses in the three cities. There was room for new housing developments inside the city limits of New York, primarily in underdeveloped portions of Queens and even Brooklyn, which meant that at least some of the "white flight" from older neighborhoods to new ones could occur without leaving the political jurisdiction of the city.[50] Open land was mostly toward the periphery of the "city/county line" of Los Angeles or in closer-in locations that had opted out (de-annexed) from the city's jurisdiction.[51] Within the city limits, such expansions took place in the San Fernando Valley, which periodically sought, albeit unsuccessfully, to secede from the city. And the open land for new developments was almost exclusively beyond the city limits in underbounded Chicago, which led to a clear politico-racial differentiation between the city and its suburbs.

This trend of white exodus, whether to the outer boroughs, unincorporated areas, or suburbs, generalized the preconditions for the second form of race riot (the "ghetto revolt"), where violence occurs chiefly *within* segregated minority areas that can be effectively cordoned off from the rest of the city. Although often "dated" to the 1960s, as we have already noted, it had its precedents in New York in the Harlem "riots" of 1935 and 1943.

The Riots of the 1960s

New York, Chicago, and Los Angeles were among the hundreds of cities whose "ghettos" exploded in anger and frustration in the 1960s. Many in the black community were impatient that "progress" in civil rights was much too slow and were distressed to discover that Johnson's "Great Society" was being hijacked by the war in Vietnam that diverted resources from his "war on poverty." They also recognized that the bodies in the body bags there were disproportionately black. Opposition to racial injustice and to the Vietnam War began to converge.

Instead of asking why riots became so widespread in the mid-1960s, the question can be turned around, as Kenneth Clark did in an article published in the *New York Times Magazine* in September 1965, entitled "The Wonder Is That There Have Been So Few Riots." In it he noted:

> It is one measure of the depth and insidiousness of American racism that the
> nation ignores the rage of the rejected—until it explodes in Watts or
> Harlem. The wonder is that there have been so few riots, that Negroes
> generally are law-abiding in a world where the law itself seemed the enemy.[52]

Clark also quotes Senator Robert Kennedy as saying, after the Watts riot, that all
these places—Harlem, Watts, and the South Side of Chicago—are riots waiting to
happen. This required little prescience on his part, since of the three cities he
mentioned, only Chicago's "big" riot had not yet occurred, and when it did in
1968, its chief location was not the South Side but west of the Loop.

New York was among the first cities to experience the ghetto revolts that
began in the early 1960s. The so-called Harlem/Bedford-Stuyvesant uprising of
1964 was both a continuation of the riot-cum-politics repertoire of New York and
a precursor to the wide-scale revolts in many other cities throughout the nation.
It was followed by the Watts riot of 1965 in Los Angeles and the West Side riots in
Chicago between 1966 (albeit by blacks and Latinos separately) and 1968 (by
blacks). Some analysts suggest that in the North, the turning point came after
1963, as the southern-based civil rights movement turned its attention to northern cities, to address issues of segregation, poverty, and police brutality.[53] All
three of these issues had been festering for decades.

Police brutality had been an issue in New York for a long time.[54] It had
triggered the revolt of 1935 and been implicated in the 1943 riot, and it was to set
off the Harlem/Bedford-Stuyvesant riot of 1964.[55] The trigger was an altercation
between a young black student, attending a high school summer program on the
predominately white Upper East Side, and a white building superintendent that
escalated after an off-duty white policeman shot and killed the youth.[56] The
mobilized protests at the school and in Harlem spread to Bedford-Stuyvesant, a
zone that could not be as conveniently isolated as Harlem.

Even though one could claim in retrospect that the Harlem/Bedford-
Stuyvesant riot marked the opening round of the hundreds of race riots or ghetto
revolts that took place in the late 1960s, it is significant that it was less destructive
than those in many other cities (for example, Newark) and that New York has
since been relatively immune to subsequent wide-scale riots, even in response to
the Rodney King verdict that sparked the South Central insurrection in 1992,
which was mirrored in cities around the nation, many of which had no history of
racial strife.[57]

Nevertheless, Kenneth Clark called the 1964 response

> more frightening than a race riot and the participants' deliberate mockery
> more threatening than a mob.... There was an eerie, surrealistic quality, a

silence within the din, punctuated by gunfire and sporadic shattering of glass, a calm within the chaos, a deliberativeness within the hysteria. The Negro...behaved as if he had nothing to lose.[58]

While it may be that the riots could not bring about the larger changes, as was usual in New York, Clark's "Negroes" had something to gain. The community was eventually "cooled out" by visits but less than adequate gestures from Mayor Robert Wagner (who returned hastily from abroad when the riot broke out). Similarly, in April 1968, when city after city went up in flames after King's assassination, New York remained relatively calm, reassured by Mayor Lindsay, who walked through the ghettos in shirt-sleeves, expressing sympathy and promising reforms.[59]

New York was not altogether free of interracial conflict in 1968, but it took a different form. It focused on a concession that had earlier been instituted by Mayor Lindsay to experiment with giving minority neighborhood schools greater control over their faculties and curriculum. This put them into conflict with the Jewish-dominated teachers' union. The shorthand name for this controversy was Ocean Hill–Brownsville, to be discussed in greater detail in chapter 5.[60]

W. E. B. Du Bois had not predicted racial violence in Los Angeles. He visited the city in 1913 and, in fact, had called it a heaven for black persons, in comparison to the bad state of race relations in other cities of the nation. But only one year after the Harlem/Bedford-Stuyvesant riots, a bloody and prolonged ghetto uprising erupted in Watts/South Central, leaving 34 people dead, over a thousand injured, close to 4,000 arrested, and property damage estimated at $40 million. It was suppressed six days later, and only after the National Guard had been called in. As had occurred periodically in New York, the explosion in Los Angeles was triggered by police brutality, but this time against a motorist and his mother, who had come to defend him. Watts was, therefore, a true precursor to the 1980 Miami riot that followed the arrest of a black motorcyclist.[61]

The Harlem riot of 1964 and the Watts riot of 1965 were not just about police brutality, however. Both occurred in the context of an economic recession whose effects appeared first in black areas but subsequently spread to the wider U.S. economy. It was almost as if blacks were the "canaries in the mines" signaling economic retrenchments. Furthermore, the particular form these uprisings took was deeply affected by the civil rights movement, which was changing course and geographic focus and becoming more militant.

In this context, the Watts riot of 1965 was only one in a large series of ghetto revolts, from which it did not deviate greatly except by its longer duration and the extent and range of its destruction, which was as great as that of the Detroit riot of

1943. But—unlike the earlier Detroit case but similar to other riots of the 1960s—Watts was not a battle between white and black residents but rather one between some members of the local community and the "forces of law and order," including the largely white police and fire services and even the National Guard. In this it resembled the "typical" riot of the 1960s, in which destruction was confined to the riot zone.

Michael McCall offers some explanations for why the Watts riot was so destructive, claiming that the spatial ecology of low-density Los Angeles prevented the police from employing the techniques of riot control that had proved so effective in urban centers of the East.[62]

> Police have learned how to deal with riots in Eastern urban centers. The same tactics were not so successful in Los Angeles. The most important technique for riot control [in dense eastern cities] has been containment of the riot area.... Containment has been accomplished by closing bus service to the riot area, and stationing officers on streets that lead into the area.... The tactic of containment can be quite successful in a city whose major form of transportation is the subway or the bus. In New York's Harlem riot in 1964, police closed subway stops in the area.... In a city like Los Angeles where there is virtually no public transportation and where "everyone" drives a car [sic], it is much more difficult to seal off the riot...area.... Most people who came to the riot area drove there, leading one newspaper correspondent to label the Los Angeles riot a "drive-in" riot. Thus, containment did not work well in Los Angeles...because people can retreat to their yards, streets are too wide to be controlled by the police, and water and soapsuds can't fill enough space to keep crowds back.

As I will show in chapter 6, however, one cannot blame the destruction that occurred in South Central in 1965 on "space" alone. The administration seemed to have been caught off guard, apparently unaware of or indifferent to the discontent brewing in the ghetto. The governor was out of the country. After being notified that there was trouble in South Central, the acting governor still chose to attend meetings out of town, as did the mayor, who absented himself to give a lecture in San Francisco. With little direction, the police withdrew to their defensive perimeter, which allowed the uprising to rage unchecked until it was finally put down by the National Guard.

One need not posit a "subculture of rioting," as does McCall, to explain why matters should have spiraled out of control. Indeed, in the multiple post-mortem studies (which became a cottage industry for Los Angeles university professors), one of the most surprising findings, in retrospect, was the widespread belief within the African American community—among "rioters" and mere spectators alike—that the riot would do some good by calling attention to their grievances. The postriot neglect of the massive need to rebuild the destroyed area would soon destroy their illusions, thus setting the seeds for a reexplosion some 27 years later.

That the inability of Los Angeles' police to respond to the Watts uprising was due simply to the unique spatial ecology of that city is belied by a similar insensitivity to growing unrest and frustrations in Chicago's West Side ghetto in 1968. There, the police and fire departments would prove equally unable or unwilling to curb the rebellion in a city of more conventional design. McCall overstates the exceptionalism of Los Angeles and thus minimizes the underlying causes for frustration that were worsening in restive ghettos throughout the nation. The deeper causes were the same: a compounding of economic difficulties in increasingly isolated ghettos that the establishment ignored, and provocative actions by police who lost few opportunities to hold lighted matches to the seething grievances, especially when they seemed on the brink of being acknowledged.

This was certainly the case in the minor riots that occurred in Chicago during the summer of 1966. In June the police broke up a rally of Puerto Ricans who were celebrating their successful first march as a community in downtown. To put an end to a fight, the police brought in not only too many reinforcements but also dogs—a tactic the Puerto Ricans deemed the ultimate insult. A riot ensued, with attacks on and looting of shops along Division Street. A month later, black residents on the West Side resisted when the police attempted to close off water hydrants on a sultry night, although as I shall show in chapter 4, the real cause was deeper. People took their grievance to the streets, resisting what they perceived as arbitrary police harassment.[63] The riot lasted several days and was quelled only after the National Guard was called in.

But the isolation and frustrated hopes would reach their climax in 1968, in the aftermath of Martin Luther King's assassination, when the gap between the pains blacks were experiencing and the relative indifference of whites was revealed with frightening clarity. The pain was particularly acute in Chicago because of the courageous role King had played in galvanizing the community to break the barriers to expansion by overcoming white resistance to open housing.

In the mid-1960s, King had moved his crusade northward and broadened its goals to encompass those for which black organizations in northern cities had been fighting for decades. From 1965 on, King became particularly involved in Chicago. His selection of that city and his decision to emphasize open housing were carefully considered, but he had perhaps chosen the country's most intractable case, for it was locked in its traditional form of conflict—the border war.

The last of these border wars, at least to date, would take place in 1968, not so much on the already substantially black South Side, where outbursts were sporadic and quickly brought under control, but in the area west of downtown, where black occupancy had been pressing, against strong white resistance, toward the city's edge. While the timing of the riot coincided with the murder of Martin Luther King and thus paralleled the general rage also exploding in African American urban communities throughout the United States, it is important to note that it was not without warning signs. It had been preceded by periodic altercations between police and members of minority communities (black and Puerto Rican) and by a series of marches for open housing on the West Side.

In some ways, one of the consequences of the 1968 rebellion was the obverse of that in 1919. It hastened the departure of whites from the far West Side, thus gaining an enlarged zone for black occupancy, without, however, addressing the persistent problems of unemployment and poverty. Although Chicago remained as residentially segregated as it had been before the 1968 riot, within only a brief period of time after it, the farther West Side—up to the city limits—became almost completely black occupied, due to white flight.[64]

The riot benefited white business and institutional interests. The destruction of some 20 square blocks on the near West Side in the course of the uprising not only led to insurance compensation to white businesses eager to leave the ghetto but opened "space" for the commercial and residential uses of the white Loop to expand into the vacuum, and for the University of Illinois not only to plan expansions into the burnt-out zone but set its sights on the Mexican area of Pilsen to its south.

As was also the case in Los Angeles after the uncontrolled burning of South Central in 1965, nothing ever came of the promises made to rebuild, and the portions of the scorched earth that were not preempted by white institutional and business uses have lain fallow as a *cordon sanitaire* or, more accurately, a demilitarized zone.

THE EARLY 1990S: INTERETHNIC TENSIONS

The exoneration of the four police officers, whose brutal beating of black motorist Rodney King had been captured on amateur videotape and widely disseminated by the media, led to outbursts of rage in many cities throughout the United States. Nowhere were the repercussions felt more strongly than in Los Angeles, in the same vast district that had been wracked by protests in 1965 and never repaired.

In 1992, South Central Los Angeles remained the poorest area of the city, and had actually deteriorated in the period between the riots. The overall unemployment rate had increased, and an estimated half of all young males were neither working nor attending school. Household incomes had risen only modestly, and the proportion of households receiving (inadequate) welfare assistance stood at one in four. In the interim, however, the ethnic/racial composition of the area had changed dramatically. In 1965, over four-fifths of the population were African American, some 17 percent were white, and there were very few Latinos and Asians. By 1990, the proportion of whites had dropped to under 3 percent, and only 45 percent of South Central's residents were black. The area had become about half Latino but remained a ghetto of the deprived. Riot participants would be drawn from both communities, and in fact, the number of Latinos arrested exceeded that of African Americans, in part because, under the guise of restoring order, the Immigration and Naturalization Service took advantage of an opportunity to round up and deport undocumented aliens.

It may appear, at first glance, that the participation of Latinos (in this instance, primarily of Mexican/Central American origin or descent) belied the racial character of the uprising and the depth of resentment toward the police. Although some analysts have suggested that Mexicans in 1992 were more likely to have joined the looting than to participate in arson and violence, this would underestimate resentments based on the long history of Anglo oppression of Mexicans, who suffered from discrimination and police profiling in Los Angeles long before African Americans. It would also ignore an equally long history of Latino protests.

This is not to deny growing tensions between blacks and Latinos, which also surfaced during the 1992 South Central riot. This may signal the start of a new cycle of conflict likely to play out in cities where a zero-sum game seems now be to be setting up—one where less educated, underemployed African Americans are being marginalized from the productive economy and the political power system by the immigration of unskilled and vulnerable workers from the "third world" and by growing numbers of Hispanic voters.[65] While there was apparent mutual participation by blacks and Latinos in the South Central uprising, my suspicions are that this alliance of convenience may only be temporary. In Chicago, New York, and Los Angeles, I suspect that future eruptions are possible at the social and physical boundaries between poor blacks and incoming Latinos, for a variety of reasons that will be explored in later chapters.

A second development in the 1990s has been growing tension in all three cities between poor African Americans and Latinos on the one hand and certain Asian immigrants who have found economic niches in small businesses that either serve the ghetto communities or employ Latinos (and to a lesser extent blacks) in service or production jobs. While the tensions are not new, the ethnicity of ghetto business operatives had changed between the 1960s and the 1990s.

In the 1992 Los Angeles riots, Korean shopkeepers in South Central, who had taken over many of the small liquor and convenience grocery stores in the ghetto that Jewish owners abandoned in the aftermath of 1965, had inherited not just the stores but the pent-up anger (and envy) of their neighbors.[66] One year before the riots, a Korean owner of a convenience store in South Central had received only a very light sentence, on the grounds of defensive homicide, for the shooting death of a young black shopper she accused of shoplifting. This case exacerbated ongoing interethnic tensions and came to symbolize to blacks that they could expect justice neither from the police nor the courts. When in the uprising of 1992 anger was vented on many Korean-owned stores, not only in South Central but in the nearby business strip of Koreatown, the media showed armed Korean men (some presumably veterans from the Korean War) on the roofs above their stores as they tried to protect them from looters. The Koreans defended their actions by complaining that the Los Angeles police had withdrawn all protection not only from South Central but from Koreatown, which then forced them to take the law in their own hands. What the media did not present clearly is that although Koreatown hosted ethnic businesses along its main commercial strip, the primary residents of the district were Latinos. This, together with the fact that South Central by 1992 was inhabited by equal numbers of blacks and Latinos, explains why, in the arrests that followed the riot, slightly more than half of those arrested were Latinos; the rest were African Americans and a small number of whites.

In New York, tensions have also been recorded between Korean shopkeepers and African American ghetto residents, but the plot line has been quite different.[67] The contrast between Los Angeles and New York is not only attributable to differences in their ghettos but due to the fact that in New York the economic niche of Koreans, albeit heavily specialized in greengroceries, is citywide. Korean shopkeepers were not exclusively associated with ghetto exploitation, nor are most perceived as exploiters.[68] In Chicago and New York, ongoing tensions between Puerto Ricans and African Americans have been more salient than between Asian shopkeepers and a combination of Latino and black customers, making a joint riot less likely. Nor have Koreans in Chicago specialized in ghetto stores. More common in the interethnic relations in that city have been Korean owners of garment sweatshops and factories and their largely Latino workers, a phenomenon also replicated in Los Angeles.

One final inter-group tension, unique to New York, must also be added: that between blacks, primarily from the Caribbean, and Hasidic Jews, who share physical space in the Crown Heights neighborhood, but rarely mix. A major but localized riot in 1991 followed the traffic death of a black youngster run over by a procession of Hasidic cars containing the chief rabbi of the sect and exacerbated by the random revenge knifing death of a Hasid visiting from Australia.

RACIAL PROFILING: THE GREAT UNIFIER

Despite interethnic conflicts among the "not quite white" minorities that now constitute the majority of residents in at least the center cities of the three major metropolitan regions, there is one issue that often brings them together, and that is racial profiling, with its attendant risk of police brutality. Their common demand is to make police more accountable and equitable in their behavior toward minority "suspects" and to overcome the thin blue line that separates the police from those they are supposed to protect.

This issue has become particularly salient in New York, due to several well-publicized cases involving black immigrants. In 1998, for example, Abner Louima, a Haitian immigrant, was brutalized in the precinct headquarter's bathroom by white arresting officers. In long-drawn-out trials, Louima was awarded a large compensation from the city and the chief offending police officer given a very long jail sentence. (A second officer received a shorter sentence for false testimony.) And in 1999, an unarmed African immigrant, Amadou Diallo, was shot 41 times and killed by four white special street crime officers. The latter incident and several other unprovoked shootings of unarmed black men have triggered mounting demonstrations against police. Local African Americans latched on to these clear cases of innocent immigrants being mistreated just because they were black.

Antipolice demonstrations have received support from leading black politicians, from Latinos (some darker-skinned, for example, the Dominicans, but also paler-skinned Puerto Ricans), and even from a wider base including union members and liberal whites. Reverend Al Sharpton emerged as leader of a broader coalition against then mayor Rudolph Giuliani and his police chief. Under attack, the two responded by initiating an (impossible) program to radically change the racial character of the police force. By 1999, it was still 67 percent white, whereas minorities constituted 65-plus percent of the city's population. Since that time, progress has been made in rectifying this imbalance by preferential recruitment. New tax surcharges were imposed to expand the police force. The deaths of police responders to the World Trade Center disaster on 9/11 created an unusual number of vacancies that have been filled by minority recruits.

Particularly in the late 1990s, the issue of police brutality has come up time and again in cities all over the country. There is no question that "targeting" of minorities, whether based on scientifically derived profiles of probability or upon racist assumptions of policemen (who, in most cities with large minority proportions, are still predominantly white) is a fact of the contemporary period. While there is hardly anything new in this practice, the solutions are hard to find. Civilian review boards are one solution, but New York, where the most recent concentration of events and protests has occurred, already has a civilian complaint board and a history of extremely high financial settlements awarded by the courts to individual victims of police brutality. The question is not only how to punish policemen for torturing or killing innocent victims but also how to prevent the systematic harassment (frequent frisking, presumption of guilt before innocence) that many minority men are subjected to.

The deeper persisting problem is explored by David Cole, author of *No Equal Justice,* who traces the various steps through which the poor and black receive unequal justice—from higher rates of search and seizure to higher rates of arrest, lower quality of defense attorneys, unfairly constituted juries, greater rates of conviction and longer sentences for similar crimes, and being the victims of police use of deadly force more often than white citizens.[69] Cole faults more than police misbehavior; rather, he sees a basic double standard in the administration of the criminal justice system, which is highly functional for the privileged. He argues that

> while our criminal justice system is explicitly based on the premise and promise of equality before the law, the administration of criminal law . . . is in fact predicated on the exploitation of inequality. . . . *[O]ur criminal justice system affirmatively depends on inequality.* Absent race and class disparities, the privileged among us could not enjoy as much constitutional protection of our liberties as we do; and without those disparities, we could not afford the policy of mass incarceration that we have pursued over the past two decades.[70]

He further argues that unless these inequalities are addressed, many of those who suffer from them will be reluctant to accept the legal system as legitimate. Force and massive incarcerations can only go so far to prevent urban rebellions. Greater justice could build more peaceful communities, and making the criminal justice system more responsive to the needs and norms of oppressed communities is one way to proceed.

I return to these themes in chapter 8, when I examine how each of the three cities has been experimenting with some variation of this solution, but with varying degrees of commitment and success. Perhaps the fitting conclusion to this introductory chapter is the slogan often shouted in demonstrations: "No justice, no peace."

Notes

1. A precise count is impossible, given the fluid definition of "riot" and the absence of an agreed-on total. This number is suggested in one of the most carefully researched books on the riots of the 1960s. See Joe R. Feagin and Harlan Hahn, *Ghetto Revolts: The Politics of Violence in American Cities* (New York: Macmillan, 1973), p. 99.
2. The Kerner Report (U.S. Riot Commission, *Report of the National Advisory Commission on Civil Disorders*. New York: New York Times, 1968; reprint, Pantheon Books, 1988) was subsequently republished several times. I have consulted the 1968 and 1988 editions The pagination of the text in both editions is the same, although the 1988 edition includes updated introductions and omits the unpaged appendix of charts showing time lines and violence levels in the 23 cities selected for more detailed analysis.
3. Kerner Report, p. 1. The phrase "is moving toward" is astonishing—as if racial segregation and inequality were new or increasing! The same phrase, more accurately expanded, became the title of Andrew Hacker, *Two Nations: Black and White, Hostile, Separate, and Unequal* (New York: Simon & Schuster, 1992).
4. See Kerner Report, pp. 35–202. The substance of their research findings is contained in the first two lengthy chapters (pp. 35–200), which yield wordy but extremely disappointing efforts to tease out comparisons. Chapter 3 consists of only two pages, including the all-important but still tentatively phrased conclusion that *"the urban disorders of the summer of 1967 were not caused by, nor were they the consequences of, any organized plan or 'conspiracy.' Specifically, the Commission has found no evidence that all or any of the disorders or the incidents that led to them were planned or directed by any organization or group, international, national or local"* (p. 202, italics added).
5. Thus dismissing any fundamental redistribution of political power, although this is exactly what the riots were about!
6. Kerner Report, p. 413.
7. Ibid., pp. 414–15; italics added. See chapter 8 below, where this solution is being reinvented.
8. Ibid., p. 419.
9. Ibid., pp. 424–56.
10. Quoted by Feagin and Hahn, *Ghetto Revolts,* p. 221, from Johnson's 1971 memoir *The Vantage Point* (New York: Holt, Rinehart and Winston), p. 173.
11. This quotation appears, significantly, on the very last page of the Kerner Report (p. 483), perhaps highlighting their shared despair.
12. The work of Douglas Massey has consistently emphasized the importance of spatial segregation in cities throughout the country. I am indebted not only to his book coauthored with Nancy Denton, *American Apartheid* (Cambridge, Mass.: Harvard University Press, 1993) but to his many articles that measure segregation levels of

African Americans and Hispanics in a variety of cities, including the three discussed in this book.

13. The classic article in this mode remains Stanley Lieberson and Arnold R. Silverman, "The Precipitants and Underlying Conditions of Race Riots," *American Sociological Review* 30 (December 1965), pp. 887–98, although few of the riots they analyzed date from the 1960s. For a more recent application of this approach, see Susan Olzak, *The Dynamics of Ethnic Competition* (Stanford, Calif.: Stanford University Press, 1992), manipulating coded statistical measures for a massive number of interethnic conflicts over time. Most recently and more germane, however, Olzak, Suzanne Shanahan, and Elizabeth McEneaney have analyzed event-histories of 154 race riots that took place between 1960 and 1993 in the 55 largest SMSAs in the United States. See their "Poverty, Segregation, and Race Riots: 1960–1993," *American Sociological Review* 61 (August 1996), pp. 590–613. For work reflecting the renewed interest in race riots and the innovation of event-history analysis, see also Daniel J. Myers, "Racial Rioting in the 1960s: An Event History Analysis of Local Conditions," *American Sociological Review* 62 (February 1997), pp. 94–112. In a recently published work, Max Arthur Herman builds a statistically based argument for common causes of riots in Chicago, Detroit, Los Angeles and Miami. See his *Fighting in the Streets* (New York: Peter Lang, 2005).

14. References to many of these fine case studies can be found in my general bibliography.

15. This book has grown directly out of my larger comparative history of the three cities, *New York, Chicago, Los Angeles: America's Global Cities* (Minneapolis: University of Minnesota Press, 1999), and may be viewed, in part, as a sequel. That earlier book, while it did not directly focus on race riots, provides a sufficient contextual background to allow a deeper understanding of the special (and spatial) features of collective actions in each city, their precise manifestations, the timing of their eruptions, their locations and geographic range, and their sociopolitical outcomes.

16. Some have suggested that major wars run on a similar cycle and might be attributed to "generational forgetting." If the hoped-for exit of American forces from Iraq coincides with an economic recession and with continued losses in jobs needed to absorb demobilized soldiers, past experience predicts an increase in interracial/interethnic conflict.

17. This excuse makes its appearance in many discussions on reparations to descendants of slaves and even in arguments about whether affirmative action is needed.

18. Indeed, recent DNA research confirms our common origins and substantial overlaps, suggesting that skin color differences originated in environmental adaptations to climate conditions, as Africans moved to increasingly sun-deprived regions. On a less abstract level, there is a wide range of intermediary skin pigmentations among those who identify themselves or are classified by others as "black," evidence of "mixed" origins. The dichotomy is empirically false.

19. People from the eastern hemisphere (the zone "excluded" by the 1919 change in U.S. immigration laws) were not admitted as immigrants until 1965. An even earlier Chinese Exclusion law prevailed from the late nineteenth century.

20. Mexicans in the censuses of 1920 and 1930 were classified as belonging to the white race, but after that, various attempts to distinguish them separately as Mexicans, or to include them in the successive categories of "Spanish surname," and eventually

"Hispanic" (black or white) have been experimented with. Darker immigrants from the Caribbean, among others, Jamaicans, Haitians, and Dominican Republicans, tend to be elided with blacks. Since September 11, 2001, Arabs and other persons from the Middle East and Pakistan, *inter alia,* have become "racialized," in a reversal of their previously less marked identities.

21. But recall W. I. Thomas's wise observation that admittedly arbitrary "definitions of the situation" are real in their consequences.

22. Defined by W. E. B. Du Bois as *the* problem of the twentieth century, but persisting into the twenty-first.

23. I use the term "caste" in a loose parallel to India, fully recognizing that it does not apply. Caste, while presumably linked to descent, is neither genetic nor based on color. Furthermore, there are known cases of entire castes improving their standing within the hierarchical system of occupational specialization, as well as individuals claiming higher caste origins and thus social mobility. Indeed, the original status of blacks in American society was more parallel to that of the "untouchables" of India who were excluded from society but indispensable to perform ritually unclean work.

24. This, indeed, is the definition used by Paul Gilje, in his detailed *Rioting in America* (Bloomington: University of Indiana Press, 1996), p. 4. Despite its promising title, the book includes so many brief narrations of "riots," small and large and occurring over centuries, that it is difficult to generalize or even categorize them accurately.

25. David Halle and Kevin Rafter, "Riots in New York and Los Angeles, 1935–2002," in David Halle, ed., *New York and Los Angeles: Politics, Society, and Culture: A Comparative View* (Chicago: University of Chicago Press, 2003), pp. 341–66. Quoted from p. 347.

26. Ibid., p. 348.

27. Therefore, I exclude from Halle and Rafter's list of New York riots those that occurred in Newark and other New Jersey towns in the 1960s. I also exclude the New York blackout riot of 1977 (the nadir of New York City's economic difficulties) as not racially triggered, although looting occurred in many poor areas occupied by minorities; a similar blackout in the city in 2003 was relatively free of looting and property damage.

28. St. Clair Drake and Horace Cayton coined this term in their classic book *Black Metropolis: A Study of Negro Life in a Northern City* (New York: Harcourt Brace, 1945).

29. The term was used by Arnold R. Hirsch in his fine book *Making the Second Ghetto: Race and Housing in Chicago, 1940–1960* (Cambridge: Cambridge University Press, 1983).

30. According to *A Report by the Governor's Commission on the Los Angeles Riots* (formally known as *Violence in the City—An End or a Beginning?* but known informally as the McCone Commission Report, dated December 2, 1965), 89 percent of Los Angeles' "Negro" population was segregated inside this cordoned-off area in 1965.

31. Martha Biondi's detailed history of African American activism in that city, *To Stand and Fight: The Struggle for Civil Rights in Postwar New York City* (Cambridge, Mass.: Harvard University Press, 2003), includes an important prologue linking members of the earlier Harlem Renaissance to the origins of the civil rights movement.

32. I use the county of Los Angeles, rather than the city, as my unit of analysis because the city consists of a set of neighborhoods interspersed with "independent" (and would-be "independent") suburbs, whereas the county subsumes all of them. Furthermore, the county contains roughly the same number of inhabitants as Metro Chicago and

New York's five boroughs, and runs many "urban" institutions, including the unified school system. The police forces of city and county call on each other in crisis situations.

33. I am thus ignoring slave rebellions and the systematic use of force to control them.

34. I depend for this classification system on the interesting small book edited by Joseph Boskin, *Urban Racial Violence in the Twentieth Century* (Beverly Hills, Calif.: Glencoe Press, 1969). This is an edited collection of short pieces gathered thematically and arranged chronologically. By "successive" I am not suggesting that older patterns disappear when new types materialize. Rather, there is a relative decline in earlier ones as the proportions shift.

35. The incidence of lynchings, according to Feagin and Vera, peaked in the period between the 1860s and 1916, when between 50 to 161 black deaths by lynching were recorded annually. By the 1930s, this number had dropped to 10–24 annually, and even lower from the 1950s on, although records are clearly incomplete. See Joe Feagin and Hernán Vera, *White Racism: The Basics* (New York: Routledge, 1995), p. 11.

36. Both these organizations were founded jointly by liberal white and black professionals. See, among others, Gunnar Myrdal, *An American Dilemma: The Negro Problem and Modern Democracy* (New York: Harper, 1944), pp. 819–42.

37. The fact that black "scab" workers were trucked in to break the strike of 1906–7 in the Chicago stockyards suggests that factory owners exacerbated racial tensions by playing what is today known as the "race card."

38. In New York, the Triangle Shirtwaist Company fire of 1911, in which more than a hundred young immigrant women died, was a significant marker in union organizing, but parallel developments were taking place in Chicago without the aid of a singular disaster. It should be noted, however, that African Americans were still excluded from the garment trades.

39. The listing, entitled "Minor Racial Violence in 1919," appears in Arthur Waskow, *From Race Riot to Sit-In, 1919 and the 1960s* (Garden City, N.Y.: Doubleday, 1966), pp. 303–7. His information was assembled from NAACP files.

40. See Herman H. Long and Charles S. Johnson, *People vs. Property: Race Restrictive Covenants in Housing* (Nashville: Fisk University Press, 1947), for their studies in Chicago and St. Louis. To some extent, however, New York's cooperative apartments served a similar exclusionary function without being subject to court challenge.

41. A slogan that would be echoed in the early civil rights struggles of the South.

42. There is an interesting story about the suppression of this hard-hitting commission report (which was never officially adopted) and its rediscovery in the 1960s. Although copies of it disappeared from the city archives, the text had been reproduced in the *Amsterdam News* (African American newspaper) of July 18, 1935. A xeroxed copy of this text was found in the Columbia University library by scholars preparing a series of documents on mass violence in America. A transcript was published in book form in the Mass Violence in America series in 1969 (cited throughout as the Mayor's Commission report), titled *The Complete Report of Mayor LaGuardia's Commission on the Harlem Riot of March 19, 1935* (New York: Arno Press and the New York Times, 1969). The report parallels, in many ways, the 1922 report on Chicago's race riot of 1919, *The Negro in Chicago*.

43. Particularly violent hostilities were to recur in that city during the summer of 1967; indeed, the narrative on Detroit's 1967 riot, included in chap. 2 of the Kerner Report, is the lengthiest and most detailed of the cases it chronicles.

44. For an explicit statement of the linkage between the Detroit riot and the establishment of the Chicago Mayor's Committee on Race Relations, see, *inter alia,* the introductions to its early annual reports—for example, one by its renamed successor, the Chicago Commission on Human Relations, *The People of Chicago: Five Year Report 1947–1951* (Chicago: Chicago Commission on Human Relations, 1953), p. 3. A section headed "Fires and Fears" reads: "Back in the summer of 1943 the flames of racial hatred flared suddenly and burned hotly in the neighboring city of Detroit, Michigan," which made Chicago afraid that "the 1919 riot would be repeated here."

45. Mauricio Mazon, *The Zoot-Suit Riots: The Psychology of Symbolic Annihilation* (Austin: University of Texas Press, 1984).

46. The fullest account of the 1943 riot is Dominic J. Capeci, Jr., *The Harlem Riot of 1943* (Philadelphia: Temple University Press, 1977). The best source comparing the 1935 and 1943 Harlem riots is Cheryl Greenberg, "The Politics of Disorder: Reexamining Harlem's Riots of 1935 and 1943," *Journal of Urban History* 18 (August 1992), pp. 395–441.

47. Unlike the case of Chicago, where the city council was able to block the locations of the city's postwar public housing projects by its power to approve or veto *every* individual site, the Board of Aldermen in New York, due to the overwhelming power of housing czar Robert Moses, could only approve or reject *all* proposed sites in a given block of proposed projects. The goal of Chicago legislators was to use public housing projects as a mechanism for increasing the concentration of blacks in the ghetto. The result of New York's policy was to scatter such projects throughout large parts of the various boroughs.

48. These points were stressed by Aldon D. Morris, *The Origins of the Civil-Rights Movement: Black Communities Organizing for Change* (New York: Free Press, 1984); see especially chaps. 1–6.

49. Ella Baker was a brilliant scholar and fine administrator who had formerly been associated with the NAACP and had spent many years in New York City, where her political education had been further honed. However, a male minister was appointed executive director. See Morris, op. cit., pp. 102–4, but see also the fine book about Ella Baker by Charles M. Payne, *I've Got the Light of Freedom* (Berkeley: University of California Press, 1995).

50. White flight was also constrained in New York by the preponderance of rental housing and the existence of rent control legislation.

51. This gives the map of the city a surrealistic shape, carved out of contiguous urban developments.

52. Excerpt reprinted from this article, in August Meier, Elliot Rudwick, and John Bracey, Jr., eds., *Black Protest in the Sixties: Articles from the New York Times* (New York: Markus Wiener, 1991), pp. 107–15.

53. Police provocation was almost always a trigger. In Manhattan an off-duty policeman killed a black high school youth in the "wrong place at the wrong time"; in Watts a year later, police harassed a black motorist and arrested him and his mother; in 1966 in Chicago, police cracked down on protests that erupted after Martin Luther King, Jr.,

had addressed an overflow audience in Soldier Field, kicking off his campaign for open housing in Chicago.

54. For detailed documentation, see Marilynn S. Johnson, *Street Justice: A History of Police Violence in New York City* (Boston: Beacon Press, 2003).

55. The fullest account of this ghetto uprising thus far is by the journalists Fred C. Shapiro and James Sullivan, *Race Riots: New York 1964* (New York: Crowell, 1969). A more scholarly research-based book by historian Michael Flamm is in preparation. See also Johnson, *Street Justice*, chap. 5.

56. The Kerner Report makes very little of this "riot," devoting only 22 lines on p. 36 to this event so crucial to New York.

57. A modest march southward from Madison Square Garden in 1992, on the day the Los Angeles police involved in beating Rodney King were exonerated, fizzled into isolated window-breakings only as it neared its end in Greenwich Village and Tompkins Square Park (personal observation).

58. Kenneth B. Clark, *Dark Ghetto: Dilemmas of Social Power* (New York: Harper and Row Torchbook, 1967), p. 16.

59. This pattern of mayoral solidarity set the tone for later symbolic gestures. In the 1992 Crown Heights case, David Dinkins, the black mayor, went to the neighborhood to help placate Jamaicans, although in the process he angered the Hasidic Jews. Mayor Giuliani's failure to react sympathetically to the Louima and Diallo cases was all the more infuriating because he deviated from what had come to be expected.

60. For a detailed and sober account of this controversy, see Jerald E. Podair, *The Strike That Changed New York: Blacks, Whites, and the Ocean Hill–Brownville Crisis* (New Haven: Yale University Press, 2002).

61. See Alejandro Portes and Alex Stepick, *City on the Edge: The Transformation of Miami* (Berkeley: University of California Press, 1993), chap. 1.

62. Michael McCall, "Some Ecological Aspects of Negro Slum Riots," (1968) reprinted in Joseph R. Gusfield, ed., *Protest, Reform and Revolt: A Reader in Social Movements* (New York: Wiley, 1970), pp. 345–362. Quotation from pp. 353–54. In this perceptive article, McCall refutes an earlier thesis of Allen Grimshaw that the New York riot of 1943 was an exception rather than a prototype for later ghetto revolts.

63. The Kerner Report erroneously attributed this to the closing of the hydrants, when in actual fact it followed the euphoria generated by King's rally in Soldier Field, attended by some tens of thousands, and his subsequent march to City Hall to demand open housing.

64. An account of white resistance in Garfield Park is Amanda Seligman, *Block by Block: Neighborhoods and Public Policy on Chicago's West Side* (Chicago: University of Chicago Press, 2005).

65. Actually, the Miami riot of 1980 might, in some ways, be considered a forerunner to the Los Angeles riot of 1992, but as Alejandro Portes and Alex Stepick emphasize in their book *City on the Edge*, the interethnic competitions (among Cubans, African Americans, and Haitians) in Miami are so different from most other places that the case does little to illuminate the more typical patterns of conflict in Los Angeles, New York, and Chicago. Atypical cases abound, however, and each has its own insights to contribute.

66. By far, the best analysis of the Korean–black/Latino conflict in the 1992 riot (albeit chiefly from the perspective of the Koreans) is Nancy Abelmann and John Lie's brilliant *Blue Dreams: Korean Americans and the Los Angeles Riots* (Cambridge, Mass.: Harvard University Press, 1995).

67. See Claire Jean Kim, "Cracks in the Gorgeous Mosaic: Black-Korean Conflict and Racial Mobilization in New York City" (Ph.D. diss., Yale University, 1996), subsequently published as *Bitter Fruit: The Politics of Black-Korean Conflict in New York City* (New Haven: Yale University Press, 2000).

68. According to *Crains New York Business* (May 21, 1990), some 90 percent of the city's 2,000 greengroceries were Korean owned and operated in 1990. Although Koreans also occupy this niche in the ghetto, their city-wide dispersion and the fact that other ethnic enterprises are also present in the city's ghettos and barrios means that there is no exclusive association between the specific business role and a generic ethnic identity. In addition, New York has no identifiable area like Koreatown which could become a target for hostilities.

69. David Cole, *No Equal Justice: Race and Class in the American Criminal Justice System* (New York: New Press, 1999).

70. Ibid., p. 5; italics in original.

Part 1

Chicago's Struggles to
Control Space

2

The Bloody Riot of 1919 and Its Consequences

In the twentieth century, Chicago experienced two *major* (and many more minor) race riots: the 1919 riot, which took place primarily on the South Side; and the 1968 uprising that, while not confined to the West Side, was allowed to rage out of control *only* there. The dates of these events bracket a period of interracial tensions in the city, marked by what might be termed border wars—a state of almost constant sniping over turf that occasionally flared up into significant battles from suppressed, but never quenched, embers. Changes in the immediate *casus belli* and in the protagonists, as well as the deflections in location, tell us much about the transformation of spatial segregation and race relations in the city and its region that had occurred in the interim.[1] And yet there is certainly continuity: both riots served primarily to redefine the territories and terms of racial apartheid.

In perhaps no other major city in the nation, with the possible exception of Detroit, have space, race, and riots been so intimately connected. And again, with the exception of Detroit and possibly Newark, in no other major urban region have persisting racial tensions been resolved so completely by a separation of the "combatants." But whereas the city proper of Detroit was eventually ceded to its minorities in the aftermath of successive riots in, *inter alia,* 1943 and 1967, not only in terms of space but in terms of the power structure, the struggle for the prize of political power and economic dominance in the Chicago region continues as an unequal contest.[2] Indeed, since Mayor Harold Washington's death in 1987, the balance of power appears to have returned to whites, in perhaps a more "compassionate" way dictated by demography, but skewed toward the interests of business.

Is Chicago fundamentally different from other American cities where competition, and sometimes battles, over land between contending interests or groups of people are "the name of the game"? I suggest that it may be, certainly in degree, if not in kind. In Chicago, as in other major cities, the "real estate game" is waged for unearned profits, for higher capitalist returns based on a monopoly over "higher use" land. In Chicago, however, this game is compounded by competition for space based on race, which time and again has trumped class and indeed has served to reproduce and even advance white privilege.

Therefore, simplified explanations based on land economics alone fail to capture the spatial story of Chicago. Nor do simple mechanistic models that emphasize tensions in labor competition resulting from a large influx of undifferentiated newcomers explain very much. The hypothesis that racial tensions are exacerbated by the influx of large numbers of "blacks" who then challenge an originally dominant "white" population is belied in Chicago, as it is in New York, as we shall see. The outbreak of a severe and prolonged race riot" in 1919 occurred at a time when African Americans constituted only about 4 percent of Chicago's population. Nor was that conflict largely between well-situated whites and excluded blacks. At that time, "ethnic" whites and blacks were both marginal to the power structure, which perhaps intensified the animosities between them. And today, simple mechanistic models that emphasize tensions in labor competition and exclusion of blacks from the productive economy, or even the selective deployment of public powers to "reconquer" space in the center city for "whiter" residential, institutional, and finance/business uses, do not fully explain why race remains the decisive variable in Chicago.

The riot of 1919 was a sign that Chicago had a special problem, one to be explored in this chapter. One of the most violent and prolonged in the history of our country, it became the object of an official investigation by a newly organized Chicago Commission on Race Relations, which issued a very long and carefully researched and documented report, *The Negro in Chicago: A Study of Race Relations and a Riot.*[3] This is one of the richest sources in riot literature and has been drawn on freely by every subsequent author who has written on the early development of the African American community in Chicago and its fate during and after the riot. Included in this remarkable document was a detailed map showing the scattered locations of African American residences at the time hostilities broke out, where the "battles" took place, and where fatalities occurred. (Newer techniques of scanning and reduction have made it possible, for the first time, to reprint this as map 2.1a here.)

But before proceeding to this story, I want to preview changes that occurred between 1919 and the riot of 1968 (covered in chapter 3), because these suggest the persistence of intractable interracial tensions in Chicago that seem even more extreme than in most American cities. These tensions were independent of the number of African Americans and their proportion in the population. In the course of the half century between 1919 and 1968, the proportion of African Americans in the population of the city increased eightfold, from about 4 percent in the census of 1920 to 33 percent in the census of 1970. By 1980, it had risen to close to 40 percent, where it remained in 1990, although it had dropped to 38 percent by 2000, because continued white flight was offset by increases in the Latino and Asian populations. By that year, even though the combined black, Latino, and Asian populations brought the "minority" total up to a "majority" of over 60 percent, the political and economic power of minorities in the city still lagged sorely behind their numbers. Their struggle for space, housing, and access to quality public facilities and services continues. For only a few brief years, during the mayoral administration of Harold Washington (1983–87), did minority groups succeed in making progress to redress these inequities.[4]

Chicago has been relatively but not completely free of major direct racial confrontations or riots since 1968;[5] but this is no firm indicator that racial tensions in the city have mysteriously been resolved. Rather, the evidence suggests that in the interim, the "combatants" increasingly have reached a *modus vivendi*, maintained largely through their separation in geographic and political space. For the most part, minorities are confined to specific sections of the city and, more recently, have come to constitute pluralities in a handful of isolated towns within Cook County. The white "Maginot line" of border wars—which retreated earliest and most completely on the South Side and later more grudgingly on the West Side—now stands between Cook County and the farther-out "collar counties" (Will, Lake, Du Page, Kane, and Henry) that encircle it. The latter remain overwhelmingly white. And in place of direct confrontations, it appears that the strategies and tactics of localized "race wars" at the margins of black settlement have shifted. The weapons are now largely: (1) selective public and private economic investment and disinvestment strategies that have marginalized or even removed a substantial proportion of poor blacks from the productive economy; and (2) the selective deployment

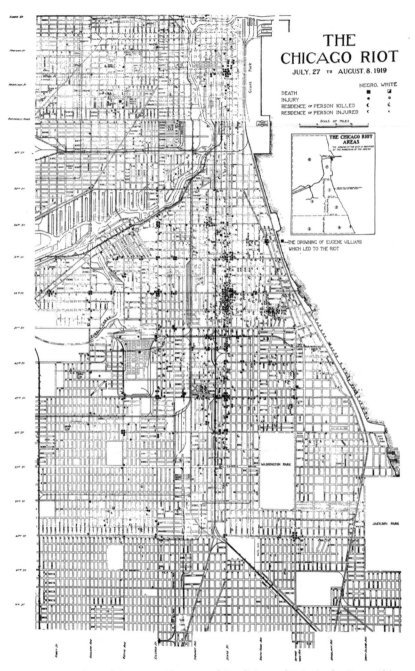

Map 2.1a.   Location of Negro Residences and Fatalities and Injuries by Race, Chicago Riot of 1919.

Source: Charles S. Johnson, *The Negro in Chicago: A Study in Race Relations and a Race Riot in 1919*. Copyright: University of Chicago Press, 1922.

of public powers to "reconquer" space in portions of the city center (an expanding Loop and the northern and northwestern quadrants) for "whiter" residential, institutional, and finance/business uses.

The 1919 riot may be seen as signaling the start of two trends in racial conflict that would intensify in the ensuing decades. The first was a new militancy on the part of the black community to resist the typical white-on-black violence that had hitherto been the dominant form racial tensions had taken. But the second, paradoxically, was the increased "ingathering" of blacks within a more fully segregated ghetto, as white violence drove scattered black residents from other areas of the city in which they already lived. This ingathering soon transformed a nascent South Side "black belt" (which in 1910 had still contained many whites) into a predominantly black-occupied portion of the city, according to the censuses of 1920 and 1930 (see maps 2.1b, 2.1c, and 2.2).

Given this concentration and the subsequent rapid growth of the African American community, it was inevitable that accommodation could be attained only through the "conquest" of more and usually contiguous territory. Thus, for the next few decades, the South Side "black belt" expanded in the only direction open to it, pressing southward to absorb larger and larger zones formerly occupied by whites. Without the operation of a dual housing market, this transition could have proceeded differently.[6] But the roots of its dynamics lay deep in the race-conscious soil of Chicago.

"BLACK LAWS": NINETEENTH-CENTURY ROOTS OF CHICAGO'S RACISM

The early distribution of blacks in the city—their poverty and the initial tendency for African Americans to be relegated to shacks between the railroad tracks on Chicago's South Side—requires a historical explanation, one in which racism must be recognized as constituting a bedrock element. Some even trace Chicago's racism to Illinois's origins as a "southern" state. Illinois, originally a colony of Virginia, shared more with its southern neighbors than its northeastern ones.[7] That may be one reason why, even though Chicago's black population long preceded the arrival of immigrants, their relative status remained inferior to them.[8]

> One year after Illinois became a state [in 1818] ... it instituted severe "Black laws." Under such laws it was necessary for blacks to have a certificate of freedom to become a resident of Illinois. Failure to produce said document could have resulted in being sold for a period of one year. Blacks had very little protection under these laws. Blacks could not vote and travel was restricted to local areas.[9]

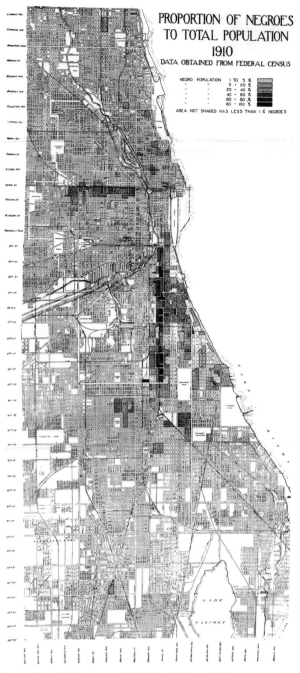

Map 2.1b.   Proportion of Negroes to Total Population, Chicago 1910.

Source: Charles S. Johnson, *The Negro in Chicago: A Study in Race Relations and a Race Riot in 1919*. Copyright: University of Chicago Press, 1922.

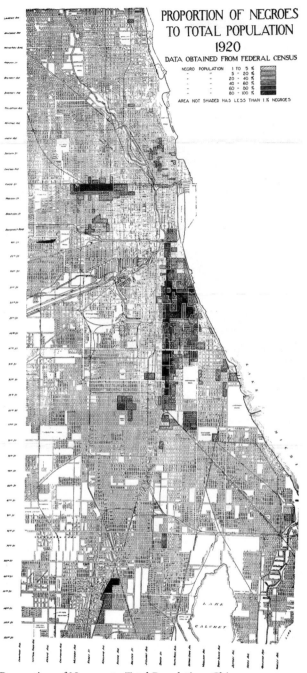

Map 2.1c.   Proportion of Negroes to Total Population, Chicago 1920.

Source: Charles S. Johnson, *The Negro in Chicago: A Study in Race Relations and a Race Riot in 1919*. Copyright: University of Chicago Press, 1922.

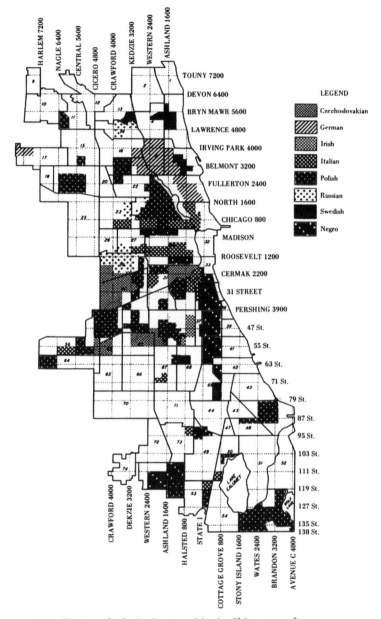

Map 2.2.   Distribution of Ethnic Communities in Chicago as of 1930.

Source: Thomas Lee Philpott, *The Slum and the Ghetto*. Copyright: Oxford University Press, 1978.

These disabilities persisted into the second half of the nineteenth century. Philpott summarized the disadvantages:

> A state law of 1858 forbade free Negroes to enter Illinois. Negroes who already resided there or who slipped in undetected by the authorities were subject to "black codes." They had no civil rights. They could not vote, serve on juries, testify against whites, or intermarry with them.... It was 1870 before Negroes could vote. The State of Illinois did not ban school segregation until 1874, and it waited another ten years to prohibit racial discrimination in public accommodations.[10]

Nevertheless, within the city of Chicago at least, the abolitionists were strong and active. In 1850, the city passed a resolution that said the police were not obligated to help recover escaping slaves. By then, two underground railway stations were operating in the city, in which blacks played important roles.[11] (One of these stations was in suburban Evanston, which accounts for the longstanding small ghetto on the west side of that town.)

But throughout the nineteenth century, numbers remained small. And since most of Chicago's blacks were employed in personal or domestic service, some living in or near the homes of their employers, there was no large or centralized ghetto. Only in the 1890s, when a new migration from the South began, did segregation intensify, and it was only after the tentative entry of blacks into heavy industry as strikebreakers that the preexistent racism intensified among the "new ethnics."

THE FORMATION OF THE BLACK BELT

By 1900, "several of the old colonies had merged to form a long, narrow Black Belt" along State Street between 12th and 39th Streets, a quarter of a mile wide and some three miles long and completely surrounded by railway tracks.[12] In the next decade, the black population increased from about 30,000 in 1900 to 44,000 in 1910, but the area open to it did not expand. The newcomers from the South settled between State Street and the Rock Island Railroad tracks to the west, the poorest and most run-down part of the black belt. Even before the great migration, rents were high and hostile whites surrounded the black belt.[13]

By 1915, when the black population had increased to over 50,000, the South Side ghetto had taken on a clearer geographic shape. As Spear notes, although in the late nineteenth century "most Negroes lived in certain sections of the South Side, they lived interspersed among whites; there were few all-Negro blocks.

By 1915, on the other hand . . . a large, almost all-Negro enclave on the South Side, with a similar offshoot on the West Side, housed most of Chicago's Negroes."[14] It was at that point that the great migration began.

By 1920, the black population exceeded 109,000. Ten years later, it would approach 234,000. White resistance to their residential expansion stiffened, and "the black population piled up in a ghetto circumscribed as no immigrant enclave had ever been."[15] The source of these new migrants had also changed. Although some 80 percent of the 30,000 native-born nonwhites in Chicago in 1890, like their white counterparts, had come to the city from elsewhere, most hailed from "upper south border states," and these areas continued to provide newcomers in the decades of slow migration that followed.[16] But in the period between 1916 and 1919, the size and composition of the black community changed drastically. During these short years, some 50,000 newcomers, recruited chiefly from Mississippi, Louisiana, and Arkansas, were crowded into the existing ghetto, whose boundaries proved impermeable.[17]

A labor shortage in Chicago had become especially critical after America entered the war early in 1917, and the steel mills, foundries, and packinghouses sent recruiters south for more workers.[18] The industrialization of Chicago's black population was dramatic. As late as 1910, more than half of black males had worked in domestic or personal services; 10 years later, only little more than a quarter did, whereas the proportion of blacks engaged in manufacturing and trade had tripled.[19]

These economic gains were not translated into more and better housing, however. Indeed, they triggered increased hostility and resistance from white neighbors and coworkers.

> Instead of expanding the boundaries of the Negro districts, the migration converted the old South Side black belt from a mixed neighborhood into an exclusively Negro area. There was remarkably little . . . change in the areas of Negro settlement despite the 148 per cent population increase . . . [resulting in a] sharp rise in the density.[20]

This overcrowding resulted in rapidly deteriorating housing quality accompanied by inflated rents. The festering slum east of State Street became even worse, and the Prairie Avenue mansions inherited from the old elite quarter were divided up and subdivided again, to accommodate the "better off."[21] Some of Chicago's earliest "border wars" were fought as the black belt expanded slightly at its edges into white districts, arousing white hostility and intensifying efforts to tighten the noose. All these served as preludes to the race riot of 1919, the bloodiest in the city's history to that date.

AN OVERSIMPLIFIED DESCRIPTION OF THE SPATIAL STRUCTURE OF CHICAGO

As every student of urban sociology knows from the oft-reproduced diagram sketched by Ernest Burgess in the early decades of the twentieth century, Chicago's simplified form is hemispherical, with the lake constituting its eastern half. The city itself occupies an elongated half circle expanding westward from the shoreline along radial lines established naturally by the north and (former) south branches of the Chicago River, a radial pattern solidified early on by the transportation system of rails, then streetcars, and then highways.

These radial lines divide the city roughly into three major sectors. The north-by-northwest sector is still a predominantly white district that merges imperceptibly into a set of prosperous suburban communities. Due west of downtown, but separated from it by the Chicago River, lies the formerly proletarian sector contained between the branches of the river. South by southwest, radiating from the southern edge of the downtown (the Loop), is the zone in which the overwhelming majority of Chicago's black population has become concentrated.

In general, areas along the lake shore evolved by careful planning into what I have elsewhere called the façade of the city. In contrast, the industrial zones and associated districts of proletarian housing originally followed the branched paths of the Chicago River, while south of the Loop, railroad lines and rail yards preempted much of the close-in ring beyond the central business district, intensifying the discontinuity between the high-rise and commercial Loop and the remaining, mostly residential, quarters. During the latter part of the nineteenth century, when Chicago's Fordist industrial base was being laid, Chicago's "dual city" of façade and backstage was established, a cleavage solidified in the early twentieth century.

The backstage city was essentially constructed when massive immigration from the European semiperiphery (south and east) swelled the ranks of the "white ethnics" who entered the burgeoning heavy industrial sector and settled in nearby residential quarters. These new industrial workers were, to some extent, segregated "on the job" by an ethnic pecking order that correlated roughly with their time of arrival, and were also roughly segregated residentially by affinity, differential vacancies, and institutional (primarily religious) and consumption specialization.[22]

The weakness of industrial labor unions and the collusion between Chicago's decision-makers and its industrial elite (often the same people) meant that public powers were frequently invoked to quell strikes and other labor actions in the proto-Fordist industries, the most important of which were concentrated in the Union Stockyards along the south branch of the Chicago River. Lockouts and the hiring of new, vulnerable laborers to break strikes were the major mechanisms factory owners used to discipline their workers. Thus, use of blacks as temporary strikebreakers in the 1904 stockyards strike is often cited as intensifying antiblack feelings. But entry via the role of scab did not necessarily preclude eventual inclusion. For example, Polish strikebreakers employed in the stockyards strike of 1894 were kept on after the strike was settled, and animus toward their role was subsequently muted.[23]

THE BEGINNINGS OF BLACK LABOR RECRUITMENT

"Ethnic succession" in the Chicago region's largest Fordist industries (the stockyards and later, the steel mills on the far south side) had been occurring during the second half of the nineteenth century, as Irish and German craft workers were threatened by newcomer Slavs, recruited first as strikebreakers in 1894 but then integrated into the labor forces as production processes were rationalized and deskilled. During labor disputes, intergroup hostilities were stoked. But in the acrimonious stockyards strike of 1904, when African American workers were first introduced in significant numbers as strikebreakers, the usual pattern of retaining strikebreakers did not apply. For two weeks,

> trainloads of several hundred Negroes, accompanied by officers of the law, arrived daily.... The role of the Negro in the strike of 1904 differed from that which he had assumed in 1894. *He was at the center of attack from the moment the strike began....* To the striking union men no scabs were as loathsome as the Negroes who took their jobs.... At the close of the struggle ... the colored deserters were herded into special trains which carried them to the Black Belt. The packers preferred white laborers and hired them to replace the Negroes whose services as strikebreakers were no longer required.[24]

It was, then, not until the labor shortage of World War I that African Americans were finally recruited in any number to the large-scale industries in the city. Hostilities intensified between "white ethnics" and blacks, who were discriminated against and who consequently retained a healthy suspicion of the unions that had opposed their hiring and, indeed, had first excluded them.[25] Some of the simmering interracial hostilities that erupted in the race riot that wracked Chicago between July 27 and August 2 in 1919 can be traced directly to tensions that built up in large workplaces, especially in the stockyards, ostensibly over unionization.[26]

WHY CHICAGO? WHY 1919?

That a widespread and prolonged outbreak of racial hostilities should have occurred in Chicago in 1919 was almost "overdetermined." First, as we have seen, tensions between male "blacks" and working-class "white ethnics" had been building from before the turn of the century and were manifested in workplaces and neighborhoods where competition over jobs and residences simmered. Second, the black population, although still small, grew rapidly during the labor shortage in the World War I period, when industrial recruiters were sent to rural areas of the Deep South to entice migrants. According to Tuttle, the school census of May 1914 had counted fewer than 55,000 blacks in Chicago, a number that had doubled to about 110,000 by the census of 1920.[27] The new residents, mostly rural folk drawn from the South, were scarcely welcomed, and this dramatic infusion of blacks certainly exacerbated existing tensions. A not atypical response was a blatantly racist headline in the *Chicago Tribune*: "Half a Million Darkies from Dixie Swarm to the North to Better Themselves."[28] And third, in the housing shortage of wartime, such "darkies" faced insurmountable barriers in gaining access to living space.

Thus, both job and residential conflicts were brewing. Charles Johnson (the black sociologist from the University of Chicago responsible for the pathbreaking early study of the 1919 riot, *The Negro in Chicago*) and William Tuttle, Jr. (author of *Race Riot*, the best later history of the same riot), disagree somewhat in evaluating the relative importance of these two forms of competition. Both Johnson's *Negro in Chicago* and Allan Spear's *Black Chicago* on the growth of the Chicago ghetto, influenced by the "ecological" framework of the Chicago School (in which both were trained), emphasize struggles over residential space, whereas economic historians such as Herbert Guttman and especially William Tuttle, Jr. tend to emphasize the threats that new Negro workers posed to unionized labor. As Tuttle notes, "contrary to . . . the Commission report [Johnson's], upwards of 20,000 black workers, or from 50 to 75 percent more than the 12,000 black [union] members in 1919, would have had to be unionized in order to have been on a par with the proportion of white union members."[29] In this debate, I agree more with the economic historians. Economic competition was a fundamental "cause" of the riot.

UNDERLYING ECONOMIC CONDITIONS

In the immediate postwar period, the combined force of four macroeconomic conditions therefore brought such tensions to a head.

1. The recent massive recruitment of black labor from rural areas of the Deep South during wartime, which more than doubled the black population in a few short years, albeit to only 4.1 percent of the total by 1920
2. The rapid demobilization of white and black soldiers from the armed forces after the war, which brought heightened competition between returning servicemen and black war workers (and the subsequent displacement of blacks from their newly gained industrial jobs)
3. A new militancy among black former servicemen, who understandably resented being "demoted" in the labor market after having served their country in war
4. An economic downturn immediately after the war, in which labor strife and fears of joblessness combined to make white ethnic labor more militant and blacks less accepting of their reduced status

These underlying conditions were certainly not confined to Chicago. It is important to recognize that in the late war and early postwar years, interracial violence was also escalating in many other U.S. cities that had configurations of economy and space somewhat different from Chicago's. Just as in the 1960s, when the peaking of racial violence signaled widespread discord and a reordering of race relations, so the period during and after World War I similarly witnessed multiple "explosions." The Chicago riot had been preceded by a bloody one in East St. Louis in 1917, and just after Chicago's, the "next major riot of the Red Summer erupted in Omaha, Nebraska," a meatpacking center like Chicago, but with a much smaller black population, albeit one that had doubled during the war from southern migration.[30]

Waskow's excellent study lists in chronological order the following race riots that occurred around the same time as Chicago's.[31]

1. Berkeley, Georgia. Attempted lynching on February 28, 1919. One Negro killed, four whites (would-be lynchers) killed.
2. Millen, Georgia. April 13–14, 1919, two days of race riots. Two white men and four Negroes killed. One Negro lynched.
3. New London, Connecticut. June 13, 1919, street battle between white and Negro sailors; police and firemen unable to stop riot, but the Marines, called in, stopped it.
4. Bisbee, Arizona. July 5, 1919. Clash between Negro cavalry and white policemen: three Negroes and two whites wounded. "Fourteen Negroes arrested and turned over to the military authorities."
5. Dublin, Georgia. July 12, 1919. "Attempted lynching of one Negro ended in killing of white by another Negro."

6. Coatsville, Pennsylvania. July 8, 1919. Race riot (rumor of attack on young white girl, attempted lynching from prison). "'More than 500 Negroes voiced protest.... Later nine Negroes on their way to City Hall with baseball bats were arrested.'"

7. Philadelphia, Pennsylvania, July 8, 1919. "Small racial incident started free-for-all fight. Whites, finding themselves outnumbered, retreated, but returned with reinforcements. General riot call sent out and 100 police stopped the trouble. Eight colored men arrested."

8. Port Arthur, Texas, July 14, reported in paper July 15, 1919. Clash between 20 whites and 14 Negroes; 2 seriously injured Negroes hospitalized.

9. Norfolk, Virginia, July 22, 1919. In a celebration of the homecoming of Negro troops, "clash between Negroes and white policemen started when policemen tried to arrest Negroes fighting among themselves."

10. New Orleans, Louisiana, July 23, 1919. Police broke up a fight between Negroes and whites.

11. Syracuse, New York, July 30–31, 1919, quoted from newspaper: "Rioting broke out between striking moulders [sic] and Negro strikebreakers at the plant of the Globe Maleable Iron Co. The rioters were subdued by the police and four men were arrested."

12. Montreal, Canada, an entry I have omitted as out of place.

13. Ocmulgee, Georgia, August 29, 1919.

14. Baltimore, Maryland, October 2, 1919.

15. Wilmington, Delaware, November 14, 1919.

16. Bogalusa, Louisiana, November 23–25, 1919 (related to a labor conflict).

While the newspaper accounts of these incidents are not necessarily to be trusted, nor is the list necessarily complete, I have included this enumeration to indicate that 1919 was tense in other places as well, and that such tension, at least outside the South, could be attributed in part to labor competition. But in Chicago, the situation was much more complex.

CONFRONTATIONS BY CLASS, RESIDENCE, AND POLITICS

However, because ethnicity was the organizing principle of the backstage neighborhoods of Chicago, and because representatives elected by wards to the Chicago city council had significant power to defend neighborhood interests, interethnic tensions at the workplace were often projected into residential space and vice versa. Furthermore, members of the city council, heavily weighted to the "back city," and the technocrats and elite executives and administrators who lived mostly in the city of the façade were often at odds.[32] It would be a mistake, therefore, to separate class from residential and political factors. We have seen how the proletarian role of masses of European immigrants intersected with Chicago's rapid industrialization. The formation and distribution of ethnic communities along the industrial river and railway corridors can largely be explained by how immigrants of different origin groups were inserted into the industrial labor force, and thus settled near their jobs. Segregation occurred in both physical and social space, as can be seen from map 2.2 above.[33]

The Chicago elite of transplanted northeasterners found the toleration of gambling parlors, saloons, and brothels by machine politicians from the "immigrant wards" as offensive as did their counterparts in New York, and they agitated against vice and for civil service and ballot reforms. They achieved modest reforms briefly in the 1890s, "when the police department was reorganized, gambling was curbed, [and] the merit system was adopted for municipal employment."[34] But their efforts were essentially undermined once "Big Bill" Thompson succeeded in taking over municipal government in 1915, leaving the Chicago Civic Federation and the Municipal Voters' League in disarray. Among Mayor Thompson's strongest supporters were African Americans, and during his regime this support was reciprocated, as a few black politicians made gains as loyal servants of Thompson's Republican machine.[35] Although in general, black voters were ignored by both machine politicians and civic reformers, during the 1919 riot, Irish gangs (notably Ragen's Colts), supported by Democratic politicians, played a particularly active role in antiblack violence.

THE RACE RIOT OF 1919

Economic developments and spatial segregation thus almost overdetermined that a "race war" would break out in 1919. In the recession of 1919, Chicago's black industrial workers suffered severe setbacks. "In the spring of 1919, the packing houses paid off 15,000 workers—a large proportion of them Negroes."[36] Although the recession was short-lived, blacks were not rehired. Racial tensions were building, an explosion soon to come. Between July 1, 1917, and July 27, 1919 (the day a black swimmer, hit by an object thrown by a hostile white, drowned off a South Side beach), there had been 24 racially motivated bombings, "more than half of them in the six months just prior to the race riot."[37]

During the six days between July 27 and August 2, white gangs made raids on the black belt, and battles erupted outside it, wherever blacks had to travel to reach their jobs. In these occurrences, spatial patterns proved highly significant. Some of the worst violence occurred in relation to the stockyards, since workers from the black belt had to go through intervening Irish quarters to get to work there. "White mobs molested blacks returning home from the stockyards . . . and after a transit strike the next day stopped violence on public transportation . . . African Americans had to walk through hostile, Irish-dominated neighborhoods in order to reach their jobs in the stockyards." There were even racial clashes between workers in the livestock pens![38]

Eventually, by the time the Illinois state militia put down the rioting, the body count at the end of hostilities stood at 15 whites and 23 blacks dead. The toll would have been even higher had not Big Bill Thompson made efforts to station police along the borders of the South Side settlement. But in the long run, the true toll was to be measured in terms of its effects on future race relations in the city. After the riot, blacks and whites withdrew more firmly within their own "borders," and the black community on the South Side proceeded to develop its own institutions, essentially becoming a city within the city.

The Precipitating Events That Touched Off the 1919 Riot

With summer temperatures in the nineties for several successive days, Chicagoans had, as usual, taken themselves to the beaches along Lake Michigan to cool off. But instead of reducing the heat of mounting racial animosities, the lake provided the spark for a major "border war" between blacks and whites. The "trigger" was an altercation on July 27, 1919, between blacks and whites at the "unwritten" dividing line of racial segregation along the southern shore of Lake Michigan, the 25th Street beach, which was "designated" for "Black" users, and the 29th Street beach, "reserved" for "Whites." What ensued were five days of street battles, eventually suppressed by reinforcements from the Illinois State Militia. Not until 10 days after the riot began was sufficient calm restored for the militia to be withdrawn.

As in all accounts of the etiology of intercommunal strife, there are at least two versions. One of Tuttle's accounts reflects the official view, placing the onus on black actors. I reproduce it here.

> Defying the unwritten law which designated the [29th Street] beach as exclusively white, several black men and women had strolled to 29th Street determined to enter the water. Curses, threatening gestures, and rocks had frightened the intruders away. Minutes later, however, their numbers reinforced, the blacks reappeared, this time hurling rocks. The white bathers fled. But the blacks' possession of the beach was only temporary; behind a barrage of stones white bathers and numerous sympathizers returned. The battle that ensued was frightening in its violence but it merely anticipated

Chicago's long-feared race war. Sparked by the conflict at the beach, all the racial fears and hates of the past months and years would explode in bloody warfare.[39]

But it should be noted that a somewhat different sequence is also accepted, one that identifies the trigger as a drowning death of a black youth in an area *between* the two beaches. This version is also included in Tuttle's account. Certainly exacerbating the ongoing tensions was the undeniable death by drowning of a black teenager, Eugene Williams, who, along with three friends, had been swimming and piloting a homemade raft in the waters of a "nonbeach" no-man's land off 26th Street, behind the Keeley Brewery and Consumers Ice plant. According to this account, a white man standing at the end of the breakwater at 26th Street started to throw rocks at the swimmers as their raft floated south. Williams was struck on the forehead by one of the rocks and went under, bloodied. His friends, unable to save him, raced to report the accident to a lifeguard at the 25th Street Beach. It was half an hour before Eugene's body was finally recovered by divers.[40]

The enraged boys, accompanied by a black policeman from 25th Street, walked to the 29th Street beach, where they

> pointed out the man they believed to be the rock thrower to the white policeman on duty, Daniel Callahan. But Callahan not only would not arrest the man; he even refused to permit the black policeman to arrest him. As the policemen argued, Harris and his friends ran back to 25th Street and "told...what was happening and they started running"...to 29th Street.[41]

The boys ran home in fear, but at 29th Street, the white (Irish) policeman still refused to arrest the alleged perpetrator and, adding insult to injury, "arrested a black man on the complaint of a white." By this time, rumors were circulating furiously all over the South Side, and in response, "hundreds of angry blacks and whites swarmed to the beach.... Then a black man, James Crawford, drew a revolver and fired into a cluster of policemen, wounding one of them. A black officer returned the fire, fatally injuring Crawford.... The gunfire had signaled the start of a race war."[42]

Space and Race in the Riot

Although the race war had broken out at the north-south dividing line of tension, the recreational border between two beaches, the actual war would be waged along an east-west residential border (a Maginot line?) along Wentworth Avenue that separated the nascent black belt to its east from the almost exclusively white and largely Irish working-class neighborhood to its west. In graphic language, Wentworth Avenue was referred to at the time as the "Dead-Line."[43] The location of this line is easily found on map 2.1a above. It is the darkest north–south line on the map, indicating maximum injuries, fights, and fatalities.

As Tuttle points out:

> To the west, across Wentworth Avenue, were the Irish, whose hostility excluded blacks from that [housing] market. This hostility was so intense that the population in one Irish-dominated neighborhood bordering on Wentworth would tolerate only twenty-nine blacks out of 3,762 residents, while in the neighborhood just on the other [eastern] side of Wentworth, 1,722 out of 3,711 residents were black.[44]

The large, predominantly Irish district to the southwest of the black belt was "protected" by Ragen's Colts, young "party hacks" who were financially supported by Frank Ragen, a popular Democratic Cook County commissioner. During the riot, Ragen's Colts actively attacked blacks across the "Dead-Line" and harassed and beat blacks venturing into Irish turf.[45]

The spatial boundary between Irish and black areas proved particularly significant during the riot days, since by 1919, blacks who lived primarily in the South Side black belt made up about one-fourth of the labor force at the Chicago Union Stockyards (albeit at the lowest levels and mostly outside the labor unions). In order to get to their jobs, they had to pass through the turf of Ragen's Colts. And although they usually traveled by streetcars, they were harassed on the first day of the riot, and when the streetcar workers went out on strike just after the riot began, they had either to walk through hostile turf or stay home. Almost all stayed home—so many that the meatpacking companies later had to set up pay stations at Jesse Binga's "black" bank to pay their workers the back wages they desperately needed to survive.

If racial, ethnic, and religious differences defined the east-west dead-line, class boundaries, compounded by race, operated just south of the expanding black belt, in the area of Hyde Park and the University of Chicago, where property owners were trying to organize to exclude the expansion of blacks in their area.

The Sequence of the Riot Itself

On the evening of the drowning and altercation at the lake, white gang members from west of Wentworth went on a rampage, beating and injuring some 27 blacks.[46] Most were the victims of Ragen's Colts and other "west-of-Wentworth gangs." Seven blacks were stabbed and another four wounded by gunfire.

The report of the Chicago Commission on Race Relations (Johnson, *The Negro in Chicago*) later observed that had it not been for the activities of these gangs, "it is doubtful if the riot would have gone beyond the first clash." I disagree. Given my earlier analysis of underlying causes, it is very likely that Chicago would have "blown" anyway, because tensions were so "ripe."

Most of these injuries were incurred chiefly when whites "invaded the territory of the black belt or threatened its peripheries. Blacks usually employed such individual tactics as sniping, while whites resorted to mob warfare. Their primary weapons were thus firearms and knives, while those of whites were bricks, stones, fists, baseball bats, iron bars, and hammers."[47]

But hostilities were not confined to invasions of the black belt. By the next day, Monday, the scene of action moved to the gates of the stockyards as white gangs awaited blacks leaving after their shift. "Pouncing upon black workers as they passed through the gates, the mob viciously assaulted their prey. Some blacks escaped, managing to elude their pursuers by outrunning them or boarding streetcars just in time. Others, however, were not so fortunate." For example, a crowd of some 2,000 followed the hard core of the attackers, who tackled John Mills (who had just boarded a streetcar to take him east to the black belt) and pummeled him to death.[48] According to Johnson, 41 percent of all clashes occurred in the stockyards area, 34 percent in the black belt, and the rest were scattered throughout the city.[49] This suggests that this was not just a struggle over residential turf. Tensions at work were more important than one might have expected.

By Monday evening, however, carloads of whites were speeding through the residential streets of the black belt, discharging their weapons as they passed. When Mayor Thompson returned hurriedly from Montana in the early morning hours of Tuesday, he assigned most of the Chicago police force to the border of the black belt to cordon off traffic. But "white mobs snowballed in size throughout the city that evening,"[50] and with 80 percent of the police massed on the South Side, violence raged unrestrained elsewhere. Finally, the mayor called on the governor to mobilize the state militia. In response, 3,500 troops filtered into the city, but they remained in local armories, since the mayor had still not requested their use.[51]

To make matters worse, mass transit workers struck, and all streetcars and elevated lines ceased running at 4 a.m. in the morning. Without streetcars, black workers could not get to their jobs at the stockyards Tuesday morning without walking through hostile white territory; frightened, they stayed away.[52] But despite their withdrawal to circle the wagons, by that evening, violence had spilled over to other parts of the city.

Italian residents on the West Side...set upon a black youth who happened to ride by on his bicycle. His body riddled with bullets and stab wounds, the boy died an awful death.... Race rioting also erupted on the North Side, where nearly 5,000 whites hunted down black people in the streets. On the South Side, however, few men and women ventured outside their homes. Parts of the district were closeted in darkness, the result of rioters having shot out most of the street lamps.[53]

By early Wednesday, the death toll had climbed to 31, yet the mayor had still not called for support from the state militia. Finally, that night, largely in response to requests from the black leaders themselves, Thompson activated the militia, because there "was the fear of a widespread plot to burn the black belt; the fire department reported thirty-seven conflagrations in five hours that evening, many of them set within a few minutes on the same evening." Just before 10 p.m., some "6,200 troops...in the city moved out of the armories and into the region bounded by Wentworth and Indiana, and 18th and 55th Streets." The troops cracked down on the white athletic clubs, and then it began to rain. "After that, the violence was sporadic and sparse."[54]

But by Thursday morning, it was still unsafe for black workers to return to the stockyards. "Truckloads of fresh food, milk, and ice entered the black belt, and on Friday the meat packers established emergency pay stations at the Urban League, Wabash YMCA, and Jesse Binga's bank."[55] Even though the transit strike ended on Friday and streetcar and elevated service resumed at 5 a.m. Saturday morning, it was still not safe for blacks to go back to work. In any case, the plants were closed on Sunday.

By Monday, the militia was beginning to get the hostilities under control, but the atmosphere was still heavy with threats.[56] It was not until Friday, August 7, that the militia could begin to withdraw. The troops were all gone by Sunday, August 9, which officially ended the 14 days of rioting. The final "body count" was 38 dead: 23 of them black men or boys (of whom seven had been killed by the police), the remaining 15 whites stabbed or shot by blacks in self-defense. Of the 537 wounded in the hostilities, 342 were black.[57]

But the true costs were to intensify the segregation of the African American population within Chicago's South Side black belt and to fuel the mutual suspicions and animosities that would persist for the next 80 (and still counting) years. The unsigned somber introduction to *The Negro in Chicago* put "The Problem" in the starkest terms possible.

Countless schemes have been proposed for solving or dismissing this problem, most of them impracticable or impossible. Of this class are such proposals as: (1) the deportation of 12,000,000 Negroes to Africa; (2) the establishment of a separate Negro state in the United States; (3) complete separation and segregation from the whites and the establishment of a caste system or peasant class; and (4) hope for a solution through the dying out of the Negro race. [But white readers were reminded that]...Negroes alone of all our immigrants came to America against their will;...that the institution of slavery was introduced, expanded, and maintained...by the white people and for their own benefit; and that they likewise created the conditions that followed emancipation.... [The Negro problem has not been made by the Negro...its solution does not lie with him. ...] It is of the first importance that old prejudices against the Negroes, based upon their misfortunes and not on their faults, be supplanted with respect, encouragement, and co-operation, and with a recognition of their heroic struggles for self-improvement and of their worthy achievements as loyal American citizens.[58]

THE CHICAGO SOLUTION—THE "ATLANTA" SOLUTION

This plea was not likely to fall on receptive ears in Chicago. Of the four alternatives, Chicago's whites chose the third. Indeed, on Tuesday, August 5, when the battles were raging most fiercely, "*an Irish alderman sought to capitalize on the rampant racial antipathy by introducing a motion that the city council establish segregated zones, but his resolution was ruled out of order.*"[59] In other sources, this proposal is referred to as the "Atlanta Solution." While no official resolution was ever adopted by the Chicago city council, Chicago's white citizens pursued by de facto means what they could not achieve by de jure methods. On the legal front, they began to strengthen the barricades by deed and residency restrictions; on the physical front, they manned those barricades with firebombs, isolated threats and victimization, and, when matters grew too threatening, by massed oppositions, putting their bodies on the line. After 1919, Chicago instituted the Atlanta solution with a vengeance, giving rise to the borders wars that filled the time gap between 1919 and 1968.

The Period of Border Wars

Struggles over turf did not end with a return to relative calm. After the riot of 1919 subsided, bombings became more frequent—both of black-occupied buildings outside the black belt and of realtors' offices involved in selling houses in white areas to black buyers. The often-mentioned "cure" for Chicago's race problem was to separate the races by increasing segregation.[60] Not without significance is that Chicago property owners borrowed from St. Louis its 1910 innovation, the racial restrictive covenant, in which property owners within a given district signed pledges not to sell or rent to Negroes. The peak five-year period for setting up such covenants in St. Louis had been between 1920 and 1924, when 170 deed restrictions were signed. The first 88 covenants signed in Chicago came in the peak five-year period between 1925 and 1929.[61] Segregation would actually intensify in the years leading up to 1948 and did not decline, even after racial deed restrictions could no longer be legally enforced. The degree to which the Atlanta solution led to virtual apartheid accounts for the fact that Chicago's 1960s riots would take place in an even more segregated city than in 1919.

The Role of Catholicism and the Irish

It is difficult to avoid addressing the issue of Irish Catholic versus black hostilities. If one considered the 1919 riot in isolation, one would be forced to conclude that there were special animosities between Chicago's Irish Catholics and its Protestant blacks. Certainly, during that altercation, politically supported Irish gangs played a prominent, albeit far from exclusive, role. But one also needs to place that in a larger context. Such conflict had appeared earlier in the 1863 draft riots in New York, when it was chiefly "new" Irish immigrants who led the "search-and-destroy missions" against black New Yorkers.[62] But it is one thing to construct situational explanations, another to make an essentialist claim.

Such a claim, however, is suggested by John T. McGreevy in his *Parish Boundaries*.[63] This book makes the point that for urban Catholics, the residential neighborhood is primarily a parish with which they identify strongly; thus, an incursion into the neighborhood is seen not only as a secular threat but also as a sacred one! In a review of McGreevy's book, Richard Wightman Fox praised McGreevy for performing

> the difficult feat of getting us to understand Catholic racism without condoning it, and to perceive the blinders worn by Catholic liberals without denying the ultimate justice of their anti-racist cause.... Catholic traditionalists were not being primitive or irrational, Mr. McGreevy suggests, when they defended neighborhood churches against the modernizing ideology of geographical mobility. For them the parish was sacred space. God's work was done not in thin air, but in particular buildings and byways.[64]

McGreevy also suggests that the high rate of Catholic home ownership in the late nineteenth and early twentieth centuries was partially due to their desire to stay in a chosen parish. First might come the church itself, with the neighborhood forming around it. But the priest might urge parishioners to buy and then hold on to property in the area, in order to solidify ties. Thus, the infatuation with real estate may be part of an "incarnational" outlook in which things of this world are holy.

But there were other reasons why white Catholics remained in their original neighborhoods with such constancy, not only during the Great Depression but even after World War II, when so many other whites were flocking to new suburban developments. After all, the formation of new Catholic parishes in the suburbs was not unheard of! But two factors may have intervened. First, class mobility for Catholics tended to come later than for Jews, with whom they sometimes shared neighborhoods; second, and perhaps more significant, their high use of Catholic schools insulated them from some of the pressures to move that other whites felt because of school desegregation orders. Was anything more involved? It is difficult to judge, nor is it necessary for us to answer this question before getting on with our story.

WORLD WAR II AND BORDER WARS: 1943

The labor shortage in Fordist Chicago during the World War II had much the same effect as it had had in the previous war: the opening of industrial opportunities for resident blacks and inducements to southern blacks to migrate, which caused a rapid increase in the African American population. The year 1943 was one of sporadic racial tensions in many northern cities, and Chicago was not immune to the contradiction between the importance of African American workers and soldiers to the war effort and their frustrated struggle for a commensurate status in society.

While the 1943 "blowup" at Cabrini Homes (a newly constructed housing project located on the northwest side in an Italian district known as Little Sicily) was hardly on the order of magnitude of the "great" race riot in Detroit in that year,[65] or even the less violent explosion in Harlem at the same time, it was emblematic of the tendency for Chicago's violence to focus on any attempts by blacks to break out of their two "ghettos" on the South and West Sides. The housing project had been initiated as part of a slum clearance scheme, with displaced Italians promised the new quarters. But by the time construction was completed, America had entered the war, and the priority shifted from ethnic replacement to war effort contribution. Therefore, a small number of blacks were assigned units in the project, which elicited a hostile reaction from the Italian community. Although the hostilities were suppressed, Chicago's politicians were fearful that the city would recapitulate 1919 or be "infected" by Detroit's events.

This did not happen, in part because Chicago's politicians took precautionary measures. A "Mayor's Committee on Race Relations" (later changed to Human Relations) was hastily organized, with a blue-ribbon staff and considerable funding. In its first annual report, the committee acknowledges its origin as a reaction to the Detroit riot. At first, this committee operated effectively. In addition, a training program in "race relations" was instituted in the police department (spearheaded by University of Chicago sociologist Joseph Lohman), in recognition of the role policemen often played as instigators of racial conflict.

The roles that better housing and city planning could play in ameliorating racial problems were also acknowledged. In February 1944, four sessions of a "Mayor's Conference on Race Relations," chaired by Edwin Embree, chairman of the Mayor's Committee on Race Relations, were held at City Hall, with a stellar cast of presenters.[66] Some 100 city officials and about 125 "other leaders of the community" were in attendance, and hundreds of "interested parties" were seated in the galleries. These sessions were held with the full support of the mayor, Edward J. Kelly, and were intended to engage city planning in human relations. "Our slogan: 'understanding leads to cooperation.'"[67]

But gradually, support for the committee's work declined. The annual reports became thinner with time, ending in brief mimeographed accounts of individual conflicts resolved by a small staff. By the time of the next major "communal blowups" in Chicago in the late 1960s (not that things were all that quiet in the interim), its impotence was revealed. During the 1968 uprising, it acknowledged that it could do little more than observe and then serve the narrow function of "rumor control headquarters."[68]

POSTWAR DEVELOPMENTS

With the end of the war, the struggle for space was resumed in earnest, and since white Chicagoans engaged in both fight and flight, it was fought block by block. (See maps 2.3 and 2.4, showing how the expansion of the ghettos was related to incidents of white violence.)

Chicago's public housing and urban renewal programs, instead of ameliorating conditions, often exacerbated conflicts. In the immediate postwar period between 1946 and 1950, Chicago experimented with the construction of small, low-rise public housing projects on open land toward the periphery of developed zones. However, each one of these raised the ire of white neighbors when black families were moved in or their assignment was anticipated. In 1947, for example, there was an "antiblack" riot at Airport Homes, and another in Fernwood Park the following year, indicating that whites would enforce apartheid by violence, if necessary.

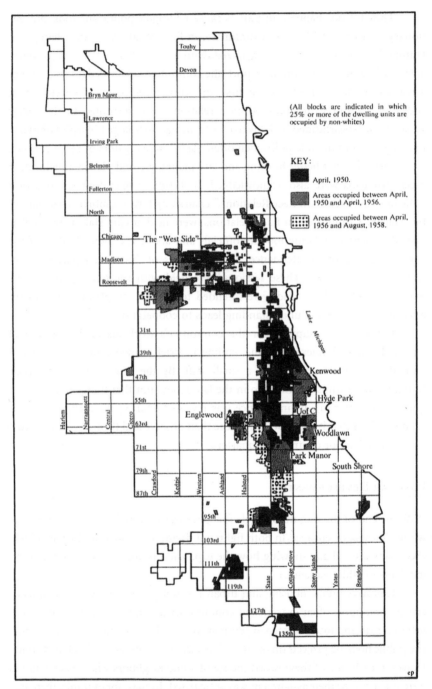

Map 2.3.   Expansion of the Chicago Ghettos between 1950 and 1958.

Source: St. Clair Drake and Horace Cayton, *Black Metropolis* (appendix added to the single volume edition of 1993). Copyright: University of Chicago Press, 1993.

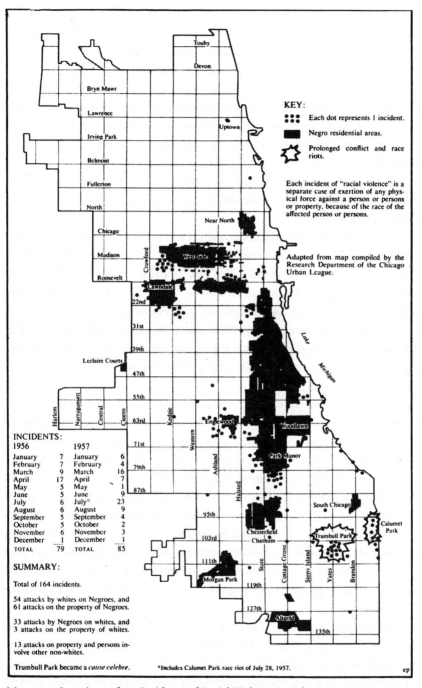

KEY:

::: Each dot represents 1 incident.

▬ Negro residential areas.

✦ Prolonged conflict and race riots.

Each incident of "racial violence" is a separate case of exertion of any physical force against a person or persons or property, because of the race of the affected person or persons.

Adapted from map compiled by the Research Department of the Chicago Urban League.

INCIDENTS:

1956		1957	
January	7	January	6
February	7	February	4
March	9	March	16
April	17	April	7
May	5	May	1
June	5	June	9
July	6	July°	23
August	6	August	9
September	5	September	4
October	5	October	2
November	6	November	3
December	1	December	1
TOTAL	79	TOTAL	85

SUMMARY:

Total of 164 incidents.

54 attacks by whites on Negroes, and 61 attacks on the property of Negroes.

33 attacks by Negroes on whites, and 3 attacks on the property of whites.

13 attacks on property and persons involve other non-whites.

Trumbull Park became a *cause celebre*.   °Includes Calumet Park race riot of July 28, 1957.

cp

Map 2.4.   Locations of 164 Incidents of Racial Violence in Relation to Negro Residential Areas, 1956–1957.

Source: St. Clair Drake and Horace Cayton, *Black Metropolis* (appendix added to the single volume edition of 1993). Copyright: University of Chicago Press, 1993.

By 1949, two national programs were in place that would eventually increase racial apartheid in Chicago. During the Depression, well-meaning reformist urban housing experts had recommended clearing the worst urban slums and replacing them with subsidized public housing. (In 1937, federal legislation established the U.S. Public Housing Administration to further this end.) This plan made much sense for that era, characterized as it was by abandonment and vacancies caused by doubling up to economize. In the postwar period, this plan was anachronistically revived, but under drastically different conditions and with decidedly different beneficiaries. The 1949 Urban Redevelopment Act initiated a federal program, ostensibly designed to clear "blighted areas" and to stimulate their rebuilding with improved but still affordable housing. The scheme, however, had several basic defects.

First, clearance was to be undertaken at a time of a critical housing shortage and overcrowding in the so-called blighted areas, which were then dispropor-tionately occupied by minorities. Put into practice in cities throughout the nation, this program became notorious as "Puerto Rican Removal" in New York, as "Negro Removal" in Chicago, and as "Mexican Removal" in Los Angeles. Furthermore, cities were empowered to select, condemn, and clear areas they determined to be "blighted," which left the criteria vulnerable to decisions that depended more on potential real estate profits than on objective measures of relative deterioration.

Second, private developers were invited to buy the city-cleared land at bargain prices, in return for promising to build decent housing for poor or middle-income tenants. In 1949, a new agency, the Chicago Land Clearance Commission, was established and put in charge of acquiring properties in "slum areas," clearing the land of structures (and residents), and reselling the vacant land to developers. This opened enormous opportunities for collusion between the city and major real estate interests. Furthermore, there were only loose controls over the uses to which the improved land could be put. Eventually, redevelopers concentrated on more profitable middle-income housing, or even high-income housing and commercial uses, rather than the affordable housing the law had required them to provide in return for their subsidies and generous loan terms.

Third, the law wisely required that persons to be displaced by "slum clearance" were to be relocated in standard housing before their homes were destroyed—a patent impossibility unless new public housing could first be built on vacant land. In actual practice, such vacant land was at a premium within the built-up limits of Chicago and, given the pattern of racial apartheid, was located in zones in or near resistant whites.

In 1949, the Chicago Housing Authority (CHA), under a promising reformist administration, proposed to construct some 40,000 federally subsidized
dwelling units on vacant sites to accommodate those who would be displaced by
slum clearance. This proved impossible, temporally and politically. There was not
sufficient time to clear and relocate simultaneously, which meant that residents of
cleared zones were simply crowded into adjacent slums. But the political barriers
were even more forbidding. Because the Chicago City Council had "veto" rights
over site selection and white aldermen were adamantly opposed to introducing
black residents into white areas—the only sites that were vacant—virtually no
sites were approved.[69]

The struggle for public housing sites in integrated areas was thus decisively
lost in the late 1940s and early 1950s, and Chicago's efforts to construct public
housing ground to a halt over the issue of segregation. Eventually, under new
leadership, the CHA proceeded to construct a solid phalanx of projects that
"thickened," without dispersing, the existing black belts.

> Of thirty-three CHA projects approved between 1950 and the mid-1960s,
> only one when completed was in an area less than 84 per cent black; all but
> seven were in tracts at least 95 per cent black; more than 98 per cent of
> apartments were in all-black neighbourhoods. The CHA...was building
> almost a solid corridor of low-rent housing along State Street and near-by
> streets.... By 1969 a judge found that CHA family housing was 99 per cent
> black-occupied, and that 99.5 per cent of its units were in black or transi-
> tional areas.[70]

Thus, the South Side black belt was solidified in its thickened form and
expanded farther to the south—albeit skipping over the redevelopment efforts in
the vicinity of the enclave of the University of Chicago, which created a mostly
white interruption in its flow. White flight permitted a steady infusion of mostly
middle-class blacks into the formerly Jewish South Shore.[71]

The West Side ghetto was flanked by public housing projects, divided by
major highways and an enclave created for the University of Illinois Circle
Campus, which displaced Italians as well as Latinos and blacks.[72] A solid phalanx
of mostly black-occupied high-rise public housing projects was built along the
major east-west corridors of Roosevelt Road and Madison Avenue—the very
streets that would later explode in the uprising of 1968.

All these developments were ignored in the Kerner Report issued in March
1968, only a month before the riots that followed King's assassination. Its references to Chicago were confined to two anecdotes, neither of them accurately
reported. The "white riot" that occurred in suburban Cicero in 1951, when whites

set fire to a house recently occupied by a black family and drove them out, is ignored, whereas the black protests in August 1964 in suburban Dixmoor receive coverage.[73] There is only slight reference to a black "minor riot" in July 1966, which the authors attribute to a conflict between the police and West Side youths over the opening of fire hydrants. As we shall see in our next chapter, this account was inaccurate in the extreme.

SOUTH SIDE BORDER WARS DECLINE; WEST SIDE TENSIONS BUILD

By the 1960s, the border wars on the South Side had essentially been "won" by blacks, as white residents decamped. Indeed, the South Side black belt had taken over even more territory than it "needed," although disinvestment and arson were creating significant zones of desolation, especially in the vicinity of the University of Chicago, which would use its role as the single largest property owner in Hyde Park and Kenwood to begin to "redevelop" the area and to push back the east-west border decisively to Cottage Grove Avenue (later to be renamed Martin Luther King Boulevard!), where it had stood in the 1940s. Some interracial housing was produced in Hyde Park–Kenwood in the aftermath, but under carefully class-controlled eligibility. Only the area south of 61st Street could not be "guarded." Buildings on 63rd Street (which was by the 1960s a "black" commercial street) eventually were burned down—one of the few South Side arson targets in the 1968 uprising. The brunt of that uprising, however, would be experienced in the Second Ghetto.

NOTES

1. Loic Wacquant, in a provocative article, identifies the period between 1915 and 1968 in northern ghettos as the era of free mobile labor, and the post-1968 period as the era of the hyperghetto—a return to semislavery through the imprisonment of chiefly male surplus labor. "From Slavery to Mass Incarceration," *New Left Review* 13 (January/February 2002), pp. 41–60. His analysis fits Chicago and Detroit very well, although it may not be so neatly generalized to New York and Los Angeles.

2. Among the sources that can be consulted on Detroit are: David Allan Levine, *Internal Combustion: The Races in Detroit, 1915–1925* (Westport, Conn.: Greenwood Press, 1976); Robert Shegan, *Detroit Race Riot: A Study in Violence* (Philadelphia: Clifton, 1964); Benjamin Singer, *Black Rioters: A Study of Social Factors and Community in the Detroit Riot* (Lexington, Mass.: Heath Lexington Books, 1970); Leonard Gordon, comp., *A City in Racial Crisis: The Case of Detroit Pre- and Post- the 1967 Riot* (Dubuque, Iowa: W. C. Brown, 1976); John Hersey, *The Algiers Motel Incident* (New York: Knopf, 1968); and Thomas J. Sugrue, *The Roots of the Urban Crisis: Race and Inequality in Postwar Detroit* (Princeton, N.J.: Princeton University Press, 1996). Detroit's second major riot in the

twentieth century began on July 23, 1967, after a raid by white police officers on an after-hours drinking and gambling club in a black neighborhood. Five days of hostility followed. After a week, 683 buildings across the city had been damaged, and whites deserted the city in earnest. See, *inter alia*, Robyn Meredith, "Five Days in 1967 Still Shake Detroit," *New York Times*, July 23, 1997, p. A10. Today, Detroit is 76 percent black with a black mayor, but large areas remain vacant. Rich and middle-class whites have gone, along with their taxes, and Detroit is now the "nation's poorest big city."

3. Originally published under this title in 1922 by the University of Chicago Press, with the Chicago commission identified as the author. It is now acknowledged that the primary organizer and author of this remarkable document was its "assistant" executive director, Charles S. Johnson, a mature African American graduate student being mentored by Robert Park in the University of Chicago's Sociology Department. Dr. Johnson later went on to a distinguished career that culminated in the presidency of Fisk University. I have therefore taken the unauthorized liberty of citing the commission's report under his name.

4. See Pierre Clavel and Wim Wiewel, *Harold Washington and the Neighborhoods: Progressive City Government in Chicago, 1983–1987* (New Brunswick, N.J.: Rutgers University Press, 1991).

5. An exception was the so-called Bulls riot in 1992. Although ostensibly related to the victory of Chicago's basketball team, it did take on racial dimensions in various parts of the city. See Michael J. Rosenfeld, "Celebration, Politics, Selective Looting and Riots: A Micro-Level Study of the Bulls Riot of 1992 in Chicago," *Social Problems* 44, no. 4 (November 1997), 483–502.

6. Up through the 1950s, growing black demand exceeded the space yielded to it, resulting in inflated rents and a doubling-up in occupancy in zones grudgingly ceded to blacks. Whites at first resisted but then yielded, sometimes in "panic," to inroads of black advancement. A similar expansion of the West Side ghetto began to occur in the 1950s. With the stabilization of black population in northern industrial cities, the dual housing market "premium" disappeared, often leading to "neighborhood blowout" through arson and abandonment. The immigration of Latinos and others has partially arrested this process, so common in the 1970s.

7. At least, this is what James Dorsey has argued. He points out that southern Illinois is actually *in* the South (as far south as Maryland, Virginia, and the northern part of North Carolina) and is close to Missouri and Kentucky, and that the "socio-cultural values in the region were essentially southern." See James Dorsey, *Up South: Blacks in Chicago's Suburbs, 1719–1983* (Bristol, Ind.: Wyndham Hall Press, 1986).

8. Dorsey, *Up South*, pp. 6–8, summarizes the earliest history of slavery in the state. He notes that when the French conquered the Mississippi valley in the seventeenth century, many of the first pioneers were black, albeit slaves who were legally recognized by the French government in the eighteenth century as real property (p. 6). When the French ceded their Illinois territory to the English in 1763, they sold their slaves before departing. In 1778, Illinois became a part of Virginia, but was ceded to the U.S. government in 1784. Even though the 1787 Northwest Ordinance prohibited slavery and involuntary servitude in the Northwest Territory, old settlers continued to hold slaves, although they were euphemistically called lifetime indentured servants (p. 7). "When the Illinois

Territory separated from Indiana in 1809 it adopted the regulations concerning indentured servitude stipulated by the Indiana Territory... [in legislations] of 1803, 1805 and 1807." These permitted the indenture of Negro males for up to 35 years and females up to 32 years, although some indentures might last as long as 99 years! The Illinois state constitution of 1818 prohibited slavery but did not speak to the status of existing slaves (p. 8).

9. Dorsey, *Up South*, p. 10.

10. Thomas Lee Philpott, *The Slum and the Ghetto: Neighborhood Deterioration and Middle Class Reform, Chicago, 1880–1930*. (New York: Oxford University Press, 1978), pp. 118–19.

11. Dorsey, *Up South*, p. 24.

12. Philpott, *The Slum and the Ghetto*, p. 121. "The Black Belt, as people were already calling it, stretched southward from the downtown railroad yards to another block of railway property just below 39th Street. The broad embankment of the Rock Island Railroad sealed it from the working-class immigrant communities to the west, and the South Side Elevated Railroad walled it off from 'the white belt of aristocracy and wealth' to the east.... The tracks were racial barricades, but only because there were white people on the other side to man them. It was the color line, not any railroad line, that checked the free movement of Negroes. A train track was simply a convenient place to draw the line. *The railways were merely instruments of folkways*" (pp. 147–48, italics added).

13. Dominick A. Pacyga, *Polish Immigrants and Industrial Chicago: Workers on the South Side, 1880–1922* (Columbus: Ohio State University Press, 1991), p. 213.

14. The concentration on the South Side was not new. By 1850 more than four-fifths of all blacks lived in the zone "bounded by the Chicago River on the north, Sixteenth Street on the south, the South Branch of the river on the west, and Lake Michigan on the east." Allan H. Spear, *Black Chicago: The Making of a Negro Ghetto, 1890–1920* (Chicago: University of Chicago Press, 1967), pp. 11–12.

15. Philpott, *The Slum and the Ghetto*, p. 120.

16. Spear, *Black Chicago*, pp. 13–14, table 2.

17. William Tuttle, Jr., *Race Riot: Chicago in the Red Summer of 1919* (1970; reprint, Chicago: Illini Books, 1996), pp. 75–76.

18. This venture was vigorously supported and assisted by the *Chicago Defender*, Chicago's black newspaper.

19. Spear, *Black Chicago*, p. 151. Detailed figures appear on pp. 152 and 154, table 12. Women's occupations changed less; by 1920, some 64 percent were still engaged in domestic service, although by that year 15 percent worked in factories.

20. Ibid., pp. 140, 146.

21. The movement of Chicago's robber barons from the South Side to the north shore of the lake was not a flight from blacks. The odoriferous effluent at the north channel of the Chicago River was eliminated when, toward the end of the nineteenth century, the flow of that stream was reversed away from the lake. This opened the way for building Chicago's "Gold Coast," to which the elite promptly moved. Some prosperous blacks moved into the mansions on Prairie Avenue they had abandoned.

22. For more details and full documentation, see my *New York, Chicago, Los Angeles: America's Global Cities* (Minneapolis: University of Minnesota Press, 1999), especially chaps. 5 and 8.

23. The introduction of strikebreakers, protected by civil and military forces, led to the defeat of union efforts in the strikes of 1886, 1894, 1904, and 1921. The 1904 strike was the focus of Upton Sinclair's novel *The Jungle*.

24. The quotation has been assembled from Alma Herbst, *The Negro in the Slaughtering and Meat-Packing Industry in Chicago* (Boston: Houghton Mifflin, 1932) pp. 24–27. Herbst reports that 50 strikebreakers had been recruited by a single agent who was paid 50 dollars a head. However, it is testimony to basic racism that although in the earlier strike of 1894, when most scabs were "Poles," the chief targets of picketers' wrath were the small number of black scabs.

25. An account far more sympathetic to the plight of blacks vis à vis unions than Herbst's can be found in James Grossman, "The White Man's Union: The Great Migration and the Resonances of Race and Class in Chicago, 1916–1922," in Joe William Trotter, Jr., ed., *The Great Migration in Historical Perspective: New Dimensions of Race, Class and Gender* (Bloomington: Indiana University Press, 1991), pp. 83–105. Grossman acknowledges that blacks resisted unionization but claims this was not true up to 1919 among the "old" black workers, who tended to join unions at about the same rate as whites. He argues that it was the "new" black migrants from the South who were most resistant, because their prior experience with white craft unions in the South, which totally excluded them, had made them very suspicious of such efforts (p. 89). Indeed, Grossman concludes that "Whatever the benefits of unions, they were . . . 'no good for the colored man.' *They were white institutions*" (p. 97; italics added). The black community did not condemn black strikebreakers, and news of strikes was not covered in the *Chicago Defender*, the leading newspaper of the black community, because the black elite was unsympathetic to unions.

26. Herbst, *The Negro in the Slaughtering and Meat-Packing Industry*, p. 45. Nevertheless, between 1921 and the Depression, African Americans constituted about 30 percent of stockyard workers and had begun to form separate unions. However, by then they were already beginning to be displaced by Mexicans.

27. Tuttle, *Race Riot*, pp. 75–76.

28. Quoted in Johnson, *The Negro in Chicago*, p. 530.

29. Tuttle, *Race Riot*, pp. 109–11, with the quotation taken from p. 111.

30. Ibid., pp. 243–44.

31. See the table titled "Minor Racial Violence in 1919," in Arthur I. Waskow, *From Race Riot to Sit-in, 1919 and the 1960s* (Garden City, N.Y.: Doubleday, 1966), pp. 303–7, compiled from NAACP files.

32. The "classic" work on this is John Allswang, *A House for All Peoples: Ethnic Politics in Chicago* (Lexington: University of Kentucky Press, 1971).

33. For a sensitive account of the politics of immigrant-versus-black competition in Chicago politics of the time, see Ira Katznelson, *Black Men, White Cities: Race, Politics, and Migration in the United States, 1900–1930, and Britain, 1948–68* (1973; reprint, Chicago: University of Chicago Press, 1976), esp. chap. 6, "Black Politics and Political Power in Chicago," pp. 86–104. But see also the excellent analysis of black leaders' complicity in William Grimshaw, *Bitter Fruit: Black Politics and the Chicago Machine, 1931–1991* (Chicago: University of Chicago Press, 1993).

34. Frederic C. Cople, *The Urban Establishment: Upper Strata in Boston, New York, Charleston, Chicago and Los Angeles* (Urbana: University of Illinois Press, 1982),

pp. 504–6, quotation from 505. The conservatism of Chicago's reformers was obvious. "They had supported and funded the use of the militia to break the Railroad Strike of 1877, had opposed the Eight Hour Day walkout of 1885, and took a hard line against the Haymarket prisoners . . . [and were strongly] antiunion" (pp. 506–7).

35. Loyal to the party of Lincoln, black voters helped to elect the notorious Thompson (bane of Chicago's elites) to three terms as mayor, during which they were "paid back" by patronage and party support for several seats on the city council (Spear, *Black Chicago*, p. 187). During the riot, blacks therefore counted on Thompson's protection. The traditional black support for Chicago Republicans was slow in eroding. It was not until well into the Great Depression that the allegiance shifted to Democrats. For a fuller treatment, see Harold E. Gosnell, *Machine Politics: Chicago Model* (Chicago: University of Chicago Press, 1937; reprint, 1968).

36. Spear, *Black Chicago*, p. 158.

37. Pacyga, *Polish Immigrants and Industrial Chicago*, p. 214.

38. Ibid., pp. 215–17.

39. Tuttle, *Race Riot*, pp. 5–6, cites as his sources Peter M. Hoffman, comp., *The Race Riots: Biennial Cook County Coroner's Report, 1918–1919* (Chicago: n.p., n.d.); *Chicago Daily Tribune*, July 28, 1919; *Chicago Defender*, August 2, 1919; and an unpublished M.A. thesis by Joseph A. Logsdon. I have been unable to consult these sources.

40. Here I paraphrase and condense Tuttle, *Race Riot*, pp. 6–7, on the drowning of the boy, knocked off his raft by a rock thrown by a white bystander, and the angry response of black observers.

41. Ibid., p. 7.

42. Ibid., p. 8.

43. In 1919 more than half of the residents in the putative black belt were white. This proportion would change dramatically after the riot. The term "dead-line" apparently dated back to the Civil War, when it was used to designate the point at which any unidentified interloper would be shot.

44. Tuttle, *Race Riot*, p. 167.

45. Political sponsorship and funding for clubhouses and athletic activities for young white "ethnic" males was a common feature of Chicago's political machines. The divisions in political space were almost as strong as the divisions in ethnic and racial space. The major religious "border" at that time was between Protestants (both black and white) and Catholics (Irish primarily, but eastern Europeans as well), although the two or more subgroups of ethnically identified Catholics were by no means without their own interethnic animosities, just as white and black Protestants, though both supporting Mayor "Big Bill" Thompson against the Catholics, were still separated by the stronger line of race.

46. The account in this section is based largely on Johnson, *The Negro in Chicago*, chap. 1, and Tuttle, *Race Riot*, chap. 2.

47. Here Tuttle, *Race Riot*, cites not only Johnson, *The Negro in Chicago*, but also several articles by Allen D. Grimshaw. See his footnote 4, p. 34. The same footnote also gives the following information: "in only two cases were Negroes aggressively rioting found outside the 'Black Belt'" (a quotation from Johnson, *The Negro in Chicago*, p. 18). From p. 21 of the same source, we learn that "among white men, 69 per cent were shot or

stabbed, 31 per cent beaten; almost the opposite was true for black men, the figures being 35 and 65 per cent respectively.

48. Tuttle, *Race Riot*, p. 37.

49. Johnson, *The Negro in Chicago*, p. 598.

50. Tuttle, *Race Riot* p. 41.

51. One can ask why the state militia did not intervene immediately. The explanation lay in the longstanding political feud between Big Bill Thompson and Frank O. Lowden, the governor of the state. Although the governor had called up the state militia when the rioting looked out of hand, he could only quarter them in local armories until he received a formal request for help from the mayor. It was several days before Thompson swallowed his pride and requested aid.

52. On Tuesday morning, only "nineteen blacks of the 1,500 employed at Armour punched in for work, and only twenty-three of the 2,500 at Swift." Other plants were similarly affected. Tuttle, *Race Riot*, p. 44.

53. Ibid., pp. 49–50.

54. Ibid., pp. 53–55; quotation from pp. 54 and 55.

55. Ibid., p. 57.

56. There was a bomb scare, mobs paraded in the streets with signs reading "Kill the Coons," and blacks living in contested neighborhoods received threatening letters that warned them to get out (ibid., p. 61).

57. Ibid., p. 64.

58. Johnson, *The Negro in Chicago*, pp. xxiii–xxiv.

59. Tuttle, *Race Riot*, p. 63, italics added.

60. Ibid., p. 250.

61. Herman Long and Charles S. Johnson, *People vs. Property: Race Restrictive Covenants in Housing* (Nashville: Fisk University Press, 1947), p. 13, table 1.

62. The trigger, as we shall see in chap. 4, was conscription, from which blacks were exempted and for which the well-to-do could pay $300 to "buy" a replacement. This was a sum poor Irishmen could never afford. See Iver Bernstein, *The New York City Draft Riots* (New York: Oxford University Press, 1990). A fascinating novel that brings this conflict dramatically to life is Kevin Baker, *Paradise Alley* (New York: HarperCollins, 2002).

63. John T. McGreevy, *Parish Boundaries: The Catholic Encounter with Race in the Twentieth-Century Urban North* (Chicago: University of Chicago Press, 1996).

64. *New York Times Book Review*, August 25, 1996.

65. Gunnar Myrdal, in *An American Dilemma: The Negro Problem and Modern Democracy* (New York: Harper, 1944), published in 1944 but completed before the 1943 major Detroit riot. The only reference to Detroit appears on p. 568, noting that in the spring of 1942 there had been a "clash" in Detroit when Negroes, "trying to move into a government defense housing project built for them . . . were set upon by white civilians and police. . . . Encouraged by the vacillation of the federal government and the friendliness of the Detroit police . . . and stimulated by the backing of a United States congressman and such organizations as the Ku Klux Klan, white residents of the neighborhood and other parts of the city staged protest demonstrations against the Negro housing project, which led to the riot." Although the passage goes on to

speculate that "it does not seem likely that there will be further riots, of any significant degree of violence, in the North," only one year later Detroit experienced its most violent explosion. This intensified Chicago's fear that hostilities might spread from the minor spark in Cabrini Homes.

66. Participants included Louis Wirth (a University of Chicago sociology professor); Charles Johnson (invited back from his position as head of the Social [Research] Institute at Fisk University); Horace Cayton (who would later coauthor *Black Metropolis*); Robert Taylor, later chairman of the CHA (after whom the infamous Robert Taylor Homes would be named); and Robert Weaver, director of the Mayor's Committee on Race Relations (who would later head the federal Department of Housing and Urban Development [HUD]).

67. See Edwin R. Embree, unpaged foreword to *Proceedings of the Mayor's Committee on Race Relations* (Chicago: Mayor's Committee on Race Relations, February 1944).

68. This apologetic "definition of itself" was widely noted in the newspaper accounts of that time. However, it claimed that it had fielded some 40,000 inquiries over the course of 10 days.

69. Except one, for spite, in the home ward of a liberal member representing the North Side! This sordid tale of the frustrating search for vacant sites acceptable to the city council is told by Martin Meyerson and Edward Banfield, in their *Politics, Planning and the Public Interest: The Case of Public Housing in Chicago* (Glencoe, Ill.: Free Press, 1955). Meyerson had taken a leave of absence from his position as professor of planning at the University of Chicago to assist the reformist Elizabeth Wood, the new director of the Chicago Housing Authority. He left in disgust, recognizing that the city council had outwitted him. She was later fired.

70. Peter Hall, "The City of Permanent Underclass," *Cities of Tomorrow: An Intellectual History of Urban Planning and Design in the Twentieth Century* (Oxford: Blackwell, 1988), pp. 383–84.

71. See Peter Rossi and Robert Dentler, *The Politics of Urban Renewal: The Chicago Findings* (Glencoe, Ill.: Free Press of Glencoe, 1961), on Hyde Park and Kenwood; and Harvey Molotch, *Managed Integration: Dilemmas of Doing Good in the City* (Berkeley: University of California Press, 1972), on the South Shore.

72. See Gerald Suttles, *The Social Order of the Slum* (Chicago: University of Chicago Press, 1968).

73. When the white owner of a liquor store in Dixmoor had a "Negro woman arrested for stealing a bottle of whiskey, he was accused of having manhandled her. A crowd gathered in front of the store, broke the store window, and threw rocks at passing cars. The next day, when the disturbance was renewed, a Molotov cocktail set the liquor store afire. Several persons were injured." Kerner Report, pp. 36–37.

3

The Black Uprising after King's Assassination in 1968

One might use the military phrase "low-intensity war" to describe the interim period between the mid-1950s and mid-1960s in Chicago, during which there were forays and retreats but few confrontations involving great violence. Sporadic battles erupted at the expanding borders of the black belt on the South Side, as the South Shore, formerly the domain of a well-to-do white community including many Jewish residents and institutions, experienced "racial succession." Attempts to prevent mass white withdrawal were mounted in an ultimately unsuccessful effort to stabilize the area's interracial composition,[1] but a rear-guard battle was won by the University of Chicago to insulate its Hyde Park vicinity from the entry of too many poor blacks.[2] It would have been difficult to predict that, given the successful achievement of greater space and a strong reconstitution of the black metropolis's multiclass community, that cumulative resentments might explode into racial warfare. Jobs had not yet disappeared from the area, and Black Muslims, among others, were engaged in rebuilding the commercial infrastructure.

That was not the case on the West Side, the much poorer Second Ghetto, which was absorbing into its ancient housing stock and its newer public housing projects minorities who could not afford the better housing and more organized community on the South Side. It was chiefly on the West Side that low-intensity warfare would be transformed into open hostilities after the murder of Martin Luther King, Jr., in April 1968. The signs of dissent were already apparent in the years before that massive response.

THE ANTECEDENTS TO THE RACE RIOT OF APRIL 1968

Between the triumphant mid-1950s and the mid-1960s, the civil rights movement alternated between unrealistic hopes and more realistic despair occasioned by disappointing failures in President Johnson's "War on Poverty" and escalating suppression of dissent against the war in Vietnam. Waskow's *From Race Riot to Sit-in, 1919 and the 1960s,* is a good general source on the early 1960s, even though he failed to predict that, as the wind went out of the sails of the civil rights movement by the mid-1960s, sit-ins would be displaced by the new form of race riot—the ghetto uprising.

By far the best book dealing with the disillusionment of the civil rights movement in Chicago in 1966 and 1967, and thus of the factors that would eventually yield the 1968 ghetto uprising, is Alan B. Anderson and George Pickering's *Confronting the Color Line.* Unfortunately, the book's coverage ends by September 1967, some seven months before the explosive events of early April 1968. But their study demolishes the myths that blacks were "rioting for fun and profit" (one of the most egregiously derogatory characterizations of that dark moment in American race relations)[3] or that the explosions were sudden, surprising, and irrational. They were riots of protest, frustration, and despair.

The somber conclusion of Anderson and Pickering's detailed analysis of the hopes and mobilizations in Chicago that were unleashed by the civil rights movement (beginning in 1954 with the school desegregation decision and culminating in the 1964 civil rights law) is that by 1966–67 the struggles for open housing and school desegregation in Chicago had failed.

> [T]he movement was strained internally and isolated politically. The leadership was uncertain of its mandate, its possibilities, and its support.... [T]he path was unclear in every direction.... [I]n the open housing marches, the Chicago civil rights movement had mobilized a minority, but it had gained broader civic support more in name than in fact. None of the various combinations of persuasion and coercion it had attempted had proved

effective. The movement had been unable to specify affirmative duties and unable to enact negative ones. The tensions among advocates of integration, desegregation, and black power had become open rifts. Thus, whether the terms were those of black dignity, constitutional duties, or white culture, the Chicago movement was encountering futility in relationship to every aspect of democratic social change.[4]

We must ask how this sorry state had arrived, and why Martin Luther King, Jr., despite his best efforts, was unable to reverse its course. The answer to that question must be sought in the context of an overall "collapse" (or reworking) of the first phases of the civil rights movement.

Douglas McAdam has contrasted what he calls "the heyday of black insurgency 1961–65" with "the decline of black insurgency 1966–70."[5] He attributes the strength of the early period to the building of a diverse but increasingly organized, unified program by the four dominant organizations seeking reform (the NAACP, CORE, the SCLC, and, to a lesser extent, the Student Non-violent Coordinating Committee [SNCC]). The monopoly that the NAACP had had over initiating the legal phase between 1954 and 1960 was broken, and during the next half decade, three-quarters of all initiated events were organized by the NAACP, CORE, or SCLC.[6] McAdam attributes their success to the fact that they focused their activities on the South[7] and on goals that had wide support in other regions of the country. They were therefore able to attract significant financial backing from northern whites.

It was not until movement-initiated actions diversified to other urban regions of the North and Midwest that white liberal support declined and a northern white backlash set in.[8] Furthermore, the North already had numerous more radical (not so compliant and thus more threatening) black organizations, with wider goals and different mechanisms of protest that were not easily disciplined by the more traditional organizations.

Finally, national interest in civil rights was declining. Whereas public opinion polls between 1960 and 1965 placed race relations at or near the top of a list of the most important issues facing America, this priority had been displaced downward as concern with and opposition to the Vietnam War increased.

> In spite of the evidence of continued tension and growing polarization, the racial conflict that had seemed to threaten American society soon dropped from its preeminent position in public concern. Vietnam, ecology, inflation, the Arab-Israeli conflict, the energy crisis, and Watergate took their turns in preempting both the headlines of the newspapers and the interest of white Americans.[9]

Civil rights were going out of fashion, and political repression and state force were increasingly accepted as a means to fight dissidents.

It was just during these unpromising times that Martin Luther King, Jr. decided it was time to expand his movement from the South to the black ghettos of the North and to the issue of housing integration, which had accounted for no more than 1 percent of all issues addressed by movement-initiated events in 1961–65 and again in 1966–70.[10] The times, place, and goals were scarcely propitious for King's decision to move north.

MARTIN LUTHER KING, JR., SELECTS CHICAGO AS HIS NORTHERN "CASE"

Chicago's ghettos may have been "in need of attention," but so were those in many other cities at the same time. One must therefore ask: Why Chicago? The answer is recounted in James R. Ralph, Jr.'s detailed book, based on archival and newspaper accounts, as well as interviews with the principals.[11] One could not ask for a fuller and more accurate account. Most interesting is his discussion of how Chicago happened to be chosen as the "test" case, after SCLC decided it was time to expand its activities to some northern city. The year 1964 was pivotal.

> The upsurge of northern civil rights protests and the summer rioting prompted King to stress SCLC's obligations to northern blacks at the organization's annual convention in the fall of 1964. He did not propose a [specific] northern project, but it was clear that northern racial problems would become more prominent in SCLC's agenda.[12]

King's vision was broadening to encompass even more ambitious goals. In October, King was awarded the Nobel Prize. In his acceptance speech, he outlined his expanded agenda, stressing "the necessity of eliminating war and poverty as well as racial injustice from the world."[13]

By the spring of 1965, because SCLC had attracted considerable contributions after its success in Selma, it could finally afford to staff an expanded operation in northern cities. Initially, five northern cities were considered: Chicago, Cleveland, Philadelphia, Washington, D.C., and New York. King therefore made an "exploratory, fact-finding swing through the north,"[14] but all except Chicago were eventually eliminated. In the end, it was decided that Cleveland was too small to attract adequate attention; it seemed counterproductive to focus on Washington, D.C., since President Johnson was still seen as a civil rights ally; and neither Philadelphia nor New York welcomed King's overtures. The black president of the NAACP in Philadelphia was a maverick, apparently threatened by competition. The opposition in New York was far more serious, based on what its black leaders viewed as King's almost traitorous (too conciliatory) behavior with respect to that city's 1964 riot.

> When a New York City riot—the first major black uprising [there] since 1943—threatened to spiral out of control, Mayor Robert Wagner pleaded for King to use his influence to help calm the city. Even though the rioting had already subsided, King acceded to Wagner's request and traveled to the city, where he quickly found himself embroiled in controversy. As King headed to Gracie Mansion to see Wagner, Harlem leaders lambasted him for neglecting them and for allowing himself to be used by the "white power structure." It would not be the last chilly welcome King would receive as he became more active in the North. King consulted with Wagner, but he also cooled the tempers of local black leaders by meeting with them and touring New York's black communities.[15]

In marked contrast, King was greeted enthusiastically in Chicago. On July 24, 1965, he spoke at churches and neighborhood rallies and even addressed almost 10,000 mostly white listeners on the village green in wealthy suburban Winnetka. Audiences "cheered as King denounced the perpetuation of Chicago's slums and urged his listeners to dedicate themselves to social reform." The next day he led 15,000 marchers through Chicago's downtown.[16]

> Soon after King's Chicago visit, Adam Clayton Powell, one of black New York's power brokers, informed reporters that he had recently told King not to visit New York City. Powell...sharply criticized King for his role in the aftermath of the 1964 riots.... "I told him [King] to go to cities where they had no real Negro leadership—like Chicago, Cleveland, and Washington," Powell explained.[17]

Given the enthusiastic welcome he had received in Chicago, there was no contest.

But the decision was reinforced by other considerations as well. Some of the activists in the movement came from Chicago and had links to local leaders; King's receptions there had always been enthusiastic; and Mayor Daley had such great power that King believed he was capable of instituting reforms, if he decided to. In addition was the challenge. "The enormity of Chicago's race problems whetted his desire to work there. Attacking the northern capital of segregation would make for better drama."[18]

The choice of Chicago was announced on September 1, 1965. The following January, King made two short visits to Chicago to prepare for the coming campaign, to be waged in the Second Ghetto—the West Side.

WHY THE WEST SIDE?

By 1965, two-thirds of Chicago's black population lived in the more established South Side "ghetto," which enjoyed well-developed community and religious institutions and contained a wide range of classes. In contrast, the quarter of a million blacks living in the West Side Second Ghetto, many of them poorer and of more recent arrival, were less organized and underrepresented by leaders of their own choice. William Grimshaw refers to the four black wards on the West Side as "plantation wards," that is, those whose African American aldermen were completely under the discipline of the Irish-dominated "Democratic machine" and whose exclusive function was to produce those wards for the Democratic Party.[19]

A good account of the demographic changes on the West Side can be found in the 1980 *Local Community Fact Book,* which reproduces (and updates) earlier historical vignettes about Community Areas 27 (East Garfield Park), 28 (the Near West Side), and 29 (North Lawndale)—the very areas that were involved in the 1966–68 West Side uprisings.[20] (See map 3.1.) I summarize these to set the scene for the emergence of the Second Ghetto.

The Near West Side, just west of the Loop across the Chicago River, had a long history of ethnic succession. By the 1850s, the original Irish settlers had been joined by German and Scandinavian immigrants in an enlarged zone that extended from the river to Halsted Street on the west and Roosevelt Road on the south. The population soon peaked at about 160,000.

> The area east of Halsted Street, south of Harrison Street had become a slum, which it was to remain for a century.... In the decades that followed, new immigrants from southern and eastern Europe arrived, mostly Italians, and Russian and Polish Jews. [Halsted and Maxwell became a Jewish commercial core.]...By 1900 more Greeks were moving in....The Near West Side was completely built up by 1895. Inhabitants were poorly housed and badly overcrowded....After the turn of the century, the Eastern European Jewish community began to break up. As the Jews vacated the Near West Side ghetto, their place was taken by blacks and Mexicans. By 1930, when the population had dropped to 152,000, blacks constituted about a sixth of the total.[21]

During the depressed 1930s, the population dropped even more, and by 1940 close to 26,000 black residents there constituted a fifth of the total. Then came a new wave of migrants, mostly poor blacks from the South, who could not afford housing on the South Side. By 1950, the population was back up to 160,000, of whom 40 percent were black.

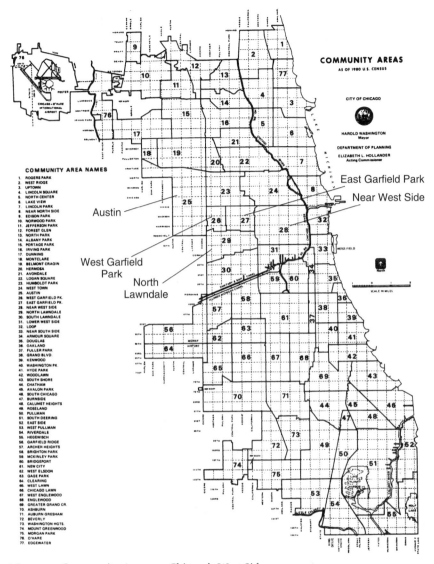

COMMUNITY AREAS
AS OF 1980 U.S. CENSUS

CITY OF CHICAGO

HAROLD WASHINGTON
Mayor

DEPARTMENT OF PLANNING
ELIZABETH L. HOLLANDER
Acting Commissioner

East Garfield Park

Near West Side

Austin

COMMUNITY AREA NAMES
1. ROGERS PARK
2. WEST RIDGE
3. UPTOWN
4. LINCOLN SQUARE
5. NORTH CENTER
6. LAKE VIEW
7. LINCOLN PARK
8. NEAR NORTH SIDE
9. EDISON PARK
10. NORWOOD PARK
11. JEFFERSON PARK
12. FOREST GLEN
13. NORTH PARK
14. ALBANY PARK
15. PORTAGE PARK
16. IRVING PARK
17. DUNNING
18. MONTCLARE
19. BELMONT CRAGIN
20. HERMOSA
21. AVONDALE
22. LOGAN SQUARE
23. HUMBOLDT PARK
24. WEST TOWN
25. AUSTIN
26. WEST GARFIELD PK.
27. EAST GARFIELD PK.
28. NEAR WEST SIDE
29. NORTH LAWNDALE
30. SOUTH LAWNDALE
31. LOWER WEST SIDE
32. LOOP
33. NEAR SOUTH SIDE
34. ARMOUR SQUARE
35. DOUGLAS
36. OAKLAND
37. FULLER PARK
38. GRAND BLVD.
39. KENWOOD
40. WASHINGTON PK.
41. HYDE PARK
42. WOODLAWN
43. SOUTH SHORE
44. CHATHAM
45. AVALON PARK
46. SOUTH CHICAGO
47. BURNSIDE
48. CALUMET HEIGHTS
49. ROSELAND
50. PULLMAN
51. SOUTH DEERING
52. EAST SIDE
53. WEST PULLMAN
54. RIVERDALE
55. HEGEWISCH
56. GARFIELD RIDGE
57. ARCHER HEIGHTS
58. BRIGHTON PARK
59. MCKINLEY PARK
60. BRIDGEPORT
61. NEW CITY
62. WEST ELSDON
63. GAGE PARK
64. CLEARING
65. WEST LAWN
66. CHICAGO LAWN
67. WEST ENGLEWOOD
68. ENGLEWOOD
69. GREATER GRAND CR.
70. ASHBURN
71. AUBURN GRESHAM
72. BEVERLY
73. WASHINGTON HGTS.
74. MOUNT GREENWOOD
75. MORGAN PARK
76. O'HARE
77. EDGEWATER

West Garfield
Park

North
Lawndale

Map 3.1.   Community Areas on Chicago's West Side.

Source: Local Community Fact Books of Chicago. Public domain.

This politically powerless zone was a defenseless and therefore a favored site for public housing construction. Jane Addams Homes, a low-rise project for 304 families, had been built in 1938; the 834-unit Robert Brooks Homes went up in 1942; and in the 1950s "the Chicago Housing Authority built Maplewood Courts, 132 units, Loomis Courts, 126 units, Abbott Homes, 1,218 units, and Governor Henry Horner Homes, 920 high-rise units to which 745 more were added in the early 1960s.... [By 1980] *the Near West Side [would have] one of the highest concentrations of public housing in the city, exceeding 20 percent of its total housing stock.*"[22] Puerto Ricans and even small numbers of Mexican immigrants also vied for locations on the Near West Side, but residential space was disappearing. The number of residential units in the area declined from some 41,000 in 1950 to 37,000 10 years later, and the resident population decreased from over 160,000 in 1950 to 126,610 in 1960.

This was because land continued to be cleared, not only for the projects but also for highways and new institutional uses. By the early 1960s, a wide swath of territory had been cleared to make room for the Kennedy Expressway on the east, and the University of Illinois on the west made plans to preempt even more for the construction of its Chicago campus. The old housing stock was also being cleared for other nonresidential uses, such as a vast Medical Center District, and eight different urban renewal projects initiated in the 1950s by the Chicago Land Clearance Commission, most of them designed for light industrial, commercial, or institutional development.

The biggest cause of displacement, however, was the construction of the Chicago campus of the University of Illinois, beginning in the early 1960s in the Harrison and Halsted redevelopment district.[23] The result was to drive out the former white residents (although new ones associated with the medical and university complexes later moved into protected enclaves)—thereby increasing the proportion of blacks in the reduced total. By then, the long-planned Congress Street highway (now joining the Eisenhower Expressway) had bifurcated the Second Ghetto into two linear strips of public housing into which blacks were crowded.

North Lawndale (Community Area 29), which stretches southwest from the Near West Side to Chicago's border with Cicero, underwent a similar transition process from white to black occupancy, although slightly later. This area had begun as a separate suburb in the late nineteenth century, but after the elevated lines were extended to it and it was annexed to the city, it became more urbanized and industrial. During the first two decades of the twentieth century, "North Lawndale experienced a tremendous population surge" as Russian Jewish residents moved there from the Near West Side. By 1930, the population had peaked at 112,000, of which 46 percent were Jewish. When that group moved on in the 1940s and 1950s to its "second settlement" area on the North Side (e.g. Rogers Park), blacks began to take their places. By 1960, the racial "transition" was virtually complete. "The white population of North Lawndale dropped from 87,000 in 1950 to less than 11,000 in 1960," whereas its "black population increased from 13,000 to more than 113,000." By 1960, some 90 percent of the people crowded into this densely packed and deteriorated quarter were African Americans.[24] (See maps 3.2. and 3.3.)

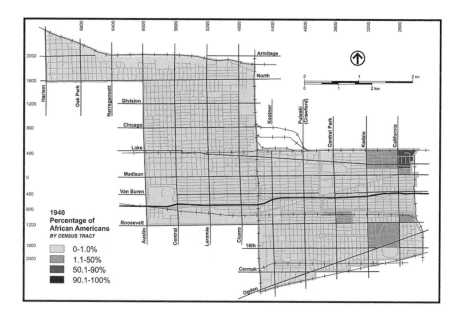

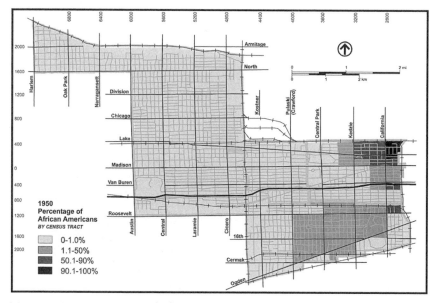

Map 3.2.   Low Proportions of African Americans Living in the Community Areas of North Lawndale, East Garfield Park, West Garfield Park, and Austin in 1940 and 1950.

Source: Amanda I. Seligman, *Block by Block: Neighborhoods and Public Policy on Chicago's West Side* (Chicago: University of Chicago Press, 2005). Copyright: Board of Regents of the University of Wisconsin System.

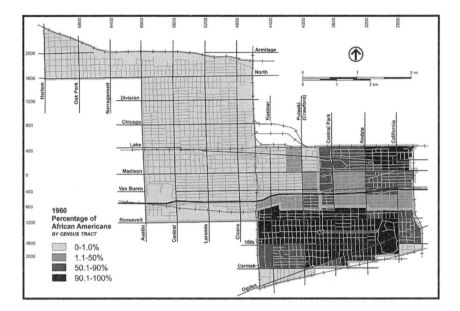

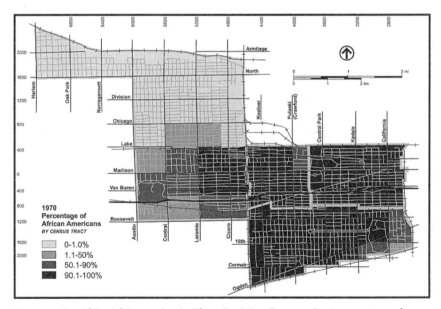

Map 3.3.   Rapid Racial Succession in These Far West Community Areas, 1960 and 1970.

Source: Amanda I. Seligman, *Block by Block: Neighborhoods and Public Policy on Chicago's West Side* (Chicago: University of Chicago Press, 2005). Copyright: Board of Regents of the University of Wisconsin System.

In contrast, resistance to the westward spread of the ghetto was greater in the three westernmost community areas of the city: East Garfield Park (Area 27), West Garfield Park (Area 26), and Austin (Area 25), all north of North Lawndale at the City of Chicago's westernmost boundaries (with Cicero to the south and west and Oak Park due west).[25]

The expansion of the West Side ghetto was blocked for some time in all but East Garfield Park, a largely commercial zone just north of North Lawndale. Its racial composition had already begun to change between 1950 and 1960. In that decade, the proportion of blacks rose from 17 to 62 percent, concentrated in the blocks closest to North Lawndale. The racial transition was not completed, however, until after the riot. By 1970, 98 percent of its residents were black.

The story of white resistance to black "invasion," especially in West Garfield Park where no blacks had lived in 1950, has been eloquently told by an empathetic historian, Amanda Seligman, who also suggests that the heightened interest of white residents in housing code enforcement, fighting blockbusting by unscrupulous real estate agents, and devising other mechanisms to slow white flight may not only have reflected the largely Catholic population's attachments to their homes and neighborhood parishes but may also have provided a more acceptable cover for some blatant racial animosity.[26]

Nevertheless, as we shall see later, although resistance began to crumble in the 1960s, it did not give way along this "last frontier" until the 1968 riot. As late as 1960, only 16 percent of West Garfield Park's population was black, concentrated in blocks adjacent to North Lawndale; by 1970, that percentage had increased to 97. Even Austin, whose population was the most insulated and resistant to black residents, would be affected by the riot. Its black population increased from 0 percent in 1960 to almost a third 10 years later.

I return to this discussion below, because this displacement of African Americans from the Near West Side to the Far West Side was one of the most immediate and important consequences of the April riot of 1968. It is ironic that, just as violence during the white-on-black riot in 1919 had served to ingather frightened African Americans within the South Side ghetto, so the explosion in 1968 frightened the white ethnic residents on the Far West Side into flight, thus yielding their defended turf to those who may have been displaced from the Near West Side.

THE WEST SIDE HEATS UP IN THE SUMMER OF 1966

Significantly, the opening volleys of several hot summers occurred not in the black area of the West Side but in an area just to its north, primarily occupied by Puerto Ricans. During the 1960s, the Puerto Rican population in Chicago had been increasing rapidly and, due to their displacement by urban renewal projects from various places of their prior residence and the expansion of the black population in other areas, was "ingathering" in "El Barrio" (the West Town/ Humboldt Park areas around Division Street) just northwest of "downtown."[27] That is where the first explosion occurred.

The Puerto Rican outburst, dubbed the Division Street riot (since most of the damage to property occurred on Division Street between Western and California avenues) but also known as the Humboldt Park riot, began on Sunday night, June 12, 1966. The day before, the first Puerto Rican parade in Chicago's history had been held downtown, with the mayor leading the march. But the next night, police were called to break up a fight among teenaged males (alleged to be gang members) holding a rally at Humboldt Park. The police, claiming to have been threatened by a gun, shot one of the youths, and then matters escalated, as 100 to 150 policemen were called to the scene and faced off against a putative 1,000 angry residents. Each side claimed that the "other" was responsible.

The journalist M. W. Newman identified the zone on the near Northwest Side (from Ashland to California and Haddon to Potomac) as "the Ghetto That Nobody Knew," an area that by 1966 housed an estimated 35,000 Puerto Ricans— their largest concentration in the city.[28] Newman alleges that nobody realized there were that many, and nobody expected any hostilities. "A week long carnival had just ended and the neighborhood was in a state of elation. On Saturday June 11th, the Puerto Rican community had organized a downtown parade—the first such display in the city's history—with Mayor Richard J. Daley at its head." Still exhilarated, large numbers congregated in Humboldt Park the following night for a rally. Apparently in response to a fight between young men, possibly from rival gangs, police were dispatched to break it up. But matters were soon out of hand, as a crowd of perhaps a thousand angry neighbors fought 100 police sent as reinforcements. No one was killed, but one policeman and two in the crowd suffered gunshot wounds, 13 more persons received minor injuries, and four police cars were rocked and set afire. The climax came when the police brought in the K-9 unit (police dogs), which was viewed as a total affront. On Monday the 49 persons arrested appeared in court. That night, crowds again gathered at the park and then took off along Division Street, breaking some 200 shop windows and looting stores.[29]

Newspaper accounts are hardly the most accurate and unbiased sources. Nevertheless, the main outlines are not disputed, and the grievances presented on June 28 by some 200 Puerto Ricans who marched from their neighborhood to City Hall to meet with the mayor stressed that: "the recent occurrences in the Puerto Rican community have indicated very strongly that the poverty program in this city has not touched our people." Among their other complaints were: first, the insult of the use of dogs, which really charged their emotions, and second, the lack of Spanish-speaking policemen, which had led to misunderstandings. In response, Mayor Daley offered them some concessions.

One month later, blacks on the West Side followed suit, but unlike the Puerto Ricans, they received no satisfaction from Mayor Daley.[30] Activist Kathleen Connolly is bitter in her account of what happened. She recalls that although "in the case of the embarrassing Puerto Rican riot, calm came about through the promise of a redress of grievances, the Negro riot was put down with 4,000 National Guard troops."[31] How had this happened? One would be hard pressed to answer that question if one consulted the Kerner Report, which attributed the July 1966 riot to a struggle between the police and neighborhood youths over an open fire hydrant.[32] This was hardly the case. The stakes were much higher, and the struggle between King and Daley was at its roots.

From the beginning, there was a subdued "war of wits" between Mayor Daley and Reverend King. When the latter moved into his North Lawndale apartment in early 1966, he took over an "illegal trusteeship" of the building to fix it up for its six other families. An embarrassed Mayor Daley countered with his own "plan" to send in exterminators and repairmen to the North Lawndale ghetto.[33] Then followed a series of nonviolent marches into nearby white neighborhoods, met routinely by catcalls and, on occasion, by thrown stones, but no police actions. But King was only in Chicago for relatively brief visits, and it seemed that the movement was stalling, confined to a small set of regular marchers.

To reinvigorate the campaign, a massive rally was organized for July 10, 1966, in the enormous lakefront Soldier Field (usually used for athletic events), at which King addressed a crowd of some 40,000 (estimates vary).[34] After the rally, King led 30,000 followers in a march on City Hall, where he posted

> "The Program of the Chicago Freedom Movement (for) An Open and Just City" with scotch tape and withdrew.[35] A ceremonial encounter with the Mayor ensued the next day. Daley agreed with the bulk of the thirty-five demands and insisted that his reforms were already affecting those areas.[36]

But the self-justifying claims of the canny political "boss" were not to be believed. The following night, Chicago's West Side erupted in violent protest.

Interestingly enough, the Kerner Report omits any mention of the Soldier Field rally and its open housing demands. Instead, it attributes rising tensions to the heat and a consequent fight between the police and neighborhood youths over an illegal opening of a fire hydrant! Its brief account reads in its entirety as follows.

On the evening of July 13, 1966, the day after the fire hydrant incident, rock throwing, looting and fire-bombing began again. For several days thereafter the pattern of violence was repeated. Police responding to calls were subjected to random gunfire. Rumors spread. The press talked in highly exaggerated terms of "guerrilla warfare" and "sniper fire." Before the police and 4,200 national guardsmen manage to restore order, scores of civilians and police had been injured. There were 533 arrests, including 155 juveniles. Three Negroes were killed by stray bullets, among them a 13-year-old boy and a 14-year-old pregnant girl.[37]

King had evidently failed to cool out "his masses," more radical than he. In Connolly's words,

> Pleading for concessions to end the violence, Dr. King seemed outmaneuvered again as Daley bought peace for the price of one portable swimming pool and ten hydrant sprinklers. As the water cooled off West Side youngsters, the Chicago Freedom Movement picked up all the broken pieces and put together the action phase of the Movement. The goal—open housing.[38]

Despite this partial defeat, King continued to lead a series of open housing marches into the heavily ethnic, white areas that circled the massive black districts. Marchers were attacked with rocks and bottles, and King himself was struck while walking through Gage Park on the Southwest Side. Furthermore, Daley obtained a court injunction limiting the demonstrations and then convened a summit conference with King to discuss open housing.[39] The much-publicized August 1966 open housing "summit" meeting between King and Daley proved a deep disappointment, and blacks felt betrayed by the lack of any tangible gains.

The title of chapter 11 of Anderson and Pickering's analysis says it all: "The Politics of Failure: January–April 1967"[40]—although it would be easy to invert the terms to "the failure of politics." The momentum was going out of the local voter registration campaign, possibly because that political path had yielded too little fruit, and while the white media pointed proudly to "progress," its views were shared neither by black leaders nor their constituents.

One year later, his promise not yet fulfilled, King was gunned down at a motel in Memphis—far from Chicago. His assassination touched off the largest black protest riot in that city since the "white riot" in 1919; its reverberations were felt in hundreds of other cities in the United States. Psychologically, it was as if the Kerner Report's belated warning of the growing chasm between two "separate" nations was already being revealed. The only analogy I can think of is the death of Lincoln: deep mourning in the North, jubilation or at least modest or passive responses in the South. The isolation African Americans felt in their grief and anger, and the fears and precautionary measures taken by white local governments (who recognized the grief and anger but did not share it), exacerbated the cleavage. Insensitivity and lack of empathy may not have "caused" the riots, but they confirmed the existing distance between the two "nations."[41]

The Riot of April 1968: "Ethnic Cleansing" on the Near West Side

It is remarkable that, in contrast to the detailed documentation of the Chicago race riot of 1919, no scholarly reconstructions exist of the riot in April 1968 that destroyed an enormous swath of territory in the Second Ghetto on the West Side after King's assassination.[42] While reactions of despair and anger triggered demonstrations in virtually all areas of Chicago where blacks lived, only in the West Side Second Ghetto did events spin out of control in arson and looting, leaving some 20 square blocks along West Madison Street and Roosevelt Road in rubble. At the risk of sounding paranoid, I am tempted to suggest that, because this area stood in the path of white "desire," this consequence may have been intended.

Given the lack of reliable secondary sources, I have depended on newspapers accounts of the time, which vary drastically by source,[43] and on the far from neutral post-mortem *Report of the Chicago Riot Study Committee to the Hon. Richard J. Daley*,[44] which is largely based on police records and interviews and is oriented toward policy recommendations for how to avert but also how to suppress future uprisings more effectively. All of these sources are too close to the events. They provide no long-term perspective on the growing frustrations within Chicago's black community, as the civil rights movement was reaching a dead end by 1966–67. Nor do they convey the rising animosities between blacks and City Hall—tensions that would reveal themselves at the height of the 1968 riot in Mayor Daley's bald directive to his police chief "to shoot to kill arsonists and shoot to maim looters" (see below).

The "murder" (the unambiguous term used by the *Chicago Defender*) of Martin Luther King, Jr. on the evening of April 4 set off reactions in black communities throughout the country, and it was scarcely unexpected that one of the most violent would be manifested in Chicago, given its large black community and the uneasy race relations that were endemic to the city. The only puzzling anomaly was that rioting on the South Side, which contained by far the largest proportion of African Americans in the city, was relatively sporadic and quickly suppressed, whereas the much smaller Second Ghetto of the West Side went up in flames.

I try here to reconstruct the sequence of events from the emotional, almost hysterical, day-by-day newspaper accounts and the day-by-day bland summaries of official actions, chronicled later in the Mayor's Riot Study Committee report. It should be obvious that there are discrepancies among these accounts, both in terms of fact and interpretation, some arising innocently from limited information, some more self-serving. I shall try to identify these discrepancies, not only because they reveal perspectives but also because they lay bare the struggle—not just for turf but for truth.

Thursday Evening, April 4, and Friday Morning, April 5: How and Where the "Riot" Began

According to the April 5 edition of the *Chicago Daily News,* the riot began on the West Side the morning of April 5, when black high school students walked out of their classes en masse and marched to nearby schools to disrupt their "normal routines."

Contrast this with the *Chicago Defender*'s account (weekly edition of April 6–12), which reported that on the night of April 4, within one hour of the announcement of King's death (the headline, in large bold type, reads "King Murdered"), the South Side experienced the first responses. There were arson attempts at Dunbar High School (at 3000 South Parkway), windows were broken at 39th, 41st, and South State streets, and at 47th and South Calumet; damage was also done to a beauty parlor at 47th and South Parkway. Police reinforcements were sent to both the south and west sides that first night.[45]

South Side leaders were certainly not quiescent. Another *Defender* article in the same issue reported on a hastily called memorial service that evening at the Liberty Baptist Church at 4949 South Parkway "where black power advocates openly defied moderate ministers who were calling for peace.... The minister was interrupted by shouts of 'Black Power,' 'Damn the Hunkies,' 'No more Hunkies by Sunday.'"[46] Evidently, the clergy had lost control of the ceremony.

The Chicago administration was also actively preparing for violence the night of April 4, although they apparently did not realize that it had already begun. According to the Mayor's Riot Study Committee report, April 4 was when their work began. Although King was shot (they use the term *assassination,* not murder) about 6 p.m. Chicago time and died an hour later,

> during the night and early morning hours of April 4 and 5, the citizens residing in the near north Cabrini-Green housing complex, the west side areas surrounding West Madison Street and West Roosevelt Road, and the south side area including 63rd Street from Stony Island Avenue to Halsted Street were off the streets watching television, listening to the radio or

discussing Dr. King's death quietly among themselves.... During the balance of the night of April 4, and into the morning hours of April 5, the black communities were on the whole abnormally quiet.[47]

In contrast to this "abnormal quiet," all through that night, government officials were in panicky communication with one another, "alerting appropriate personnel of the possibility of civil disorder." Officials also debated about whether to close the schools. Underestimating the depth of grief and despair in the black community, they decided to open the schools but to order them to organize "a service in memory of Dr. King." But by the time schools opened on Friday,

> absenteeism was unusually high in the ghetto high schools.... Early in the school day, the first of numerous false fire alarms were set off in some of the schools by students especially bent upon disrupting the *normal routines*. With each succeeding alarm and the resulting evacuation of high school buildings, the high school population dwindled as many students failed to return to classes. Throughout the morning, beginning around 9:00 o'clock, principals of a number of the high schools in the black communities were forced to call upon the police for assistance in quelling vandalism and responding to some few actual and threatened physical assaults by black students on whites.... By noon, most of the Chicago public high schools with predominantly black populations were closed.[48]

School walkouts were not restricted to the West Side. On the South Side that morning, students from Hirsch, South Shore, and Chicago Vocational high schools gathered at the grounds of the latter, then moved west to Stony Island Avenue, "breaking some store windows as they went." Police intercepted students from Hyde Park High School who were moving "in large numbers toward nearby predominantly white Mt. Carmel High School." In fact, an article in the *Chicago Daily News* reported that the violence occurring on the South Side was as bad as, if not worse than, that on the West Side. It noted that eight South Side schools from 63rd to 87th streets and Blue Island to Ashland avenue were closed and that about 400 students broke the windows of 100 stores as they moved along West 63rd street. "Most were students from Harper High School, joined by others from Lindbloom.... Police reported students from Parker were wrecking windows near 63rd and Woodlawn."[49]

Despite this, attention focused almost exclusively on the West Side—in large measure because expansion of the riot from there could possibly threaten nearby white businesses in the Loop, whereas on the enormous South Side it could be contained. This assumption proved well founded:

As early as 9:00 A.M. on April 5 some white businessmen along West Madison Street began to close their stores and shops and leave the area. They continued to do so throughout the morning. By noon many had left. . . . [They] sensed that the trouble would be manifested largely by acts of vandalism and violence directed against white businessmen.[50]

But the movement of the growing protest march was initially westward rather than toward downtown. When it reached Austin High School, the march encountered police resistance, which inevitably intensified the building anger.[51]

> Shortly after 11:00 A.M. a large group of students, mostly from Marshall High School, proceeded west on Madison Street toward Austin High School in relatively peaceable fashion but with the avowed intention of causing the dismissal of Austin. On its way to Austin this group stopped in Garfield Park [where speeches were made that left the group] in a more violent and angry frame of mind. When this group reached Austin, it was met by a small contingent of police. There was then some confusion during which *shots were fired in the air by the police.* The group then left Austin High School and proceeded east on Madison. As the group moved east on Madison, and particularly in the neighborhood of Madison and Kedzie, it did considerable damage to stores and shops.[52]

Note that it was only after the police fired that the march changed course, proceeding eastward along West Madison Street toward the Loop, the central business district, passing City Hall and the Civic Center area. Groups of ex-marchers then "wandered about the Loop and near Loop areas, making considerable noise and causing some minor property damage . . . [and using] abusive language . . . [until they were] dispersed . . . early in the afternoon."[53]

Police protection of downtown was massive, intimidating the crowd but also signaling businesses and banks to close early. A headline in the *Chicago Daily News* the following day read "Rush Hour Early: Loop Empties as Rumors Spread Fear." Perhaps partly as a result of this show of force, few arrests were made downtown; instead, window breakage, looting, and eventually arson were reported principally back along unguarded West Madison Street within the ghetto.

Friday Afternoon and Evening, April 5, through Early Saturday Morning, April 6

It was during the afternoon of April 5 that the mass media began to construct its image of "rioting for fun and profit." The *Chicago Daily News* of April 6 reveled in

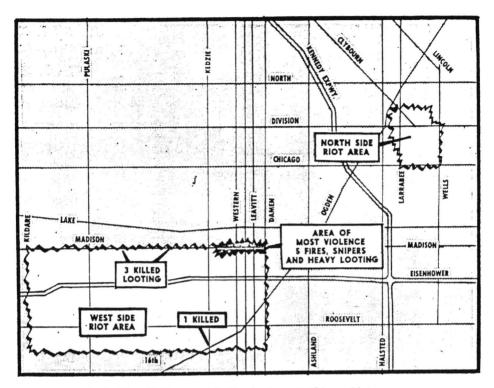

Map 3.4.   Blocks Virtually Destroyed by Fire in the 1968 Chicago Riot.

Source: Frank San Hamel's map from the *Chicago Daily News*, April 6, 1968, p. 5.

its description of "bedlam." The Mayor's Riot Study Committee report narrative begins with "looting." It describes how "crowds began to gather and to encourage each other to participate in a more and more open and organized fashion in the looting of stores ... [such as] clothing and appliance, general merchandise, liquor stores, grocery stores and pawn shops operated by whites." It was not until "about quarter of four ... [that] fire broke out in ... [a previously looted] furniture store ... [on] West Madison Street near Western Avenue ... apparently begun by a Molotov cocktail thrown into the building from the street."[54] (See map 3.4 for the extent of fires.)

How well the fire department handled the spreading fires is a matter of debate. The Mayor's Riot Study Committee report claims that the usual contingency plans were immediately put into place, as fire trucks from city stations raced to the scene and suburban firefighters moved into the city to cover "partially vacated outlying fire stations within the city limits, so that at all times during the weekend the overall fire protection being accorded the city outside the areas affected by the disorders remained adequate."[55] The fire chief claimed that 40 percent of the city's firefighting equipment was eventually deployed in the West Side. But apparently the contingency plans did not work. *Chicago's American* on Saturday, April 6, reported on the fires that had raged through the preceding night. A front-page article by William Garrett called it "a night of hell for Chicago firemen" and quoted the fire commissioner as saying "This was the worst night in the history of the fire department since the great fire of 1871." Another front-page article by Don Harris in the same paper has the subhead "9 Die. Hundreds Injured in Night of Fires, Looting." The article describes how troops were called from outside the city to dampen the fires and stop the looting on the West Side. Headlines on page 2 for the story's continuation read "Police Outnumbered, West Side Looters Run Wild." Another article on the same page is headed "Newsmen Flee Mobs, Tell of W. Side Terror."[56]

Why 4,000 firemen found the fires "too much" remains unexplained. Firefighters claimed they were under attack by snipers. However, the picture just above McHugh's critical article in the *Chicago Daily News* shows a national guardsman threatening bewildered passersby with his bayonet rather than any threats from a mob or even snipers.[57]

Mobilizing the Troops and Cordoning Off the West Side

By April 5, the Illinois National Guard was fully mobilized and authorized to use tear gas to disperse the rioters/looters. More details were provided in the *Chicago Daily News* edition of April 6. The bold front-page headline reads "1,500 New Troops Here," which brought the number of troops on duty in Chicago to almost 7,000.

As early as the evening of April 4, Brigadier General Richard Dunn, commander of the Illinois Army National Guard, had been in touch with the deputy superintendent of Chicago police but had been assured that the Guard would not be needed. However, as troubles escalated on Friday, the mayor changed his mind. "About 2:00 P.M. Mayor Daley called Acting Governor Shapiro to advise that the National Guard would be needed."[58] (The acting governor called the riot an "insurrection.")

> The afternoon of the 6th, General Dunn requested the mobilization of additional National Guard.... At the same time, the Acting Governor at Mayor Daley's request asked for federal troops, whereupon President Johnson immediately signed the necessary executive proclamation federalizing

the Illinois National Guard (thereby placing them on the budget of the federal rather than the state government) and ordered regular troops to duty in Chicago.[59]

The guard was mobilized and began to be dispatched within the next hour or two. But the same traffic jam that had delayed exit from the Loop also slowed down the assembly and movement of troops. It was midnight by the time the first national guardsmen appeared on the streets and well into the next morning before the force had risen to 6,900, joining an estimated 5,000 army troops already in Chicago from nearby camps.

In the meantime, the fires spread and the looting continued. In the meantime also, the isolation of the West Side grew more extreme. Bus service to 12 square miles of the West Side (from Chicago Avenue to Cermak Road and from Ashland Avenue to Cicero Avenue) was suspended by 6:30 p.m. for fear of snipers and smoke. Weary firemen, unable to control the fires, with their hoses on fire or losing water pressure and their trucks running out of fuel, began to give up. Electricity service "in portions of the west side area was interrupted for a number of hours during the evening and night."[60] By then, substantial numbers of (the first) arrestees arrived at Central Police Headquarters for processing. Their numbers would rise to thousands by the end of the outbreak. The morning edition of Chicago's *Sunday American* carried photos of the West Side destruction on the front page and, in a box, reported that fatalities had risen from 9 to 18 (incorrect), that hundreds had been injured, and that fires and looting had cost millions of dollars of property damage.

Who was responsible? According to the authors of the Mayor's Riot Study Committee report,

> the Committee [found] that ... [a] relatively small number of so-called "natural leaders" among the young blacks of high school age were generally the catalysts and leaders of the April disorders. ... A few older blacks joined them in this destructive "leadership" role. ... [D]uring the first hours of the disorder on April 5 the followers ... were predominantly young people. Later on April 5 and on April 6 many older residents of the riot areas joined in the looting. The handful of riot arsonists were apparently older than high school age; some if not all were in their twenties. Throughout the weekend some leaders and followers merely had in mind that *Dr. King's death provided a handy excuse for lawlessness, destruction and violence* [!]. Many others were principally motivated by a sense of rage and a resulting desire to strike back; their targets became "whitey" in general

and white-owned and operated business establishments in particular. . . . But there was no conspiracy.[61]

The report does not raise the question of whether there could have been a "conspiracy" on the part of the city officials to inflame tempers on the leaderless West Side by mobilizing their weapons of war and their massive "shows of force." It is worth noting that police, army, and national guard forces were lighter and relatively less provocative on the South Side, where order was more easily restored.[62] The Mayor's Riot Study Committee report claimed that "during the afternoon on the south side there was relative peace and calm, though tensions were high," and noted that "the 63rd Street area and the South Side generally were free from uncontrolled vandalism and looting."[63] Protests also sputtered out quickly at Cabrini Green housing project, isolated on the north side in an area so poor that there was nothing the police thought needed to be protected.[64]

The Day and Night of Saturday, April 6

Between 2 a.m. and 8 a.m. on April 6, "vandalism, looting and arson activity in the west side area was substantially reduced. Beginning after 8:00 A.M., looting activity increased again and some additional fires were set."[65] The police and national guard made a substantial number of arrests. On the Near North Side, limited acts of vandalism and some looting occurred on Saturday morning. On the South Side, and particularly near the corner of 63rd and Halsted streets, "looting began to occur late in the morning, increased during the afternoon and late in the day became fairly widespread. . . . [But it was] highly selective and directed almost entirely toward white-owned and operated business establishments, especially those known for or thought to engage in sharp sales and credit practices."[66] That afternoon, Daley announced a curfew "on all residents of the city under the age of 21, effective each night from 7 P.M. to 6:00 A.M. the following morning."[67]

Sunday, April 7: More Troops and the Curfew

The US Fifth Army brought in federal troops from Texas and Colorado; these arrived by April 7, but not all were deployed. Some remained in their bivouac areas at O'Hare Field and Glenview Naval Air Station, while others, assigned to patrol in the South Side area, were bivouacked in Jackson Park. Relative calm was restored by means of the federal troops and the "federalized" Illinois National Guard. On the West Side, demolition of unsafe buildings and cleanup began. The curfew was extended for the second night.[68]

Monday, April 8, through Wednesday, April 10: Winding Down

On Monday, schools were reopened, and some held the memorial services that had been scheduled for the previous Friday, although attendance was low in some areas.[69] Security remained heavy, especially on the West Side, where large numbers of police and national guardsmen continued to patrol. The court system continued to struggle with the processing of approximately 3,000 riot-related arrestees.

On Tuesday, the Chicago public schools were *finally* closed in memory of King, and many shops in riot areas were shuttered all or part of Tuesday. By Wednesday, Mayor Daley declared the official emergency terminated, and the departure of federal troops and the demobilization of the national guard began. The curfew was lifted, but the "war" between Mayor Daley and the black community was to continue.

The Controversy Reignited: "Shoot to Kill Arsonists and Maim and Detain Looters"

It is hard to imagine why, once he had ruthlessly suppressed what he called an insurrection of lawlessness, Mayor Daley chose to further inflame the black community by petulant (but threatening) remarks he delivered at a press conference less than a week after "order" had been restored. The ostensible purpose of the conference, on Monday, April 15, was to announce his appointments to a committee charged with investigating the riot. Nevertheless, he also publicly expressed his annoyance that the superintendent of police (James Conlisk) had not followed his orders to "shoot to kill arsonists and maim and detain looters" when the riot first started. He is quoted as saying, in his usual awkward English,

> I have conferred with the superintendent of police [Conlisk] this morning and I gave him the following instructions, *which I thought were instructions on the night of the 5th that were not carried out.* I said to him very emphatically and very definitely that an order be issued by him immediately and under his signature *to shoot to kill any arsonist or anyone with a Molotov cocktail in his hand . . . and to . . . maim or cripple anyone looting any stores.*[70]

Daley expressed distress that Conlisk had not carried out his earlier orders to issue these instructions to his police; instead, he said, "I found out this morning" that Conlisk had told police to make their own judgments, "so I am again telling him to issue my instructions! In my opinion, policemen should have had instructions to shoot arsonists and looters—arsonists to kill and looters to maim and detain."

Incendiary remarks! They were immediately greeted with horror by New York's Mayor John V. Lindsay, who, by restraining police and (the myth says) walking through New York's ghettos in his shirt-sleeves to offer his condolences, had single-handedly averted a riot in his city after King's death. Lindsay was quoted as saying: "In times of trouble we intend to respect human life as much as our obligation to maintain public order. We are not going to turn public disorder into chaos through the unprincipled use of armed force. In short, we are not going to shoot children in New York City."[71]

Tuesday's editorial in the *Chicago Daily News,* under the heading "Daley's Dubious Order," complimented the mayor for appointing a committee to pay special attention to the role of police in the recent riot but asked why "he has already prejudged the police department and found it guilty of laxity" because it ignored his draconian order to shoot and maim? The editorial reminded its readers (and indirectly the mayor) that the Kerner Report had "warned specifically against the excessive use of deadly weapons in a civil disorder" because it "may be inflammatory and lead to even worse disorder."[72]

By Wednesday, April 17, the mayor had "backed up" a little. In the text of a statement read to the city council, he announced that he "stood corrected," but then he only made matters more obscure. His amplification did little to influence either praise or condemnation from a polarized citizenry. According to a City Hall operative, a Mr. Reilly, 584 telegrams, 3,164 letters, and 753 phone calls were received on Wednesday endorsing the mayor's directive, while only 90 telegrams, 221 letters, and 93 phone calls opposed it.[73]

On the other hand, as might be expected, Daley was strongly reprimanded by the NAACP, which called on him to apologize to the Negro community. In his telegram to the mayor, Sydney Finley, field representative of the NAACP,

> called the mayor's statements irresponsible and untimely.... His second, and supposed toned down statement still gives license to law enforcement to act as judge, jury, and executioner.... [W]e of the NAACP believe the personal affront and abasement to the black citizens of America is deserving of a public apology.[74]

The front-page editorial in the same issue of the *Chicago Defender* attacked Daley for his callousness and lack of understanding. The large banner headline that day read: "NAACP Leader [Sidney Finley] Hits Daley, Calls for Public Apology," with the subtitle "Thinks Negroes Should Remember At Vote Time."

> There is a deepening realization that slum uprisings are caused by despair, frustrations, mental anguish, hopelessness and stark poverty. Against this

background of tragic deprivations, *it is difficult to understand the circumstances that led to Mayor Daley's inhumanly harsh "shoot-to-kill" orders against arsonists.* Though he had modified the statement as a concession to the storm of resentment that it provoked, the people of the black community in particular are still broiling over the intent and effect of the original dictum.[75]

He added that even the board of governors of the conservative City Club of Chicago criticized the mayor's statement as deplorable, conflicting with standing police orders. "Intemperate exhortations to greater violence render a disservice to the effort to maintain order," and "shooting, killing and maiming are not the proper tools of authority except as other means completely fail." The members of the Riot Study Committee did not entirely agree.

The Recommendations of the Riot Study Committee

In light of these criticisms of Daley's statements, one might ask whether the police were really as "restrained" as Daley claimed, and would the Mayor's Riot Study Committee report urge greater restraint? Hardly. Less than three months after the riot, the report not only "whitewashed" the police of culpability but focused on recommendations for how the police might "improve" their performance by becoming more effective. After acknowledging the grievances that had led to the protest riot and making some positive suggestions for "studying" its causes, the committee's report concentrated on more and better police fighting!

The report's final chapter (pp. 15–21) includes a summary of its 39 principal recommendations. The first three deal with schools, recommending that they be immediately closed in the ghetto areas if any triggering incidents like the King assassination should recur. They also advised improving rapport with black students and funneling more resources and special education programs to ghetto schools. The recommendations managed to be both threatening and condescending at the same time! The fourth and fifth recommendations deal with the national guard, recommending that it be called in early and kept in constant touch with the police and other city authorities.

Recommendations 6 through 18 are a strange mix of pious hopes and nitty-gritty equipment improvements to help the police do their job. The police department should regulate deadly force by continuing General Order 67-14 (coming down on the side of Conlisk, not Daley's intemperate order). It should be given more radio frequencies to improve coordination. It should be given more vans and squadrols to transport arrestees. It should review its procedures for handling looted goods to prevent police from being falsely accused of looting. Instead of making sweeping arrests, police should go for the leaders "whose arrest would have a sobering effect on . . . other persons in the area." Whites and blacks should be treated equally. A backup auxiliary force should be developed for emergencies. "*Overwhelming manpower rather than fire power should be used except in rare circumstances*" (italics added), thus leaving the riot committee sitting on the fence in the controversy between Daley and Conlisk. There should be intensive study of the use of chemicals for riot control, but until that is done, tear gas should be used rather than mace. Communication between police and the community should be improved. "Police must increase their understanding of the degradations and frustrations which the very poor, black and white, feel" and why these lead to crime. Disarming and granting of annual amnesty for turning in guns are recommended. The police should "aggressively . . . implement the recommendations contained in the report of the 1967 Citizens Committee to Study Police-Community Relations."

The next two recommendations concern the fire department. It needs a better "alert" system, and there must be better cooperation between fire and police departments to protect firemen entering riot areas.

A laundry list of assorted suggestions follows, none of them particularly original. The Commission on Human Relations should improve its capacity as a center for rumor control. The Urban Progress Centers should handle food and clothing distributions in emergencies. Ghetto aid programs should involve more Negro participation, especially among "young people." It would be desirable to train "ghetto area residents for more self-determination and local community control. The skill, experience and financial support of downtown institutions (private as well as public) must be made available to the ghetto communities in this connection." Citizens' organizations should work to establish or strengthen "autonomous community organizations in those ghetto areas, such as the west side of Chicago, where they are desperately needed." Businessmen and merchants should increase efforts to develop black ownership and expand franchises to blacks in ghettos. There should be better government policing of and "Better Business Bureau" enforcement against fraudulent merchandising practices by ghetto merchants. More consumer education in schools is needed.

Singling out the insurance industry, the report recommended full implementation of new state and federal legislation making available casualty insurance coverage in ghetto areas. And turning to the role of the media, the committee urged journalists "to dispel rumors" and give correct information during large-scale civil disturbances.

The next eight recommendation raise judicial issues: how the courts should handle riot arrests, attorneys, bonds, complaints, mass arrests, disposal of cases in district police stations in future riots, public defenders, decentralized detention and processing centers. These recommendations stress the need for an overall plan of coordination of judicial procedures.

The committee concluded its report with the question: "Are the April Riots Likely to Recur?" Worried that they might, given the deep-seated resentments in the ghetto communities, their political impotence, and their communication isolation from City Hall, the authors repeated their earlier recommendation that a new "standing commission" be appointed

> with the sole purpose and function of examining into the needs of the ghetto areas, determining the appropriate and necessary methods of meeting those needs and checking upon the extent to which governmental and non-governmental agencies are taking steps to meet such needs; such a commission should be composed of representatives of the ghetto areas and of the general community, as well as of organizations within and outside the ghetto which are committed to ghetto improvement. It is recommended that such a commission have a full-time, paid Negro as its executive director.[76]

This bypassed the by then impotent and financially strapped Mayor's Committee on Race (Human) Relations, set up initially in 1943 to do this job.

And finally,

> Chicago should not tolerate violence and disorder, property destruction, theft and assault as a means of rectifying injustices in the ghetto areas. At the same time, the problems of the ghetto are real and serious and have brought this city as well as the rest of the country to a crisis of relationships between peoples so serious that the Committee calls upon our fellow citizens to support the leaders of our city in finding the necessary new and radical solutions to the unprecedented circumstances which confront us.[77]

You would think that this resounding if florid call to "arms" and to research-based ameliorative programs designed to integrate marginalized blacks into mainstream power organizations, coming as it did from his handpicked advisers, would have made an impression on the mayor to whom it was directed. But outside of its support for more and better equipment for the police department and advice on strategies for "nipping a riot in the bud," the report's recommendations were ignored.

CONTRASTING THE BLACK AND WHITE RIOTS OF 1968

Earlier I noted how surprised I was not to find any independent secondary account of the April 1968 Chicago riot. Whenever I searched library catalogues, the only entries I found under "Chicago, Riots, 1968" were to the Grant Park antiwar protests of August 23–28, held in clear view of the Democratic Party Nominating Convention. This riot was covered in great detail in a document variously named *Violence in Chicago: The Walker Report* but also *Rights in Conflict: The Violent Confrontation of Demonstrators and Police in the Parks and Streets of Chicago during the Week of the Democratic Convention.* I shall refer to it under its shorter name, *The Walker Report.*

This dense 362-page study was produced with a massive and, we can only assume, well-paid staff. From Max Frankel's introduction we learn that Daniel Walker's resources were virtually unlimited.

> Starting with the F.B.I.-trained staff of his Chicago Crime Commission—a distinguished citizens group that has devoted itself to fighting gangsterism and exposing the links between business interests and crime syndicates—Mr. Walker built a study team of 90 full-time and 121 part-time interviewers and researchers. Many lawyers and trained investigators were lent to him, at no cost, by prestigious law firms and banks. Together they took 1,410 statements from eyewitnesses, reviewed 2,017 others provided by the Federal Bureau of Investigation, and studied 180 hours of motion picture films, more than 12,000 still photographs and thousands of news accounts. They began work on September 27, 1968, and...completed the Report 53 days later, on November 18.[78]

Frankel's introduction starts from the unexamined preconception, perhaps drawn from the earlier report to Daley, that "when Negroes rioted in April, 1968, his [Daley's] policemen handled the situation efficiently and with restraint." But in handling that riot, the Chicago police had been too restrained and were later chastised by Mayor Daley in his famous "shoot to kill arsonists, shoot to maim looters" statement. It was here that, according to *The Walker Report,* much of the trouble began, which "culminated in the riot of the police themselves" in the Democratic Convention riot.[79]

In the section identified as Summary, the same myth about how "restrained" the police had been in the April 4–10 riot (a myth to which no one who observed it could have subscribed) is repeated. *The Walker Report* blames Daley's rebuke of the superintendent of police in April 1968 for unleashing an uninhibited display of police brutality, not only several weeks later on April 27, when the police attacked demonstrators, bystanders, and media representatives at a Civic Center peace march, but eventually at the Democratic Convention protests in late August.

Since there is no evidence that police brutality was greater against white "protesters" than against black "rioters" and, in fact, the opposite was true, this alerts us to a double standard of judgment and helps to explain why the Democratic Convention received such detailed study, whereas the causes of the larger and more lethal black riot were ignored. It also explains why potential black participants were reluctant to join in planning for the convention demonstration.

In early February 1968, there was an attempt to merge peace and black movements via a meeting in Chicago to which Tom Hayden and Rennie Davis invited leaders of SNCC, CORE, and the Black Caucus.[80] "But shortly after the Lake Villa meeting [in March], prospects for the demonstration of a united black-white front in Chicago disintegrated. The change of direction may, perhaps [sic], have been related to the assassination of . . . King and the ugly aftermath of riots, including the use of guardsmen and federal troops to quell disturbances."[81] Nevertheless, the National Mobilization for the antiwar demonstration still tried to involve blacks in their planned demonstration. They largely failed.

> Many blacks felt that demonstrations like those planned for Chicago, focusing on the war in Vietnam, were traditionally conducted by whites and were remote from the problems which plagued the black man—problems which have to be dealt with by blacks themselves. *Still others feared the heavy security forces which were expected to be amassed in Chicago and wanted to avoid what they thought could develop into a massacre of blacks.* . . . Many black leaders expressed dismay at the prospect of a march through the ghetto which might bring troops with them—a grim reminder of the April riots.[82]

And indeed, "one leader of a black community organization said that complaints of police brutality received by that organization increased dramatically in the week or so before the convention." Nevertheless, the Black Panthers urged participation, although the leaders of other organizations, such as the Blackstone Rangers, actually left the city to avoid more crackdowns, especially since they had been under "preventive surveillance."[83]

The antiwar demonstration/riot did include some blacks, but in overwhelming numbers participants were young, white, and middle-class. And despite the allegations that the police had been more brutal than during the King "black protest riot," casualties and arrests were considerably lower.[84] First, no one was killed by police guns, and despite the public outrage and media alarms, only a relatively small number of demonstrators were injured by police batons. The records of injuries are of course incomplete, but the police reported 192 police injured, most hit by flying objects at the height of battle on Wednesday, of whom 49 were hospitalized. Most police injuries occurred at Balbo and Michigan and the vicinity of the Hilton, 78 percent occurred on August 28 (Wednesday), and 63 percent were from thrown objects. There was a less complete enumeration of injured demonstrators, but Chicago area hospitals reported 101 demonstrators admitted (of whom 58 were from Chicago and 43 from more distant locations; 23 were 16–19 years old, 48 were 20–24 years old; only 6 were 40 or older). Some 668 persons were arrested, most of whom

> were under 26 years of age, male, residents of Metropolitan Chicago, and had no previous arrest record. Two-thirds of the arrests were made of persons ranging in age from 18 to 25, with those under 17 comprising 9.6 of the total. Men outnumbered women almost eight to one.... Forty-three per cent of the arrested were employed, 32.6 per cent were students, and 19.9 per cent were unemployed. The employed represented a wide range of occupations including teachers, social workers, ministers, factory laborers and journalists.[85]

Given the large size and prolonged duration of the confrontation, these figures seem modest indeed, especially when compared to those of black protesters after King's assassination.

THE ECHO RIOT OF 1969: RELATIVE POLICE BRUTALITY

It would be foolish to argue that police behavior, independent of the race of rioters, had changed either for better or for worse. True, only nine persons arrested in the Grant Park demonstration carried knives or guns, and most police were threatened by thrown bottles, not snipers. But there seemed to be one set of "rules of engagement" for police dealing with whites and an entirely different set for dealing with young and equally unarmed blacks. This was demonstrated only eight months later on the first anniversary of King's murder, when the city administration reverted to the old but "improved rules of engagement" deemed suitable for its black citizens.

Given that between April 4, 1968, and April 3, 1969, no rebuilding of the West Side took place and very little economic assistance, much less political power, was extended to those most hurt by the uprising of April 1968, it is not surprising that on the first anniversary of King's death an "incipient riot" was again threatened. Although in the interim the mayor still had not learned from the Kerner Report to give help to troubled minority communities (as he had been reminded by his committee's report), the police department had taken seriously the set of final recommendations directing it to counteract any threat with dispatch and with maximum force. Thus, this "echo" riot, which repeated many of the activities of the prior year, was ruthlessly and even more efficiently suppressed by a city administration that immediately deployed maximum manpower, including the national guard. (Possibly those extra communications networks, better coordination with the national guard, and more patrol cars and decentralized booking courts did the trick.)

Discouraging Conditions on the West Side before the Echo Riot Began

The *Chicago Tribune* of March 30, 1969, carried an article by Michael Smith that included the following observation: "In a tour of the area hardest hit, a *Tribune* photographer team found dozens of square blocks totally vacant. Even the smallest heaps of rubble had been taken away. Not one of the buildings that once filled these blocks has been replaced." The article showcased two photos of the 3300 block on West Madison Street, one taken when the fires were raging in April of 1968, the second showing the same extensive area, now cleared and absolutely empty.[86] Another article by Lois Wille in the *Chicago Daily News* of March 28, 1969, came to the same conclusion.

> Nothing has been built in the two main areas destroyed by flames last April.... Madison St. between Kedzie and Homan is largely a barren field of glass and rubble. Roosevelt Road from Kedzie to Homan is just as desolate. Only one building stands on the block between Spaulding and Homan—a tavern with apartments upstairs that was spared by the flames. On April 9 [1968], two days after the riots subsided, city housing and planning officials announced [a] crash rebuilding program to begin "immediately." But... [no] specific construction plans have been drawn. The burned-out land has not yet been acquired by the city. It still belongs to the original owners, who have no intention of rebuilding in an area they consider hostile.[87]

Wille noted conflicts between city agencies and black neighborhood groups over future developments, with the city favoring a shopping mall, whereas blacks wanting more housing—and with their input.

> Two initial steps for rebuilding the Madison-Kedzie area have been completed in the year since King's death. On Jan. 16 the city received a $38,989,954 federal grant for improving 24 areas, including the burned-out site. Ten months after the riots, on Feb. 11, the City Council declared the area a slum—a necessary step before the city can draw urban renewal plans.... The Chicago Housing Authority is building 186 three-story apartments on scattered sites in Lawndale near some of the burned-out areas. [But these] were planned before the April riots.[88]

Is it any wonder that, given these daily reminders of the city's neglect of their interests, tensions should have resurfaced on the anniversary of King's murder?

How the Echo Riot Began

On Thursday, April 3, 1969,[89] students of Crane High School on West Madison Street met in their lunchroom to protest a decision by the faculty not to hold a school-wide ceremony to mark the anniversary of King's death. The next day, the *Chicago Daily News* published a menacing-looking multicolumn photo in its "Third Page Section," showing some of the "100 heavily armed policemen" chasing students near Crane High School (on West Jackson) after police cleared and closed the school on Thursday, April 3; the caption identified the protest as "a lunchroom rampage."[90]

An accompanying article under Henry De Zutter's byline was a bit more helpful.[91] He pointed out that Crane was one of the few all-black city schools where teachers and administrators had decided against holding a special assembly, preferring to "honor Dr. King by conducting observances in each classroom." Crane also housed a branch of Chicago City College, and the college conducted its own memorial service in the high school auditorium, at which Charles Hurst, a black psychologist and newly appointed president of the Crane branch, and two members of the Black Panther Party spoke under heavy police guard. Armed police (who had been stationed in the school since the troubles of the previous year!) barred high school students from joining the service, an action students took as clearly provocative.

We shall never know exactly what happened next. The police accused the invited members of the Black Panthers of starting a riot by breaking windows and overturning furniture, although according to De Zutter, "Hurst and one of the Black Panthers invited to speak...denied that any panther was responsible for the violence."

The version of the "story" that appeared in the Friday, April 4, edition of the *Chicago Sun-Times* was somewhat different.[92] That paper reported that students of seven high schools on the west and north sides had walked out of their schools on Thursday, and that "after incidents of window-smashing, looting, scattered shooting and attacks on motorists and policemen," almost 5,000 national guard troops were ordered to active duty and another 2,000 troops were held at the ready in armories outside the Chicago area. It was evening, however, before motorized patrols of guardsmen could be deployed on the West Side and around the Cabrini Green housing project. (The accompanying photo shows an armored truck with armed guardsmen patrolling West Division Street on Thursday night.) Tear gas was used at one point "to disperse a group of youths.

Mayor Daley once again imposed a curfew for all persons under 21 from 8 p.m. until 6 a.m. He also imposed restrictions on the sale of firearms, ammunition, gasoline and liquor." By 10:30 that evening, "both the West and North sides were relatively calm," and bus service was restored. Emergency mass-arrest court procedures handled the 243 persons, mostly juveniles, who had been arrested.

By Saturday night, "emergency restrictions enforced since disorders broke out Thursday on the West and Near North sides were called off [and] . . . the 7,000 Illinois National Guardsmen . . . were deactivated." The mayor said proudly, "The calm over the last 36 hours . . . has clearly shown that *all* [*sic*] *of the citizens of Chicago* have a fervent and genuine desire for peace in their neighborhoods and city."[93]

The attentive reader may feel a bit of déjà vu, and an inattentive one may be tempted to check whether he has lost his place. The echo riot began in much the same way as the original, but it was "better handled," taking to heart the real advice given by the mayor's committee. The incipient riot had been "nipped in the bud," largely by applying the tactics of suppression that had been the major focus of the recommendations in the Mayor's Riot Study Committee report, submitted in response to the previous year's events. The authorities put all of them into operation, including the draconian call-up of the national guard and the intimidating use of surveillance helicopters.

DID THE RIOTS ACHIEVE ANYTHING?

The riots (the originals of 1966 and 1968 and the echo riot of 1969) did have certain effects, but not necessarily those intended by the participants. Three major consequences can be singled out.

Reclaiming Formerly Black-Dominated Zones

First, the fires left a *cordon sanitaire* between a much-reduced black ghetto on the Near West Side and the rest of the city, thus furthering the reconquest that had been initiated in the 1960s (by the siting of the intersection of the east-west Congress Street highway, now called the Eisenhower Expressway, and the north-south route of the Kennedy Expressway, further clearing of land for the University of Illinois Chicago Circle Campus and the expansion of a medical facility to its west). The areas nearer the Loop in the Second Ghetto, destroyed in the 1968 riot, were easily cleared and being rebuilt with glistening office towers and high-priced condos. Only one "problem" remained "unsolved." A reduced and isolated black ghetto, primarily housed in the phalanx of public housing projects along the main avenues involved in the 1968 riot, constituted a residual impediment to West Side gentrification. A solution to this "blight," however, had to await federal funding. In this, Chicago would be rewarded, years later, for its sorry history of having constructed and then neglected hypersegregated public housing.[94] I reserve this discussion for the epilogue to this chapter.

Improved Riot Control Procedures

Second, the riots galvanized Chicago's police to develop better (more oppressively "efficient") techniques of riot control. While this did not end riots (see my discussion of the 1992 Bulls riot below), it certainly cowed potential participants. In the process, many black leaders, especially of the South Side community that was no longer under pressure from "white resistance," were coopted into the system and, as they had done in 1968 and 1969, were willing to help restore order quickly to their "own" turf.

Racial Succession on the Far West Side and Expansion on the South Side

A third consequence was the further flight of resisting, but now fearful, whites to other parts of the city and especially to the (mostly white-) collar counties. For the West Side, the most important "unintended" consequence was the expansion of the West Side ghetto all the way to the city limits at still-resistant Cicero (see maps 3.2 and 3.3 above and table 3.1). Ironically, the very areas where white residents had offered the greatest resistance to King's marches for integrated housing have now turned into equally segregated zones, but for black residents. To some extent, this has been a Pyrrhic victory, since the zone is now devoid of the factories and workplaces that had supported its former working-class white residents. The results of this racial succession can be seen on maps 3.5 and 3.6.

Grieving for lost homes, displacement, and denied job opportunities accumulated in Chicago's ghettos of despair, despite some undoubted mobility

Table 3.1 Racial Change on the Far West Side, Chicago, 1930–80.

| | PERCENTAGE WHITE OCCUPANCY | | | | | |
	1930	1940	1950	1960	1970	1980
East Garfield Park	97	95	83	38	2	1
West Garfield Park	100	100	100	84	3	1
Austin	100	100	100	100	66	21

Source: Figures have been assembled by the author from sequential editions of *Local Community Fact Books*.

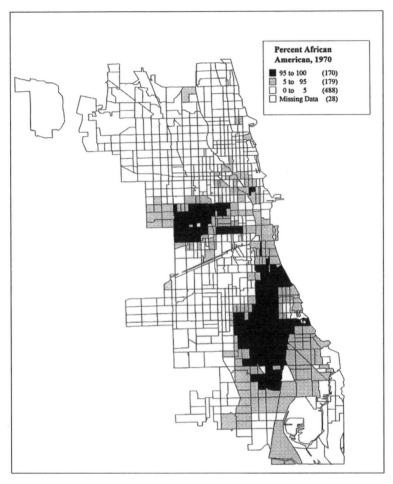

Map 3.5.   Extent of Primarily Black-Occupied Census Tracts in Chicago, 1970.

Source: Courtesy of Jeffrey D. Morenoff, "Neighborhood Change and the Social Transformation of Chicago, 1960–1990," master's thesis, University of Chicago, 1994.

for the growing black middle-class population that was spreading to the city limits and beyond on the South Side. Grievances over deteriorating conditions would surface in an unlikely time and place—during Chicago's 1992 celebrations over the repeated triumphs of Michael Jordan's great basketball team. But other than that, Chicago has thus far been spared a massive race riot. Why?

REVIVING THE ATLANTA SOLUTION—ON THE WIDER COUNTY SCALE

By the early 1990s, the city of Chicago had undergone a cycle of political power realignment and had experienced significant racial/ethnic changes. After the brief

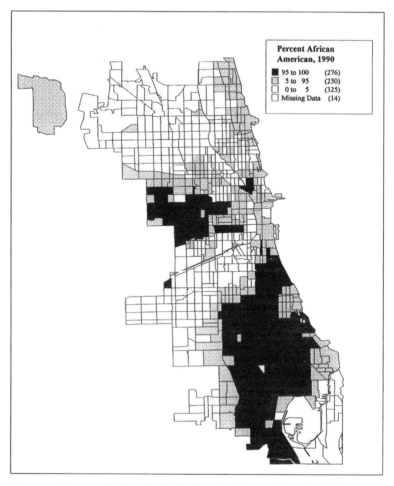

Map 3.6.   Extent of Primarily Black-Occupied Census Tracts in Chicago, 1990.

Source: Courtesy of Jeffrey D. Morenoff, "Neighborhood Change and the Social Transformation of Chicago, 1960–1990," master's thesis, University of Chicago, 1994.

capture in 1983 of the mayor's office by Chicago's first and only black mayor, Harold Washington,[95] his five-year interregnum was cut short by his untimely death one year into his second term, and power reverted to the Irish and, eventually, to the son of Boss Daley. The old white growth machine was restored—involving further territorial conquest of areas immediately south and west of the Loop for white institutions, businesses, and housing,[96] even though the proportion of whites residing in the city of Chicago and its containing Cook County has continued to decline.

Table 3.2 Distribution of Various Racial/Ethnic Populations (in Percentages) in Chicago and the Surrounding Area, 1990. Based on 1990 U.S. Census Data.

Race/Ethnicity	CMSA	PMSA	Chicago	Suburban Counties
White NH	66.7	62.3	37.9	82.1
Black NH	18.9	21.7	38.6	7.7
Amerind NH	0.2	0.1	0.2	0.1
Asian NH	3.0	3.6	3.5	3.3
Other NH	0.1	0.1	0.1	0.1
Hispanic	11.1	12.1	19.6	6.6

NH = Non-Hispanic. The area covered is Chicago, Il.-Ind. and Wisc. CMSA; the Chicago PMSA; the City of Chicago and Cook County; and the surrounding Illinois counties (Cook Co. minus city of Chicago, Du Page, Kane, Lake, and Will counties). Calculations mine. I have calculated so as to separate the portion of Cook County that falls within the city limits of Chicago from that portion outside the city. This suburban Cook County residual has been added to Will, Kane, Du Page, and Lake counties, and the composite of these suburban regions immediately surrounding the city has been summed and then calculated.

Source: U.S. Department of Commerce, Bureau of Census, 1990.

Table 3.3 Racial/Ethnic Composition of the City of Chicago, Chicago PSMA (Chicago Plus Cook County), and the Surrounding (Collar) Counties, 1990 (%).

	City of Chicago	Chicago PSMA	Collar Counties	Total CMSA
White non-Hispanic	37.9	62.3	82.1	66.7
Black non-Hispanic	38.6	21.7	7.7	18.9
Hispanic	19.6	12.1	6.6	11.1
Asian non-Hispanic	3.5	3.6	3.3	3.0

As can be seen in tables 3.2 and 3.3, by 1990, the new Maginot line of apartheid had moved outward to the line dividing Cook County from the four surrounding Illinois counties (called the "collar") of Du Page, Will, McHenry, and Kane, although portions of Cook County near the northern and north-western borders adjoining the wealthy and white suburbs remained unwelcoming to blacks and Hispanics. Even these figures overestimate the degree of suburban integration, because blacks remain largely concentrated in the five suburban "towns," associated originally with railroad construction, that were known for their early and exclusive black occupancy.

The separation of the "races" is therefore virtually complete, as the South Side "Black Metropolis" has expanded even beyond the city limits and the West Side "Second Ghetto" has retreated westward up to the city limits. The populations in both zones are more than 95 percent black, and both areas have experienced the draining away of employment opportunities. Black unemployment rates in the city are three times higher than those for whites. If Chicago is "spared" further ghetto uprisings, it is because apartheid writ large has made it easier for whites to reclaim the valuable land on the Near West Side while abandoning the enlarged South Side and Far West Side ghettos to the African American community.

Epilogue

The Bulls Riot of 1992: Echo of Rodney King

Chicago experienced no immediate repercussions of the April 1992 Los Angeles South Central riot until the evening of Sunday, June 14, 1992, the night the Chicago Bulls basketball team won the National Basketball Association championship for the second year in a row.[97] All over the city, celebrations began, with people of all shades of skin taking to the streets.

> Outside the downtown area [where police were trying to calm whites who were rambunctiously celebrating by getting drunk], in the South Side and West Side ghettos of Chicago, however, the night took a different turn: hundreds of stores were looted, more than 1,000 people were arrested, and 90 police were injured. . . . Data gathered from court records shows that 98% of those arrested for felony looting that night were black. . . . The quantity of arrestees and extent of the property damage easily place the Bulls riot of 1992 into Spilerman's (1976) category of most severe riots, although the apolitical nature of the precipitating incident (a basketball game) naturally raises questions.[98]

Rosenfeld rightfully attributes the events that occurred in isolated portions of the south and west side ghettos to the interaction of several factors. The most basic and persistent variable was the level of ongoing disaffection and resentment growing out of the continued neglect of the problems of housing and jobs. This anger was exacerbated on April 1, 1992, "when the largest welfare cut in Illinois history went into effect," despite the angry opposition of Chicago's black leaders. Closer to the event, however, was the acquittal on April 29 of the Los Angeles policemen who had been accused of beating black motorist Rodney King. The beating and the subsequent trial had been heavily covered in the media, and the outrage at the verdicts stoked anger in black communities throughout the United States. The outbreak of rioting in Los Angeles itself was immediate and was graphically portrayed on television. In Chicago, Korean storekeepers in ghetto areas braced themselves for similar attacks, closing their stores on May 1, anticipating riots and looting—that did not occur. They were merely postponed.

In the window of opportunity provided by the chaos of the celebrations of the Bulls' victory and temporarily deflected by the attention police were devoting to out-of-bounds white behavior in the bars of "Old Town," the ghettos again erupted. The causes were familiar ones: mounting resentments over persisting poverty, lack of opportunities, and the presence of alien shopkeepers in the ghettos (notably Arabs and, more recent comers, Koreans). The "rioters" on the west and south sides employed the by-now-familiar repertoire of actions honed since the 1960s. Much may have changed in the distribution of whites and blacks in the Chicago metropolitan region, but apartheid has not diminished, nor has the brutality of the police (as measured by arrests and injuries) in putting down civil disorders in Chicago's black ghettos decreased. Hopelessness fueled protest, and fear fueled response.

The Paradox of Police Reforms and More Prisons

As in other cities, there have been efforts in Chicago to reform the police, sparked by the black patrolman's organization, and there have been academic and governmental studies, as well as experimental programs seeking to strengthen community policing and other suggested panaceas for Chicago's problems. But so long as minorities remain disproportionately poor, underserved at best, harshly disciplined at worst, it is not unlikely that "ghetto uprisings" and "police riots" may recur in Chicago. Alternatively, the police may "cull" the potential rioters (young unemployed minority males) by remanding them to the expanding prison-industrial complex. I return to these themes in chapter 8.

Dispersing Poor Minorities by Destroying Public Housing

I have noted above the impediment to further West Side gentrification posed by the selective postriot survival of the massive public housing projects along the east-west avenues.[99] Indeed, this is perceived by many in local government to be only part of a more general problem, for which a "solution" is now being tried. Since the original text of this chapter was written, a new strategy has appeared in Chicago that seeks to avoid future "riots" or insurrections, not by eliminating the causes of black dissatisfaction and distress but by destroying the "breeding grounds" that presumably have allowed the riots to ignite in and spread from the "infamous" public housing projects.

Ironically, federal subsidies for public housing had initially been defended in the 1940s and 1950s on the grounds that replacing teeming slums with sanitary and safe housing would not only improve the physical health of the "deserving" poor but also improve their social behavior. The assumption was that "respectable" tenants would be selected, those who had the will and funds to maintain their apartments in decent condition. Over the years, however, admissions became less selective, maintenance was neglected, and occupants were drawn almost exclusively from nonwhite minorities. Although these changes occurred in many places, in few other cities (with the exception of New York, which has not sought to tear them down) were facilities so concentrated in high-rise apartment complexes.[100]

Disdainful of its tenants, the Chicago Housing Authority, over the years, neglected maintenance and managerial control, especially because the projects primarily served poor minorities with little power and had been carefully "insulated" from white territory. So bad did the CHA's reputation become that it was ranked the worst public housing authority in the country and was finally placed into federal receivership.

Enter HOPE VI. Misdiagnosing the problems of poverty, welfare (now to be redefined as workfare for single mothers), the disappearance of jobs, and localized economic implosion as due to poor housing and the isolation of the poor from the good "moral" influence of their betters, HUD opened the door to a new opportunity—to once again clear the "sick" slums, remove their inhabitants, and, in the words of the old urban land economists, reclaim land values and restore the tax base.

In 1989, a National Commission was appointed by Congress to evaluate severely depressed public housing. Three years later, HOPE VI (Housing Opportunities for People Everywhere!) was set up and funded, and by 2003, HUD had already approved some 135,000 public housing units for demolition, far more than the commission had anticipated.[101] Chicago became one of the most enthusiastic applicants.

By 1997, Chicago had its required "Plan for Transformation" in place, that included the destruction of Cabrini Green on the highly desirable and mostly white North Side, the clearance of multiple projects west of the Chicago River, also on prime land, and even the enormous Stateway Gardens, Robert Taylor Homes, and Ida B. Wells projects on the less desirable Near South Side. When the money came, the plan was put into action. Now those projects are being leveled to return the land to the tax rolls and more profitable uses. An early September 2005 special edition of the *Chicago Reporter* estimated the number of units already destroyed and the relative booms being experienced in prices, values in new mortgage loans, and racial changes from black to white within a few blocks of each of the districts where housing projects have been leveled.

Relocation of the displaced project residents is a disaster, as history might suggest. Funds for those "eligible" will come from Section 8 (the only remaining form of housing subsidies), but the number of units in Chicago or its immediate vicinity is far below what will be needed, their quality is not assured, and most of the new "refugees" are already crowding into remaining poor areas of existing ghettos.[102] There is evidence that many displaced families have already left the city for more depressed small towns in southern Illinois or Wisconsin where Section 8 units may be more plentiful. Rebuilding at half the densities means that even if the displaced meet the stringent eligibility requirements (e.g., have a valid lease, are current with rent and utility charges, and, if on welfare, participate in workfare and have a "good housekeeping record"), it is estimated that "fewer than 20 percent will be able to return to their old neighborhoods, and most will continue, if not to "grieve for a lost home," at least to suffer from the uprooting from familiar turf and support networks. To my mind, this has all the markings of a new Atlanta Solution, as the reconquest of inlying districts of central Chicago is extended to land that can now be redeveloped, thanks to the destruction of the "projects" and the scattering of their "dangerous" tenants. Whether intentionally or not, this may serve to postpone, if not prevent, Chicago's next race riot.

NOTES

1. See Harvey Molotch, *Managed Integration: Dilemmas of Doing Good in the City* (Berkeley: University of California Press, 1972).
2. Space for new university-sponsored housing was cleared in Hyde Park in the aftermath of arson and neighborhood blowout. For a sympathetic account of the university's activities, see Peter Rossi and Robert Dentler, *The Politics of Urban Renewal: The Chicago Findings* (Glencoe, Ill.: Free Press, 1961).
3. See Edward Banfield, "Rioting for Fun and Profit," in *The Unheavenly City: The Nature and Future of Our Urban Crisis* (Boston: Little, Brown, 1968), reproduced without change in his *The Unheavenly City Revisited* (1978), pp. 185–209.

4. Alan B. Anderson and George Pickering, *Confronting the Color Line: The Broken Promise of the Civil Rights Movement in Chicago* (Athens: University of Georgia Press, 1968), p. 310.

5. These are the titles, respectively, of chaps. 7 and 8 of Douglas McAdam, *Political Process and the Development of Black Insurgency, 1930–1970* (Chicago: University of Chicago Press, 1982).

6. Ibid., p. 154, table 7.4.

7. Some 71 percent of movement-initiated actions were in the South and were directed to expanding voting rights and to dismantling Jim Crow. Ibid., p. 190, table 8.3.

8. Between 1965 and 1970, the number of movement-initiated actions in the South dropped to only a third of the total, whereas the proportion in New England and the Middle Atlantic region rose to about a third, and to 21 percent in the East North Central region. Ibid., p. 190, table 8.3.

9. Here, McAdam, *Political Process*, p. 197, is quoting from Lewis M. Killian, *The Impossible Revolution: Black Power and the American Dream* (New York: Random House, 1975), p. 146.

10. Ibid., p. 187, table 8.2.

11. See James R. Ralph, Jr., *Northern Protest: Martin Luther King, Jr., Chicago, and the Civil Rights Movement* (Cambridge, Mass.: Harvard University Press, 1993), on which the following account is based.

12. Ibid., p. 32.

13. Ibid., p. 33.

14. Ibid., p. 34.

15. Ibid., p. 32.

16. Ibid., pp. 34–35.

17. Ibid., p. 35.

18. Ibid., p. 39.

19. See the excellent analysis of William J. Grimshaw, *Bitter Fruit: Black Politics and the Chicago Machine, 1931–1991* (Chicago: University of Chicago Press, 1992), esp. chap. 6.

20. Chicago Fact Book Consortium, eds., *Local Community Fact Book: Chicago Metropolitan Area 1980, Based on the 1970 and 1980 Censuses* (Chicago: University of Illinois Press, 1984).

21. *Local Community Fact Book 1980,* pp. 75–79, on Community Area 28 (the Near West Side). This account is largely based on narratives that appear in earlier editions of the *Local Community Fact Book,* duly updated. Quotation from p. 75.

22. Ibid.; italics added.

23. Gerald Suttles's *The Social Order of the Slum* (Chicago: University of Chicago Press, 1968) captured this turf war in full swing, as residents of this multiethnic area failed to unite behind a dynamic Italian American woman who sought to block displacement by the campus.

24. *Local Community Fact Book 1980,* p. 82.

25. For the nineteenth-century origins of the Far West Side as a suburban flank and its transformation in the early decades of the twentieth century into an industrial and commercial zone hospitable to Catholic working-class residents, see Amanda Seligman, *Block by Block: Neighborhoods and Public Policy on Chicago's West Side* (Chicago:

University of Chicago Press, 2005), pp. 18–30. Her book focuses primarily on the resistance of West Garfield Park's white residents to African American newcomers prior to the riot, although she also includes some material on Austin. Only the final three pages, added belatedly to her excellent book, mention the riot of 1968. She is now researching a book on that riot.

26. Recall my discussion in chap. 2 of John McGreevy, *Parish Boundaries: The Catholic Encounter with Race in the Twentieth-Century Urban North* (Chicago: University of Chicago Press, 1996).

27. On the growth and distribution of the Puerto Rican community in Chicago and its collection into El Barrio, see Felix M. Padilla, *Puerto Rican Chicago* (Notre Dame, Ind.: University of Notre Dame Press, 1987), esp. pp. 83–93.

28. See M. W. Newman, "Behind the Rioting, a Ghetto," *Chicago Daily News*, June 18, 1966, in the files of the special Chicago Municipal Reference Collection, pagination missing.

29. I assembled this account from photocopied Chicago newspaper clippings for June 13–16, 1966, in the files of the special Chicago Municipal Reference Collection (formerly Library), now housed in the Harold Washington Main Chicago Public Library, not all of which were fully identified.

30. David J. Garrow, ed., *Chicago 1966: Open Housing Marches, Summit Negotiations, and Operation Breadbasket*, with a preface by Garrow (Brooklyn: Carlson, 1989). The interior title page reads *Martin Luther King, Jr. and the Civil Rights Movement.* This work contains, *inter alia,* an informative article by Mary Lou Finley, "The Open Housing Marches: Chicago, Summer '66," pp. 1–48.

31. Much of the following account is based on Kathleen Connolly, "The Chicago Open-Housing Conference," in Garrow, *Chicago 1966*, pp. 49–96, although Hirsch, in *Making the Second Ghetto: Race and Housing in Chicago, 1940–1960* (Cambridge: Cambridge University Press, 1983), pp. 264–65, treats it as well.

32. Kerner Report, pp. 38–39.

33. Connolly, "The Chicago Open-Housing Conference," pp. 57–58.

34. Taylor Branch, in his much-honored *At Canaan's Edge: America in the King Years: 1965–68* (New York: Simon and Schuster, 2006), devotes only brief pages to the activities of Martin Luther King, Jr., in Chicago, and he may not have checked primary sources. See his chap. 30, "Chicago, July–August 1966," pp. 501–22, where he minimizes the size of the crowd and the subsequent march to City Hall.

35. The parallel to his namesake was not unintentional.

36. Connolly, "The Chicago Open-Housing Conference," p. 59.

37. Kerner Report, p. 39. Interestingly enough, the 1966 Puerto Rican riot received no mention.

38. Connolly, "The Chicago Open-Housing Conference," p. 61.

39. Hirsch, *Making the Second Ghetto*, pp. 264–65.

40. Anderson and Pickering, *Confronting the Color Line*, pp. 311–25.

41. A modest parallel to the split reactions in the two communities might be the O. J. Simpson trial. I am not suggesting that no whites mourned King's death, but merely that the depth of their response was incommensurate.

42. I was shocked to find that this was the case. I therefore had to reconstruct the course of the riot from newspaper and other primary documents. My account here combines

(and distinguishes between) these sources and the official Mayor's Riot Study Committee report. Since this chapter was written, a few other reconstructions have come to my attention. See, for example, Adam Cohen and Elizabeth Taylor, *American Pharaoh: Mayor Richard Daley: His Battle for Chicago and the Nation* (Boston: Little Brown, 2000), which depends heavily on Gary Rivlin, "The Night Chicago Burned," *Chicago Reader*, August 26, 1988. I am grateful to D. Garth Taylor for calling them to my attention. I have not attempted to revise my own reconstruction but offer it as an independent account, based on not only my sources but also my independent observations, since I was in Chicago, teaching at Northwestern University, when the riots occurred.

43. The chief contrast is between the accounts of white newspapers, and particularly the conservative *Chicago Tribune*, which, as might be expected, simply exaggerated and condemned the uprising, and the *Chicago Defender*, the leading black newspaper in the city, which was more sympathetic to the causes but hardly "inflammatory," counseling calm and compromise. I am grateful to Michael Rosenfeld, who sent me some of the clippings from the *Defender*. I have been unable to access more radical black informal papers, which would require considerable search. Existing studies contrasting newspaper coverage of the 1968 events, such as they are, similarly lack the more fugitive material. Among the relatively thin studies I have been able to locate are: Robbin E. Washington, Jr., "The *Chicago Defender* and the *Chicago Tribune*'s Coverage of the West Side Riot of April 1968" (master's thesis, Governor State University, 1980) (26 pages); James Flannery, "Chicago Newspapers' Coverage of the City's Major Civil Disorders of 1968" (Ph.D. diss., Northwestern University, 1971), which concentrates most heavily on the 1968 Democratic Convention riot of October; and Thomas J. Kelley, "White Press/Black Man: An Analysis of the Editorial Opinions of the Four Chicago Daily Newspapers toward the Race Problem: 1954–1968" (Ph.D. diss., University of Illinois at Champaign-Urbana, 1971).

44. The report, dated August 1, 1968, was only 121 pages of large type with wide margins and focused chiefly on diagnosing where the police had gone wrong and how they might respond better to future threats to law and order. Unlike Johnson's voluminous work *The Negro in Chicago*, the Mayor's Riot Study Committee report treats the event as "essentially uncaused" and dismisses it as "unproductive." The conclusions appear up front, on p. 2, where the authors call the "disorders . . . clear and plain violations of law," "shocking events" that "solved nothing." The authors admonish "Chicago's black citizens" to recognize "that riots are destructive for everyone including themselves" (Mayor's Riot Study Committee report).

45. Donald Mosby, "Threats of Violence Hit City after News," *Chicago Defender*, April 6–12, 1968, pp. 1–2.

46. See Betty Washington, "Uproar at First Memorial Rites for King," *Chicago Defender*, April 6–12, 1968, p. 22.

47. Mayor's Riot Study Committee report, pp. 5–7. This committee was appointed by Daley and instructed "to conduct a complete and detailed factual investigation into the events immediately preceding, on and subsequent to April 4, 1968, in Chicago in order to determine precisely 'what, why and how' the disorders of April 5–7 occurred, without repeating the studies made by (i) the National Advisory Commission on

Civil Disorders, known as the Kerner Commission, and (ii) the Citizens Committee to Study Police Community Relations (in Chicago), known as the Mulroy Committee." The committee held 10 days of hearings and heard 47 witnesses, whose testimonies yielded "approximately 1,900 pages of transcript [never released]. In addition, the volunteer staff of the committee, headed by Chief Counsel Charles A. Bane, estimates that more than 900 persons were interviewed, exclusive of members of the police department.... With respect to the police, the Committee's staff submitted a detailed, lengthy questionnaire to, and received answers from approximately... 476 policemen. Personal interviews were conducted with the Superintendent of Police and his staff, as well as with commanders of the three police districts in which the principal April disorder occurred" (p. 1).

48. Ibid., pp. 6–7, 9, italics added. "Normal routines" for abnormal times?

49. *Chicago Daily News*, April 5, 1968, p. 12. Unfortunately, byline and p. 1 are missing from the Chicago Municipal Reference Collection's clipping files.

50. Mayor's Riot Study Committee report, p. 7.

51. The role of the police in triggering or at least intensifying riot behavior has been confirmed by many studies summarized in Joe Feagin and Harlan Hahn, *Ghetto Revolts: The Politics of Violence in American Cities* (New York: Macmillan, 1973), esp. pp. 151-59.

52. Mayor's Riot Study Committee report, p. 8; italics added.

53. Ibid.

54. Ibid., pp. 9–10.

55. Ibid., p. 10.

56. Clippings from Chicago Municipal Reference Collection files.

57. John McHugh, "Too Much for 4,000 Firemen," *Chicago Daily News*, April 6, 1968, p. 5.

58. Mayor's Riot Study Committee report, p. 12.

59. Ibid., p. 16.

60. Ibid., p. 15.

61. Ibid., p. 3; italics added.

62. An article by Dorothy Collin, "United Gangs Patrol for Peace on City Streets," *Chicago's American*, Monday April 8, pp. 1, 7, suggested that the Blackstone Rangers and the East Side Disciples were "patrolling for peace" on the South Side.

63. Mayor's Riot Study Committee report, p. 15. This claim is belied by witnesses who saw the burning of S. 63rd Street, of which substantial remnants exist to this day.

64. According to the Mayor's Riot Study Committee report (p. 15), there was very little looting or arson on the Near North Side "dominated by the Cabrini-Green Housing complex.... This looting and arson activity was... principally directed toward white-owned and operated business establishments." During the late evening, some sniper fire came from Cabrini, but the police did not respond.

65. Ibid., p. 16.

66. Ibid., pp. 16–17.

67. Ibid., p. 18.

68. Ibid., p. 18.

69. Ibid., p. 19.

70. His remarks, accurately quoted, appeared in a boxed item headed "What Daley Said," *Chicago Daily News*, April 17, 1968, p. 1. Other sources confirm the gist of his remarks.

71. Joseph Zullo, "New York's Mayor Opposes Daley's Police Get-Tough Order," *Chicago Tribune*, April 16, 1968, n.p. In Chicago Municipal Reference Collection.

72. "Daley's Dubious Order," editorial, *Chicago Daily News*, April 16, 1968, p. 14.

73. James Strong, "Letters Back Daley 15 to 1, Reilly Says," *Chicago Tribune*, April 19, 1968, p. 10.

74. *Chicago Defender*, April 20–26, 1968, p. 1.

75. Ibid.; italics added.

76. Ibid., pp. 120–21. I think they are reinventing the inquiry of Johnson's *The Negro in Chicago*!

77. Ibid.

78. Max Frankel, introduction to *The Walker Report*, p. x. The only reason it wasn't published earlier or officially was its inclusion of obscenities!

79. Ibid., p. viii.

80. This meeting seems to have been observed by the F.B.I., since knowledge of it is revealed in *The Walker Report* (p. 25).

81. Ibid., pp. 28.

82. Ibid., pp. 55–56; italics added.

83. Ibid., p. 57. The reluctance of blacks to participate made enormous sense, given that as early as January 1968, confidential sources were already playing on racial paranoia. "Examples are: 1. Reports that black power groups were allegedly meeting to discuss the convention and the assassination of leading political figures. 2. Unnamed black militants in the East were reported to have discussed renting apartments near the Amphitheatre for use as sniping posts. 3. An organization was reportedly organized to secure weapons and explosives and to plan a revolution to coincide with the convention." The list continued with another six "rumors," culminating in a plot to put LSD in the Chicago water supply (p. 97).

84. For a breakdown of those injured and arrested, see "Supplement to the Walker Report," pp. 351–58.

85. Ibid., p. 356.

86. Michael Smith, "West Side Riot Area Rubble Is Gone but Not the Scars," *Chicago Tribune*, March 30, 1969, sec. 1, pp. 1, 3.

87. Lois Wille, "Ruins of 1968 Rioting Still a No-Man's Land," *Chicago Daily News*, March 28, 1969, pagination missing from clipping in the Chicago Municipal Reference Collection's file.

88. Ibid.

89. April 4 that year fell on Good Friday, when schools were to be closed.

90. "Third Page Section," *Chicago Daily News*, April 4, 1969. The headline reads "Crane Initial Trouble Spot: How Students' Rampage Began."

91. Henry De Zutter, *Chicago Daily News*, April 4, 1969. Title and page number are missing from the file in the Chicago Municipal Reference collection.

92. Richard Foster, "Guardsmen Patrol Disturbance Areas," *Chicago Sun-Times*, April 4, 1969, pp. 1, 6, 12, 13.

93. Francis Ward, "Daley Calls Off Curfew," *Chicago Sun-Times*, April 6, 1969; italics added.

94. On the Chicago Public Housing Authority's policy of increasing segregation, see my discussion in *New York, Chicago, Los Angeles: America's Global Cities* (Minneapolis: University of Minnesota Press, 1999), *pp.* 223–26; 348–50.

95. His election was a "fluke," although it had excellent results. A three-way race in the Democratic primary split the "white" vote, allowing the maverick Washington to win. See Pierre Clavel and Wim Wiewel, eds., *Harold Washington and the Neighborhoods: Progressive City Government in Chicago 1983–1987* (New Brunswick, N.J.: Rutgers University Press, 1991).

96. To the south was the renovation of Dearborn Station and development of expensive loft dwellings in what used to be Printers' Row; to the west, new glass office edifices and upscale condominiums such as Presidential Towers were constructed on the western side of the Chicago River, formerly beyond the pale of the Loop.

97. I draw in this section on the excellent research of Michael J. Rosenfeld, "Celebration, Politics, Selective Looting and Riots: A Micro Level Study of the Bulls Riot of 1992 in Chicago," *Social Problems* 44, no. 4 (November 1997), pp. 483–502.

98. Ibid., p. 484.

99. In the following account, I draw on my "Commentary: What Is Special about Chicago?" *City and Society* 17 (2005), pp. 289–303.

100. In the 1950s and 1960s, to forestall greater integration and still avail itself of federally subsidized redevelopment programs and public housing, Chicago had won a concession—to clear dense but low-rise "slums" in its two major ghettos, and to construct in their place and along their margins massive high-rise public housing projects where poor minorities could be stacked and basically neglected.

101. An excellent account can be found in Sudhir Venkatesh and Isil Celimli, "Tearing Down the Community," *Shelterforce Online,* no.138 November/December 2004.

102. See the critical article by planning professor Janet Smith, "Cleaning Up Public Housing by Sweeping Out the Poor," *Habitat International* 23, no. 1 (1999), pp. 49–62.

Part II

New York's Struggles for Equity and Social Justice

4

The Harlem Revolts of 1935 and 1943

*R*acial tensions have been recurring phenomena deeply embedded in New York City's past, as they have been in American history in general. Among others, there were significant protests in Harlem in 1935 and again in 1943 (to be treated in this chapter) that prefigured the types of ghetto revolts that would come to be characteristic in other cities only in the late 1960s. These culminated in the 1964 Harlem riot that spread almost instantaneously to the city's "Second Ghetto" in Brooklyn, Bedford-Stuyvesant (covered in chapter 5).

But before proceeding to those detailed cases, one must acknowledge that just as New York was older than Chicago (and both were older than Los Angeles as an American city), its history of race riots stretches farther back in time. These antecedents help to highlight differences in the status of blacks in Chicago and New York, which may partially explain the different manifestations of racially charged events in the two cities.

Are Antecedents Precedents?

The most noteworthy differences between Chicago and New York can be traced back to the very earliest histories of slavery in the two states. In that comparison, New York's laws stand out as far more liberal than those of Illinois. Under Dutch administration, free blacks were clearly identified, and even those who were classified as slaves were still allowed to work on their own account in their "free" time. Even though a harsher brand of slavery was to prevail during British rule, the city continued to house black freemen whose numbers increased after the Revolutionary War, since slaves who had fought in the struggle against British rule were eligible to receive their freedom when independence was achieved.[1]

In addition, whereas slavery persisted well into the nineteenth century in Illinois, albeit eventually to be replaced by the outrageous "Black Laws" that validated a system of indentured servitude that was slavery in all but name, New York state was among the first in the nation to abolish slavery. It did so in 1827, at the same time England did, although the ambiguous status of the freed slaves still deprived them of full citizenship. Abolitionists were very active in New York in pre–Civil War days, and free blacks engaged in a range of occupations, including commercial clerking, especially in the port, in semiprofessional services, and even in modest craft production in New York's generally small-scale industries.

The Draft Riots of 1863

These greater opportunities, however, did not prevent a certain amount of residential concentration, nor did they offer much protection to vulnerable blacks during the Civil War draft riots of 1863. That summer, recently arrived Irish and German workers, protesting conscription into the Union army, vented their grievances, *inter alia,* against blacks who were permitted to enlist but were otherwise exempted from the draft.[2] On July 13, the day on which the conscription lottery was scheduled to begin, Irish workmen, too poor to afford the $300 required to buy an exemption from service, at first expressed their anger at the exact site of the draft lottery. This explosion spread in two social directions: upward toward wealthier New Yorkers who could afford to purchase exemptions, and laterally or downward toward "Negroes" who, because they did not yet enjoy full citizenship rights, could not be drafted.

> For five days in July 1863, armed mobs interrupted enforcement of the first
> federal conscription and struggled with authorities for sway over the nation's
> manufacturing and commercial capital. What began on the morning of
> July 13 as a demonstration against the draft soon expanded into a sweeping

assault against the local institutions and personnel of President Abraham Lincoln's Republican Party, as well as a grotesque and bloody race riot.[3]

Joseph Boskin emphasizes the contextual character of racial violence, reminding us that the 1860s was a period of general national stress when hostilities toward blacks were likely to "erupt with the slightest provocation," as they did not only in New York but also in many other northern cities.

> Fearful of job competition from free blacks, anticipating that emancipation of the slaves would cause the depression of wages and the employment market, distrustful of Negroes because of alleged immoralities and angered over the use of Negroes as strikebreakers, white laborers attacked Negroes in many northern and midwestern areas. Race riots occurred in Chicago, Detroit, Cleveland, Buffalo, Philadelphia, Boston, and in other smaller cities. *The worst outbreak took place in New York City in 1863.*[4]

By the time the New York draft riots had come under control five days later, some 105 New Yorkers lay dead. At least 11 of the enumerated fatalities were black males. Thus, even though these racially directed hostilities seem to have resulted in particularly vicious lynchings, blacks were by no means the exclusive casualties. Nevertheless, their estimated 11 percent of all identified fatalities was far in excess of their representation in Manhattan's population at that time, which was only 1.5 percent.

But blacks were not segregated into a single quarter. As can be seen from table 4.1 (constructed from data in Iver Bernstein's excellent study of the 1863 riot),[5] in both 1860 and 1865, New York City's African American population lived throughout the city. True, Five Points and the West Side port-wholesaling zones of Lower Manhattan (Wards 5, 8, and 14) accounted for the largest proportion of blacks (some 43 percent of the total), and there was a second-settlement concentration farther north in Ward 20 (a port area/tenderloin zone that housed an additional 12 percent). These few wards thus accounted for more than half of the city's black population. But significantly, there was no ward from which they were excluded.

For the most part, however, white rioters pursuing blacks did not systematically seek them out in areas of black residential concentration but rather attacked them in zones where they were few. This suggests that whereas isolated blacks in the path of the general riot had a higher probability of being victimized, there seems to have been no systematic search for black targets. Of the six black fatalities that occurred in the 15 wards south of 14th Street (Lower Manhattan), only one took place in a ward with a sizeable number of black residents. To put it another way, the four dockside wards below 14th Street that experienced six black

Table 4.1 Distribution of New York Black Population by Ward in 1860 and 1865, Compared to the Distribution of 11 Named Blacks Killed in the 1863 Riot.

| Ward Number | BLACK POPULATION | | Black Deaths, 1863 |
	1860	1865	
1	111	78	0
2	67	34	0
3	24	45	1
4	67	48	0
5	1,396	865	1
6	334	289	0
7	141	70	2
8	2,918	2,174	0
9	424	476	2
10	198	96	0
11	225	124	0
12	263	436	0
13	562	302	0
14	1,075	683	0
15	778	962	0
16	629	721	0
17	308	253	0
18	404	302	0
19	563	295	0
20	1,471	1,224	3
21	368	258	2
22	146	208	0
Total	12,472	9,943	11

Source: Data from Bernstein, *The New York City Draft Riots*, app.

fatalities (or 55 percent of all known black fatalities) then contained only some 17 percent of all black residents in the city. The remaining five fatalities (45 percent) occurred in the two wards between 26th and 40th streets (the center of rioting), even though these wards housed only 15 percent of the black total. Three of the five black fatalities that occurred in the vast zone north of 14th Street took place in Hell's Kitchen, a West Side dock area where Irish and blacks coexisted; the remaining two occurred on the East Side nearer the site of the conscription lottery, a zone in which few blacks lived. No fatalities occurred in the two wards between 14th Street and 26th Street, where 1,033 blacks lived, or in the three large and sparsely populated wards north of 40th Street that housed only 972 black residents.

Did attacks on blacks in 1863 lead to their greater "ingathering" to segregated quarters in New York, as would the 1919 riot in Chicago? It is difficult to trace the effects of the 1863 riot on the reconfiguration of segregation in New York, because the Civil War itself had led to a modest depopulation of the city. Between 1860 and 1865, the number of whites in the city decreased by 10 percent, while the number of blacks dropped by 20 percent. The decline in the latter, however, was more marked in those wards that had experienced riot fatalities. The number of black residents in wards where fatalities had occurred declined by 24 percent (from 3,867 to 2,938) in the five-year interval, whereas the wards free of race-riot-related deaths dropped by only 19 percent (from 8,605 to 7,005). One must conclude that race per se was not the exclusive focus of the New York riot, nor were the changes in spatial distribution in its aftermath as severe as those precipitated by Chicago's 1919 riot.

THE RIOT OF 1900

The case was somewhat different with respect to the race riot that occurred in New York in 1900. By 1890, the black population of Manhattan had recovered from its post–Civil War decline and had increased to some 25,674.[6] But by that time the proportion of nonwhites was still only 1.7 percent of the total, because of the massive influx of European immigrants, who by then constituted over 42 percent. Another 10,000 blacks lived in Brooklyn, still a separate jurisdiction until the consolidation of the five boroughs in 1898. After 1898, the addition of Brooklyn, Queens, the Bronx, and Staten Island brought the total population of New York City to 3,437,202. The census of 1900 reported that 67,304 (or under 2 percent) were nonwhite, including almost 10,000 who had been born abroad, chiefly in Jamaica. Again, however, these numbers were dwarfed by the 36 percent who were whites born abroad.

It is therefore hard to account for the 1900 race riot in New York by sheer numbers or by the rate of growth of the black population. More likely, Irish port workers may have felt threatened by job competition.[7] The immediate trigger, however, was one that would become increasingly familiar in the years to come: an altercation between a policeman and a black male. As James Weldon Johnson recounts the story:

> On the night of August 12 [1900] a coloured man named Arthur Harris left his wife on the corner of Eighth Avenue and Forty-first Street for a moment to buy a cigar. When he returned he found her struggling in the grasp of a white man. Harris engaged the man and was struck by him over the head with a club. He retaliated with a pocket-knife and inflicted a wound which proved fatal. He thereupon ran away.[8]

The victim was revealed to be a popular Irish police officer in plain clothes, whose "funeral [on August 15] was attended by a large contingent of the police force, in addition to a great throng of friends, sympathizers, and those drawn by morbid curiosity." Since the perpetrator was still missing but demands for vengeance were mounting during the day, by nighttime

> a mob of several thousands raged up and down Eighth Avenue and through the side streets from Twenty-seventh to Forty-second. Negroes were seized wherever they were found, and brutally beaten. Men and women were dragged from street-cars and assaulted. When Negroes ran to policemen for protection, even begging to be locked up for safety, they were thrown back to the mob. The police themselves beat many Negroes as cruelly as did the mob.... The riot of 1900 was a brutish orgy, which, if it was not incited by the police, was, to say the least, abetted by them.[9]

This account bears similarities to those of the Chicago riot of 1919.

Johnson rightly points to national-level economic problems as an underlying cause of these interracial tensions. Certainly, such problems persisted and would soon be intensified during World War I by the "great migration" that infused northern industrial centers with African Americans drawn from the South. But even before that infusion, the riot of 1900 seems to have accomplished what the riot of 1863 had not: it increased racial segregation of blacks in the city. By 1911, Mary White Ovington could write that whereas

> fifty years ago... the colored were scattered throughout the city today we find them confined to [five] fairly definite quarters [in Manhattan]: Greenwich Village, the Middle West Side [Hell's Kitchen], San Juan Hill,[10] the

upper East Side [now the Barrio], and the upper West Side [Harlem]. Brooklyn has a large Negro population, but it is more widely distributed and less easily located than that of Manhattan.[11]

Ovington described the Greenwich Village community as much proletarianized since the early days when it had housed the elite of the Negro community.[12] Due to the selective outmigration of more successful blacks to other settlement areas in the city, by 1910 this remnant community represented those who had "been left behind in these old forgotten streets."[13] On the Lower East Side, also, where Negroes had earlier "dwelt near the whites as barbers, caterers, and coachmen, as laundresses and waiting maids," there were almost no Negroes left, since the elite they served had long since moved uptown and immigrants had poured into the zone. By 1880, the midtown settlement from 6th Avenue to the Hudson had already become the "center of the Negro population," but it remained an important racially mixed district. This zone also contained the notorious vice district known as the Tenderloin.[14] The third zone of concentration was located on the West Side in the fifties and above; this had formerly been a white district, which whites had deserted only after the construction of a noisy elevated line there. "From there one ascends to San Juan Hill in the sixties along the Hudson."[15] And finally, Negroes occupied mixed-race tenement quarters east of 3rd Avenue and north of 43rd Street, a zone where occupancy was becoming increasingly black, especially in the mixed tenement zone above 96th Street. Ovington describes how the exodus of upwardly mobile Jews and Italians to the outer boroughs had recently opened up space in fairly good tenements along the upper east and central (Harlem) sides, a transition that was particularly rapid between 1906 and 1911.[16]

EARLY GROWTH OF HARLEM

Because the growth of Harlem as an area open to black occupants (other than as servants attached to wealthy white households) had just begun, it did not receive much attention in Ovington's account. However, it would shortly outdistance all areas of preferred black settlement, becoming by the 1920s perhaps the world's most famous "black metropolis."

The contrast between the origins of Harlem and the formation of Chicago's black belt could not be sharper. The latter began as an unattractive shack town between rail lines and solidified as a zone that ingathered a defensive population driven from other parts of the city in 1919. In contrast, Harlem began as a highly desirable and elegant quarter to which New York's blacks moved voluntarily, taking advantage of a real estate crisis that generated a bonanza for them.

The bucolic village of (New) Harlem, founded originally by Peter Stuyvesant, became a fashionable neighborhood only after the Civil War, when an elevated line was extended to it.[17] It enjoyed a brief interlude as an elegant suburb, until the panic of 1907, combined with the speculative overbuilding in the area, opened the zone to a new group of residents—blacks. However, it was not until the 1930s that the zone became largely black.[18] Then, during World War II, an "influx of Southern Negroes... crowded nearly all the remaining white residents out of Harlem." As Shapiro and Sullivan remind us in their study of the New York riot of 1964, "Harlem once offered the finest housing in New York City and many of those fine old homes are still there," even though by the 1960s their still fine exteriors largely concealed "disreputable" and overcrowded rooming houses. And although rich and middle-class blacks continued to live in the zone, a significant proportion of its residents were poor and welfare dependent.[19]

The early development, spread, and increased black occupancy of Harlem are well described in three basic sources. There is the small gem of a book by James Weldon Johnson, an important figure in the Harlem Renaissance of the 1920s.[20] There is a "Chicago School" description produced by the black sociologist E. Franklin Frazier, written in the aftermath of the 1935 riot.[21] And there is a later sociological and historical account by Gilbert Osofsky that draws heavily on Johnson and Frazier.[22] From these accounts, it is clear that during the first few decades of Harlem's existence as an elegant area, blacks were still in the minority and were rigidly excluded from the area west of Lenox Avenue.

This would begin to change during World War I, with the migration from the South of African American workers needed to meet wartime labor shortages. As Johnson informs us, "every available method was used to get these black hands, the most effective being the sending of labour agents into the South, who dealt directly with the Negroes, arranged for their transportation, and shipped them north, often in consignments running high into the hundreds." Johnson himself witnessed a "consignment" of 2,500 being shipped on a single train from a single southern city.[23]

But the migrants imported to New York were not the "rural cotton folk" who went to Chicago. Drawn more from southern cities on the Atlantic seaboard, they were considerably "better prepared to adapt themselves to life and industry in a great city." A goodly proportion were also attracted selectively from among the better educated classes in the British Caribbean[24]—a group that eschewed migration to industrial cities such as Chicago or Detroit. By then, Harlem was beginning to serve as a magnet for ambitious blacks and as a cultural icon whose fame would spread worldwide in the 1920s.[25] It well deserved that reputation, since its beauty, good housing, and accessibility to the rest of the city contrasted

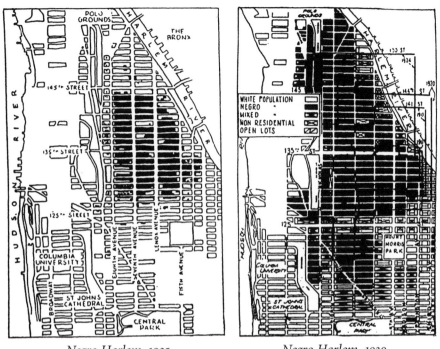

Negro Harlem, 1925   *Negro Harlem, 1930*

Map 4.1.   The Growth of Black Harlem between 1925 and 1930.

Source: James Weldon Johnson, *Black Manhattan*. Original copyright: Knopf, 1930.

dramatically with the minority slums in other cities. Not unexpectedly, it grew apace, both in population and extent.[26]

Map 4.1 shows black Harlem as still tiny in 1925 compared to its vast extent by 1930. Johnson stresses that this "city within a city," which had developed only in the preceding fifteen years (i.e., since 1915), was taken without violence.

> In Chicago, Cleveland, and other cities, houses bought and moved into by Negroes were bombed.... Although there was bitter feeling in Harlem during the fifteen years of struggle the Negro went through in getting a foothold... there was never any demonstration of violence that could be called serious. Not since the riot of 1900 has New York witnessed, except for minor incidents, any interracial disturbances. Not even in the memorable summer of 1919 ... did New York, with more than a hundred thousand Negroes grouped together in Harlem, lose its equanimity.... It is apparent that race friction, as it affects Harlem as a community, has grown less and less each year for the past ten years; and the signs are that there will not be a recrudescence.[27]

He also contrasts the beauty, centrality, and good housing of Harlem with the peripheral slums of other cities.[28]

Johnson attributed the low racial friction in New York to both the enviable quality of Harlem's black residents and the liberalism of the city's white population. Noting that Negroes saved, worked hard, and invested in property, he also attributed their better status to the types of employment opportunities open to them. "Employment of Negroes in New York is diversified; they are employed more as individuals than as non-integral parts of a gang. This gives them the opportunity for more intimate contacts with the life and spirit of the city as a whole."[29] Johnson also praised what he called "the psychology of New York, the natural psychology of a truly cosmopolitan city, in which there is always the tendency to minimize rather than magnify distinctions."

> New York, more than any other American city, maintains a matter-of-fact, a taken for granted attitude towards her Negro citizens. Less than anywhere else in the country are Negroes regarded as occupying a position of wardship; more nearly do they stand upon the footing of common and equal citizenship. It may be that one of the causes of New York's attitude lies in the fact that the Negro there has achieved a large degree of political independence; that he has broken away from a political creed based merely upon traditional and sentimental grounds. Yet, on the other hand, this itself may be a result of New York's attitude.[30]

Being part of the Harlem Renaissance itself, Johnson perhaps underestimated the cumulative effects of the political consciousness and organizational strengths of the more radical black figures in the 1920s and 1930s, whom Martha Biondi credits with laying the groundwork for the maturation, in the 1940s, of the civil rights movement, long in advance of other cities.[31]

Johnson's small book ends on an optimistic note, remarking that

> more than two hundred thousand Negroes live in the heart of Manhattan ... and do so without race friction ... an integral part of New York citizenry. They have achieved political independence and without fear vote for either Republicans, Democrats, Socialists, or Communists. . . . Politically they have begun to fill important government posts and their artistic achievements have smashed stereotypes. . . . The Negro in New York ... still meets with discrimination and disadvantages. But New York guarantees her Negro citizens the fundamental rights of citizenship and protects them in the exercise of those rights. Possessing the basic rights, the Negro in New York ought to be able to work through the discriminations and disadvantages.[32]

But what Johnson failed to foresee was that the United States would fall prey to a worldwide depression when the New York stock market crashed in October 1929. The results were devastating for all, but worse for America's blacks. And even though New York state, under the governorship of Franklin D. Roosevelt, led the way in designing and implementing relief measures, blacks did not benefit in proportion to their needs. They faced greater hardships but were less likely to receive aid, either from the private charities that first rushed into the breach or from the public relief funds provided to workers who lost their jobs in the formal sector of the economy.

THE DEPRESSION AND THE HARLEM RIOT OF 1935

Between October 1930 and May 1931, the Welfare Council of New York City surveyed some 900 social workers and public health nurses to find out how the depression was affecting their clients. Among the findings were that a significant "downgrading" of housing standards had occurred as families moved to smaller, cheaper quarters or doubled up with relatives. This was especially the case in Harlem, where housing was already overcrowded. Furthermore, diet and health were deteriorating, and families were suffering from severe psychological distress and strife.[33]

When Mayor La Guardia, formerly the congressman representing East Harlem (then still occupied primarily by Italian and Jewish renters), became the mayor in 1934, he inherited a city in great distress. Municipal aid lagged behind the state's, and its relief programs were riddled with graft and corruption. By the end of 1933, a fiscal crisis was imminent, and the city had to be rescued from receivership.[34] There was much to be done, and the city turned to Washington for help. It received it, thanks to the political coalition of Franklin D. Roosevelt, Harry Hopkins, and Fiorello La Guardia that had already been established, even before Roosevelt put together his New Deal, which built in part on experiments begun in New York state. This close relationship between New York City and Washington greased the wheels for numerous programs that often began in New York City before they became national policies.[35]

One area in which New York innovated was in the construction of subsidized housing, in order not only to "make work" but also to contribute to the supply of affordable housing. One large-scale project, to be built on vacant land, was immediately planned: the Williamsburg Houses in Brooklyn, intended for white occupancy. It took the Harlem riot of 1935 to precipitate Mayor La Guardia's announcement of a similar project for blacks, Harlem River Houses.[36] This illustrates another distinctive feature of the next two "race riots"—or really ghetto revolts—in New York, the interconnection between violence and politics that Karl von Clausewitz aphorized at the international level: war as politics by other means.

This theme of riots as a form of political action is made explicit in the title of Cheryl Greenberg's article "The Politics of Disorder: Reexamining Harlem's Riots of 1935 and 1943."[37] There can be no question that New York's black community was more organized politically than that in almost any other city, although the 1935 riot suggests that when conditions deteriorated enough, political organization could be turned in another direction. It is hard, then, to accept the somewhat complacent judgment of Dominic J. Capeci, Jr., that "from 1933 to 1943 race relations in New York City were not ideal, but they were more harmonious than in other urban centers. *This was partly due to the combined efforts of black leaders* [such as Adam Clayton Powell] *and white public officials* [such as La Guardia]."[38]

What Capeci tends to ignore is that long before the brief "riot" in 1935, the legitimate grievances of Harlem's population were being articulated by its leaders, albeit ignored by the city's political actors, and that a mass-based, political culture of activism had emerged that "spread from traditionally political black organizations to the black community at large."[39] New groups joined with the churches, the Communist Party, and the NAACP to channel "the political energy of Harlem into demands for fair hiring by relief agencies, higher relief grants, an end to employment discrimination, and a race-blind job placement system for city-run employment agencies."[40] Demonstrations, rent strikes, boycotts, and marches drew large numbers of participants.

> These angry groups often clashed with the police, and violence and arrests were common.... Perhaps the most far-reaching of these political efforts was the "Don't Buy Where You Can't Work" campaign.... In early 1931, a "group of serious and determined women," the Harlem Housewives League, approached several chain stores in Harlem, showing them the volume of black business they did and asking them to hire blacks. When these demonstrations of black purchasing power failed to move business owners, other community groups [including Marcus Garvey's Universal Negro Improvement Association] moved into action.... Although neither of these efforts brought significant change, both attracted many middle-class and moderate blacks.... The buy-black campaign also brought nationalists and black business leaders into the coalition.[41]

Their efforts were joined more than a year later when black nationalists established the Harlem Labor Union, which organized the picketing of white-owned stores.

In the summer of 1934, the target was Blumstein's, Harlem's largest department store, where for four months running, hundreds of picketers at a time marched in front. Finally, the store capitulated, and "the boycotts and demonstrations spread to other establishments on or near 125th Street.... *At the end of 1934, however, the courts ruled that the picketing was illegal*... [and] the jobs campaign quickly disintegrated,"[42] leaving supporters indignant and angry. What was worse, the gains that had been so hard to achieve were lost. The store owners "did not hire the promised black clerks, but because of the injunction against picketing, the League was powerless to force compliance. A month after the cessation of the pickets, 400 black clerks who had been hired lost their jobs." As Greenberg concludes,

> thus Harlemites were left in early 1935 with a strong sense of common grievance and a recognition of the potency of mass action but no organized way of channeling the struggle that had a broad appeal. Yet thousands of Harlemites were now accustomed to mass meetings, to listening to street corner orators define problems and offer solutions, and to breaking the law. In 1935 this newly popular street action exploded into full-blown rioting. Calm was restored within twenty-four hours, but the riot brought more public attention to black grievances than had any previous event. Ironically, the riot, product of the collapse of organized protest groups, brought many of the victories those groups had sought in vain.[43]

The Immediate *Casus Belli* of the Harlem Riot of 1935

It is common in cases where longstanding grievances have accumulated and organized attempts to ameliorate them have clearly been blocked that conditions are ripe for response—even though the immediate trigger may be less provocative than the quickly spreading rumors allege. This was certainly the case the afternoon of March 19, 1935, when a 16-year-old boy was apprehended and accused of stealing a penknife from Kress's variety store on the busy commercial thoroughfare of 125th Street in Harlem. The comedy (tragedy) of errors, misinterpretations, and police bullying that led this "relatively unimportant case of juvenile pilfering" to escalate into a full-scale protest riot is described in the first chapter of the Mayor's Commission report (*The Complete Report of Mayor LaGuardia's Commission on the Harlem Riot of March 19, 1935*).[44]

The boy was caught and the knife was removed from his pocket by two white employees; when they held and threatened him, he began to struggle and "bit the hands of his captors." The police were called, and the arriving officer, Patrolman Donahue, in order to avoid the curious and excited spectators, took the boy through the basement to the rear entrance on 124th Street. But his act only confirmed the outcry of a hysterical Negro woman that they had taken "the boy to the basement to beat him up." Likewise, the appearance of the ambulance which had been summoned to dress the wounded hands of the boy's captors not only seemed to substantiate her charge, but when it left empty, gave color to another rumor that the boy was dead. By an odd trick of fate, still another incident furnished the final confirmation of the rumor. . . . A hearse which was usually kept in a garage opposite the store on 124th Street was parked in front of the store entrance while the driver entered the store to see his brother-in-law.[45]

Such a minor event escalated, with further antagonism between the irate crowds and the police, into a full day of rioting, some spontaneous and some organized by various groups with speakers and flyers.

That afternoon, crowds continued to assemble in front of the (by now closed) Kress store and spread along 125th Street from 5th Avenue to 8th. The already agitated and increasingly inflamed (both by speakers and by police) crowd began to break windows and to loot from white-owned stores. Police reinforcements were called. "They arrested seventy-five people, mostly black, for 'inciting to riot, felonious assault, malicious mischief and burglary, all the direct result of the disturbance.' Fifty-seven civilians and seven policemen sustained injuries, and 626 windows were broken."[46]

Ironically, although the rumor of the first boy's death was eventually revealed as untrue, one tragic consequence of the ongoing riot was the fatal shooting by police of another 16-year-old boy as he was innocently returning from the movies that night. (The Mayor's Commission report condemned the shooting of Lloyd Hobbs "as inexcusable and brutal on the part of the police.")[47] This was the sole fatality of the 1935 Harlem riot. Within less than 24 hours, the riot had run its course or been suppressed by the police.

La Guardia took the uprising seriously enough to appoint an interracial committee (which included, among others, the poet Countee Cullen and the powerful union leader A. Philip Randolph) to inquire into the causes of the riot, to diagnose problems faced by Harlem's population, and to suggest possible ways to redress grievances. The committee divided up into six subcommittees (to look into, respectively, employment discrimination, inequity in the distribution of Home Relief, housing, poor educational and recreational facilities, deficient hospitals and health services, and crime and police misbehavior). These topics are reported on in chapters 3–8 of the report. E. Franklin Frazier, the distinguished sociology professor from Howard University, was assigned a staff of 30 to conduct a study of the appalling socioeconomic conditions in Harlem, hardest hit by the Depression.[48] Not surprisingly, the investigators concluded that the problems of blacks were due chiefly to *inadequate incomes coming in part from discrimination.* The centrality of unemployment to other ills was summarized by Capeci as follows.

> Discriminatory hiring practices deprived AfroAmericans of adequate employment and . . . [therefore] of nourishing foods, decent lodging, necessary medical care, and a healthy family relationship. Hence many became wards of the state, depending upon others, often the discriminators, for charitable assistance. . . . During the first week of September 1935, 43 percent of Harlem's black families were on relief. Throughout the state that year, two-and-a-half times as many blacks as whites were on relief because of unemployment. . . . Blacks registering as unemployed in 1937 constituted 40 percent of all gainful AfroAmerican workers, while the corresponding percentage for all other groups was 15.[49]

Blacks thus suffered, only in more intense fashion, from all the ills exacerbated by the Depression. They doubled up in overcrowded and fast-deteriorating housing; their poorer health was inadequately treated in Jim Crow hospitals. Their overcrowded and dilapidated schools were segregated and lacked adequate teaching materials. In addition, students often had unsympathetic white teachers and read textbooks filled with demeaning images of blacks.[50]

There was also endemic tension with the police, who "were overzealous in arresting black youth." In return, young blacks tended to view the police as "the boldest examples of northern racism. . . . Critics of the police compared large concentrations of patrolmen in black ghettos to 'an army of occupation' and complained of constant brutality."[51] Given these conditions, it was not surprising that the Harlem riot of 1935 "brought to the surface aggressive, resentful feelings. Unlike earlier disorders in which whites attacked blacks, Harlem's was a hostile outburst 'against racial discrimination and poverty in the midst of plenty.' "[52]

WHY WAS THE REPORT SUPPRESSED?

The substantive research chapters of the Mayor's Commission report, one prepared by each subcommittee, were unlikely to give offense, even though their awkward writing styles and uneven content left much to be desired. The report was nowhere as competent as Johnson's study *The Negro in Chicago,* produced in the aftermath of that city's 1919 riot. The real reason why the Mayor's

Commission report was never released, as suggested in the introductory paragraphs to the coverage in the *Amsterdam News*, was the refusal of one commission member, a Catholic priest, to sign any report that cleared the Communist Party of responsibility for the riot. Furthermore, the recommendations made in chapter 9 were viewed as too specific and "radical," which required a toning down of rhetoric.[53] It is therefore worth examining the recommendations originally made in chapter 9, which in no way would strike a contemporary reader as inflammatory! Indeed, they sound eminently sensible and humble, and, as we shall learn, La Guardia did pay attention to some of them.

SUMMARY OF RECOMMENDATIONS MADE IN CHAPTER 9

Employment and Home Relief

To address the problems of corruption and inequities in the distribution of relief funds, the Harlem community must be better represented on the city's Home Relief Bureau. A Negro should be appointed without salary to give publicity "to the present discrimination in work relief" and to dismiss those responsible for it.

Housing Conditions

(1) The New York Housing Authority should be "empowered to plan" for a housing program for Harlem; (2) the city should enforce its housing codes better; (3) tenants of Harlem should organize and protest against exorbitant rents, and "if such protests are ineffectual...they [should] refuse to pay rentals until some equitable agreements are reached."[54]

Educational and Recreational Facilities

(1) Tear down P.S. 89 and erect a modern school building either on the site or nearby; (2) request (and obtain from Washington) emergency funds to build educational and recreational facilities for Harlem; (3) open additional school buildings (some empty and immediately available) in order to reduce class sizes; (4) secure additional playgrounds and hire the soldiers at the 367th Infantry armory to properly supervise play and games; (5) keep the playgrounds open and supervised until 6 p.m. in term time and all day long in the vacation period; (6) use unemployed teachers to conduct groups of children to "more remote parks" for supervised recreation; (7) increase the staff of teachers and especially visiting teachers as fast as possible; (8) abandon the present policy of paying school custodians a lump sum because it leads to political corruption; (9) the Board of Education should devote greater attention to the problems of Harlem and a Negro should be appointed to the Board "whenever this becomes possible";

(10) organize a conference of agencies that deal with delinquents and "deficient or backward" children to consider how to meet the needs of similar Negro children.

Health and Hospitals

With respect to health and hospitals, the commission recommends that (1) "colored doctors and nurses be admitted to all municipal hospitals" in accordance with the law "that prohibits racial discrimination in tax supported hospitals"; (2) either double the size of Harlem Hospital or supplement it with a new one of equal size and capacity; (3) bring the number of nurses in Harlem Hospital's training school up to "the quota demanded by nursing standards"; (4) Negro nurses in Harlem Hospital should be "given the identical provisions for affiliated training on contagious diseases and psychiatry that exist for all other nurses in training."

Crime and Control of Police

(1) Instruct the police in Harlem (and back up these instructions with disciplinary measures) that it is "not their business to interfere with the association of whites and Negroes"; (2) the police in Harlem should "close up pleasure dens that cater to the vices and disreputable pleasures of white patrons" and also close up "any cabaret, dance hall or any other institution for entertainment in Harlem that refuses to admit Negroes"; (3) have the commissioner of police arrange to appoint a "committee of from five to seven Harlem citizens of both races to whom colored people may make complaint if mistreated by the police."

RIOTING PAYS IN NEW YORK

Even though the Mayor's Commission report was never adopted officially and indeed seems to have disappeared from the archives, La Guardia was apparently well intentioned in his appointments and instructions, the commission was provided with a staff, albeit not very competent, and at least some of its recommendations that were within the power of the city government and for which funds could be found were actually followed.

> Within three months of the riot, for example, the director of the Emergency Relief Bureau (ERB)...established an Advisory Committee on Negro Problems...[which] successfully convinced the ERB to raise the number of blacks "in responsible positions" and corrected cases in which black supervisors earned less than whites. The head of the WPA in New York took similar steps. A new Harlem Health Center building opened, and Harlem Hospital

received a new wing. Within a year of the riot, the city budget included appropriations for four new schools in the area. The Harlem River Houses, the first black public housing project, were quickly completed and opened in 1937. The state created a Temporary Commission on the Condition of the Urban Colored Population, and city hospitals agreed to accept black nurses.[55]

The relationship between the riot and La Guardia's decision to build public housing for blacks was very transparent, as Peter Marcuse's history of early public housing in New York reveals. In 1933 the Housing Division of the Public Works Administration had already selected a site in Williamsburg, Brooklyn, and had begun to acquire land on which to build subsidized housing for 1,622 white working-class families.

> Harlem River Houses had a different history. It was intended for Negroes...but it was hardly built out of benevolence; the event that precipitated its announcement was the Harlem riot of March 19 and 20, 1935. Within a month of the riot, the Authority was assuring the community that [it] was doing everything it could to hasten a Harlem project. Within two months of the riot, Mayor LaGuardia gave a firm commitment that the very next housing project to be built would be in Harlem.[56]

Vacant land for the project was found on the northeastern edge of Harlem between the developed areas and the Harlem River, which ensured speedy construction but also insulated it from white areas in the Bronx across the narrow river. The empty land was taken by eminent domain from a Rockefeller interest, which speeded up its construction.[57] Some 15,000 families applied, so admission could be highly selective. However, since the unemployed and persons in "atypical" households were disqualified from admission, even if much more public housing had been built, it could never have solved the problems of the shortage and high rents in Harlem nor of the unemployment generated by the depression, although it could, and did, give work to construction workers.

These accomplishments were tangible evidence that protests could be partially successful in drawing attention to the plight of specific neighborhoods and in obtaining redress through the political process. The black community, through its political organization and its overt expressions of anger, met with responsiveness from the city's government in ways that minorities in Chicago and Los Angeles never elicited. The city, however, could not create sufficient jobs during the depression to address the deeper issues of poverty and dependence. That would have to await the stimulus to the local economy created by the next war.

INTENSIFIED POLITICAL MOBILIZATION IN THE 1940S FORESHADOWS THE NEXT RIOT

Although the New York economy did not benefit as much as did industrial Chicago and Detroit from the heightened demand for heavy war materiel, its port became the chief beneficiary of increased exports under President Roosevelt's lend-lease program, and the city received an inflow of southern migrants seeking jobs and housing. Blacks, however, failed to benefit equally from the improved conditions, being the last to be hired and thus the last to move off relief. Nevertheless, some progress could be noted by the early 1940s.

> By 1940, the Harlem River Houses, the... Harlem Health Center building, the Women's Pavilion at Harlem Hospital, and two Harlem schools were completed. Also, the number of black nurses and attendants of the Hospital Department doubled and that of black physicians and medical board members tripled.... Blacks were also receiving better employment opportunities in the civil service.... Perhaps most important were mayoral appointments of blacks [to high positions].[58]

But the basic complaints about job discrimination and poor-quality housing, now intensified by overcrowding, continued to fester. La Guardia tried to address the problem of discrimination in hiring. Responding in part to pressures from the black labor union and other organizations that had long advocated policies to prohibit racial discrimination in hiring, La Guardia wrote the draft for Executive Order 8802, issued by Roosevelt, which "reaffirmed a federal policy opposed to discrimination in the employment of workers in defense industries or government and created an apparatus to enforce that policy." This order of nondiscrimination was quickly adopted as New York City's official policy.

> [I]n May 1942, the City Council enacted Local Law No. 11, which required the [private] agencies to record discriminatory placement orders, to open their records to the license commissioners, and to identify the clients of such employment [discriminatory] advertisements. *A year later, a* [state] *constitutional provision forbade the denial of equal protection of state laws to any person "because of race, color, creed, or religion."*[59]

Given the cessation of housing construction due to the war, however, it was unlikely that much could be done to relieve the growing shortage of apartments in Harlem and resulting rent increases, but the community was particularly resentful of La Guardia's support for Stuyvesant Town. At the beginning of the riot-torn summer of 1943, La Guardia finally came to an agreement to use the city's powers of eminent domain to clear a congested site near the Lower East Side and then turn the land over to the Metropolitan Life Insurance Company to build a large rental housing complex over which the company would have full rights to select tenants. Blacks feared—on the basis of Metropolitan's traditional discriminatory employment practices and a public statement by its chairman—that they would be excluded, "thus setting a precedent for discriminatory tenant selection in future quasi-public projects."[60] Their opposition proved prescient. (When the project was completed, black applicants were routinely rejected, and it took decades and several court cases before nonwhite tenants gained modest entry to this desirable project.)[61]

So by the summer of 1943, although conditions had theoretically been improved by legal and administrative reforms, many grievances remained, not only over housing but especially with respect to employment and police harassment. The outbreak in June of the deadly Detroit riot, in which whites attacking blacks had police protection and even assistance, put fear into blacks and city governments elsewhere. I have already described in chapter 2 how the Detroit riot threw the fear of God into Chicago's politicians, who out of concern that the unrest might spread, immediately set up the Mayor's Commission on Race Relations, intended to defuse tensions. Some observers expected that New York City, given its more "liberal" attitudes and laws, would be immune to the racial tensions developing elsewhere, but most of the precipitating grievances were not location specific.

> As 1943 began, the city's unemployment problem was far from solved . . . only 1.3 percent of all defense production workers in the state were black, and those mostly unskilled. . . . Gradually, some advances were made, particularly by black women, in defense industries and in other occupational categories.[62]

Things may have been getting a little better, but not fast or enough, and there was a new militancy. The irony that blacks, even as they were called on to risk their lives for their country, were subjected to segregation and discrimination in the armed services was not lost on them. Nor was the traditional animosity of police toward blacks erased by a mere uniform. Thus, although the city took precautions to avoid a Detroit-type riot, setting up its by-then-routine interracial committees, it failed.[63] The pressures had been building up for too long, and the community was well organized and prepared for action. As Biondi noted,

> the struggle for Negro rights in New York relied on Black communal organization and strength. Activists utilized the[se] institutions and resources. . . .

Black New Yorkers in the 1940s had higher levels of membership in institutions that encouraged social consciousness and political activities. . . . According to NAACP executive Walter White, "Negro militancy and implacable determination to wipe out segregation grew more proportionately during the years 1940 to 1945 than during any other period in the Negro's history in America."[64]

THE HARLEM RIOT OF 1943

Harlem in 1943 was considerably more populous, larger in extent, and more segregated in character than it had been in 1935. By 1940, almost half a million residents, some 6 percent of the city's population of almost 7.5 million, were black. Although over 100,000 lived in Brooklyn, most lived in Harlem, which had expanded to include almost 400 city blocks—from 110th to 155th streets and between Third and Amsterdam avenues. In this vast area, 80 percent of the residents were black; central Harlem alone "accounted for 63 percent of the borough's entire black population."[65] Tensions were building. Capeci quotes Malcolm X's 1943 comment that "one could almost smell trouble ready to break out."[66]

And by this time it would be unlikely to involve black-white conflict between civilians. Given the enormous geographical extent and increasingly segregated character of black Harlem, the only whites who really *had* to enter a combat zone would be armed police. When, indeed, a large-scale riot erupted in Harlem the night of August 1, it was precipitated by a police officer and was suppressed in about 12 hours only by heavy and massive use of the police force.

The immediate *casus belli* was an altercation between a white policeman and a (female) client at a local hotel. The police report of August 1 gave the following details. That evening, at about 9:30 p.m.,

> a white police officer arrested a black woman in Harlem for disorderly conduct. A Mrs. Roberts interfered with the arrest. Her son, Robert Bandy, a soldier in uniform, threatened the officer and punched him. The policeman placed him under arrest as well. By then a small crowd had gathered. An unidentified man hit the police officer from behind, and Mr. Bandy ran. The officer threw his nightstick at Bandy, then drew his gun and shot. The wounded soldier was then brought to the hospital, still under arrest.[67]

Rumors (that later turned out to be false) spread that a white policeman had killed a black soldier, and by 10:30, the reaction had begun—in an area that, although it centered on commercial 125th Street (the "main drag"), extended all the way from 110th to 145th streets along 8th, 7th, and Lenox avenues. Windows were broken and stores looted, after their "protective iron gates were ripped from their hinges.[68] Fires [were] started.... The air was filled with screams and laughter, sounds of people running...distant fire trucks, shooting, shattering glass. [T]he battles continued into the next day. By then...[t]he scene was one of smashed windows, wrecked stores, and cluttered sidewalks, with broken glass, foodstuffs, clothing, and assorted debris everywhere."[69]

How the Riot Was Handled

Capeci attributes the short duration of the riot to La Guardia's prompt and decisive response.

> When shifts changed at midnight, all patrolmen were held on duty.... Security police were...assigned to each car of the...[subway] serving Harlem, and military police cleared the area of servicemen. Firemen were also held on duty.... [Adjacent precincts added police to the area, and in half an hour of this order, after 1 a.m.], 5,000 police were in the zone of disorder. [La Guardia also ordered all bars to close as well as all liquor stores.] In time the riot zone was sealed off. Traffic was diverted around the entire area of West Harlem.... As rioters burned themselves out on the morning of August 2, the Mayor moved to prevent a recurrence.... [His radio broadcast] carefully [avoided] any condemnation of the ghetto's citizenry as a whole [and described] measures taken to restore full order. Traffic would be limited and nonresidents denied entrance to Harlem. Liquor stores would be closed indefinitely.

Capeci also credits La Guardia with planning for postriot reconstruction "almost as soon as the disturbance occurred." Medical services, emergency rooms, and hospitals were alerted; blood supplies were secured, and police were assigned to drive ambulances. Emergency food was provided. A day after the riot, milk deliveries in Harlem were 90 percent restored, pushcarts and emergency shops were operating, and vendors were allowed to enter. "By August 6, there was 'no shortage.' " Black volunteers played a significant role in helping to restore order and in supervising relief measures. Thanks to the speed with which hostilities ended, the 8,000 New York State guardsmen who were on standby at city armories never had to be deployed.[70]

When the curfew the city had imposed on the quarter was finally lifted some two weeks later, the toll listed six African Americans dead, hundreds injured, and more than 550 blacks arrested (mostly for looting or receiving "stolen goods").

Property damage was estimated at $2 million. Although not inconsequential, this in no way matched the damage the white-on-black riot in Detroit had caused two months earlier. The Detroit riot had involved some three-fourths of the city's area, suffered from more than 100 fires that were allowed to burn out of control, left some 34 dead (including 25 blacks, most killed by the police), injured more than 700, and finally had to be put down by federal troops.[71]

Many New Yorkers blamed the uprising on "hoodlums" and congratulated themselves on how well the city had weathered the crisis. But as Capeci notes, while this "eased their consciences," it also caused them to *disregard reasons for ghetto resentment and the need for measures to improve the living conditions of black residents.*"[72] There was a growing discrepancy between what blacks were expected to contribute to the war effort and how little they benefited from it. Segregation in the military, exclusion from defense jobs, and an inflationary spiral in prices and rents (which they blamed on white landlords and shopkeepers) were a few of the more obvious underlying grievances.

Capeci reported the results of a survey conducted in Harlem by Kenneth Clark just after the riot, which found that at least a third of blacks queried thought the riot might trigger some positive results.[73] Perhaps they were right.

POSTRIOT REFORMS

Up to that time, New York had not imposed rent controls or price regulations, although many other cities had already done so.

> Within one week of the riot, the Office of Price Administration announced plans to open an office in Harlem.... In addition, the *OPA announced in mid-September "that a special study was being made of the possibility of establishing rent control in New York City."... Federal rent control was also implemented before the year ended, making New York the last major city to be regulated.*[74]

And, as had happened after the 1935 riot, additional public housing was promised on a nondiscriminatory basis. Delivery had to await the end of the war, however.

SPACE MATTERS

Social scientists engaged in the "growth industry" of analyzing American racial tensions have singled out the 1943 Harlem riot as the paradigmatic event presaging the series of racial uprisings that would wrack American cities in the second half of the 1960s. Capeci is explicit in drawing this connection between the Harlem riots and the "transition from the communal to the commodity type of riot" of the 1960s. "The Detroit riot of 1943 demonstrated characteristics of each type of disturbance, but it was the Harlem upheavals of 1935...and [even more so] 1943 that ushered in Watts, Newark, and the second Detroit."[75]

Later, in the 1960s, naïve observers were to question why "they" were destroying "their own communities." Leaving aside the symptomatic "they" and an implied "us," this question ignores the spatial changes that, between World War II and the 1960s, had vastly expanded the boundaries of segregated areas of black occupancy in the post–World War II era, a physical expansion that not only allowed the police to follow a control strategy of cordoning off "riot" areas, keeping blacks in and whites out, but also made it impossible for blacks to choose alternate targets.[76]

Among the analysts who have explored how space has mattered is Allen Grimshaw, who focused on race riots before and during World War II.[77] Michael McCall has summarized Grimshaw's findings, critiquing him perhaps unfairly for failing to predict how different the riots of the 1960s would be.[78] According to Grimshaw, urban riots before and during World War II began in "spontaneous brawls over an immediate disturbance among 'bystanders' and progressed into 'mass, uncoordinated battles' between groups of one race and isolated individuals of the other." Most violence occurred in the three following situations: an isolated white victim was beaten up when passing through a black ghetto; white gangs invaded a Negro slum and were fought by black defenders; battles took place between black subgroups and then with the police who were sent in to quell violence. He acknowledged that "both the Detroit riot of 1943 and the Chicago riot of 1919 saw a great deal of looting and property damage in the slum, including arson and bombing, with considerable numbers of casualties."[79]

McCall criticizes Grimshaw for dismissing the 1943 Harlem riot as a deviant case,[80] not recognizing that something new, as yet undefined and unnamed, was being foreshadowed: namely, the ghetto uprising. However, Grimshaw recognized the importance of Harlem's large size and isolation, which implied little black-white civilian violence, although it would take a powerful police presence to put down the major form of the riot: looting and general property destruction. In short, the 1943 Harlem riot did not have white civilian attacks on Negroes, was contained within the ghetto area, was characterized more by battles between the police and black civilians, and involved a large amount of looting and property damage. *"The outstanding fact that emerged from analysis of the recent major riots was that the 'Harlem pattern' is the new pattern for Northern urban riots.* Far from being a deviant case, it is now the most general pattern."[81]

Between 1943 and 1964, when a more prolonged riot would erupt in Harlem and would spread to the Bedford-Stuyvesant section of Brooklyn (New York's "Second Ghetto"), the city's minority population underwent enormous growth and diversification, and the metropolitan region underwent a dramatic spatial transfiguration. It was in the context of these changes during the postwar period that the next and, so far, the last New York race riot would occur.

NOTES

1. According to James Weldon Johnson, *Black Manhattan* (New York: Knopf, 1930), during the Revolutionary War "the Legislature of New York passed an act granting freedom to all slaves who served in the army for three years or until honorably discharged" (pp. 10–11).
2. Race was not specifically mentioned in the Conscription Act, which merely specified "able-bodied male *citizens* of the United States." See Iver Bernstein, *The New York City Draft Riots: Their Significance for American Society and Politics in the Age of the Civil War* (New York: Oxford University Press, 1990), p. 9 (italics in the original). But because blacks were *not* citizens, the result was to exclude them from mandatory registration and the draft.
3. Ibid.,p. 3.
4. Joseph Boskin, introduction to Boskin, ed., *Urban Racial Violence in the Twentieth Century* (Beverly Hills, Calif.: Glencoe Press/Macmillan, 1969) (unpaged introduction, italics added). Note that Boskin mentions "the use of Negroes as strikebreakers," although there were no industrial unions in the 1860s.
5. Bernstein, *The New York City Draft Riots*, appendix.
6. Of whom almost 4,000 were of foreign birth (chiefly Jamaica and other parts of the Caribbean), pointing to one of the characteristics that distinguished New York's black population from the beginning and which remains significant.
7. This is one of the arguments of Noel Ignatief, *How the Irish Became White* (New York: Routledge, 1995), who stresses that the upward mobility of the Irish was partially achieved by blocking the entry of more blacks into occupations in which they had already achieved footholds. But job competition also seems to have been at the root of other riots—in Springfield, Ohio, and Atlanta, Georgia, in 1906, and in Springfield, Illinois, in 1908, where the Irish were not necessarily involved.
8. Johnson, *Black Manhattan*, first quotation, p. 126; second quotation, p. 127.
9. Ibid., p. 127.
10. According to *The WPA Guide to New York City* (new ed., New York: Pantheon, 1982), "a Negro community, west of Columbus Circle, has been popularly known since the turn of the century as SAN JUAN HILL, a folk tribute to the exploits of Negro soldiers in the Spanish-American War" (p. 160).
11. Mary White Ovington, *Half a Man: The Status of the Negro in New York* (New York: Longmans, Green, 1911), p. 18. An excerpt from pp. 18–26 of this book is reprinted in John Bracey, Jr., August Meier, and Elliot Rudwick's valuable edited volume *The Rise of the Ghetto* (Belmont, Calif.: Wadsworth, 1971); see pp. 32–37.

12. Some of these early residents had even owned their own (mostly domestic) slaves. See Sherrill D. Wilson, *New York City's African Slaveowners: A Social and Material Culture History* (New York: Garland, 1994), which concentrates especially on the elite who lived on Thompson Street in Greenwich Village but also contains valuable information on the status of blacks in the early city, which contrasts markedly with the situation of the "Black Laws" of Illinois. Wilson attributes the more liberal New York antecedents in New Amsterdam to the Dutch policies, which recognized free blacks, permitted slaves to own land, livestock, and other property, to work on their own account, and to enjoy the protection of the law. See especially her chap. 3.

13. Ovington, *Half a Man*, as reprinted in Bracey et al., *The Rise of the Ghetto*, p. 32.

14. This was the chief location for the 1900 riot.

15. Ovington, *Half a Man*, as reprinted in Bracey et al., *The Rise of the Ghetto*, p. 34, gives a quite different account of the origin of this name from that of the *WPA Guide;* she claims the name was first used "by an onlooker who saw the policemen charging up during one of the once common race fights." Ovington's description reveals her concern over "social disorganization" in this "rough neighborhood." She wrote: "the people on the hill are known for their rough behavior, their readiness to fight, their coarse talk.... Boys play at craps unmolested, gambling is prevalent, and Negro loafers stand about the street corners and largely support the Tenth Avenue saloons" (p. 35).

16. Ibid., pp. 36–37.

17. Fred Shapiro and James Sullivan, *Race Riots: New York 1964* (New York: Crowell, 1964), pp. 17–19. But see also pt. 2 of Gilbert Osofsky, *Harlem: The Making of a Ghetto, Negro New York 1890–1930*, 2nd ed. (New York: Harper Torchbooks, 1971) (originally published 1963), who, in turn, draws on Johnson's *Black Manhattan*. I can detect few discrepancies between these accounts.

18. On the transition from Jewish to black occupancy, see Jeffrey S. Gurock, *When Harlem was Jewish, 1870–1930* (New York: Columbia University Press, 1979).

19. Shapiro and Sullivan, *Race Riots*, pp. 21–25. In the 1990s, these early brownstones were being reclaimed by gentrifiers.

20. Johnson, *Black Manhattan*.

21. E. Franklin Frazier, "Negro Harlem: An Ecological Study," *American Journal of Sociology* 43 (July 1937), pp. 72–88. Frazier directed a large staff charged with investigating conditions there, begun in the wake of the 1935 Harlem riot.

22. Osofsky, *Harlem*.

23. Johnson, *Black Manhattan*, p. 151.

24. Ibid., p. 152.

25. Among those drawn to Harlem who served to boost its standing in the so-called renaissance was Robert Park's protégé Charles Spurgeon Johnson, author of *The Negro in Chicago*, who migrated to Harlem at the age of 26 to join the Urban League and became a leading facilitator of black cultural developments and editor of the League's journal, *Opportunity*. See, for example, David Levering Lewis, *When Harlem was in Vogue* (New York: Oxford University Press, 1979; reprint, 1981), esp. pp. 45–47; 89–98, for a description of Charles Johnson's numerous roles.

26. Much of this account has been drawn from Johnson, *Black Manhattan*, esp. pp. 145–59.

27. Ibid., pp. 155–56.

28. Ibid., pp. 148–49, tells the familiar story of the overbuilding of Harlem, the effects of the stock market crash of 1929, and the role of Negro realtors who bailed out over-extended white landlords.

29. Ibid., p. 157.

30. Ibid., pp. 157–58.

31. See Martha Biondi's outstanding history of this movement in *To Stand and Fight: The Struggle for Civil Rights in Postwar New York City* (Cambridge, Mass.: Harvard University Press, 2003).

32. Johnson, *Black Manhattan,* pp. 181–82.

33. Welfare Council of New York City, *An Impressionistic View of the Winter of 1930–31 in New York City* (New York: Welfare Council of the City of New York, 1932).

34. Thomas Kessner, *Fiorello H. La Guardia and the Making of Modern New York* (New York: Penguin Books, 1978), pp. 217-20. The "austerity" measures imposed by bankers to keep the city afloat were very similar to those that would be imposed by financiers in the 1975–76 fiscal crisis.

35. The personal relationship between Roosevelt and La Guardia also greased the wheels for federal appropriations to New York. " 'Our Mayor is the most appealing man I know,' said President Roosevelt of La Guardia. 'He comes to Washington and tells me a sad story. The tears run down my cheeks and the tears run down his cheeks and the first thing I know he's wangled another $50 million' "; quoted in David Gelernter, *1939: The Lost World of the Fair* (New York: Free Press, 1995), p. 2 (original source not identified).

36. See Peter Marcuse, "The Beginnings of Public Housing in New York," *Journal of Urban History* 12 (August 1986), pp. 353–90, esp. p. 369, where he cites *New York Times,* May 23, 1935, for this correction. At that time, government policy and accepted usage dictated that the racial composition of a neighborhood should be reproduced by future occupants. A third project, Red Hook Houses, was built for white occupancy. During wartime, defense workers received priority placements.

37. Cheryl Greenberg, "The Politics of Disorder: Reexamining Harlem's Riots of 1935 and 1943," *Journal of Urban History* 18 (August 1992), pp. 395–441.

38. Dominic J. Capeci, Jr., *The Harlem Riot of 1943* (Philadelphia: Temple University Press, 1977), quotation from p. 3; italics added.

39. Greenberg, "The Politics of Disorder," p. 400.

40. Ibid., p. 401. This observation is supported by detailed evidence in Biondi, *To Stand and Fight,* which notes the important influence of communists in the growing militancy.

41. Greenberg, "The Politics of Disorder," pp. 402–3.

42. Ibid., p. 405 (italics added). The court ruling against picketing would not be reversed until several years later—too late.

43. Ibid., p. 406.

44. After the riot, the mayor appointed a distinguished biracial commission on "conditions" in Harlem that conducted 25 hearings and listened to 160 testimonies from witnesses. It is hard to interpret the "mysterious disappearance" from official city archives of the commission's report. It was never officially released, and its preservation and eventual publication (a typed transcription copied from the complete account that appeared in the July 18, 1936, issue of the *Amsterdam News*) is a wonderful piece of luck *cum*

scholarship. A photocopy of that issue of the black newspaper was discovered in the files of Columbia University's library by Robert Fogelson and Richard Rubenstein, the editors of the Mass Violence in America series, who published the transcription under its original title (New York: Arno Press and the New York Times, 1969). My page references are to this published and presumed accurate transcript.

45. Mayor's Commission report, quotations from pp. 1–2.

46. Police reports, as cited by Greenberg, "The Politics of Disorder," p. 17.

47. Mayor's Commission report, p. 15.

48. See E. Franklin Frazier, *The Negro Harlem: A Report on Social and Economic Conditions Responsible for the Outbreak of March 19, 1935,* cited by Capeci as a part of the subsequently suppressed *Report of the Mayor's Commission on Conditions in Harlem.* The following summary account comes mostly from Capeci, *The Harlem Riot of 1943,* esp. chap. 2. However, the bulk of the background analysis is also contained in Mayor's Commission report, chaps. 3–8, which I assume was written by the researchers under Frazier's direction, although there is no attribution of authorship.

49. Capeci, *The Harlem Riot of 1943,* pp. 34–35.

50. "The Reverend John W. Robinson, chairman of the Permanent Committee for Better Schools in Harlem, pointed out how school districts had been gerrymandered to ensure segregation and how Harlem students were relegated to high schools "where the curriculum relegated them to a marginal economic status in society.... Robinson's committee found that almost four hundred books in the city's schools depicted blacks as slaves, 'lazy, [and] shiftless.' " Quoted in ibid., p. 40.

51. Ibid., pp. 38–41. The final quotation is from p. 41. For a fuller discussion of police–community conflicts during the Depression, see Marilynn Johnson, *Street Justice: A History of Police Violence in New York City* (Boston: Beacon Press, 2003), chap. 5.

52. Capeci, *The Harlem Riot of 1943,* p. 43. Only the phrase "in the midst of plenty" seems unwarranted.

53. Chap. 9 of the Mayor's Commission report, pp. 122–35. In its introduction to the earlier version of the Mayor's Commission report, the *Amsterdam News* (July 18, 1936, p. 1) asserts that the mayor had found the original version of chapter 9 "too hot, too caustic, too critical, too unfavorable... [so it was] allegedly revamped... to make it more to his liking."

54. The rent strike was a standard mechanism of tenant activism in Manhattan. See Joseph Spencer, "New York City Tenant Organization and the Post–World War I Housing Crisis," pp. 51–93, and Mark Naison, "From Eviction Resistance to Rent Control: Tenant Activism in the Great Depression," pp. 94–133, both in Ronald Lawson, ed., *The Tenant Movement in New York City, 1904–1984* (New Brunswick, N.J.: Rutgers University Press, 1986).

55. Greenberg, "The Politics of Disorder," p. 418; based on detailed archival sources.

56. Marcuse, "The Beginnings of Public Housing in New York," quotation from p. 369.

57. The 574 units of the Harlem River Houses were constructed on vacant land that John D. Rockefeller owned, between built-up Harlem and the Harlem River and adjacent to the Dunbar Co-ops, which Rockefeller had earlier constructed for middle-class blacks (a project undergoing foreclosure proceedings). The federal Public Works Administration (PWA) contracted with the New York City Housing Authority to plan and design

the project, but the PWA actually built the project before leasing it back to the New York City Housing Authority to operate. Ibid., pp. 369–75.

58. Capeci, *The Harlem Riot of 1943*, p. 8.
59. Ibid., pp. 11, 12–13; italics added.
60. Ibid., pp. 13–14.
61. See Arthur Simon, *Stuyvesant Town, U.S.A.: Pattern for Two Americas* (New York: New York University Press, 1970). Update: in October 2006, Stuyvesant Town and the adjacent Peter Cooper Village, both subsidized rental projects covered by the rent control/regulation laws, were purchased for $5.4 billion by private firms and banks—the highest price ever paid in New York's history. Occupants, including a small number of blacks, most of whom had initially gained access through subletting, were in panic that the buyers planned substantial upgrading that would remove the rent-regulation ceiling or would convert the units to condominiums.
62. Capeci, *The Harlem Riot of 1943*, pp. 61–63.
63. For details on those committees, see ibid, chap. 4.
64. Biondi, *To Stand and Fight*, pp. 15–16.
65. Capeci, *The Harlem Riot of 1943*, p. 32.
66. Ibid., p. xi.
67. As cited in Greenberg, "The Politics of Disorder," p. 426.
68. At that period, almost all stores in Harlem belonged to nonresident whites; a large number of the store owners were Jewish, so they bore the brunt of the anger.
69. Capeci, *The Harlem Riot of 1943*, pp. 101–2.
70. Ibid., pp. 104–7, first long quote: p. 104.
71. Ibid., pp. 68–70.
72. Capeci's analysis appears in chap. 7, entitled "Police, Hoodlums, Race, and Riot." Ibid., pp. 115-33. Quotation from p. 115, italics added.
73. Ibid., p. 130.
74. Ibid., pp. 158–59; italics added. It should be noted also that New York remains one of the few cities in the country that still has kept rent controls, duly modified, in force.
75. Ibid., pp. 170–71.
76. Not until the 1992 riots in South Central Los Angeles would this system break down.
77. See Allen Day Grimshaw, "Urban Racial Violence in the United States: Changing Ecological Considerations" (1960), as reprinted in Allen Grimshaw, ed., *Racial Violence in the United States* (Chicago: Aldine, 1969).
78. Michael McCall, "Some Ecological Aspects of Negro Slum Riots" (1968), as reprinted in Joseph R. Gusfield, ed., *Protest, Reform and Revolt: A Reader in Social Movements* (New York: Wiley, 1970), pp. 345–62.
79. Grimshaw's analysis as summarized by McCall, pp. 346–47.
80. Ibid., p. 347. Implicit in the idea that the 1943 Harlem riot was a "deviant" was that a race riot, in the strict sense of the term, should involve direct conflict between white and black civilians. But given the large size of Harlem and the skill of police in isolating the zone, no whites except the police were involved. This interpretation was shared by New York's mayor and even by black politicians such as Adam Clayton Powell, Jr., who denied it was a "race riot." See Capeci, *The Harlem Riot of 1943*, pp. 115, 119.
81. McCall, "Some Ecological Aspects," p. 347.

5

The Harlem–Bedford Stuyvesant Uprising of 1964

etween the end of World War II and the early 1960s, significant redistributions of New York's racial and ethnic groups occurred. The termination of the wartime housing construction moratorium, coupled with the return of veterans whose home purchases were facilitated by low-interest loans guaranteed by the Veterans Housing Administration, led to an unprecedented churning of population in the New York region. Many young newly formed families of working-class whites did not return to the neighborhoods in which they had grown up, although their parents tended to stay on, thanks to the bargains of rent-controlled apartments and their attachments to neighbors and to religious and other local facilities. Others, both young and old, "decentralized" from the already built-up outer-borough neighborhoods in Brooklyn, the Bronx, and Queens, where they had established roots, to more outlying, previously undeveloped portions of those boroughs where new garden apartments and single-family houses were being built. Still others, mostly demobilized veterans, took advantage of federal loan incentives to buy houses in the raw, mass-produced suburbs on Long Island, and some even moved into what had been thought of as "exurbia."

A similar decentralization, albeit almost entirely within the city limits, was occurring among minorities who had previously been concentrated heavily in the northern part of Manhattan. But because the net growth rates for minorities within the city limits exceeded those for whites, there was a gradual shift in racial proportions between 1940 and 1960. As late as 1940, 94 percent of the city's total population was classified as "white." Manhattan, due to Harlem and, to a lesser extent, such enclaves as Chinatown and other small "minority" pockets, was the only borough with a significant proportion of "nonwhites" (17 percent). In contrast, the outer boroughs, while containing large numbers of "ethnics" (mostly Jews, Italians, and Irish),[1] were overwhelmingly white: 95 percent in Brooklyn; 98 percent in the Bronx and Staten Island; and 97 percent in Queens. And yet it was from those boroughs that the majority of suburban settlers were recruited.

The vacancies thus created opened up housing opportunities in the outer boroughs and allowed for partial (and very spotty) decentralization of Manhattan's overcrowded black population. But because of additional migration to the city by nonwhites, the proportion of whites decreased throughout the city. By 1960, 85 percent of New Yorkers were still classified as white. The highest proportions of nonwhites were found in Manhattan (with 26 percent), followed by Brooklyn (15 percent). Staten Island, Queens, and the Bronx still remained overwhelmingly white (95, 91, and 88 percent, respectively).[2] (See the discussion below on the "ambiguous" racial definition of Hispanics, at that time primarily Puerto Rican.)

The redistribution of nonwhites was not a random affair, however. Rather, certain subareas within Brooklyn and the Bronx changed "complexion" in radical fashion, while leaving other parts of the borough almost untouched. The role that postwar public housing projects played in "opening up" these boroughs increased the "spottiness" of this distribution (see below). Brooklyn's Bedford-Stuyvesant section provides a relevant example, in part because it was among the first locations of the "new round" of urban uprisings that exploded in several hundred American cities in the course of the 1960s. Although Los Angeles scholars often claim that the Watts riot of 1965 fired the opening shot of this later sequence, events in Harlem and "Bed-Stuy" (as well as in New Jersey) actually preceded it by more than a year.[3]

NEW YORK'S SECOND GHETTO, BEDFORD-STUYVESANT

The history of Bedford-Stuyvesant's transformation into a "ghetto" is remarkably parallel to Harlem's.[4] As far back as 1663, the village of Bedford had been an agricultural and trading way station for white farmers. They were joined in the early nineteenth century by a small number of black farmers.[5] It was not until the final decades of the nineteenth century, however, that the area began to be developed as a fashionable zone of two-story houses for middle- and upper-class buyers. As in Harlem, there was much real estate speculation.

> With the influx of the upper-class, and the formation of the fashionable "Stuyvesant Heights" section and its mansions of the wealthy, came servants. And the servants needed places to live. They formed the first Negro community in the Bedford area.... The collapse of Stuyvesant Heights society came [after] the early 1920's when prices soared, and then, with the Depression, many of the lovely brownstones became too much for their original owners to maintain. They moved out and the prices dropped until the houses were within reach of Negro families.[6]

Houses were subdivided, and blockbusting was developed into a fine art. As happened elsewhere,[7] panic selling preceded the major black influx into this "in-town" leafy suburb. As early as 1940, the area around Pratt Institute had become a blighted slum. By 1950, nonwhites constituted more than half of the population. "Ten years later the percentage of Negroes and Puerto Ricans was conservatively figured at 83."[8] By 1970, this "second ghetto" had spread dramatically (see maps 5.1 and 5.2).

Confounding a simple model of "white flight" was the role of slum clearance and public housing in changing the racial composition of the area. By 1964, nine public housing projects with almost 50,000 (mostly black) residents were located in the Bed-Stuy ghetto, whose total population had climbed by then to an estimated 400,000.[9] Although the stereotypical narrative speaks in such metaphorical terms as "white flight," "racial succession," and "neighborhood burn out" and "blow out" (especially with reference to the South Bronx and Bedford-Stuyvesant, where this sequence is not totally inaccurate), its major flaws are its failure to acknowledge that New York City's "suburban" expansion in the post–World War II period took place not just in the thickening of outlying villages or the construction of new developments, and even whole towns such as Levittown beyond the city limits, but in the outer boroughs themselves, where open land was still available.

I can illustrate this by tracing the demographic changes in the vast borough of Queens, which in 1930 had a population of only a million inhabitants. Between 1930 and 1990, the total population of the borough almost doubled. However, the number of white residents did not decline but in fact rose by some 163,000. So it was essentially the *addition* of blacks and other minorities (Asian and Hispanic) that accounted for the changed racial composition of Queens—a change made

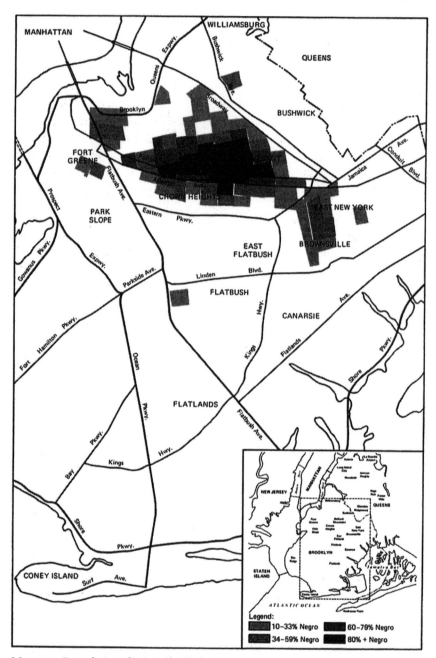

Map 5.1.   Boundaries of Primarily Black-Occupied Areas in Bedford-Stuyvesant, Brooklyn, in 1950.

Source: Harold X. Connolly, *A Ghetto Grows in Brooklyn*. Copyright: New York University Press, 1977.

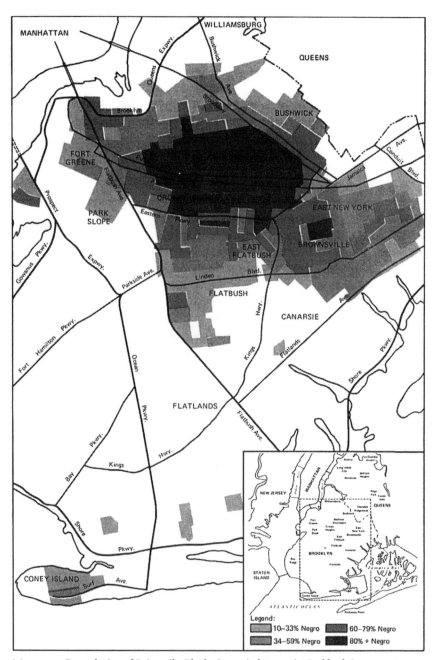

Map 5.2.   Boundaries of Primarily Black-Occupied Areas in Bedford-Stuyvesant, Brooklyn, in 1970.

Source: Harold X. Connolly, *A Ghetto Grows in Brooklyn*. Copyright: New York University Press, 1977.

possible through densification, developments on vacant land, and a re-sorting of groups. Between 1930 and 1990, the number of black residents increased from under 19,000 to almost 421,000, and "others" increased from 877 to approach 400,000. White flight thus accounts for less of the change than one might have imagined.[10] The World's Fair had stimulated interest and development in the area, and that was intensified by the 1964–65 revival (and new construction) of the old fairgrounds.

While Queens is perhaps the most extreme case, many of these observations also apply to Brooklyn and the Bronx. Outlying portions of those two boroughs also experienced not so much population succession as additional growth, as blacks and others inherited older zones and whites relocated to newer developments within the boroughs. The fact that they remained within the city limits, in contrast to Chicago, had significant implications for local politics.

Race and Ethnicity

In the above discussion (as in those of many writers), the terms "race" and "black"/"white" have been used *as if* they had transparent and firm meanings. Race, however, is acknowledged to be an ambiguous category, telling us more about the values of the society that defines and "uses" the concept than about any abstract characteristic possessed by individuals.[11]

Such generalizations as appear above are confounded in New York by two factors: first, the wide range of variation within New York's black community itself, and second, the existence of racial "infill"—constituted chiefly by Puerto Ricans, who, up to the "new immigration" since the mid-1960s, constituted New York's dominant "Hispanic" group.

Freed Slaves and the Caribbean Influx

Given New York's demographic diversity, race is an especially inaccurate concept, having very limited statistical and analytical value. Just as the category "white" was crisscrossed by dimensions of national ancestry, religion, time of arrival, class, and political power, not to mention linguistic and phenotypical characteristics,[12] so New York's "black" population challenged the boundaries of simple dichotomies. Contrary to the situation in Chicago, for example, where to be poor, of rural origin, and dark-skinned were more tightly correlated, the congruence between phenotype and nativity broke down in New York. From the beginning a sizeable number of "blacks" were of foreign origin (largely Jamaican, but also from other Caribbean islands). Indeed, many of the political leaders and entrepreneurial elite of the black community were drawn from this subgroup.

Second, native "blacks" varied widely by superficial appearance. Especially after the Civil War, the freedom of the city drew ambitious newcomers of mixed parentage, some of whom "passed," while others, of equally indeterminate appearance, remained identified with the black community.[13] From the beginning, New York "blacks" thus have varied by class, ethnicity, accent, ancestry, and, increasingly, after 1965, with an influx of Haitians and Dominicans and even Africans, by language.

Puerto Ricans Arrive: The Formation of East Harlem

The second largest "minority" in New York from the 1950s onward consisted of persons of Puerto Rican birth or descent. In this highly mixed population, race was an even less relevant marker, and immigration status was not a desideratum. The island had become a U.S. colony as a result of the Spanish-American War of 1898, and in 1917 the Jones Act conferred the rights of partial citizenship on its residents. Migration between the island and the mainland was freed of legal routines and restrictions, and eligibility for welfare, public housing, and other social services came to be the same as that enjoyed by "full" citizens.

Nevertheless, the number of Puerto Ricans in the city remained tiny. As late as 1940, Puerto Ricans in New York City numbered only some 60,000, or less than 1 percent of the total. The mechanisms of labor placement put into place during World War II assisted in "steering" Puerto Ricans into the city and into industrial jobs, but mass migration from the island really took off in the 1950s, spurred by economic involution on the island and facilitated by the institution of direct air travel which, while it actually began in 1945, became much cheaper in the 1950s. The 1950s were the years of peak migration to New York. By 1960, they numbered some 800,000, or about one-tenth of the city's population.[14] The main concentration of Puerto Ricans at that time was in East Harlem (La Guardia's old congressional district!), which by then was being referred to as El Barrio, although it was not exclusively Puerto Rican, nor did all Puerto Ricans live there, by any means.[15]

To what extent did the categories "black" and "white" overlap with this growing Spanish-speaking group? Nowhere is the issue of "race" so ambiguous as among migrants from the island, whose "racial" stock had long been "mixed." Glazer and Moynihan's discussion brilliantly captures the changing "social definitions" of racial identity within this group, and I must therefore quote at length from them:

> [W]hile in their own minds a man's color meant something very different from what it meant to white Americans, [Puerto Rican migrants] knew very

well its meaning for Americans. About one-fifth of the Puerto Rican group in New York in the thirties were listed in census returns as Negro (a slightly smaller proportion than were then listed as colored in the Puerto Rican census)...[but] by 1940, this had dropped to about 11 per cent....By 1960 the proportion of colored among the New York Puerto Ricans was only 4 per cent.[16]

This is stunning information. Since there is no reason to believe that suddenly there was a highly selective out-migration of light-skinned "Spaniards" from the island, one can only surmise that the progressive "whitening" of New York's Puerto Ricans was a social act. Given this, one must question all figures that "divide" borough populations into dichotomies of white and black.[17] Such figures both overestimate and underestimate the amount of racial integration that was occurring in various parts of the city. This is particularly true within New York's public housing projects, where Puerto Ricans (who may report themselves as "white") and African Americans now make up the largest proportion of tenants.

The "Disembourgeoisement" of the Puerto Rican Community

Distancing themselves from the presumed low status of blacks, however, did not protect the Puerto Rican community from eventually sinking to a socioeconomic status below even that of African Americans. They were to be trapped between the rock of deindustrialization and the hard place of newer immigrants willing to work for even lower wages. In the early 1950s, Puerto Ricans had "increasingly found jobs in the labor market niche of center-city blue-collar positions left behind by the exodus of workers to new industries in the suburbs or by the occupational advancement [or retirement] of existing workers. Puerto Rican migration was viewed as crucial to salvaging New York industries that depended on inexpensive labor, such as the garment industry."[18]

Labor force participation rates for men and women, mostly in the category of "operatives," were higher than those of other groups, and dual- or triple-income families seemed the only way to economic security. However, the situation began to unravel soon afterward, as such jobs increasingly disappeared from the New York economy and as circular migration stirred the pot of tenuous family arrangements, often breaking them apart as men returned to the island. Female-headed households multiplied, becoming increasingly dependent on public housing and aid to dependent children, two programs for which, because of their "citizenship" status, they enjoyed immediate eligibility. By the mid-1960s, the sex ratios within the Puerto Rican community were tipped heavily toward women, and the rates of dependency in the Puerto Rican community as a whole exceeded those of any other subgroup in the city.[19]

The plight of Puerto Ricans was further worsened by programs intended to enhance living conditions for inner-city residents. At the peak of urban renewal and urban redevelopment activities, the city engaged in large-scale slum clearance, concentrated in zones where the most deteriorated tenements were to be found. Because these were also zones in which Puerto Rican communities had formed, this entailed considerable shifting from one slum to another. If in Chicago urban renewal became known sarcastically as Negro Removal, in New York the common phrase for it was Puerto Rican Removal.

East Harlem became one of the prime targets for slum clearance, which was not an illogical choice, given that it contained an enormous concentration of badly deteriorated tenements. Kessner called it perhaps the worst area in the city:

> Here [in East Harlem] stood the ugly offscourings of American industrialism, grimy factories amidst junkyards, warehouses, used-car lots, and repair shops. Coal yards and oil storage depots belching gasseous [sic] pollutants tinted the sky an ashen gray and raw sewage fouled the river. A transient population filled East Harlem's bars and whorehouses, while its residents occupied seedy tenements and deteriorating housing.[20]

Once the Jews and Italians (who had previously predominated in the area when La Guardia had represented it in Congress) died or moved on, the Puerto Ricans inherited it. Later displaced when their tenements were razed and public housing projects built on the sites, many were able to move back eventually. On the Lower East Side, projects also replaced the tenements along the East River; and although the original inhabitants were mostly non-Hispanic, by 1980, some 80 percent of project residents in that area were Puerto Rican. A similar transformation occurred in Red Hook Houses in Brooklyn, which changed from mostly Jewish white occupancy to mixed black and Puerto Rican in the 1960s.

Increasing poverty, especially in female-headed households, and new eligibility rules for public housing accounted for these changes. Originally, unemployed persons and single mothers were disqualified from applying for public housing. Admission was highly selective, and during the war, priority was given to war workers. Over time, these rules were changed, and despite efforts by the New York City Housing Authority to retain non-Hispanic whites and to "integrate" public housing on a stable basis, gradually project occupants changed almost completely to a mix of African Americans and Puerto Ricans, as working-class whites moved out. Since public housing projects were constructed in all boroughs (some even on open land rather than slum-cleared sites), minority populations were introduced into many formerly white parts of the outer boroughs, albeit in isolated pockets.[21]

This involved substantial numbers of persons, because the New York City Housing Authority ran by far the largest public housing program in the country. As of January 1, 1989, the Authority was supervising 316 operating projects, containing a total of 179,045 dwelling units serving a population of 472,088 in 2,787 buildings.[22] Examination of the dates of completion of the 316 projects reveals that New York City has been providing public housing since 1936 (when First Houses was opened, even before passage of the federal Housing Act of 1937), that the projects are located in all the boroughs, and that they have steadily been added to.

Before 1940, the city had completed only four projects: First Houses, with only 123 apartments, Harlem Houses, with 577 units, Red Hook, with 2,545 units, and Williamsburg, with 1,630 units. During the 1940s, close to 25,000 dwelling units were added. Over 20 projects were completed in that decade, almost all containing between 1,000 to 2,000 units each. (Only four contained less than 1,000, and one, in Queens, had over 3,000.) This pattern of building large high-rise projects (usually Corbusier-type towers on super blocks with interior common green space) persisted into the 1950s. In that decade alone, New York City added the largest number of public housing units ever—over 75,000 subsidized apartments—to its public housing stock. Some 70 new projects were scattered throughout the five boroughs. Like those of the preceding decade, these projects were large-scale: they averaged over 1,000 units per project. All told, the 1950s and 1960s represented the heyday of public housing construction in the city. (Some 43 percent of all subsidized dwelling units were built in the 1950s, and another 24 percent in the 1960s.)[23]

New York Touches Off the Racial Conflict of the 1960s

Despite the construction of massive amounts of subsidized housing assigned on a nondiscriminatory basis, the existence of a longstanding and vigorous set of social and political institutions in the black community, as well as a mayor's office dedicated to defusing racial tensions and "empowering" minority leaders by appointing blacks to higher offices and to civil service positions, the city did not remain immune to the rising national racial tensions of the 1960s. But the riots that began on July 16, 1964, reveal much about the changes that had taken place in the distribution of racial groups in the city since 1943.

THE HARLEM FRUIT RIOT

Before proceeding to the riot itself, however, I must mention a little known and perhaps "trivial" one-day event that preceded the larger explosion by more than a year: the so-called Harlem fruit riot of April 17, 1963. Although the exact "facts" are still in dispute, one could have predicted that the continued racial tensions between a still virtually all-white police force and Harlem's population would be a potential tinderbox, especially at a time of rising militancy among Harlem's youth. Whereas opinions may differ about the role that police brutality and the "blue line of silence" played in exacerbating protest and violent response from the community, it should be pointed out that this continues to be a persisting issue in New York City, and increasingly in other cities as well.

A brief but poignant account of the "fruit riot" is included in Truman Nelson's book *The Torture of Mothers*, based on transcripts of testimony given by at least two involved adults. The first, Frank Stafford, a 31-year-old door-to-door licensed African American salesman, was arrested and savagely beaten by police when he and a 47-year-old Puerto Rican seaman came to the aid of three black teenagers (ages 16, 18, and 19) charged by the police with overturning a fruit cart. The second account was given by Wallace Baker, another bystander. Nelson's study illustrates the difficulties of reconstructing authoritative narratives of "riots."[24]

Nelson's book begins by contrasting two accounts of the same event that appeared, one month apart, in the same "authoritative" newspaper, the *New York Times*. On April 19, the *Times* reported that "four youths, and a man [*sic*] were involved in a free-for-all on Friday afternoon [April 17], after they allegedly overturned a fruit stand at 368 Lenox Avenue, near 128th Street." Retrospectively but no more accurately, the *Times*, in its issue of May 29, gave the following police account. On that afternoon, "about 75 Negro children on their way home from school overturned some cartons at a Harlem fruit and vegetable stand, and what might have been a minor incident grew into a riot."[25] Both accounts were flawed.

Despite the fact that the proprietor testified that the three youths who were subsequently arrested had not even been at his store, and that at least one of the adults (Frank Stafford) had witnesses to attest to his innocence and a second, Fecundo Acion, was equally uninvolved until he came to the defense of the boys, police brutality took its indiscriminate course. According to Stafford, he had just left a customer at 129th Street (Mrs. Evelyn Johnson, who corroborated his story and indeed tried to come to his rescue) when he saw "many people, many police, little boys running. In the windows people were standing and staring out. But there were more police in the street than there were people in the windows. And the police had their guns out.... The police were pointing their guns at the roofs."[26] According to Stafford, the police were beating "this kid, [so] I spoke up and asked them 'Why are you beating him like that?'" And then the police started "swinging on me." There were three policemen hitting Stafford, one on the back of his head and another on his right shoulder, and when he turned away to avoid their blows, the third struck him sharply on his eye.

His testimony was graphic. He reported that he, the Puerto Rican seaman, and the three boys were taken to a detective's private office on the second floor of the police precinct and were savagely beaten for three or four hours by shifts of police officers who had removed their jackets and badges to avoid identification. Finally, Stafford was released to Harlem Hospital for emergency care and, several hours later, was transferred to Bellevue Hospital for treatment of his badly damaged eye. He was kept there for two weeks, during which time surgery was performed. The operation failed, and his right eye had to be removed to prevent infection from spreading to his remaining eye.[27]

Wallace Baker's testimony corroborates Stafford's account.[28] He saw some small boys picking up fruit from the ground and running toward Lenox and 129th Street, followed by three policemen. One caught a boy and was preparing to beat him, so "I ran over and tried to stop him." He, too, was arrested and beaten for his troubles.

The Times reporter Junius Griffin investigated the fruit riot for four weeks, talking with the police, participants, and witnesses to piece the story together, and discussing the problem with concerned members of the Harlem community. According to Griffin,

> April 17 was a sunny Friday, and the pupils, in a holiday mood, decided to take a few apples and oranges from Joe's Fruit Stand at 368 Lenox Avenue. When two stands were overturned, the children grabbed at the spilled fruit. Four policemen tried to catch the offenders, whose cries attracted to the scene some tough teen-aged members of Harlem gangs. The teen-agers jeered the patrolmen, and reinforcements were summoned. Policemen emerged from patrol cars with pistols drawn and nightsticks swinging. Local businessmen and passersby said that a Harlem resident who tried to stop the fracas suffered injuries that resulted in loss of an eye. According to them, some youngsters who were merely onlookers were beaten on the head. Four policemen were injured. Several persons were arrested. Charges of police brutality were made by Harlem residents. Police officials have denied the brutality charges, but refused to elaborate.... The temper of central Harlem grew sullen, as residents complained about the policemen's "inept handling of a minor situation."[29]

Griffin foresaw some longer-term consequences of this ineptness. He suggested that the Harlem fruit riot "set the stage for the expansion of anti-white youth gangs, some of whose members call themselves Blood Brothers."[30] The incident served as a recruitment incentive in a Harlem whose young men were growing increasingly militant. Whereas Griffin's diagnosis of increasing militancy was obviously accurate, it underestimated the widespread extent of resentment of police brutality while overestimating the role gangs would play in the longer, more extensive and violent Harlem/Bedford-Stuyvesant riot that began on July 16, 1964, and continued for six days.

THE HARLEM/BEDFORD-STUYVESANT RIOT OF JULY 1964

Significantly, the rallying cry was once again police brutality, although the incident that triggered the prolonged and better organized protests was hardly as "minor" as a fruit riot, nor did it begin within the confines of Harlem. The only full account of the origins and development of the Harlem/Bedford-Stuyvesant riots I have been able to find was written by two white newspaper reporters, Fred C. Shapiro and James W. Sullivan, who gathered testimony from large numbers of observers, including other reporters, and were themselves present during the riots. While their account includes neither footnotes nor specific references and is by its nature only partial, enough details have been reconstructed to yield a credible "story."[31]

Thursday, July 16

The day began with the fatal shooting in Yorkville, a moderately upscale white area on the Upper East Side of Manhattan, of James Powell, a slightly built 15-year-old African American boy, by Lieutenant Thomas Gilligan, a decorated and considerably larger and fit white policeman who was off-duty and therefore in plain clothes when he fired three shots, the second of which was judged lethal. The young victim was a student attending a summer remedial reading program at the Robert E. Wagner, Sr., Junior High School, far from the Bronx Soundview public housing project where he lived.[32]

The incident had an innocuous enough start, although it was symptomatic of festering tensions between the host neighborhood, largely middle-class Irish, and the summer school students, mostly African American and Puerto Rican. As best as can be reconstructed, just before 9:30 a.m., Patrick Lynch, the superintendent of three apartment houses across from the school, perpetually annoyed by the tendency of "outsider" students to lounge on "his stoops," squirted some black students with his hose while watering down the sidewalk. (They claimed his action was intentional and was accompanied by insulting epithets.) The enraged, wet students threw some "bottles and garbage-can lids [at him], which attracted the attention of . . . three Bronx boys," including James Powell.[33] Lynch then escaped into the apartment building and was chased by Powell. A witness said that Powell "didn't stay two minutes."[34]

But as Powell exited the vestibule, he was shot three times by Lieutenant Gilligan, not on duty and not in uniform, who had raced to the scene from a nearby shop. Despite the fact that "this bloody tragedy was acted out in perhaps one minute" and "was witnessed by dozens of people," the full facts were never established. Gilligan claimed that he showed his badge and fired the first time as a warning shot, firing the next two only after Powell lunged toward him with a knife. Death was instantaneous, confirmed by Powell's friend, who rushed to him from across the street. The friend claimed he had not seen the actual shooting but denied that his friend had a knife (although a teacher later found one, not proven to be Powell's, eight feet away). Conflicting testimony was lost in the subsequent reactions of distress and anger that ensued.

Informed of the shooting, the principal of the school called an ambulance (too late), and crowds of excited students gathered on the street, running back and forth to view the body. Police reinforcements arrived, and Gilligan was rushed from the scene. Confrontations escalated between the 75 police reinforcements, who tried to keep the crowd on the other side of the street, and, by now, some 300 hysterical students.

> Garbage-can lids, bottles, and rocks began to fly, and crying girls ran back and forth in the street, while the principal and teachers begged the students to quiet down. . . . But it ended without a fight and without any arrests. Police took three hysterical girls into custody but released them after they calmed down.[35]

In the tinderbox of black discontent, however, the charges of police brutality and the use of excessive force ignited the "fire this time." Prominent in the demonstrations and protests that followed the next morning were signs calling for Gilligan's dismissal and punishment.

> The Gilligan-Powell case was the spark which fell into Harlem and, with fire-tending, intentional or unintentional, flamed into the Harlem and Bedford-Stuyvesant riots of 1964. For six nights, mobs roamed the streets in two boroughs. As many as 4,000 New Yorkers dedicated themselves to attacks on police, vandalism, and looting of stores. When it was all over, police counted 1 rioter dead, 118 injured, and 465 men and women arrested. . . . [The 1964

New York riots] can be said to have caused the riots which plagued other cities in succeeding weeks, because those riots were patterned on the ones touched off in New York.[36]

Friday, July 17

The existence of a well-organized civil rights movement and heightened militancy distinguished this riot from that of 1943, when black leadership had joined the city "establishment" to cool things out. This time, the Congress of Racial Equality (CORE) organized picketing at the school the next day to protest the violence and to demand a civilian review board to discipline the police. When the 75 or so demonstrators showed up at the school at about 8 a.m., they were greeted by about 50 policemen

> carrying nightsticks. This equipment, unusual on daytime assignment, was protested and, after conferences with a representative of the City Commission on Human Rights, the clubs were sent back to the precinct.... By noon, there were more than two hundred pickets in front of the school, many of them students.... [Chanting "Killer Cops Must Go"], their signs included "STOP KILLER COPS!...WE WANT LEGAL PROTECTION...END POLICE BRUTALITY." Several of the pickets were whites and Puerto Ricans.[37]

Saturday, July 18, through Early Morning Sunday, July 19

This anger was manifest in Harlem during the next few days, peaking on Saturday, July 18, a particularly hot day.[38] It was certainly bloody. "Louis Smith, a CORE field secretary who said he was just back from Mississippi, was at Harlem Hospital that night and was upset by what he saw. 'This is worse than anything I ever saw in Mississippi,' he said."[39]

Powell's funeral service was that afternoon. The 250 people who filed by his casket were protected by a large number of police, who had their barricades handy, in case of troubles. There were none. Nor was there trouble later on at a previously scheduled CORE rally, which changed its focus from the three civil rights workers who were missing in Mississippi to the shooting death of Powell and a protest against police brutality. According to the reporters present, the rally seemed to be ending, with "the crowd excited, but not unruly." Most reporters left. The only one who stayed on became, by default, "one of the leading authorities on the beginning of the Harlem riot."[40] According to him, the speeches became more inflammatory, eventually calling on people to march on the Twenty-eighth Precinct headquarters a few blocks away.

Deputy Chief Thomas Pendergast estimated that 250 persons marched south on 7th Avenue. At the door to the precinct, however, police barred entry, and the crowd was forced to the opposite sidewalk. A committee of five was eventually admitted and demanded the immediate suspension of Gilligan. When the police tried to disperse the crowd, a fight broke out, and a few bottles were thrown from the roofs of tenements nearby. "Policemen donned steel...helmets and moved into the tenements, went up the stairs, and took over the roofs, ending the aerial bombardment. Barricades were called for, and...a scuffle broke out, and about twenty-five people, including some policemen, fell to the pavement." Some 14 persons were arrested, but this only increased the anger of the gathering and the descent of bottles from the rooftops.[41] And when word of the battle at precinct headquarters reached the rally that was still continuing on 125th Street, it further inflamed emotions. By 10 p.m., the crowd had swelled to an estimated 1,000, and things were getting out of control.[42]

In street conflicts between police and protesters in Manhattan, the usual "plan of battle" is for police to form flying wedges to push crowds backward along the narrow streets and for protesters to escape to roofs from which loosened bricks and other informal projectiles can be flung.[43] Escalation is sure to follow, as each antagonist enrages the other. In this case, the goal of the police was to isolate Harlem from the rest of the city. After a disorganized start, they blocked traffic into Harlem, rerouted buses, and "secured" subway stations. But the crowd continued to swell, as rumors of police attacks spread to the audience then exiting the Apollo Theater. According to Shapiro and Sullivan, it was at 10:30 p.m. that a new weapon was first added to the usual mix: a Molotov cocktail. It set a fire near a police car, injuring a policeman. "The other policemen drew their guns and began to fire in the air. It was the first gunfire of the night."[44] By midnight, the gunfire

> was almost continuous in Harlem, breaking out first in one place, then a couple of blocks away, then again a couple of blocks in another direction. But the fall of bricks and bottles from roofs and windows also was almost continuous, and the streets were soon deep with broken glass, so that patrol cars were put out of action with flat tires.[45]

By 4:30 a.m., the police commissioner arrived and met with the director of the City Commission on Human Rights, a judge of the Criminal Court, and whoever among the "leadership" could be assembled at that ungodly hour. It was decided that Police Commissioner Michael Murphy "should write a letter to the people of Harlem and that it should be passed on through the churches and through sound trucks on the streets"[46]—a feeble effort, considering the seriousness of the situation! Indeed, the scene the next morning was sobering:

When dawn broke about 5 A.M., the sun illuminated a ghastly scene of broken windows; ransacked stores; streets littered with broken glass, rubbish, and empty cartridges; crowds of sullen Negroes; and tired policemen, semimilitary in their helmets. Most startling were the gates which merchants had put across their windows the night before and which now snaked crazily across the sidewalks amid the litter on Lenox, 125th, Seventh, and Eighth....
Police Commissioner Murphy [gave a press conference in which he reported] the statistics for the night: 1 dead; 12 policemen and 19 civilians injured, 30 persons arrested, 22 business places looted.[47]

Sunday, July 19, through Monday, July 20

Cleanup began the next day, but the deeper problems defied cleansing. Police Commissioner Murphy's statement, calling for an end to "these disorders" and for restoring "order in our community," was distributed widely and read in the churches, which not only failed to mollify the churchgoers but made them angry at his "implied reproach."[48] That night things got wild again, and by early Monday morning, 27 police and 93 civilians were officially listed as injured (although hospitals reported treating more than 200), 45 stores had been damaged or looted, and 108 arrests had been made.[49]

At 9 a.m. on Monday, a small, subdued group assembled at the funeral home from which Powell's body was to be removed for burial, and there was no confrontation between them and the 100 police stationed there. During the day, city officials met with various civil rights groups whose principal demand was for a civilian review board, a demand the executive committee of Manhattan's Democratic Party supported unanimously, as did Republican Senator Jacob Javits, the Workers Defense League, and the Uptown Tenants Council, as well as 75 Negro ministers.[50] The afternoon remained calm, at least until after a planned march to the United Nations headquarters was to begin. But just before the sun went down, despite the appointment of a commission of inquiry and attempts by Harlem clergy to deflect anger, rioting began again, even though all of Harlem had been cordoned off to traffic, and special units of "Technical" police were sent in—to break up crowds and to take over the rooftops, from which residents were throwing loose bricks and even Molotov cocktails.

By 11 P.M., the sound of sirens was almost continuous as streams of squad cars raced from one reported incident to another, most of them false reports, and hollow-eyed, scowling firemen...raced from one fire alarm to another, most of them also false. About midnight, a Molotov cocktail crashed through the window of a pharmacy, touching off a fire....A joyful crowd gathered at the corner, cheering the fire and booing the firemen, who fingered their axes.[51]

By 1 a.m. things were beginning to calm down. But just as things seemed to be "under control" in Harlem, the police got a call for reinforcements in Bedford-Stuyvesant. During the next few days the action shifted to the Second Ghetto in Brooklyn.

Midnight Monday, July 20, through Tuesday Evening, July 21: The Action Moves to Bed-Stuy

The Brooklyn branch of CORE met Monday evening to plan how it could respond to Powell's shooting and show support for Harlem in the face of police brutality. After the meeting broke up after midnight, about 35 members, half of them white, marched around a four-block area, singing, and drawing in curious followers. "When the marchers . . . returned to Nostrand and Fulton, CORE took over the traditional northeast corner and began its rally." Although few of the speakers could be heard, about 1,000 persons had been attracted to the corner, and the number of policemen had risen from 6 to 20. Tensions were rising, with hostility directed especially toward the black policemen, targeted as "Uncle Toms."[52] Although the CORE speakers urged the police to withdraw and the crowd to disperse, neither retreated. "The first bottles came," and police reinforcements arrived and then "charged the crowds, nightsticks poised."[53]

For the rest of the night, the battle between police and growing crowds continued, windows were broken, and some looting occurred. By 7 a.m., things had quieted down. But CORE, in asking the crowd to disperse, had promised a rally for the next evening. Both CORE organizers and the police had work to do. And Mayor Robert Wagner, who had been en route to Geneva to attend a conference, had turned around and was coming home to "mind his store."[54] Perhaps trying to put the genie back in the lamp, CORE changed the rally's venue from Brooklyn in order to join a civil rights demonstration in Manhattan. That did not deter people from assembling at the appointed corner, where, according to Shapiro and Sullivan, "militant black nationalists" filled the vacuum.[55]

Tuesday Night, July 21, through Wednesday, July 22: The Worst Day

According to Shapiro and Sullivan, it was the militants who inflamed the mounting crowds that night, encouraging them to loot and trash the commercial streets. Despite the fact that, on advice from the police, the stores on Fulton, Nostrand, Bedford and Franklin had been boarded up by Wednesday morning, this did not seem to protect them.

All Wednesday, the worst day, officials were trying to head off the expected explosion. Abe Stark, the Brooklyn borough president, tried the usual New York strategy of "cooling out" anger by holding meetings with community leaders. But the mayor, newly returned from his European trip, announced that law and order would be maintained. Mayor Wagner gave a televised address in which, at the end, he said that more minority policemen should be recruited and that incidents of police brutality would be followed up. But this was too little, too late.

> With the approach of dusk [on Wednesday night], loungers had already begun to gather on Fulton, and if the mayor's speech had little effect in getting them off the street, neither did it seem to bring anyone onto the street.... So the crowds increased, and, as on the previous night, at least nine out of ten came not to riot or loot, but "for a look-see around."... Wednesday evening they had something new to gawk at.... The cavalry had arrived. A troop of mounted police had taken over the four corners of Nostrand and Fulton.... Police had been afraid to use horses in Harlem because of their vulnerability to the Molotov cocktail, *but the lower buildings and wider streets in Bedford-Stuyvesant reduced the danger from the rooftops.*[56]

A sound truck came through from the NAACP urging the people to "cool it," but instead of having the desired effect, it seemed to restart the riot. Some observers claimed that the trigger was organized by agitators in green berets, green sunglasses, and walkie-talkies, who, according to the NAACP spokesperson, started to rock the NAACP station wagon. The police intervened massively.

> Knots of the crowd shot out in every direction into the darkness ... and after they had passed the distracted cops, the windows started to go again.... Men and women filled their arms and scuttled into the side streets.... Garbage cans lined Fulton Street, as they had the night before, and with the first wave of surging men and women this waiting ammunition was swept up.... Many cans were aimed at police, on foot, on horses, and in cars.... The trouble worked its way over to Bedford Avenue [from Nostrand] and then toward Franklin.... Officers dropped to one knee to fire in the air, and the tide of runners split.... Negroes were beaten, some brutally, in Bedford Stuyvesant that night.[57]

But Shapiro claims the police behaved with great restraint under intolerable provocation. Nor were the police the only targets. "Attacked with them were the NAACP leaders, the press, or anyone foolhardy enough to suggest withdrawal.... This was the mob's day,"[58] with massive and widespread looting of clothing stores, groceries, check-cashing facilities, and liquor stores.[59] It started to rain shortly after midnight, which ended Wednesday night's rioting. The riot was completely over by Thursday night in Brooklyn, although in Harlem it continued sporadically for a few more days.[60]

In Bed-Stuy, the three-day "box score" reported by the police was 18 injured (but they counted only policemen), 302 arrests, and 405 broken windows.[61] The combined costs of the Harlem and Brooklyn riots were 465 riot-connected arrests, a million and a half dollars of extra police expenses, and some two and a half million dollars of damage suits filed against the city.[62]

The Limitations of Coverage and Analysis

I have accepted the "play-by-play" account by these two white news reporters as the best available, given the absence of any more reliable counter-evidence. Interestingly enough, the Kerner Report barely mentions the 1964 New York riot and, in contrast to the city's response to earlier times of troubles, no committee of inquiry was appointed to report to the mayor. It is true that the journalists' account is confined to what they each observed and what they could reconstruct through unsystematic interviews with other reporters, but their book has face validity and an immediacy of recording vivid moments that cannot be duplicated at this time. Despite its incompleteness, it is the best we have.

Perhaps it is less important to verify the exact sequence of events than to evaluate their analysis. And in this, Shapiro and Sullivan fall short. They facetiously suggest a recipe for the riots that were just beginning in cities throughout the nation: "Take one ghetto, add lack of opportunity for either physical or emotional escape, mix in an unsympathetic attitude on the part of society, and heat. Some time after dark, these elements will jell into a mass thick enough almost to be tangible. Then add a spark. It does not matter what the spark is."[63] This dismisses the deep sources of disaffection and the even deeper grievances that underlie it. And their answer to the question of what stops a riot is equally superficial: "Three days and nothing less. It is like a disease, apparently, that takes three days to check."[64]

Shapiro does advance an interesting "theory" that links the short-lived and scattered rioting in New York, in comparison with "deeper" and longer riots elsewhere, to the lesser segregation in New York, where integration

> has progressed to the point where it is easier for a Negro leader to switch neighborhoods than fight. Most Bedford-Stuyvesant leaders live in integrated Crown Heights. Most Harlem leaders pack up at the end of the

day and head for Queens or Westchester. It is worth noting that the house
provided by the Black Muslims for Malcolm X...is in Queens. But the
pluperfect example of absentee leadership is, of course, Representative Adam
Clayton Powell who rules Harlem while commuting between his home in
Puerto Rico and his office in Washington.[65]

This dismisses the commitment of black leaders to broader issues of social
justice.

Two Contrasting Explanations

Two contrasting views of the "causes" of race riots in the 1960s have been
advanced. The most easily dismissed is the one set forth in Edward Banfield's
chapter entitled "Rioting for Fun and Profit,"[66] which has been the object of bitter
scorn on the part of more progressive thinkers. In it, Banfield made a supreme
effort to avoid the obvious: that a smoldering resentment of racial inequality in
economic opportunities, political power, and police treatment, underlay the
protest riots of the 1960s. He does this by an ingenious "classification" of four
"ideal types" of riots:

1. The "rampage" ("an outbreak of animal—usually young, male animal—spirits...in search of excitement").[67]
2. The "foray for pillage" ("the motive is theft...[with] boys and young adults...the principal offenders").[68]
3. The "outburst of righteous indignation" (a leaderless, spontaneous response to "what they regard, rightly or wrongly, as injustice...that is likely to go unpunished").[69]
4. The "demonstration" (whose "motive is to advance a political principle or ideology...not a spontaneous, angry response...[but rather] the result of prearrangement by persons who are organized, have leaders, and who see it as a means to some end").[70]

While admitting that these are only analytical categories and that large riots
are "compounds of two or more types," Banfield is thus able to deflect attention
away from the generalized racial bases for the New York riots of 1964, the 1965
Watts riot, and subsequent ghetto uprisings, including the yet-to-be 1968 West
Side riot in Chicago. Instead, Banfield cites approvingly the head of the Federal
Bureau of Investigation (FBI), who claimed they were not "really" race riots;
Bayard Rustin, the conciliatory head of the NAACP, who blamed the violence on
"merely a few confused Negro boys"; and the police commissioner of New York,

who claimed that "they riot either out of sheer cussedness or for criminal reasons." Banfield cites the findings of an "elaborate survey of Negro opinions made late in 1964... [that] showed that most Negroes were neither sunk in hopelessness nor consumed with anger. Only about a third were in any sense militant, and the proportion of Negroes who were strongly antiwhite was much smaller."[71]

One might ask how many blacks needed to declare to an interviewer their anger or feelings of hopelessness before the causes of their discontent would be recognized as grounded in reality? Far more persuasive was the grounded research conducted by Kenneth Clark who then headed Harlem's official community organization, Harlem Youth Opportunities Unlimited (HARYOU). In 1964, the organization published a groundbreaking study of the area's social problems that included a discussion of the consequences of powerlessness, among which were not only crime but also riots.[72]

There was, however, little new in their enumeration of Harlem's social problems. It will be recalled that after the one-day Harlem riot in 1935, the Mayor's Commission Report concluded that high unemployment, overcrowded and fast deteriorating housing, poor health, and overcrowded and dilapidated schools were the basic causes of resentment. The report singled out endemic tension with the police, who "were overzealous in arresting black youth." In return, young blacks tended to view the police as "the boldest examples of northern racism.... Critics of the police compared large concentrations of patrolmen in black ghettos to 'an army of occupation' and complained of constant brutality."[73]

This final complaint was especially applicable in the riot of 1964. Not only had the *casus belli* been a police killing of a young student, but the massive, albeit delayed, deployment of police to Harlem was poorly planned and was executed with insufficient direction. Its aggressive behavior deviated from established procedures in responding to riots. With unclear or possibly reversed directions, the hastily assembled officers panicked and abandoned their standing orders to avoid using their guns, a factor that certainly exacerbated confrontations, feeding the fires of black anger and prolonging the hostilities.[74] To some extent, the absence of experienced political figures left the police commissioner, who presumably authorized the use of guns, without the guidance that these civilian political and community leaders might have provided. Michael Flamm considers the latter's absence a contributing factor:

> Mayor Robert Wagner Jr. was traveling in Majorca and Congressman Adam Clayton Powell Jr. was [vacationing] in Switzerland.... Governor Nelson

Rockefeller was...at a family property in Wyoming. Relaxing there as well was...NAACP President Roy Wilkins.[75]

Reading accounts of how the riot was mishandled, one could sense Fiorello La Guardia turning in his grave, especially in response to the condemnatory letter issued by the commissioner of police, a provocative insult that he had meticulously avoided in the earlier riots.

The 1964 riot had its initial cause in police brutality, and in the suspicion, later vindicated, that the offending officer would go unpunished. But it was clearly compounded by the unrestrained behavior of the police during the riot itself. This reinforced demands that police be held culpable for their misbehavior via increased civilian supervision. The long struggle to establish an effective Civilian Review Board was intensified after the 1964 riot, but major reforms were not instituted until two years later, only after Mayor Wagner, reluctant to battle police resistance, was replaced by John Lindsay, who supported this vital reform. However, even he had to compromise with shared authority.[76] He also had to cope with the issue of segregated schools, unsympathetic teachers, and offensive textbooks, although police brutality remained a constant thorn in the city's politics.

THE MINIFIRES NEXT TIME (POST-1964)

In the more than 40 years since the Harlem/Bedford-Stuyvesant uprising, New York has been free of large-scale outbursts of collective violence. In April 1968, when over 100 cities in the nation exploded in frustration and anger at the murder of Martin Luther King, Jr., the response in New York's ghettos was muted, "cooled out" by Mayor Lindsay's conciliatory tone and his restrictions on the police. The iconic image was of a sympathetic mayor, walking in shirt-sleeves through the "ghettos" to extend his condolences! And as was shown in chapter 3, the harshest criticism Mayor Daley received for his controversial "shoot to kill, shoot to maim" order came from Lindsay. But Mayor Lindsay had his own troubles in 1967–68 over the issue of community control of schools: the so-called Ocean Hill–Brownsville controversy.[77]

COMMUNITY CONTROL VERSUS THE TEACHERS' UNION

Following the Supreme Court ruling of 1954, the highly centralized New York Board of Education, the largest in the nation, undertook a number of ingenious steps to balance the goal of "neighborhood" schools with mandated desegregation. (Busing was not seen as an innovative solution in the mass transit city where students are issued free subway and bus passes to travel to their assigned schools.) The board redrew school district boundaries to include catchment areas from adjacent white and minority areas, facilitated the transfer of minority students from overcrowded, primarily "black" schools to nearby, underutilized "white" schools, and even established new, "desirable" schools, especially one in East Harlem at the river's edge, designed to attract black and white students from both sides of the river. But even in this last effort, white students refused to enroll. By 1967, the board began to explore a different "solution"—community control.

Ironically, the movement for community control was born in 1963 in then virtually all-white Jackson Heights, Queens, where residents, ostensibly seeking a decentralization of the school system and greater representation in decision-making, actually sought to preserve their schools' "whiteness."[78] Only later, after black leaders had given up all hope of school desegregation, was the ideology of community control adopted to advance educational reforms in matters of curriculum, personnel, and decentralized decision-making in black neighborhoods. Supported by business groups, liberal politicians (among them Lindsay),[79] and foundations (Ford, Carnegie, Rockefeller), as well as by the mainstream press, Black Power advocates, the more moderate Kenneth Clark, and "new left" academicians, a consensus was building. The city would experiment with demonstration projects in three neighborhoods (East Harlem, the Lower East Side, and in the Ocean Hill–Brownsville section of Brooklyn) to devise new forms of community control. The experiment was funded in part by the foundations, primarily Ford.

The only group left out of the consensual loop was the 57,000 public school teachers, by then represented by the United Federation of Teachers. The union was fairly new, having been organized only in 1960, after Mayor Wagner in 1958 recognized the right of municipal employees to unionize. The union sought "professionalization" (favored credentials and competitive test scores) and job security tied to seniority, and supported the right of teachers, after five years of service, to request transfers to "more desirable" districts. It counted on its bargaining partner, the highly centralized Board of Education, to enforce the terms of its hard-won gains.

To understand how this well-intentioned "reform" ultimately turned into "the strike that changed New York" (the title of Podair's award-winning book), one must examine the wider arena of ethnic alliances, class mobility, and race in New York City. Roger Waldinger's study of "ethnic niches" in the labor force of New York explores how the various white ethnic groups used jobs in the city's expanding public sector to advance their social mobility through a "stable ethnic division of labor." In this, "Jews took over professional and technical jobs, mostly in the school system, where the 35,000 or so Jewish public educators 'set the tone.'"[80] Jews, who (according to the estimates of Glazer and Moynihan in *Beyond the Melting Pot*) constituted only about one-quarter of the city's population, were drawn to higher education and—often the first generation to attend college—were drawn to teaching. Although Podair gives no estimate of the percentage of teachers in the New York system who were Jewish, he contends that they dominated this "niche" in the complex ethnic mosaic of the city.

> There were . . . reasons for the large number of Jews in the city educational system. Excluded from many areas of the private sector, and attracted by the objective nature of the examinations and the job security offered by civil service employment, Jews had gravitated toward the New York public schools since the 1930s. . . . Jews had established an informal network that operated to draw co-religionists into the system, providing information on vacancies, job contacts, and test preparation assistance. . . . By the 1960s, in New York, it was almost an instinctive reaction for a Jewish college graduate, especially a graduate of the city colleges, to consider teaching in the city's schools as a career option.[81]

But by the 1960s, fewer than 50 percent of the students enrolled in New York's public schools were white; almost a third were black; and the rest were presumably "Hispanic" (largely Puerto Rican) or Asian. In contrast, blacks constituted only 8 percent of the teachers and less than 3 percent of the supervisors in the school system. This discrepancy was particularly evident in Ocean Hill–Brownsville, an extension of the Bedford-Stuyvesant "ghetto" that had previously been an area of Jewish residence.[82]

The crisis began when "the Governing Board of the Ocean Hill–Brownsville Demonstration School District" terminated the employment of 19 white teachers in the district schools; the letter of termination specified that the teachers should report to the head office for reassignment.[83] After unsuccessful negotiations, the United Federation of Teachers called a series of strikes that closed city schools for some 58 days and led to a polarization between blacks and their former allies, the generally progressive Jewish community.

A number of studies have been written on this controversy,[84] and for our purposes, there is no need to go more deeply into it. Suffice it to say that the union sought legal remedies in the courts, which found in their favor and ordered the school to reinstate the fired teachers. This decision was ignored by the local district board, and the union called a strike to begin in September when schools were scheduled to open. The first strike lasted for only two days before negotiations resumed. When these failed, teachers again went on strike, this time for two weeks in late September. Shortly thereafter, when union efforts again failed to gain the reinstatement of the teachers, the third and most prolonged city-wide strike began. When it was over, about five weeks later, the ethnic/ religious and racial political alliances in the city had been reconfigured, at least according to Podair's analysis.

> The strike divided the city in two important respects. First, by pulling blacks and Jews apart, and bringing Jews and white Catholics together, it reconfig-ured New York's social landscape in sharp, defining shades of black and white. Second, it brought long-simmering class resentments to the surface, arraying poor blacks and corporate, government, media and intellectual elites against the teachers and their allies in the city's white middle-class population.[85]

With so much substantive, goal-directed conflict at stake, it is understand-able why the reaction to the murder of Martin Luther King, Jr. in April 1968 was muted. The 1965 assassination of Malcolm X had affected the community more strongly than had that of King. And even when numerous cities were reacting to the clearing of the four white policemen who had been videotaped savagely beating Rodney King in Los Angeles in 1992, New York's demonstration was confined to an orderly interracial march from Madison Square Garden to Tomp-kins Square Park, which did not turn violent until it merged, in Greenwich Village, with a different protest coming from the park. New York has a tendency to focus, perhaps like a solipsist, on its own issues rather than to respond reflexively to actions elsewhere.

EPILOGUE

This is not to say that the city has been untroubled by racially charged violence, or that the relations between the black communities and the police have been peaceful. Rather, as I shall contend, New York's racial tensions explode periodi-cally, but protests have tended to be spatially contained. There have been a few more noteworthy "triggers," provocative events that transform the low-grade fever into a cumulatively angry black response. These have been treated by the political and legal apparatuses with extreme, albeit ambiguous, caution, as if to defuse growing cleavages and placate growing black militancy.

Some of these isolated incidents have resembled earlier white attacks on blacks who ventured into the "wrong" space. Among these was the chase, beating, and finally murder in Howard Beach (Queens) in December 1986 of one of four black teenagers who transgressed the territorial boundaries of informal segregation. Three of the four white youths involved were convicted of manslaughter—a neat compromise. Even more upsetting was an attack on four African American youths who ventured into Bensonhurst (south Brooklyn) in August 1989 in search of an advertised secondhand car. They were set upon by a gang of some 30–40 mostly Italian-American youths wielding baseball bats. The incident ended in the shooting death of 16-year-old Yusuf Hawkins.

Less frequent but more serious have been localized neighborhood disputes between rival groups. The most noteworthy example was the intercommunal battle in August 1991 between Hasidic Jews and Jamaicans—two normally noninteracting ethnic/racial groups that share physical but not social space in Crown Heights (Brooklyn).[86] The riot was precipitated by the death of a seven-year-old Jamaican boy who was run over by the speeding limousine of a Hasidic rabbi. When the first ambulance to arrive on the scene, one sponsored by the Jewish community, ignored the seriously injured boy to attend to the shaken up driver and passenger, the Jamaicans blamed the boy's subsequent death on this breach of medical ethics.

In the course of the three-day hostilities between the Jamaican and Jewish communities, a visiting Australian yeshiva student was stabbed to death. A 20-year-old black, Lemrick Nelson, was arrested for the crime, which he initially denied committing. In an unusual sequence of events, Nelson was tried three times. The first time, he was acquitted of the murder charge in a state court; the second time, in March 1998, he was sentenced in a federal court to the maximum of nine and a half years for "violating the civil rights" of the stabbed man; and finally, at his third trial in May 2003, this judgment was confirmed. Although only in the third trial, again for "violating the civil rights" of his victim, did he admit to the stabbing, no further sentencing could be imposed, since he had almost completed his initial sentence. The stringing-out of this sequence probably prevented further escalation. But the major casualty had been Democratic mayor David Dinkins, New York's first and, thus far, last black mayor, who was tardy in responding and was viewed by Jews as partisan to blacks.[87]

Dinkins also drew fire for mishandling conflicts between blacks and Koreans over the boycotts and picketing of Korean greengrocers in Flushing, Queens, and Flatbush, Brooklyn. Claire Jean Kim suggests that there was a connection between the election of Dinkins and the decision of Black Power advocates to boycott a Korean-owned Red Apple grocery store in Flatbush over the subduing of a black customer by the Korean store manager and his staff.

Those who had voted for David Dinkins in the hope of greater racial harmony were quickly disappointed. Set off by an altercation between merchant Bong

Ok Jang and customer Ghiselaine Felissaint, the Red Apple Boycott began on January 18, 1990, just seventeen days after Dinkins was inaugurated.... Revolutionary nationalist activists and moderate Black officials [had] joined forces in the resurgent Black Power movement to oust Mayor Edward Koch, but they had never been more than temporary bedfellows. With the election over, the December 12th Movement went back to its regular grassroots work...through campaigns like the Red Apple Boycott.[88]

The boycott, resurrected from the earlier repertoire of community control actions developed as early as 1935, used without success in a similar 1988 boycott of another Korean-run grocery store in Bedford-Stuyvesant, and mobilizing arguments from the Ocean Hill controversy, proved successful this time. It was sustained for almost 16 months, and consolidated the "movement" by drawing in immigrant communities such as the Haitians and others from the Caribbean. This alliance outlasted the boycott itself and has withstood later tests in subsequent issues involving police brutality—which recently has concentrated unduly on immigrants of African and Afro-Caribbean origin.

This building of a more broadly based movement for greater black power is one of the defining characteristics of New York's racial divisions, increasingly dependent on the diversity of the city's "black" population. Haitians, Hispanics from the Caribbean, and even African immigrants have forged a common cause in their Afro-American identities. In this, New York City differs dramatically from Chicago and Los Angeles. Al Sharpton recognized this. Dinkins, who was unsupportive of the boycotts, did not. For a variety of reasons, including his handling of the Crown Heights riot and the boycott movement against Korean shopkeepers, Dinkins failed in his reelection bid and was replaced by Republican Rudolph Giuliani, whose main platform plank was "law and order."[89] Critics contend that this gave license for stepped-up police brutality, especially by the street crime division of the New York Police Department.

But the rules of the game were changing, as large damages were collected from the city in several cases of false arrest and torture. Of these, the most notorious was the bathroom mistreatment and resulting serious injury of Haitian immigrant Abner Louima (in Brooklyn) in August 1997, for which five policemen would stand trial in various courts on various charges. As in the case of Crown Heights, three trials at different levels of court, convictions on one grounds or another, and reversed convictions strung out the crisis, doling out hope to all parties that "justice would be done." Eventually, one officer was convicted and sentenced to 20 years and a second to 5 years for false testimony. And long before that, a civil suit against the city had awarded Louima some $8 million in damages.

The most disturbing incident, however, was the inexplicable close-range shooting in 1999 of Ahmadou Diallo (this time in the Bronx), an unarmed immigrant from Africa, who died from the 41 shots policemen directed at him as he reached in his pocket to extract his identity card. In this egregious case, the officers were completely exonerated and no damages were awarded. But, as in the earlier cases, this served to mobilize protests and to catapult Reverend Al Sharpton to a prominent political role, not only in Harlem and in the black community of New York, but even to national visibility and a tentative bid to run for president, as Jesse Jackson had considered doing 20 years before.

In all these instances and more, blacks accused the police of being disinterested in enforcing the law when the victims were black and the perpetrators white, of being less than zealous in prosecuting black-on-black crime, and/or of using excessive force, especially when the perpetrators were black and the victims white.

Were the police, in fact, "out of hand," and did the famous "blue line of silence" conceal police brutality? There is not space to go into the details of each case, but some of the conclusions of an Amnesty International report of June 1996 entitled "Police Brutality and Excessive Force in the New York City Police Department" indicate that these continue to plague police-community relations.

The report, while denying its ability to affirm whether or not brutality has actually increased, verified that the

> number of claims for police mistreatment against the City of New York... increased substantially... from 977 in 1987 to more than 2,000 in 1994 [and t]he amount paid out by the city in settlements or judgments awarded to plaintiffs in police abuse cases has also risen from one million [dollars] in 1992 to more than $24 million in 1994.... Of the ninety cases of alleged excessive use of force investigated by Amnesty International between the late 1980s and early 1996, the evidence suggests that the large majority of the [victims of] police abuses are racial minorities, particularly African-Americans and people of Latin American and Asian descent. Racial disparities appear to be especially marked in cases involving taking custody for questionable shootings.[90]

TACTICS OF COMMUNITY RESPONSE IN THE 1980S AND BEYOND

Instead of wide-scale protests in the form of riots, the repertoire of New York's black community has continued to be of four types: the electoral mobilization, the protest march, the mass meeting, and the boycott. The first led to the defeat of Mayor Ed Koch, perceived by many as racist, by Dinkins in the Democratic Party primary election of 1989, clearing the way for Dinkins's short-lived triumph. The second was manifested in the marches led by Al Sharpton into the hostile turf of Howard Beach and Bensonhurst. The third took the form of organized rallies in Harlem and even at City Hall, all of which were focused on specific agendas, such as unprovoked shootings; the most recent was to protest the death of Sean Bell in Queens on the eve of his wedding. The fourth was revived in boycotts, no longer directed against Jewish owners of stores in black neighborhoods (for they had long been displaced by other middlemen) but against other minorities who had replaced them, among them a few Korean greengrocers whose networks of supply and finance were not concentrated in ghettos but had secured this niche all over the city.[91]

These tactics have evidently sufficed to give minorities confidence that they can influence events in New York without recourse to riots. At least, this has been true as of early 2007.

NOTES

1. The census is enjoined from collecting information on religious identity, which means that this distribution can only be approximate. The percentage of New York City residents of Jewish belief/descent in 1960 was estimated as high as 25; the three largest "old ethnic" descent groups—Irish, Italian, and Polish—are overwhelmingly Catholic. The Protestant "minority" is almost equally split between whites and blacks. Despite some debatable value positions the authors take, the best book on New York's "ethnics" for this period remains Nathan Glazer and Daniel Moynihan, *Beyond the Melting Pot: The Negroes, Puerto Ricans, Jews, Italians and Irish of New York City* (Cambridge, Mass.: MIT Press, 1963). See pp. 8–10 for some breakdowns by religion and national origin in 1960.

2. It was not until later (in the 1970s and 1980s) that the "complexion" of the city underwent its most dramatic shift. By 1980, whites still constituted 61 percent of the city's population, a proportion that had dropped to some 52 percent by 1990. Within Manhattan, the percentage of the population classified as "white" decreased and then stabilized at 59 for 1980 and 1990. It was in Brooklyn and the Bronx that racial succession was the most dramatic during those decades. By 1980, Brooklyn's "white" proportion stood at 56 percent, but 10 years later this had dropped to 47 percent; in 1980, a minority (47 percent) of the Bronx's residents were "white," and by 1990, the comparable figure was only 36 percent.

3. Nor were these the first. As the authors of the Kerner Report recount, as early as 1963, "serious disorders...broke out in Birmingham, Savannah, Cambridge, Md., Chicago, and Philadelphia." By 1964, Jacksonville and St. Augustine, Florida, Cleveland, and Philadelphia, Mississippi, had been added to the list. In July, New York would join, as would several cities and towns in New Jersey. See Kerner Report, pp. 35–36.

4. The following account has been largely taken from Fred C. Shapiro and James Sullivan, *Race Riots: New York 1964* (New York: Crowell, 1964), chap. 6. But see also Harold X. Connolly, *A Ghetto Grows in Brooklyn* (New York: New York University Press, 1977), esp. chap. 3 on the early history of the area.

5. Shapiro and Sullivan, *Race Riots,* p. 108.

6. Ibid., p. 109.

7. For example, on Prairie Avenue south of Chicago's Loop.

8. Shapiro and Sullivan, *Race Riots,* p. 111. "The forties also saw the emergence of the area politically and socially. Although Harlemites might still slight Brooklyn Negroes by saying 'when a colored man can't afford to live in Harlem any longer, he moves to Bedford-Stuyvesant,' the truth was that prices in both areas by then were on a par, and a new social awareness was in the making in the minds of Bedford-Stuyvesant Negroes" (p. 112).

9. Ibid., pp. 107, 115.

10. "Memories of My Queens," *New York Times,* September 3, 1995, pp. 1, 10.

11. These are brilliantly traced in Tomás Almaguer and Moon-Kei Jung, "The Enduring Ambiguities of Race in the United States," in Janet Abu-Lughod, ed., *Sociology for the Twenty-First Century: Continuities and Cutting Edges* (Chicago: University of Chicago Press, 1999), pp. 213–39.

12. Points that are legitimately emphasized in Nathan Glazer and Daniel Moynihan, *Beyond the Melting Pot.*

13. A marvelous account of this complexity can be found in the life history of a descendant, she claims, of the "first black family" to settle in a Bronx neighborhood in the 1860s. See Judith Collins, *All Is Never Said: The Narrative of Odette Harper Hines* (Philadelphia: Temple University Press, 1995). Members within this large extended clan of southern-origin "mixed bloods" ranged in appearance from blue-eyed blonds (the paterfamilias, who bought his land and built his house on it, as well as an uncle who "passed," worked on Wall Street, and made secretly arranged visits "home"), to those who more resembled their African-born ancestor, freed early by her American Indian husband. This ambiguity of classification did not prevent the author (who became chief publicist for the NAACP and later a civil rights activist) from full identification with black causes, just as Walter White's fair skin, blue eyes, and blond hair did not bar him from succeeding James Weldon Johnson as executive secretary of the NAACP in 1931. Although "passing" and "light-skinned blacks" were also found in Chicago, it seemed less common there than in New York or Philadelphia.

14. Probably the best book on the early history of this group is still Virginia Sanchez Korrol, *From Colonia to Community: The History of Puerto Ricans in New York City, 1917–1948* (Westport, Conn.: Greenwood Press, 1983). See also her definitive compressed entry on Puerto Ricans in Kenneth Jackson, ed., *The Encyclopedia of New York City* (New Haven: Yale University Press, 1995), pp. 962–63.

15. There was also a concentration on the Lower East Side.

16. Glazer and Moynihan, *Beyond the Melting Pot,* pp. 92–93. They also include a quotation from a very early source: Lawrence R. Chenault, *The Puerto Rican Migrant in New York City* (New York: Columbia University Press, 1938): "The Puerto Rican, if white or slightly colored, deeply resents any classification which places him with the Negro...."

People... in Harlem report that... the darker the person from the West Indies is [and they include Puerto Rico with this group], *the more intense his desire to speak only Spanish, and to do so in a louder voice*" (pp. 150–51).

17. Not only were the categories ambiguous and subject to individual choice, but they have been extremely unstable over time. Some of that instability can be attributed to the Bureau of the Census itself, which has tried, in vain, to impose greater precision by altering the terminologies and cross-classifications over time. But most has come from the refusal of Hispanics to accept American definitions of racial categories.

18. Christopher Mele, "Neighborhood 'Burn-Out': Puerto Ricans at the End of the Queue," in Janet Abu-Lughod et al., *From Urban Village to East Village* (Oxford: Blackwell, 1994), p. 132. Mele cites Clara Rodrigez, *The Ethnic Queue in the United States: The Case of the Puerto Ricans* (San Francisco: R and E Associates, 1974), p. 121.

19. An excellent collection of studies of East Harlem over time, and therefore of the changing situation of Puerto Ricans concentrated there, is Judith Freidenberg, ed., *The Anthropology of Lower Income Urban Enclaves: The Case of East Harlem* (New York: New York Academy of Sciences, 1995).

20. Thomas Kessner, *Fiorello H. La Guardia and the Making of Modern New York* (New York: Penguin, 1978), p. 134.

21. This contrasts markedly with the situation in Chicago, described in chap. 3 above.

22. New York City Housing Authority, *Project Data: January 1, 1989*. The total number of residents is considered definitely an undercount, because of an acknowledged but unknown number of illegal subfamilies doubled up in legally resident households.

23. One is tempted to think of an ironic parallel with Marx's observation that one unintended consequence of the increasing scale of capital and the concentration of workers in large factories was a rise in workers' class consciousness. Could the amassing of large numbers of poor people in larger and more amorphous housing projects have contributed to the discontent and mobilization of the 1960s?

24. See Truman Nelson, *The Torture of Mothers,* with notes provided by Junius Griffin (New York: Garnisson Press, 1965). There is no reason to doubt the testimony of Stafford, but Baker's account should probably be dismissed. Junius Griffin was a well-respected reporter for the *New York Times* and one of the few African Americans employed by that paper. His notes appear on pp. 103–21. Griffin later observed and reported on the Harlem/Bed-Stuyvesant riots as well.

25. Ibid., p. 2.

26. Ibid., pp. 3–4.

27. Stafford's verbatim testimony is reproduced in ibid., pp. 4–8.

28. Baker's testimony appears in ibid., pp. 9 et seq.

29. Junius Griffin, notes, in ibid., pp. 103–4.

30. According to Griffin's notes, Wallace Baker was one of three Blood Brothers and three other youths who were later indicted for the murder of a white proprietor of a used clothing store on 125th Street in Harlem. Ibid., p. 107.

31. In the section that follows, I depend heavily on Shapiro and Sullivan, *Race Riots,* and on the "Text of Report by District Attorney of New York County," reproduced in ibid., pp. 209–22, as an appendix. The report by the district attorney summarizes the findings

of the grand jury investigation of the events that found Lieutenant Gilligan "not criminally liable for the killing of young Powell" (210).

Unfortunately, I have found no other book-length study of this riot. Only one article has come to my attention. Historian Michael Flamm, who is writing a book on the 1964 riot, referred me to the only essay he has published thus far: Michael W. Flamm, "New York's Night of Birmingham Horror: The NYPD, the Harlem Riot of 1964, and the Politics of Law and Order," in Richard Bessel and Clive Emsley, eds., *Patterns of Provocation: Police and Public Disorder* (New York: Berghahn Books, 2000), pp. 81–98. Marilynn Johnson devotes only four paragraphs (pp. 234–36) of her book *Street Justice: A History of Police Violence in New York City* (Boston: Beacon Press, 2003) to this important case. Most of her chap. 7, "Storming the Barricades: The 1960's," is devoted to mobilizations to alter the composition of and strengthen the authority of a civilian board to review police behavior and to the student antiwar rebellion at Columbia University.

32. See Shapiro and Sullivan, *Race Riots*, pp. 1–7.

33. Ibid., p. 3.

34. Ibid., p. 6.

35. Ibid., p. 7.

36. Ibid., pp. 1–2. Here I disagree somewhat with the role the riot played in touching off successive racial struggles. The causes were deep and pervasive—the frustrated dreams of the civil rights movement, coupled with the beginnings of economic weakness.

37. Ibid., pp. 12–13.

38. "There is a definite correlation between heat and Negro Riots. If that day had been a cool one, there very likely would have been no riot. But it was a sizzler." Ibid., p. 43. This is certainly a suspect theory, even though revolutions and uprisings of all kinds, including the American Revolution, have been more likely to occur in hot weather!

39. Quoted in ibid., p. 61.

40. Ibid., pp. 43–46; quotation from p. 46.

41. Ibid., pp. 46–47.

42. Ibid., p. 49.

43. Space matters! One can read similar descriptions as far back as the 1863 draft riots.

44. Shapiro and Sullivan, *Race Riots*, pp. 51–52. The gunfire could be traced only to the police, since the authors later state that the crowds had neither guns nor knives. Flamm, "New York's Night," tells us that police firings were so excessive that they needed several supplies of additional munitions.

45. Shapiro and Sullivan, p. 53.

46. Ibid., p. 61.

47. Ibid., p. 62. These statistics, except with respect to police casualties, proved to be wild undercounts.

48. This letter, with its condescending tone and implied condemnation, was widely distributed before the mayor could return from abroad. It simply served to further inflame tempers. Ibid., p. 65.

49. Ibid., p. 83.

50. Ibid., pp. 85–86.

51. Ibid., p. 97, as observed by Sullivan.

52. Ibid., pp. 128–29.

53. Ibid., p. 130.

54. Ibid., p. 136. The parallels with the Watts riot a year later were striking, with mayor, governor, and police chief all absent from their posts, underestimating the danger of the situation. See chapter 6.

55. Shapiro and Sullivan, *Race Riots,* pp 137–38.

56. Ibid., p. 159; italics added.

57. Ibid., pp. 162–5; quotation is from pp. 164–65.

58. Ibid., p. 167.

59. Ibid., pp. 168–69.

60. Ibid., pp. 173, 182.

61. Ibid., p. 199.

62. Ibid., pp. 205–6. Omitted from this list was the black civilian who died from a police bullet.

63. Ibid., p. 192.

64. Ibid., p. 193.

65. Ibid., p. 196.

66. In *The Unheavenly City: The Nature and Future of Our Urban Crisis* (Boston: Little, Brown, 1968), pp. 185–209. In today's catch phrase, Banfield would be called a "neocon."

67. Ibid., p.187.

68. Ibid., p. 189.

69. Ibid., p. 190.

70. Ibid., p. 191.

71. Ibid., p. 194. Here Banfield cites Gary Marx, *Protest and Prejudice* (New York: Harper and Row, 1967), p. 300, note 25, which refers to a summary of the survey findings that appeared in a special issue of *Fortune Magazine,* December 1967. I believe that the 1964 survey being referred to may be William Brink and Louis Harris, *The Negro Revolution in America* (New York: Simon and Schuster, 1964).

72. See Harlem Youth Opportunities Unlimited (HARYOU), *Youth in the Ghetto: A Study of the Consequences of Powerlessness and a Blueprint for Change* (New York: HARYOU, 1964).

73. Dominic Capeci, Jr., *The Harlem Riot of 1943* (Philadelphia: Temple University Press, 1977), pp. 38–41; final quotation is from p. 41.

74. Flamm, "New York's Night," claims that Police Commissioner Murphy personally gave his approval for the police to use their guns, an unprecedented directive for the New York Police Department, which in both the 1935 and 1943 riots had ordered officers not to draw their guns unless they were in immediate danger.

75. Ibid.

76. See Johnson's *Street Justice* for the complex history of these still ongoing struggles to gain absolute civilian control over the police.

77. The best book on this controversy is Jerald Podair, *The Strike That Changed New York* (New Haven: Yale University Press, 2002).

78. Parents and Taxpayers (PAT) was organized in Jackson Heights, Queens, and ironically, by 1966, served as a model for its opponents, the civil rights movement, "to launch

the campaign for community control of schools in black neighborhoods that climaxed at Ocean Hill–Brownsville." See Podair, *The Strike That Changed New York*, pp. 26–30.

79. Aristocratic mayor John Lindsay had been vice chairman of the National Advisory Committee that produced the Kerner Report, and was "responsible for its best known passage: 'Our nation is moving toward two societies, one black, one white—separate and unequal.' " Ibid., p. 36.

80. See Roger Waldinger, *Still the Promised City? African-Americans and New Immigrants in Postindustrial New York* (Cambridge, Mass.: Harvard University Press, 1996), esp. p. 217.

81. Podair, *The Strike That Changed New York*, pp. 155–56.

82. Ibid., p. 155. I have taken these estimates from Podair, but they should be used with caution. See my note above regarding the ambiguity of Puerto Rican reporting on race, especially before the census changed its categories. It is significant that of the three demonstration experimental neighborhoods, the Lower East Side and East Harlem contained significant numbers of Puerto Rican students. Only Ocean Hill–Brownsville was predominantly black. It may not be surprising, then, that the conflicts between Jewish teachers and black residents reached a crisis stage only in the latter.

83. Podair reproduces the letter, ibid., p. 2.

84. See, among others, Derek Edgell, *The Movement for Community Control of New York City's Schools, 1966–1970: Class Wars* (Lewiston, N.Y.: Edwin Mellen Press, 1998); the works of Marilyn Gittel, who was involved in the Ford-funded study, including her *Local Control in Education: Three Demonstration School Districts in New York* (New York: Praeger, 1972); and her collection edited with Maurice Beube, *Confrontation at Ocean Hill–Brownsville* (New York: Praeger, 1969). See also Jane Anna Gordon, *Why They Couldn't Wait: A Critique of the Black-Jewish Conflict over Community Control in Ocean Hill–Brownsville, 1967–1971* (New York: Routledge, 2001). See also Claire Jean Kim, *Bitter Fruit: The Politics of Black-Korean Conflict in New York City* (New Haven: Yale University Press, 2000). She is far more sympathetic to the genuine dedication of black activists, including militants, to achieving better education in black schools than is Podair, but both conclude that the experiment failed because its foundation and political backers really never intended for the school districts to exercise "real" autonomy and power.

85. Podair, *The Strike That Changed New York*, p. 123.

86. The two communities had coexisted uneasily only because the Hasidim preferred isolation and kept their children in religious, not public, schools.

87. Dinkins had won the mayoralty race against Rudolph Giuliani in 1989 by the narrowest margin ever. The election returns of that year confirmed the racial/ethnic polarization that had begun in the Ocean Hill–Brownsville controversy. Dinkins's plurality was achieved by overwhelming support from black voters (9 out of 10) and strong support from other minorities (about 3 out of 4), whereas Giuliani attracted significant support (75 percent) from outer-borough Jews and Catholics. Kim, "Cracks in the Gorgeous Mosaic," p. 180, table 2.6.

88. See Kim, *Bitter Fruit*, chap. 4. I consulted the earlier version of this book, her dissertation "Cracks in the Gorgeous Mosaic: Black-Korean Conflict and Racial

Mobilization in New York City" (Ph.D. diss., Yale University, 1996). See pp. 109–55 in this source; quotation from pp. 109–10.

89. Liberals, blacks, and Jews were often distressed by Giuliani's defense of police brutality, although his reputation was somewhat redeemed by his response to the September 11, 2001, crisis at the World Trade Center.

90. Amnesty International, *Police Brutality and Excessive Force in the New York City Police Department* (New York: Amnesty International, June 1996), p. 1.

91. It should be noted that the tensions between blacks and Korean owners in New York differ drastically from those that erupted in South Central Los Angeles in 1992, because of the diffuse distribution of Korean shops in New York, as contrasted with the concentration of Korean liquor stores in South Central.

Part III

Los Angeles's Futile Uprisings

6

The Watts Riot of 1965—the Beginning or the End?

The Watts riot was neither the beginning nor would it be the end of interracial violence in Los Angeles. Racial and ethnic tensions have churned beneath the surface in multiracial Los Angeles ever since the city was founded; on more than one occasion, these have erupted into pitched battles. If the first "white settler" on the site that was to become Chicago was a "black man," so the first 44 "Spanish settlers" of the small colony established in 1781 in the area they named Los Angeles were, with only a few exceptions, Indian, black, mulatto, and mestizo.[1] In the ensuing 50 years, a small number of "whites," mostly adventurous shippers from New England, joined to participate in, and indeed to control, the export of hides and tallow. But it was not until the Gold Rush of the 1840s, when demand for southern California's meat stimulated cattle ranching, that some of Los Angeles's most famous citizens—both Mexican and Anglo—arrived.

Gold intensified the American ambition to conquer California. By 1846, the United States had declared war on Mexico, which had been "liberated" from Spain only some two dozen years earlier. By 1847, American forces were in control of Los Angeles; their occupation was "regularized" by the peace treaty of 1849. But for a long time the composition of the population changed little. "Anglos" remained a distinct minority. The census of 1850 counted only 300 residents of "American ancestry" in the city of Los Angeles, with men outnumbering women three to one.[2]

> For three decades after 1849, while thousands of Americans were invading Northern California, taking possession of the land and establishing their institutions, Southern California remained virtually unchanged. Spanish continued to be used as the language of instruction in most communities throughout the sixties and seventies. Twenty years after the discovery of gold, Los Angeles was still a small Mexican town in which Spanish was spoken almost universally.... [I]t was not until the great influx [of the 1880s] that the Spanish influence began to decline.[3]

The absence of a preponderance of "Anglos" did not mean that "peaceful coexistence" reigned among the various ethnic and racial groups that constituted Los Angeles's diverse population. Los Angeles's "first racial riot took place [in 1871] on *Calle de los Negros*, but its victims were Chinese instead of Negroes."[4] Chinese indentured laborers had initially been brought to California by the builders of the Central Pacific railroad, and their willingness to work for slave wages was resented by whites. Similar persecution of the Mexican population occurred. Despite the existence of a Mexican gentry,[5] most were subject to police brutality, racial profiling, and higher arrest rates, especially after their labor on the railroads was eventually substituted for that of the Chinese. During the Great Depression of the 1930s, Mexicans drew the harshest punitive measures—many, including their American-born offspring, were placed on trains and forcibly repatriated.[6] The indiscriminate attacks on Mexican and black youths by white sailors in 1943 continued until they were put down by the military police and sailors confined to base. But none of these earlier "race riots" paralleled the one in Watts in 1965, which is more accurately described as a "ghetto revolt."

Prior to that time, hostilities were largely directed by whites (Anglos)[7] toward "minorities," that is, they were "race riots" in the original sense of that term. But immediately we are caught in the vise of racial misconceptions and ambiguities. Is the term "minority" a statistically meaningful demographic term? In the case of Los Angeles, no. It is an invidious category of lesser power, of unequal rights, of social and economic inferiority. From the start, California, and especially Los Angeles, presented paradoxes and anomalies that immediately confound conventional categories. The racial-ethnic composition of the city's population now appears to have run full cycle: the demographic minority (i.e. "Anglos") of the 1850s became the majority through the first half of the twentieth century, but since then has slipped back to minority status. And the much-touted "multiculturalism" of today's ethnic composition simply restores an original mix of Asians, Latinos, blacks, and mulattos with the latecomers (Euro-Caucasians) who, for less than a hundred years, constituted the majority.[8]

Given this distinctive history, it should not be surprising that during modern times Los Angeles's experience has been characterized by intercommunal violence. The same area of Los Angeles has been the site of two major and violent ghetto/minority revolts less than 30 years apart. The first riot erupted in 1965 in Watts, which was by then a largely "black" town near South Central Los Angeles, but it spread rapidly to adjacent areas.[9] It is acknowledged to have been the worst in the series of riots that broke out in more than 100 cities in the latter 1960s, easily as severe as the 1943 Detroit riot. It lasted for seven days, resulted in 34 deaths and over a thousand injuries. The second erupted in 1992 in South Central, just west of Watts. By the time of the second event, the district contained equal numbers of blacks and Latinos, as well as a small minority of Asians.

In many ways, the "riots" were quite similar to one another. Both erupted roughly within the same area in which deprived minorities were concentrated. The rioters engaged in arson and looting, as well as battles with motorists, firemen, and the police. The anger of the participants was especially directed toward businesses that were viewed as run by exploitative outsiders (Jews in 1965, Koreans in 1992). And the participants entertained the illusion that by revolting so visibly, they would draw attention to their needs and attract assistance; in both instances, they were to be disappointed. The differences, however, are also significant. In 1965, many of Watts's African American residents were relatively recent newcomers to the city. In the 1992 uprising in South Central, African Americans were the "old-timers"; the newcomers were chiefly immigrants from Central America. Since the 1992 uprising will be treated in chapter 7, I reserve systematic discussion of the comparisons to that chapter.[10]

THE HISTORICAL DEVELOPMENT OF WATTS

Although Watts now suffers from very poor mass transit access to downtown, it owed its initial growth to the railroads that were constructed before the turn of the century, when Mexican workers who built the Santa Fe and Southern Pacific railroads settled in the vicinity. It received a major boost at the beginning of the twentieth century when its location was selected as the intersection point of two

major rail lines of Huntington's Pacific Electric Lines; a railroad station was constructed, and the Mexican town was renamed Watts, after its major land owner.

With the building of the railroads came the settling of Mexican laborers,
most of them employed by Pacific Electric. Since transportation was close at hand
and land cheap, many of the Mexicans settled in Watts, which had been
incorporated as an independent city in 1907. About the same time, and probably
for the same reasons, a small settlement of Negroes grew up in a portion of Watts
called Mudtown.[11] Incorporated into the city limits of Los Angeles in 1926, the
district provided inexpensive housing that was still conveniently located and was
hospitable to an influx of African American migrants. Until World War II,
however, residents of the area were "about evenly divided among Negroes,
Mexican Americans, and other Caucasians."[12] It was the expanded demand for
labor in the nearby industrial district along the tracks and in the port area at
which the tracks ended that led to an influx of African Americans during and
after the war.

Between 1940 and 1965, the African American population of Los Angeles
County increased from some 75,000 to 650,000. This larger population became
increasingly concentrated in the only two areas open to it in a highly segregated
city: an already degraded Watts, and the older and somewhat better South
Central Avenue district to its west. Many of the poorest newcomers congregated
in Watts.

> Watts and the entire South Central area became the port-of-entry for this
> new multi-problem population, partly because of low-cost public housing in
> the area and partly because deed restrictions and social and job discrimina-
> tion made it difficult for Negroes to settle in other sections.... As Negroes
> moved in, there was a steady exodus of the white population...and the
> Mexican-Americans gradually resettled in...principally East Los Angeles.
> This trend continued through the two decades following World War II.
> Between 1940 and 1960 there was an eightfold increase in the Negro popula-
> tion of Watts. By 1965, the community had become a full-fledged Negro
> ghetto, with Negroes comprising 87 per cent of the total.[13]

By the later year, however, Watts had lost two of its locational advantages—
its proximity to industrial jobs and its convenient transportation access to
downtown. After the war, black workers were dismissed, and many of the nearby
industrial plants closed, as factories moved farther out to zones that were
reachable by car but not mass transit. By the early 1950s, the elevated north-
south Harbor Freeway was constructed, replacing the street-level rail lines and
forming a barely permeable barrier between a much-deteriorated Watts to the

east and the somewhat better-off areas to the west, including South Central proper. By 1961, the existing mass transit system of Los Angeles had "died" (or rather, had been consciously "killed"), supplanted by limited-access freeways that bypassed Watts. By then, Watts's population had become overwhelmingly African American, increasingly poor, and more marginalized from employment opportunities. By the time the riot broke out in 1965, the population of Watts was suffering from high rates of unemployment, dependency, and poverty. And as had been the case in Harlem, most businesses in the area were run by owners who did not live in the community and who employed few of its residents. Many of these proprietors were Jewish, and they were particularly resented as exploitative.

In contrast, the core of "South Central," just west of the Harbor Freeway, had been the "High Harlem" of Los Angeles that reached its cultural peak in the 1920s. Home to a relatively prosperous, if small, black population whose status spanned a fairly wide range, it boasted hotels, an active jazz scene, and well-organized churches and community organizations. In 1913, the "Central Avenue" core area had been heralded by W. E. B. Du Bois as the most promising of any black community in the country. While it was segregated (and certainly tightly hemmed in by racial restrictive covenants, before these were declared unenforceable in 1948 in *Shelley v. Kraemer*), its population may have been contained, but it was not marginalized.

Despite the growth of the black population during the war, by 1950 African Americans still constituted only 5.5 percent of the city's population and less than that of the county's. This proportion was only half as high as what their representation would reach in 1970 at its peak, but they were by then the poorest community in the city.[14] As suburban construction opened new areas for whites in the postwar period, the defense line along Slauson Avenue collapsed;[15] and by 1960, the "three largest black neighborhoods—Central Avenue–Furlong Tract, Watts, and West Jefferson—had coalesced." Nelson and Clark described this enlarged "black belt"

> as a massive segregated area, stretching from the southern part of downtown Los Angeles southward more than a dozen miles, and reaching from three to seven miles westward.... As is to be expected in an area of *nearly forty square miles*, much variety is present in the main ghetto of south central Los Angeles, and even its older and meaner areas do not have the appearance of slums in the usual sense... no tenements, two-thirds of the dwellings are single family houses... and even the public housing development consists of one or two story stucco buildings. West of the freeway much of the area is distinctly middle class, and on its northwestern edge in the Baldwin Hills takes in some fine homes, often with swimming pools.[16]

Prescription for Rebellion

Single-family houses and swimming pools notwithstanding, conditions in large parts of this 40-square-mile tract were appalling. The fact is that poverty does not always show the same face in different settings, but, as housing critic Charles Abrams put it in 1950, there were already "rats among the palm trees" in Los Angeles. Abrams noted that slums were not confined only to these central areas but could also be found "hidden on the hills, along side roads, or behind store fronts. Shacks made out of old crates and little garages on back alleys house thousands of recent immigrants."[17]

Inadequacies in newly constructed areas were more than matched by deterioration in already built-up zones near the center. As had happened elsewhere in the postwar era, whole inner neighborhoods underwent population succession, as better-off whites left for the periphery where, aided and abetted by deed restrictions, minimum lot size zoning, and racially restrictive covenants (and more informal mechanisms, once the restrictive covenants were deemed unenforceable), they threw up barriers to "undesirables." Blacks (and some poorer whites with few options) remained largely in South Central and Watts, and the growing Mexican population inherited much of the inlying territory east of downtown, as Jews and Italians who had previously predominated there left for greener pastures.[18]

Segregation by race and ethnicity intensified between 1960 and 1970, as the careful analysis of Massey and Mullan demonstrates.[19] But by 1970, Latinos had begun to move into zones such as Watts/South Central that had formerly been almost exclusively black.[20] Segregation of poor minorities increased the probabilities that amenities, when they were expanded, would be invidiously distributed. Even Sam Bass Warner, an otherwise uncritical admirer of the city, reluctantly acknowledged, in a mild understatement, that at the time of his writing, segregation was already a problem.

> Like all American cities, the Los Angeles metropolis does not extend its amenities equally to all its residents but reinforces sharp differences governed by class and race. . . . Los Angeles is no better than most cities when it comes to racial discrimination, segregation, and disadvantages for its poor. The county population [in 1970] is 10.8 percent black, 13.5 percent of Spanish surname. *The isolation of blacks is almost as extreme as in Chicago. The Mexican Americans are less rigidly segregated . . . than the blacks, but nonetheless they are highly segregated.*[21]

Furthermore, in the 1960s land clearance for urban redevelopment and for freeways was cutting into the zones available for minority residence and, unlike

New York and even Chicago, which at least made efforts to replace some slum housing with subsidized public housing projects, Los Angeles had done virtually nothing to avail itself of federal aid in this area. Although the city housing authority did eventually construct some public housing for minorities (exclusively in black areas), at the time that Abrams was writing (1950), the County Board of Supervisors had just turned down an offer of $300,000 from the federal government for public housing. Abrams attributed this to pressure from California's powerful real estate lobby, which had also just engineered the defeat of state-aided housing in a state-wide referendum. In short, Abrams concluded that not only did Los Angeles not admit that it had slums, but real estate interests blocked public housing because they feared racial integration. They need not have feared this, since segregation was too hardy a disease to have been so easily eliminated by the small number of projects that were eventually built, virtually all of them except senior housing in already segregated districts.[22] Indeed, one of the grievances acknowledged by the McCone Report, submitted after the 1965 riot, was the passage of Proposition 14 by two-thirds of the voters in November 1964, a referendum that repealed the Rumford Fair Housing Act and thus foreclosed the possibility of reducing housing segregation.[23]

THE WATTS UPRISING OF 1965—THE END OR A BEGINNING?

The major riot in South Central (commonly but somewhat inaccurately referred to in all the literature as the Watts riot)[24] that erupted in Los Angeles on the evening of August 11, 1965, and raged relatively unchecked until it was finally extinguished, with the aid of the California National Guard six-plus days later, was, if not the most lethal (34 dead) to date, certainly one of the best documented ghetto uprisings of the 1960's. One would think, therefore, that the "facts" of the underlying causes, the precipitating event, the sequences in time and space, the number and characteristics of the participants involved, the accompanying attitudes and consequences, and so on would have been definitively established. To this day, however, they remain contested. Ambiguities have arisen not only from the selectivity of narratives but also from the ideological filters through which events were interpreted.

The official, and therefore "authoritative," version is laid out in the report of the Governor's Commission on the Los Angeles Riots, the so-called McCone Report, submitted to Governor Pat Brown on December 2, 1965. Although it is only 109 pages long, in large print and with wide margins, it claims to be based on records and testimonies that filled 18 volumes of transcripts! Like the equally brief report of the commission Mayor Daley appointed to investigate the 1968 Chicago riot, it seems naïvely straightforward, if too accepting of a "law and order" perspective that basically exonerates the police and the national guard and instead blames the riot on the irrational and lawless behavior of ghetto residents, for which it has been severely criticized.[25]

But unlike the 1968 Chicago case, which was never independently investigated, quite a different story, in great detail that is more credible and explanatory, is told by the distinguished historian Robert Conot in his bestselling and widely acclaimed *Rivers of Blood, Years of Darkness*. Although I found it frustrating that this book lacks scholarly footnotes, his thorough methodology cannot be faulted,[26] and his narrative is more nuanced and complete than the bald summary that appears in the McCone Report. Conot tells us that he was already familiar with the area of South Central "a considerable time before the riot, and, by exercising prudence, was able to move about the area even while the riot was still in progress, thus observing some of the happenings first hand." His major and voluminous sources, assembled between August 1965 and May 1966, eventually "filled an entire filling cabinet." He studied the four-volume (over 1,300 pages) documentation by the Los Angeles County district attorney's office of the first arrests that triggered the riot and of other subsequent arrests and their dispositions. He conducted interviews and discussions with nearly 1,000 persons, as well as obtaining some 500 "written accounts of occurrences, as well as personal opinions." He had access to all documents pertaining to the actions of the California National Guard during the riot, including 16 hours of taped interviews with officers and men who were on the scene. He gathered material from the Los Angeles Fire Department, had access to some documents from the Police Department, and in addition claims to have read the complete transcript— a formidable accomplishment—of the 18 volumes of testimony collected by the McCone Commission. He also interviewed members of the Frye family and therefore obtained their version of what happened. He came to conclusions quite different from those of the McCone Report.

THE RIOT SEQUENCE

Wednesday Evening, August 11

All accounts agree on placing the "trigger time" and the "triggering event" on Wednesday evening just inside the City of Los Angeles near the border of Watts. While it would be impossible to compare in all their aspects the events described laconically and self-servingly by the McCone Report and the fuller and more critical account of Conot, it is symptomatic of their different approaches that they immediately diverge in describing how the riot was first triggered.

We look first at the bland story told by the McCone Report. Its narrative begins with the arrest, at about 7 p.m. on August 11, 1965, of 21-year-old Marquette Frye, who was stopped at 116th and Avalon (near but not in Watts) by a white California highway patrolman on a motorcycle. When Frye failed, in the judgment of the officer, to walk a straight line, touch his nose, and pass one other sobriety test not specified, he was arrested at 7:05 for driving under the influence. At the time he was apprehended, his 22-year-old stepbrother Ronald, was a passenger in the car, which belonged to Marquette's mother,[27] who lived only two blocks away. Nevertheless, the patrolman (Lee Minikus) refused to let Ronald drive the car home and radioed his partner to get a car to take Marquette to jail and to order a tow truck to impound the car. It being a hot night, many residents were outside and therefore witnessed what happened next. Ronald ran to get his mother, and they returned to the scene by 7:15, just as the second patrolman and tow truck arrived. By then the "original group of 25 to 50 curious spectators had grown to 250 to 300 persons." Mrs. Frye scolded her son for drinking. "Marquette, who until then had been peaceful and cooperative, pushed her away and moved toward the crowd, cursing and shouting.... The patrolmen pursued Marquette and he resisted."[28] Police radioed for help. As the policemen struggled with the Frye brothers, Mrs. Frye "attacked" one of them, jumping on his back and ripping his shirt. In the meantime, the other officer, who claimed to have been aiming his night stick at Marquette's shoulder, hit him on the forehead, "inflicting a minor cut." By 7:23, all three Fryes had been arrested, and other highway patrolmen and even officers of the Los Angeles city police had arrived, even though the incident took place just south of the Los Angeles city limits. By then the crowd had grown to over 1,000. Tensions escalated.

Although the McCone Report absolves the police of wrongdoing (the "arrest of the Fryes was handled efficiently and expeditiously") and confirms that ordering a car for the prisoner and a tow truck for the vehicle was "in accordance with the practices of other law enforcement agencies," perhaps they should have used less expedition and more sense, especially given what followed. The three prisoners were already in the police car, which was ready to take off when someone spat at the police.[29] Instead of departing with their three prisoners in hand, the police stopped their withdrawal, and two entered the crowd and arrested a young woman whom they thought to be the offender.[30] The McCone report concluded that "although the wisdom of stopping the withdrawal to make these arrests has been questioned, the Commission finds no basis for criticizing the[ir] judgment" (even after it ignited a riot!). The police finally withdrew at 7:40, but by then, the "now irate mob" stoned their retreat. The young woman they arrested had been wearing a smock, and rumors flew that she was pregnant.

There were rumors about how the Fryes had been mistreated at the arrest scene. For the next four hours (from about 8:15 to midnight), "the mob stoned automobiles, pulled Caucasian motorists out of their cars and beat them, and menaced a police field command post which had been set up in the area." "[Until the] early morning hours, there were sporadic reports of unruly mobs, vandalism, and rock throwing. Twenty-nine persons were arrested."[31]

Contrast this with Conot's account: first, Marquette Frye, originally cooperative with the police, even playfully charming, had reason to panic when threatened with arrest. When he was age 13, his father, a cotton farmer and then a miner at a played-out mine in a tiny interracial town in Wyoming, had migrated to Los Angeles, along with his second wife, his stepson, Marquette, and several other children. "The children, who hardly knew what a policeman was, were picked up on their first day in the city... [when] they were spotted by a truant officer." Marquette's original naïveté, his alienation from both "ghetto culture" and, once he learned how to fit in, the competing forces of law and order, were certainly not designed to enhance his faith in the latter. Picked up several times as a juvenile for petty offenses (rifling a coin machine, shoplifting, and finally purse-snatching), he was remanded to the Los Angeles County Probation Department and sent to a forestry camp, where he was kept for two years, finally being released on parole at age 19.[32] After his release, his job history was sporadic, but "he had kept his nose clean" and had just "successfully completed his two years of probation."[33] (Conot editorializes that if Marquette bolted, it was obviously in panic.)

At 5 p.m., he had picked up his stepbrother Ronald in his mother's 1955 Buick and driven to a friend's house, where they all had three or four screwdrivers (vodka and orange juice). A few minutes before 7 p.m., "Marquette decided they'd better head home for dinner," but by then "he'd had just enough vodka to make him feel as if the world was a good place to live in after all." He was driving a bit erratically.[34] Officer Leo Minikus caught up with him and, only about one block from home, Marquette pulled over to the curb, parked legally behind another car, and approached the officer with a jaunty smile, hoping to "disarm the officer by his friendly manner." However, he was unable to produce his driver's license, which he claimed he had just lost. Smelling liquor on his breath, the officer administered three DWI tests (no breathalyzer), after which he began to write up a ticket. In the meantime, Minikus's partner arrived. Marquette, "talking with his hands, and using his whole body for emphasis, the way he always did when he became excited," pleaded to be let off without a ticket, to be allowed to walk the short distance to his home, and for Ronald to drive his mother's car home.[35] Throughout this time, Ronald, newly discharged from the air force and of a less mercurial temperament than Marquette, waited in the car. But when the tow truck prepared to hitch up the car, he got out to offer to drive the car home and showed the officer his driver's license. At that point, his stepmother, alerted to the trouble, arrived out of breath and identified the car as hers, asking the tow truck driver to stop. She showed Minikus her driver's license and car registration, and he agreed to let her take her car. And then things went terribly wrong. Mrs. Frye scolded her son for drinking and demanded the car keys.[36]

> "Momma, I'm not going to jail. I'm *not* drunk and I'm *not* going to jail.". . . As he spoke to his mother, his voice broke. He was almost crying. Spotting the officers [who were approaching], he started backing away, his feet shuffling, his arms waving. . . . All his old anger, the old frustration, welled up within Marquette. . . . What right did they have to treat him like this? [He screamed at the cops,] whipping his body about as if he were half boxer, half dancer. . . . [The growing crowd identified with Marquette and] began to close in. . . . What, a few minutes before, had seemed to be an entirely innocuous situation, was taking on an ugly tenor.[37]

Now the police were in panic, and the "fog of war" set in. The arresting officers made a hurried call for reinforcements. One retrieved his baton from his motorcycle and the other a shotgun from his car, and both began pushing people back and going after the by-now-defiant Marquette with the baton. It was then that Ronald rushed to protect his brother but was jabbed in his stomach. "As Ronald doubled over, he [was] jabbed again. Ronald rolled to the ground."[38] In the meantime, Marquette had been cut on his forehead by the baton and also jabbed in the stomach. "Marquette doubled over. Instantly, Minikus caught his head in a vise" and, "with the fight gone out of him, had no trouble leading him to the patrol car," where he was thrown across the front seat and handcuffed.

Mrs. Frye, "distraught at having seen both Ronald and Marquette struck down" and believing "the latter to be under further attack in the police car," rushed to his aid. A foot shorter than Minikus, she "sprawled awkwardly across his back," and "suddenly felt herself lifted up. Struggling, the back of Minikus's shirt bunched in her fist, she was torn away by Officer Fondville. Off balance, a strip of the ripped shirt in her hand, she stumbled onto the back of Officer Wilson. Both momentarily went to the ground." Officer Fondville then "forced her over the trunk of the car . . . forced her arms behind her, handcuffed her, and placed her in the rear seat of the [patrol car]." When Ronald demanded to know what his stepmother was being arrested for, he, too, was handcuffed and put in the car.[39]

Observing all this, the growing crowd began shouting at police oppression; more highway patrolmen and Los Angeles police were arriving, sirens blaring, which lured even more spectators to the scene. Among them was Joyce Ann Gaines, a sociology student at Compton Junior College, who had run out of a nearby beauty parlor, still wearing her protective smock.[40] When one of the retreating officers felt something on the back of his neck, he decided that it was saliva and decided that it had come from Gaines. Innocent, she struggled against being pulled out of the crowd, arrested, and put into another patrol car. Jimmy Ticey, a friend of Gaines's sister, tried to come to her aid, and was also arrested.[41]

Although the exact details in Conot's account may be disputed, they have the ring of authenticity, and are far more credible (given what we know about how violence escalates in crowds) than the terse account in the McCone report. As the Kerner Commission report explains:

> Almost invariably the incident that ignites disorder arises from police action. Harlem, Watts, Newark and Detroit—all the major outbursts of recent years—were precipitated by routine arrests of Negroes for minor offenses by white police. Thus, to many Negroes police have come to symbolize white power, white racism and white oppression. And the fact is that many police do reflect and express these white attitudes. The atmosphere of hostility and cynicism is reinforced by a widespread perception among Negroes of the existence of police brutality and corruption, and of a "double standard" of justice and protection—one for Negroes and one for whites.[42]

Conot's account, although rich in anecdotes culled from official testimony and from his own interviews, unfortunately fails to provide a synthetic temporal or spatial sequence of the actual events as they unfolded. A "bare-bones" and patently inadequate summary of the temporal sequence appears in the McCone Report, although it focuses primarily on the official attempts to defuse tensions and then, when that effort failed, to suppress the rebellion.[43]

Thursday, April 12: Attempts to Defuse Anger Fail

The McCone Report commends "the work of Negro leaders, social workers, probation officials, churchmen, teachers, and businessmen in their attempts to persuade the people to desist from their illegal activities, to stay in their houses and off the street, and to restore order."[44] A meeting was held at 2 p.m. in the auditorium at Athens Park, at the invitation of the Los Angeles County Human Relations Commission, that

> brought together every available representative of neighborhood groups and Negro leaders to discuss the problem. Members of the press, television, and

radio covered the meeting. Various elected officials participated and members of the Los Angeles Police Department, Sheriff's Office and District Attorney's Office were in attendance as observers.[45]

Despite the fact that Mrs. Frye, by then released, urged calm, feelings grew restive. "The tone and conduct of the meeting shifted ... from attempted persuasion with regard to the maintenance of law and order to a discussion of the grievances felt by the Negro." The meeting ended hastily after a young black man seized the microphone to announce that "the rioters would attack adjacent white areas that evening." Needless to say, it was his "incendiary" remarks that were carried on radio and TV.[46]

A very different account of how the meeting in Athens Park originated is given by Conot. John Buggs was the black executive director of the Los Angeles County Human Relations Commission, an organization set up in 1943 in the aftermath of the so-called zoot-suit riots. As soon as hostilities had begun the night before, he and one of his consultants visited the area and decided that something had to be done to prevent the spread of the rioting. It seemed even more serious than the variety of incidents that had manifested rising tensions between the police and the black community throughout 1964.[47] He tried to avert an escalation. By 10 a.m. on Thursday, Buggs had organized help.

> Probation and parole officers were instructed to call every person for whom they were responsible and warn them to stay off the streets. Welfare workers were asked to call everyone on state aid, and hint that the checks might be withheld unless the area remained calm. Ministers were contacted in the hope that they could influence their parishioners. The Group Guidance Section went out to meet with the kids.... Key people in CORE ... [and in other organizations] were similarly called on to help. Finally, to counteract the rumors that "It's on!" Buggs decided to try to form 56 teams of neighborhood people to go around and spread the word that "It's off!" To do this he began organizing a meeting at the clubhouse in Athens Park.[48]

This is the meeting that failed. Never put into operation were the imaginative schemes Buggs designed: to reassign black undercover policemen to the area, to use trusted gang leaders to cool out tempers, and even to organize a block dance on Avalon, the scene of the previous night's violence.[49]

From then on, violence escalated, but no one in the state or local government seemed to be in charge. Governor Pat Brown was out of the country visiting Greece. His lieutenant governor, Glenn Anderson, was in Santa Barbara. Mayor Sam Yorty was giving a speech in San Diego. And William Parker, longtime chief of police, had ignored the mounting tensions in order to keep a previously arranged speaking engagement. In the absence of any counter-orders, "the police decided to set up a perimeter around the center of trouble and keep all crowd activity within that area."[50]

It was not until 5 p.m. that afternoon that Police Chief Parker was back in his office. After learning that the Athens Park meeting had failed, he "called . . . the Adjutant General of the California National Guard in Sacramento, and told him that the Guard might be needed." In response, the general sent a colonel to Los Angeles as his liaison officer and "alerted the commanders of the 40th Armored Division . . . in Southern California to the possibility of being called." In addition, because the governor was out of the country, Parker tried to reach Anderson, the acting governor, by telephone, but evidently did not make contact until the evening, after Anderson had returned to his home in suburban Los Angeles. Although Parker reported that "there were as many as 8,000 rioters in the streets," he reassured Anderson at 1 a.m. that matters were "nearing control" and at 6:45 a.m. that "the situation was rather well in hand."[51] Needless to say, it was not.

Friday, August 13: Official Neglect on the Worst Day

By around 8 a.m., large crowds of angry residents had reformed near the arrest site and the nearby business district along 103rd Street in Watts, and it was reported that "riot activity was intensifying." Nevertheless, the major officials again took off, even though this was to prove the worst day and night of the riot. Anderson flew to Berkeley to attend an early meeting of the Finance Committee of the Board of Regents of the University of California and stayed on for the afternoon meeting of the full board. Yorty took a morning flight to San Francisco to deliver a planned speech at the classy Commonwealth Club. Both were gone by 10 a.m., when Chief Parker told Colonel Quick, General Hill's liaison, "It looks like we are going to have to call the troops. We will need a thousand men."[52]

The question was: Who was empowered to call them out in the absence of the governor? It took the better part of the day and many long-distance calls back and forth before the hot potato settled in Anderson's lap; he suggested that General Hill should begin to assemble some nearby troops. It was not until 5 p.m. that the lieutenant governor signed the proclamation, officially calling up the guard.[53] By then, the governor had been reached in Athens and was advised to request activation of the guard, although legally he could not do that until he had returned to California soil! By 6 p.m., some troops were assembled in armories, but it was 10 p.m. before any were actually deployed, and it was midnight and beyond by the time troops arrived on the scene of what, by then, officials were calling a rebellion.[54]

It was true that by then the streets were out of control. The McCone Report admits that Friday was the worst night, although the violence on both sides continued well through Saturday.

> Early Friday afternoon, rioters jammed the streets, began systematically to burn two blocks of 103rd Street in Watts, and drove off firemen by sniper fire and by throwing missiles. By late afternoon, gang activity began to spread the disturbance as far as fifty and sixty blocks to the north. . . . The first death occurred between 6:00 and 7:00 p.m., when a Negro bystander, trapped on the street between police and rioters, was shot and killed during an exchange of gunfire.[55]

Conot's detailed account of this death (and several others that same night that are not mentioned in the McCone Report) is at such variance with the McCone Report and is so detailed and play-by-play that it could only have been derived from eyewitness and police reports.[56] Conot's version of this first fatality emphasizes that police forces were advancing from two different directions and that they unwittingly responded to each other's shots, assuming the gunfire was coming from snipers. Police mostly fired over the heads of the threatening crowds, but "each shot left a residue—a bullet that went up had to come down, and where it came down it was likely to be interpreted as having been fired by a sniper." Bullets fired into the air can also ricochet. This is apparently what happened to Leon Posey, Jr.,

> a wiry 20-year-old with a trim mustache and goatee, [who] was sitting in a barbershop waiting for a friend who was being tended to. Hearing the crash of glass, the sirens of police cars, a smattering of shots, seeing people start to run by the window, he stepped outside to look at what was going on. . . . [The police] aimed their shots over the heads of the mob. Leon Posey, Jr., a .38-caliber bullet ricocheting off a building wall and lodging in the back of his head, slumped to the sidewalk. He was the first to die."[57]

Thirty-three more fatalities would follow in the days to come. Conot chronicles each of the next thirty "civilian deaths," almost all of which were as irrational or accidental as that of Leon Posey, Jr.

Saturday, August 14: The City's Response Escalates

By Friday night and into Saturday, the violence of the protest and the city's response escalated. "The riot moved out of the Watts area and burning and looting spread over wide areas of Southeast Los Angeles several miles apart." By 1 a.m., some 100 fire companies were in the area, and official fatalities had begun:

Map 6.1.   The Area of the 1965 Los Angeles Riot, Showing That Major Violence and Destruction Were Confined to the Curfew Zone.

Source: Map appended to the McCone Report. Public domain.

a firefighter fell from a collapsing wall, a deputy sheriff was hit by friendly fire, and a policeman was shot by his own gun when the driver he was threatening through the window instinctively raised his arm in defense. The latter death was judged an accident.

By midnight Friday, 1,000 national guardsmen had joined police in trying to clear the streets, a number that rose to 3,336 by 3 a.m.[58] It would not be until midnight on Saturday that their full complement of 13,900 would be reached. In the meantime, until then, the patterns of looting and burning spread throughout an area of some 46.5 square miles, which was declared a "Curfew Zone" (see map 6.1).[59] The curfew "made it a crime for any unauthorized person to be on the streets in the curfew area after 8:00 p.m."[60] The massive show of military/police force, the fact that fires and "radical shopping" had left little of value in the shops, and that one could risk arrest by even appearing on the street were enough reason for things to become quieter.

Sunday, August 15, and After

By Saturday night, Governor Brown had returned home. On Sunday, to compensate for the shortages caused by the widespread destruction and denuding of shops, aid was being distributed by churches, community groups, and government agencies, and the governor walked through the riot zone "talking to residents."[61] The curfew was finally lifted on Tuesday, August 17, and by the following Sunday less than 300 guardsmen remained in the city.

ASSESSING THE DAMAGE

The six days during the long hot summer that the "riot ran its course" (between the evening of August 11 and the afternoon of August 17) left a highly visible trail of physical destruction and ruined lives in its wake. Thirty-four persons were dead, including a fireman, a deputy sheriff, and a Long Beach policeman, although none of these latter deaths was actually caused by rioters. Over a thousand were injured (773 "civilians" plus smaller numbers of police officers, firemen, national guardsmen, and persons from "other governmental agencies"). Property damage was estimated at about $40 million. Over 600 buildings were damaged by fire and looting, of which more than 200 were destroyed. Almost 4,000 persons had been arrested, "women as well as men, including over 500 youths under eighteen," most for burglary and theft. Many were acquitted or had the cases against them dismissed.[62]

The political situation in Los Angeles was also in shambles, with elected officials potentially found, if not in dereliction of duty, at least guilty of disorganization and paralysis. The absence of Governor Pat Brown, the callous decisions of Mayor Sam Yorty and Police Chief Parker to abandon their posts in favor of giving speeches and attending meetings out of town, even as violence escalated, suggested that heads might roll unless blame could be deflected to more abstract causes. The appointment of the Governor's Commission on the Los Angeles Riots, headed by a former director of the Central Intelligence Agency who was certainly sympathetic to law and order, was well designed to achieve this end.

THE MCCONE REPORT: ASSIGNING BLAME, RECOMMENDING CHANGE

The McCone Report blamed the victims—claiming that their frustrated aspirations had been encouraged by "the glowing promise of the Federal poverty program," whose projects "did not live up to their press notices." They were blamed for listening to "exhortations [by their leaders] to take the most extreme and even illegal remedies to right a wide variety of wrongs, real and supposed." The report did acknowledge the affront many Negroes "felt and were encouraged to feel" about the repeal in November 1964 of California's Rumford Fair Housing Act.[63] The report diagnosed the riot as an irrational, formless, senseless, hopeless "explosion" growing out of the

> dull, devastating spiral of failure that awaits the average disadvantaged child in the urban core, [whose] home life all too often fails to give him the incentive and the elementary experience [to prepare him] ... for school.... Frustrated and disillusioned, the child becomes a discipline problem [who] leaves school ... [and] slips into the ranks of the permanent jobless, illiterate and untrained, unemployed and unemployable.[64]

Acknowledging the need for massive and expensive efforts to improve the conditions of Negro life so that future explosions can be prevented, the report called "upon the members and leaders of the Negro community. For unless the disadvantaged are resolved to help themselves, whatever else is done by others is doomed to fail."[65]

Following from this self-serving diagnosis that attributed the causes of the downward spiral to failures of the "Negro community" itself, the report singled out three recommendations of the "highest priority and greatest importance": (1) expanded job training and employment opportunities; (2) preschool education, remedial courses, and intensive instruction in small classes; and (3) improved law enforcement to prevent crime and to handle citizen complaints and to improve community relationships.[66] These tasks could hardly be delegated to leaders of the Negro community.

Needless to say, these pious recommendations were never implemented. "Good" jobs, as well as "bad" ones, continued to disappear from the area in the next decades. As would be the case in the 1968 West Side riot in Chicago, whole blocks of damaged houses and shops were never restored or replaced. Although the ground was cleared, much of it remained empty and fallow. Commercial facilities were decimated. Shopkeepers, many of them Jewish, abandoned the area entirely, although some were eventually replaced by Koreans who would bear the brunt of the next uprising. (By 1990, the ratio of residents to shops in South Central stood at 415, as compared to the ratio in Los Angeles County of 203.)[67] Inferior schools continued to deteriorate, with larger classes, and there was little hope for preschools. The so-called spiral of despair continued its downward path. The only recommendation made by the McCone Commission that was carried out was the construction of a new hospital in South Central that by 1992 was treating mostly the Latino population.[68]

The report did make some recommendations for improving the Police Department, namely, to strengthen the role of the Police Commission, to establish a better system of handling citizens' complaints, to train police officers in human relations, and finally, to increase the number of black and Hispanic officers. And yet, 20 years later, joint hearings held by the Los Angeles County's Commission on Human Relations and the Los Angeles City's Human Relations Commission revealed little progress. Courses had been organized, and the representation of minorities in the police department was increased, but the joint commissions reported, "police-community conflict persists, and testimony indicated much remains to be done.... Presenters... cited the need for additional recruitment, hiring, and promotion of minority officers, and better procedures for responding to citizen complaints about police behavior, especially in the use of force."[69] (It should be pointed out that excessive use of force by police, and their exoneration by a white jury outside Los Angeles, would trigger a recurrence of the 1965 South Central uprising in 1992!)

THE POST-MORTEMS

Discontent with the superficial diagnosis of the McCone Report and its puerile (and unlikely to be implemented) recommendations surfaced almost immediately. To gather data on the characteristics and conditions of residents of the "riot zone," the Bureau of Census conducted a special census in November 1965, revealing the underlying poverty and joblessness that were rampant in the area.[70] Hard-hitting critiques of the McCone Report itself were issued by individuals and civic organizations.[71]

Detailed investigations by sociologists, psychologists, and political scientists in universities and civic organizations in the Los Angeles area explored attitudes and behaviors of whites and blacks during and after the riot. Of these, the largest and most ambitious research project was that undertaken by the Institute of Government and Public Affairs at the University of California at Los Angeles (UCLA), under a contract with the Office of Economic Opportunity, although other participants in the Los Angeles Riot Study also received financial assistance from other sources. I have been unable to determine exactly how many students and faculty actually participated in the combined projects that gathered background information and reported on extensive interviews via numerous protocols and questionnaires, but their loosely coordinated studies cumulated to one of the most extensive post-mortems ever conducted on an American riot. The UCLA Library contains dozens of mimeographed reports that I was able to consult. In this account, however, I draw most heavily on the two published volumes that are most accessible: *The Los Angeles Riots,* edited by Nathan Cohen, and *The Politics of Violence,* coauthored by David O. Sears and John B. McConahay.[72]

Cohen's book reports that during the five months following the riot,

> 2,070 personal interviews were collected in a survey, which sampled seven basic populations: (1) Negro Curfew Area residents; (2) Negro riot arrestees; (3) white residents of greater Los Angeles; (4) white Curfew Area residents; (5) Mexican-American Curfew Area residents; (6) social service workers; and (7) merchants who incurred damage during the riots.[73]

Of these, the most interesting for our purposes were the two-hour-long interviews with a random sample (stratified by age, sex, and income) of 585 Negro curfew area residents, conducted by specially trained Negro interviewers who lived in the area.[74]

Confirming the known fact that many of the residents of South Central had come to Los Angeles from the South or Southwest during World War II, the researchers found that about 60 percent had been brought up ("socialized in") in those regions, whereas only about 20 percent had grown up in California and another 16 percent in northern or western states outside California. Nevertheless, more than two-thirds had urban backgrounds (p. 144), and 70 percent of the men and 60 percent of the women had lived in Los Angeles for 10 or more years (p. 146). Some 55 percent of the males and almost 59 percent of the women reported having graduated from high school or attended some college (p. 147). All these belied the media stereotype of ghetto residents as illiterate recent migrants from rural farms in the south. Most of the men (72 percent) were working, albeit in unskilled, semiskilled or skilled occupations, but 15 percent were unemployed,

4 percent were students, and 8 percent were retired. The females were only half as likely as males to be employed.

Regardless of background, almost three-quarters of respondents reported numerous grievances (p. 156), among which were, in descending order, the poor conditions of streets and housing in their neighborhood, mistreatment by whites (including discrimination and police malpractice), economic conditions (low pay, high prices and rents, lack of jobs, etc.), and lack of public facilities (transportation, schools, shopping, parks, etc.). The more numerous their grievances, the more likely they were to have approved of the riot, to have participated in riot activities, and to believe that the riot, by calling the attention of whites to their just grievances, would yield an improvement in those conditions. Although three-quarters of the respondents claimed not to have been active in the riot, 23 percent of males and 20 percent of females reported that they had been very or somewhat active (p. 172). Even higher percentages reported very or somewhat favorable opinions about the riot: over 36 percent of the males and 23 percent of the females (p. 174). Some 43 percent of the males and 35 percent of the females thought that the riots had helped the Negro cause (p. 177). In answer to the question of whether the riot had made whites more or less sympathetic to Negro problems, 52 percent of the males and 49 percent of the females answered that it made whites more sympathetic, whereas only 11 and 12 percent, respectively, thought it had made whites less sympathetic (p. 179). In that form of wishful thinking, they could not have been more mistaken!

The gap between the perceptions of blacks and whites had grown to a yawning chasm—perhaps the most tragic consequence of the riot. A sample of 600 white residents in the Los Angeles region (100 each from six areas at different economic levels) were interviewed on their reactions to the riot.[75] In response to the question "Do you think the (riot) helped . . . the Negro's cause?" only 19 percent of whites said yes, whereas some 74 percent answered no (p. 489). Some 71 percent thought that the riot had actually increased the gap between the races (p. 489), even though 79 percent agreed that "since the (riot) whites are generally more aware of Negro problems" (p. 489). Sixty-six percent approved of the way the authorities had handled the riot (p. 492), and 79 percent thought Police Chief Parker had handled it well (p. 493). The authors point out that "The Negroes take an almost opposite view from the majority of whites . . . 64% of the Negroes thought the situation was handled badly" (p. 493). The 100 ghetto merchants interviewed in a separate sample were less inclined than whites to approve of the actions of authorities during the revolt: in response to how well Chief Parker handled the (revolt), only 51 percent answered "well," as contrasted with 33 percent who answered "badly." Approvals for Mayor Yorty and Governor

Brown were even lower: 28 percent and 15 percent, respectively (p. 624). The volume concludes, in chapter 13, with a discussion of the limitations to Negro power in Los Angeles and, in chapter 14, with an analysis of the "political attitudes of Los Angeles Negroes" by David O. Sears. Both confirm the actual and perceived exclusion of African Americans from the white-dominated political system of the city and county, as well as the negative attitudes of African Americans toward the mayor and the chief of police.

These political considerations receive more ample treatment in Sears and McConahay's study, which drew particularly on two samples: 586 Negro residents of the curfew zone and a sample of 124 Negro residents in the curfew zone who were arrested during the rioting. They do not claim that this sample is representative of the close to 4,000 persons arrested,[76] of whom 514 were juveniles and some adults were not Negroes.[77] (See table 6.1.)

From this comparison, it is clear that members of the arrested sample were more "exposed" to riot events, and therefore more vulnerable to arrest, than the sample of curfew zone Negroes, although more than a third of the arrestees denied that they had been very or somewhat active in the riot. Given Conot's detailed accounts of the randomness of arrests and the high rates at which their cases were dismissed, this level of denial does not seem untrustworthy.

The arrestees were more likely to estimate a higher percentage of riot participants than the curfew sample and to perceive members of their own neighborhoods as being more involved in riot activities than the curfew sample. It is not surprising that arrestees, being more in harm's way, personally witnessed more riot events (shootings, stone throwing, stores burning and looted, and crowds) than did members of the curfew sample, who reported themselves less active in the riot and more likely to have remained indoors.

Being out on the street, whether participating or simply rubbernecking, certainly did increase one's chances of being arrested, but the arrestees were little different from the Negro population of the curfew zone: Some 65 percent of the adult arrestees were raised in the South[78] (as compared to 60 percent of the curfew zone sample), but most of the juveniles had Los Angeles roots. Some 15 percent of the juveniles had dropped out of school—not that different from the curfew area sample. Sears and McConahay analyzed the characteristics of the subset of curfew area residents who reported having been active in the riot. Their data refute the "riffraff" stereotype of rioters as having been drawn from recent poor and uneducated migrants from the rural South or disproportionately from the "underclass."[79] There were no statistically significant differences in riot participation by level of one's own education, parents' education, or subjective class identification. The major significant difference in propensity to be active in the riot was age, with those

Table 6.1 Comparison between Observations and Attitudes of Black Residents and Black Arrestees in the 1965 Los Angeles Riot.

Riot Participation Sample	Curfew Zone sample (%)	Arrestee Sample (%)
Self-reported activity:		
"Very" or "somewhat" active	22	62
Perceived community involvement:		
Mean percentage of community perceived as participating	20	33
Percentage who perceived own neighborhoods as being "very" or "somewhat" active	52	82
Events personally witnessed:		
Saw shooting	20	48
Saw stones thrown	29	67
Saw stores burning	54	81
Saw stores being looted	60	87
Saw crowds of people	60	90?

Source: Sears and McConahay, *The Politics of Violence*, table 1.1, p. 11.

between the ages of 15 and 29 far more likely to report riot activity than older groups.[80] Native-born Los Angeles residents were more likely to be active than migrants, but this could have been due to their youthful age.

Conot gives us figures on the disposition of cases, as well as anecdotal information on a number of "false arrests" made at sites of conflict. The original charges against those arrested included 36 counts of homicide, 95 of robbery (including 2 juveniles), 372 of assault (including 46 juveniles), 2,865 of burglary and theft (including 417 juveniles), and 584 of misdemeanors (including 49 juveniles). "In the case of the homicides, 33 of the 36 persons had merely been on the scene at the time that police officers had shot and killed another suspect, and the homicide charges against all of these were dismissed."[81] Only one person was actually tried for murder, a 23-year-old employed navy veteran who, in a later lengthy jury trial, after being held in jail for seven months, was found not guilty.[82]

"Most of the robbery and assault cases were...tried on lesser charges, and a large proportion of the burglary charges wound up as trespassing convictions." In juvenile court, charges were dismissed in 25 percent of the cases, and 62 percent of the actual cases heard were released on probation. The remaining 13 percent were sent to camps. "In charges against adults, approximately 700 of the 2,249 felony cases were dismissed....Of the remaining 1500, 350 were found not guilty, 800 were adjudged guilty of misdemeanors, and 350 found guilty of felonies."[83] In the eventual trials of the Frye family and those who had come to their aid, all cases were dismissed, and the police were reprimanded for harassment, or at least poor judgment. In short, the massive arrests could not be sustained.

The massive destruction, on the other hand, remained a lasting and undeniable consequence of the withdrawal of police to the perimeter of the 46.5-square-mile curfew zone and their inability to protect firefighters, who also had to withdraw. Lasting, also, were the political consequences of the uprising. In 1973, Los Angeles voters put an African American into the mayor's office in the hope of buying racial peace, which it did for almost two decades, until, in the aftermath of the 1992 uprising, Bradley was replaced by a white candidate, thus ending the coalition between blacks and West Side "liberals."

Insufficiently acknowledged, unanalyzed, and poorly understood were the connections between the uprising and organizations within the black community which identified the plight of South Central's residents as due not only to economic deprivation but to the absence of real political power. Given the methodology of the Los Angeles Riot Study, which treated respondents as randomly chosen and unrelated individuals rather than as members of a loosely connected community, this was perhaps inevitable. A reinterpretation has recently been published by Gerald Horne, a black scholar, who puts the battle for South Central more explicitly within the context of the civil rights struggle.[84]

I shall return to his interpretation in the next chapter, which examines the 1992 reuprising. Indeed, although the narratives describing the events of the 1992 riot do not deviate much from those of 1965, current analysts, many of them African American, are more sophisticated in interpreting the meaning of the revolt, albeit more pessimistic about any potential alliance between African Americans and Latinos in the changing terrain of Los Angeles politics. In the previous two elections for mayor, for example, the Latino vote was aligned directly with the "white" vote, while blacks overwhelmingly supported the losing candidate. In the most recent election, with black support, "Anglo" Los Angeles elected its first Latino mayor since Cristobal Aguilar held that office in 1872. Jose

Sepulveda, the last Mexican mayor, deposed in 1848, has been restored, metaphorically, to power. Whether that alliance will hold and benefit African Americans remains to be seen.

NOTES

1. Jean Point du Sable, offspring of a French adventurer and an escaped slave mother, established the first permanent cabin on the site of Chicago in 1779. The first settlers of Los Angeles came from the Spanish colony of what would later become independent Mexico. According to Hubert Howe Bancroft's classic *History of California*, vol. 1, *1542–1880* (San Francisco, 1884), as cited in Spencer Crump, *Black Riot in Los Angeles: The Story of the Watts Tragedy* (Los Angeles: Trans-Anglo Books, 1966), p. 13, only 2 of the settlers were Spanish, 11 were Indian, 7 were of mixed Spanish and Indian "blood," 2 were listed in Spanish documents as being of "pure Negro blood," while the remaining 24 were of "Negro blood variously mixed with that of Indians and Spanish."
2. Howard Nelson, *The Los Angeles Metropolis* (Dubuque, Iowa: Kendall Hunt, 1983), p. 143. There were an unspecified number of Indians and blacks in the midst of a Mexican plurality.
3. Carey McWilliams, *Southern California: An Island on the Land* (1946; reprint, Salt Lake City: Peregrine Smith, 1990), p. 50.
4. Literally, "the street of the black ones," called by English speakers "Nigger Alley," an alley just off the original Plaza. See Crump, *Black Riot in Los Angeles*, p. 13.
5. The last mayor before the US conquest of Los Angeles was a mulatto, Jose Sepulveda, after whose family major streets have been named.
6. See Abraham Hoffman, *Unwanted Mexican Americans in the Great Depression: Repatriation Pressures, 1929–1939* (Tucson: University of Arizona Press, 1974).
7. Note that the term "Anglo" derives not from a racial distinction but from a cultural/linguistic one.
8. See Tomás Almaguer, *Racial Fault Lines: The Historical Origins of White Supremacy in California* (Berkeley: University of California Press, 1994).
9. Although the zone of eruption was not exclusively occupied by African Americans, within it were then concentrated 82 percent of the black population of the city.
10. David O. Sears, a distinguished member of the UCLA group that had investigated the 1965 riot, has written a perceptive comparison of the events in 1965 and 1992. See his "Black-White Conflict: A Model for the Future of Ethnic Politics in Los Angeles," in David Halle, ed., *New York and Los Angeles: Politics, Culture and Society: A Comparative View* (Chicago: University of Chicago Press, 2003), pp. 367–89.
11. The early history of Watts is reviewed in *Violence in the City: An End or a Beginning? A Report by the Governor's Commission on the Los Angeles Riots, December 2, 1965*, pp. 75–76. This document is commonly referred to as the "McCone Report." The text of the governor's commission report has been reprinted in full in an edition compiled by Robert M. Fogelson and published by Arno Press and the *New York Times* (New York, 1969).

12. Ibid., p. 76. Note that Mexicans were classified as Caucasians.

13. See Nathan Cohen, "The Context of the Curfew Area," in Cohen, ed., *The Los Angeles Riots: A Socio-Psychological Study* (New York: Praeger, 1970). Quotation p. 43.

14. As late as 1970, black families were even poorer than Spanish-surname families. In that year, "the median family income for blacks was $7,500; for Spanish-surname families, $8,900; and for white families, $11,400." Howard Nelson and William Clark, *Los Angeles: The Metropolitan Experience* (Cambridge, Mass.: Ballinger, 1976), p. 38.

15. *Shelley v. Kraemer* was based on a Los Angeles case, specifically at Slauson Street, which had long been the southern "wall" of Los Angeles's spatial color line.

16. Nelson and Clark, *Los Angeles*, pp. 37–38.

17. Charles Abrams, "Rats among the Palm Trees," *Nation*, February 25, 1950; quotations pp. 177–78.

18. Ibid. This is not to deny that there was also some "suburbanization" of the black population. An analysis of census figures from 1970 showed that "suburbs" of the Los Angeles Standard Metropolitan Statistical Area contained the largest number of black residents of any other major metropolitan region by 1970. See Francine Rabinowitz, "Minorities in the Suburbs: The Los Angeles Experience," Working Paper no. 31 (Cambridge, Mass.: MIT Harvard Joint Center for Urban Studies, 1975). But what should be borne in mind are the peculiar and arbitrary boundaries between center city and suburb in Los Angeles. The apparent suburbanization of the black population often involved a move from one segregated "urban" area to an equally urbanized and segregated "suburb," which fell outside the boundaries of the city because of the vagaries of irregular annexation.

19. See Douglas Massey and B. Mullan, "Processes of Hispanic and Black Spatial Assimilation," *American Journal of Sociology* 89 (1984), 836–73.

20. For the increase in the Mexican American population in Los Angeles, see California Department of Industrial Relations, Division of Labor Statistics and Research, *Negroes and Mexican Americans in South and East Los Angeles: Changes between 1960 and 1965 in Population, Employment, Income and Family Status* (San Francisco: State of California, Division of Fair Employment Practices, 1966).

21. Sam Bass Warner, Jr., *The Urban Wilderness: A History of the American City* (New York: Harper and Row, 1972), pp. 142–44; italics added.

22. Abrams, "Rats among the Palm Trees." For more details, see Donald Craig Parson, "The Development of Redevelopment: Housing and Urban Renewal in Los Angeles," *International Journal of Urban and Regional Research* 6 (1982), pp. 393–413.

23. McCone Report, p. 4. See also Donald Craig Parson, "Urban Politics during the Cold War: Public Housing, Urban Renewal and Suburbanization in Los Angeles" (Ph.D diss., University of California at Los Angeles, 1985).

24. The title of this section is the subtitle of the McCone Report, *Violence in the City*. It takes its name from the chair of the commission, John A. McCone. As far as I have been able to trace his background, he made his fortune in World War II as a shipping magnate, held posts in the Defense Department (1948) and the air force (1950–51), chaired the Atomic Energy Commission (1958–61), and served as director of the Central Intelligence Agency between 1961 and 1965.

25. As Robert Conot, author of the best account of *any* riot I have ever read, concludes, when the report appeared in December 1965, "it was criticized for being superficial, dealing in

generalities, lacking incisiveness, and certainly not being worth the almost $300,000 that was spent on it." Conot cites the particularly harsh comments of the California Advisory Committee to the U.S. Commission on Civil Rights. See Conot, *Rivers of Blood, Years of Darkness* (New York: Bantam Books, 1967, reprinted 1973), pp. 415–16, esp. n. 3, p. 416.

26. Conot, *Rivers of Blood*, describes his exhaustive methodology on pp. 467–79.

27. The McCone Report says that Ronald was Marquette's brother, but they were actually stepbrothers.

28. McCone Report, p. 10.

29. Ibid., p. 11.

30. The Kerner Report (p. 37) says that "a young Negro woman . . . was *erroneously* accused of spitting on the police" (italics added). Months later, the case against her was dismissed. Also arrested was a man who had come to her aid; his case was also dismissed.

31. McCone Report, p. 12.

32. Conot, *Rivers of Blood*, pp. 3–5.

33. Ibid., p. 6.

34. Ibid., p. 7.

35. Summarized from ibid., pp. 9–11.

36. Summarized from ibid., pp. 12–13.

37. Ibid., p. 14.

38. Ibid., p. 15.

39. Summarized from ibid., p. 16.

40. Ibid., p. 17. The smock led to rumors that she was pregnant.

41. Summarized from ibid., pp. 18–21.

42. Kerner Report, p. 206.

43. McCone Report, pp. 12–22.

44. Ibid., pp. 12–13.

45. Ibid., p. 13.

46. Ibid., p. 13.

47. Conot, *Rivers of Blood*, p. 97.

48. Ibid, p. 102.

49. These plans were proposed to the 77th Street police station but were rejected. For details, see Bruce M. Tyler, "The Watts Riot and the Watts Summer Festival," *Journal of Kentucky Studies* (September 1968), pp. 76–95. "This aborted dance soon became institutionalized as 'The Watts Summer Festival.' The dance was re-organized later to compete with the anniversary of the riot as a 'carnival' and not a 'rebellion,' and it was to compete with the emerging pro-riot advocates who sought to repeat the riot of 1965" (Tyler, p. 81).

50. McCone Report, p. 14.

51. Ibid., pp. 14–15, quotation on p. 15.

52. Quoted in McCone Report, p. 16. This request could only come from the governor's office. With Brown still out of the country and Anderson out of town, the request from Sacramento was finally issued by Brown's executive secretary. Ibid., p. 17.

53. McCone Report, pp. 18–19.

54. Ibid., p. 19.

55. Ibid., pp. 18, 19.

56. Details of arbitrary arrests, mistaken inferences of guilt, and random shootings by the police are chronicled by Conot, *Rivers of Blood*, chap. 29, pp. 239–52.

57. Ibid., quotation pp. 245–46.

58. McCone Report, p. 19.

59. A map of this vast territory, showing the locations of the buildings destroyed, looted, or damaged, was appended to the McCone Report.

60. McCone Report, p. 20.

61. Ibid., p. 21.

62. Ibid., pp. 1–2, 23.

63. Ibid., p. 4.

64. Ibid.; quotation p. 5.

65. Ibid., p. 7.

66. Ibid., p. 8.

67. Claritas is a market research firm. Its figures are cited in the special issue of the *Los Angeles Weekly*, May 8–14, 1992, p. 17.

68. Constructed in 1972, this hospital was in such bad condition by the end of 2004 that its accreditation had been withdrawn; residents were fighting for it to be fixed and reopened, since it remained the *only* hospital that was easily accessible to South Central residents.

69. "McCone Revisited: A Focus on Solutions to Continuing Problems in South Central Los Angeles," a joint public hearing in 1985 by the Los Angeles County Commission on Human Relations and the Los Angeles City Human Relations Commission (mimeo).

70. U.S. Department of Commerce, Bureau of Census, *Special Census Survey of the South and East Los Angeles Areas, November 1965* (Washington, D.C.: Government Printing Office, 1965).

71. Among others, see Robert Fogelson, *White on Black: A Critique of the McCone Commission Report on the Los Angeles Riots* (privately printed, n.d.); and Kendall O. Price, et al., *A Critique of the Governor's Commission on the Los Angeles Riot* (Inglewood, Calif.: Public Executive Development and Research, 1967).

72. Nathan Cohen, ed., *The Los Angeles Riots: A Socio-Psychological Study* (New York: Praeger, 1970); and David O. Sears and John B. McConahay, *The Politics of Violence: The New Urban Blacks and the Watts Riot* (Boston: Houghton Mifflin, 1973).

73. Cohen, *The Los Angeles Riots*, p. 1.

74. The methods of sample selection, data gathering, and data analysis used in these interviews are described in T. M. Tomlinson and Diana L. TenHouten, chap. 4 in Cohen, *The Los Angeles Riots*, pp. 127–39, and the actual findings appear in Raymond J. Murphy and James W. Watson, chap. 5 in Cohen, *The Los Angeles Riots*, pp. 140–257. Cohen, *The Los Angeles Riots*, is cited by page numbers in the text in the paragraphs that follow.

75. See Richard T. Morriss and Vincent Jeffries, "The White Reaction Study," in Cohen, *The Los Angeles Riots*, pp. 480–560, plus the interview schedule to p. 601.

76. See Sears and McConahay, *The Politics of Violence*, p. 11, table 1.1.

77. Conot, *Rivers of Blood*, devotes all of his chapter 52 (pp. 379–409) to the characteristics of arrestees and their trial disposition.

78. Ibid., p. 380.

79. See Sears and McConahay, *The Politics of Violence*, pp. 20–28.

80. Ibid., p. 23, table 2.1, p. 28, table 2.2.

81. Conot, *Rivers of Blood*, p. 381.

82. Ibid. The trial is discussed at length on pp. 390–97.

83. Ibid., p. 381.

84. See Gerald Horne, *Fire This Time: The Watts Uprising and the 1960s* (New York: Da Capo Press, 1997).

7

Riot Redux

South Central, 1992

A t 12:40 a.m. on Sunday, March 3, 1991, Rodney King was savagely beaten by four apparently out-of-control Los Angeles uniformed police officers, while some 17 other officers stood by. This scene happened to be videotaped from his well-positioned second floor balcony by amateur photographer George Holliday, who was awakened by sirens blaring in the San Fernando Valley neighborhood where the beating was occurring.[1] Widely shown on television on March 4 and 5, it shocked many viewers nationwide, although it simply reminded many local black and minority viewers of the humiliations they themselves had experienced at the hands of what they viewed as a racist, militaristic police force.

On March 6, the FBI, the Los Angeles district attorney's office, and the Los Angeles Police Department's Internal Affairs Division began their investigations. The Police Commission, a civilian panel charged with overseeing the operation of the police department, also began an inquiry. By late March, feelings were still running high, and more damage control was deemed necessary. Mayor Tom Bradley called on Police Chief Daryl Gates to resign, and the Police Commission placed Gates on leave,[2] although both moves were overturned by the city council on April 5, ostensibly to forestall a lawsuit by Gates.

On May 1, 1991, Mayor Bradley created an independent commission to investigate the case, appointing Warren Christopher, former deputy secretary of state, as chair. Christopher had been vice chair of the McCone Commission and principal drafter of its much-maligned report, but this time he was in a stronger political position.[3] Unlike the after-the-riot McCone Report, which had depended on and defended official Los Angeles Police Department records, Christopher was charged with investigating police behavior that could potentially touch off a riot. His large staff interviewed some 450 police officers (current and past) and experts on policing and law enforcement, reviewed some 1,240 personnel complaints filed against the police, examined 100,000 pages of transcripts of Mobile Digital Terminal (MDT) communications and 700 police personnel files, and held five public hearings.[4]

Some two months later, on July 9, 1991, the commission issued its report.[5] It came down hard on the Los Angeles Police Department. According to Sonenshein,

> it was a shocker. Unexpectedly, the commission issued a stinging report, which highlighted the failure of the LAPD and other city officials to rein in police brutality. Most dramatically, the commission released transcripts of police conversations on car computers. The transcripts contained numerous examples of racist and sexist phrases, including the infamous reference to "gorillas in the mist."[6]

The report, concluding that "the department suffered from a siege mentality," called on Gates to retire and recommended "greater civilian control of the police department."[7] In September 1991, the city council approved a ballot referendum incorporating many of the recommendations of the Christopher Commission Report, including greater civilian control over the police department. By early June 1992, Los Angeles voters overwhelmingly approved Proposition F to reform the Police Department and to restore civilian control over it,[8] but it was too little and much too late. The city had already exploded at the end of April in response to the trial verdict that had found the four policemen, charged with using excessive brutality, not guilty.

The Indictment and the (First) Trial

On March 14, 1991, the four officers (Stacy Koon, Lawrence Powell, Timothy Wind, and Theodore Briseno) who had been indicted by the district attorney's office on multiple criminal charges, including assault with a deadly weapon, pleaded not guilty to all charges. Koon and Powell were also charged with filing a false police report. Matters seemed to be moving along routinely, and there was only subdued street reaction, so certain were most Angelenos (including Mayor Tom Bradley) that the officers would be found guilty and punished. Police Chief Daryl Gates, who bore the brunt of the outrage, remained in office, albeit suffering growing negative evaluations of his performance and heightened calls for his resignation.

Contrary to popular expectations, however, the trial was to be a long-drawn-out process that undermined and discredited faith in the legal system.[9] The problems began with complex jury selection procedures, which in general tend to underrepresent minorities. Jury selection begins with the declaration of the district in which the trial is to take place. This should have been Los Angeles County, where the alleged crime took place. However, it is possible to request a change of venue in "notorious" cases. "Because of the publicity... and the deep emotions expressed by the residents in Los Angeles, the State Second District Court of Appeal granted a change of venue on July 23, 1991," but by the time the new venue was to be selected, the Second District Court of Appeal had removed black judge Bernard Kamins (who had favored Los Angeles County), previously assigned to the beating case, and replaced him by a white Los Angeles Superior Court judge, Stanley Weisberg. In late November, the new judge selected suburban Ventura County, having rejected alternatives such as the San Francisco Bay Area ("where racial makeup is similar to the original trial site of Los Angeles"), Orange County, and Riverside County, giving different but weak reasons for his choice.[10] It was beginning to look very suspicious, and suspicions were confirmed when Simi Valley was selected to hear the case.

> In the venue of Ventura County... blacks comprised only 2.2% of the population, Hispanics 26.1%, Asians 5.2%.... In Simi Valley City... the racial distribution is even more skewed.... For example, 79.9% of the residents are white, compared to 1.5% black, 27.7% Hispanic, 5.3% Asians.... If the trial had taken place... in Los Angeles City [as originally scheduled] greater representation of... racial minorities could have been ensured.... Specifically, minority residents [there] comprise: 13% black, 39.9% Hispanic, and 9.2% Asian.[11]

As it was, the final 12 jurors who survived "careful" scrutiny included no blacks, six white men, four white women, one Hispanic woman, and an Asian woman born in the Philippines.

> Eight had either served in the armed forces or had spouses who had been in the military.... Five... said in the questionnaires that they owned or used

guns.... Three jurors had relatives who had served in police departments, including a woman who said that her step-father was a police officer in Portland, Oregon, and another who said that his brother was a retired Los Angeles Police Department sergeant.... Seven jurors said they had been victims of crimes ranging from robbery to assault. On the questionnaires, all said that they had positive opinions of police in general and the role of police officers.[12]

This was hardly a jury of the victim's "peers," although it was well primed to acquit the perpetrators. That it did on April 29, 1992. The reaction of most recipients of the news, including President George H. W. Bush, was disbelief, and in the black community, outrage. Patricia Moore, a Los Angeles city council-woman standing on the courthouse steps when the verdict was announced shortly after 3 p.m., spoke for more than her constituents when she called the verdict "a modern-day lynching."[13]

THE SEQUENCE AND SPREAD OF THE RIOT

Wednesday Evening, April 29, to Thursday Morning, April 30

The media seemed caught by surprise when scattered protests began almost immediately and that same night Los Angeles's South Central district erupted in flames, roughly paralleling 1965.[14] Newscasters scrambled frantically to flash repetitive images on TV screens throughout America and the world, but their explanations were cast primarily in purely racial terms. In his book on the media coverage of the riot, Darnell Hunt reveals how "race shapes both television's construction of news and our understandings of it."[15]

The police department should not have been caught unawares, although once again it seemed woefully unprepared to respond to the community's angry despair. It may be that Chief Gates, knowing he was on his way out, had already abdicated responsibility, but it was even worse than that. The blue-ribbon commission later charged with investigating the police's inadequate and delayed response to the riot, headed by William Webster, a former director of the FBI and the Central Intelligence Agency, concluded that there was no meaningful prepa-ration for a riot. The commission painted a wide swathe of blame:

> City leaders and LAPD commanders alike seem to have been caught by surprise as the lawlessness escalated following the verdict.... The initial response of City officials was marked by uncertainty, some confusion, and an almost total lack of coordination.... [The] Command Staff had no specific plan in place for dealing with the potential unrest following the

verdicts.... [More immediately,] during the two hours that elapsed between the time that prosecutors were notified that the actual jury had reached verdicts [at 12:45 p.m. on April 29] and the actual reading of the verdicts [at 3:10 p.m.], little was done to prepare for the possibility of a widespread and disorderly reaction. The failure of City and police leaders to position the City's resources properly to respond to the coming firestorm, started long before this two-hour window.[16]

More critical in its recommendations, the commission stated strongly, "the across-the-board failures in the planning function at every level of the emergency response to the civil disorder that erupted on April 29, 1992, point to the very real and substantial need for a complete overhaul of the City's and the Department's planning for responding to an outbreak of civil disorder."[17]

Indeed, when the verdict was read shortly after 3:10, there were only 838 Los Angeles Police Department officers on duty in the entire city, and they had no instructions,[18] even though, within five minutes of the verdict, angry crowds were already protesting at Parker Center Police Headquarters and assembling at Fifty-fifth and Normandie in South Central.[19] According to the time line in the Webster Report, the first looting occurred at 4:15 at Florence and Normandie.[20] Over the next two hours, protests at the latter site escalated, so that the 30–35 officers seeking to disperse the growing crowds were badly outnumbered. By 5:45, the police were under attack, their squad cars being "rocked" and attacked with bottles. Lacking orders, most of the police withdrew.[21]

At 6:46, Reginald Denny, a white truck driver who blundered into the fray and then tried to turn around, was dragged from his cab and savagely beaten,[22] until he was rescued by several black good samaritans who drove him to the hospital. His beating was also taped and shown repeatedly on television. By presenting this beating as a presumed equivalent to King's, the media recast a riot protesting police malfeasance into what some whites could interpret as a "race war."

In the meantime, Gates seemed oddly oblivious. After spending time alone in his office, he put his deputy in charge and by 6:30 had left for Brentwood, an upscale white neighborhood, to address a political fundraiser.[23] With few instructions and insufficient numbers, the police regrouped at central police headquarters, which by 7 p.m. was being stormed by protesters, who smashed lobby windows and set fire to a guard shack in the parking lot. It was an hour later that officers in full riot gear finally dispersed the crowd attacking Parker Center.[24]

The police never did venture back in force into the heart of the riot zone and thus could not protect the firemen who had been trying to put out the fires that, after they retreated, would consume much of the core zone that first night. The first two fatal shootings (of innocent black passersby, attributed to "unknown assailants") occurred at 8:15 p.m. at Vernon and Vermont, the site of a Korean-run swap meet.[25] And in a major two-hour gun battle later that night between police and residents of Nickerson Gardens, the police made their first "kills."[26]

As early as 7 p.m., Governor Pete Wilson had called Mayor Bradley, offering to call up 2,000 California National Guard troops, but his offer was not accepted by the mayor until an hour later.[27] By 9:00 p.m., the guard was alerted, and 15 minutes later, the first contingent of 2,000 guardsmen was called up.[28] But they remained in their armories for most of Thursday, April 30, awaiting supplies of riot gear and ammunition and waiting for squabbles to be settled over how they were to be deployed. It was not until Thursday night, more than 24 hours later, that the first contingent arrived near the corner of Vernon and Figueroa—85 somewhat frightened guardsmen in full battle dress and armed with M-16s.[29] They would be joined by thousands more in the days to come.

> In the meantime, however, South Central was burning, and disorders had spread north toward downtown and west along Wilshire through Koreatown, lapping into Hollywood, the fringes of West Los Angeles and the San Fernando Valley. [White] Southern California was gripped by terror.... Most of the panic was born of rumor and the dread that "they" were on the way to the privileged west side, Molotov cocktails in hand. In fact, with the conspicuous exception of South Central, Koreatown, and the surrounding mid-Wilshire area, police held control of the streets. The true nightmare city was South Central, where residents stayed inside as the riots raged, and the sick and the needy were unable to obtain emergency medical or fire help.[30]

Thursday Morning, April 30, to Friday Evening, May 1

The fog of war had set in and would run for five-plus days. Just after midnight, Governor Wilson declared a state of emergency, and Mayor Bradley imposed a curfew in the same 45-plus square miles that had been delimited in the 1965 riot, restricting the sale of gasoline and banning the sale of ammunition, but the curfew was soon extended, apparently voluntarily, to virtually the entire city.[31] Needless to say, it could not be enforced in the areas where it was most needed. Conditions in South Central rapidly worsened. Just before 3 a.m.,

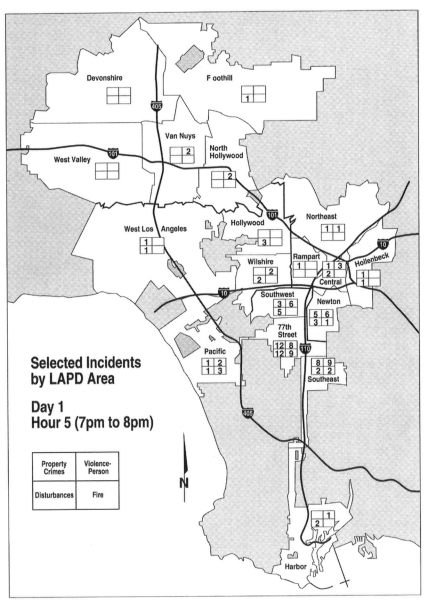

Map 7.1.   The Rapid Spread of Violence and Destruction beyond the Curfew Zone during the 1992 Riot. Number and Location of Accumulated Incidents as Reported by Los Angeles Police Department by the Fifth Hour of the First Day.

Source: William Webster and Hubert Williams, *The City in Crisis*, vol. 2, appendices, section on maps. Copyright: Webster and Williams. Reprinted by permission.

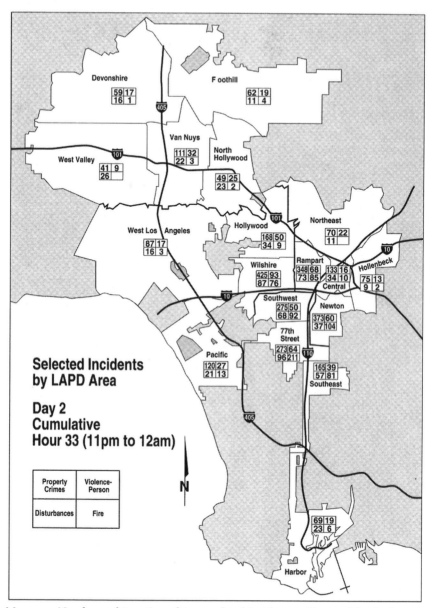

Selected Incidents by LAPD Area

Day 2 Cumulative Hour 33 (11pm to 12am)

Property Crimes	Violence-Person
Disturbances	Fire

N

Map 7.2.   Number and Location of Accumulated Incidents as Reported by the Los Angeles Police Department by the 33rd Hour of the Second Day.

Source: William Webster and Hubert Williams, *The City in Crisis*, vol. 2, appendices, section on maps. Copyright: Webster and Williams. Reprinted by permission.

transformers exploded west of Vernon to Central Avenue, leaving in the dark an area that extended from Manchester to Vernon.[32] By then, looting and arson intensified.

Throughout this period until Thursday afternoon, the Webster Report acknowledged, there were "no police present" in South Central. It was not until 1:30 Thursday afternoon that the first national guard troops were deployed to South Central.[33] But by then, riot-related incidents had spread well beyond that area. (See maps 7.1 and 7.2.) With matters still out of control by the early hours of May 1, the president federalized the national guard. By 9 a.m., Bradley renewed the city-wide curfew, extending it indefinitely.

Saturday Morning, May 2, to May 10

Gradually, the national guard, supplementing the reactivated Los Angeles Police Department and forces of the Los Angeles County Police Department, brought the "insurrection," by then virtually city-wide, under increased control. Arrests for curfew violations began to outnumber those for arson, looting, and personal violence. All in all, many considered the riot "finished." Gradually, power lines were repaired, and limited bus service was restored. The president declared Los Angeles a disaster area, and Bradley appointed Peter Uberroth to head the hastily organized "Rebuild L.A.," a coalition of public and private investors. On May 4, the emergency center was shut down and the curfew finally lifted. But it was not until May 8 that the federal troops began to pull out of the Los Angeles area and not until May 10 that federalization was lifted and mobilization finally terminated.[34]

DOCUMENTING THE RIOT

In contrast with the paucity of records on the basis of which the other five riots described in this book have been reconstructed, the 1992 Los Angeles riot was, if anything, excessively documented, albeit often by aerial surveillance photos from helicopters that transmitted its spread, and by selectively inflammatory pictures on television newscasts that were repeated in endless loops. The accounts of journalists and newspaper photographers, documenting isolated events, have been collected in books. Again, these tend to highlight specific moments without offering narratives that connect them in sequence or that offer explanations for how they moved and evolved. Instead, we have dramatic but disjointed "iconic" images.

It is perhaps understandable that no author has attempted a coherent narrative of the events. We are, therefore, dependent on the truncated chronology reconstructed from police records and interviews conducted later by the Webster inquiry, admittedly one-sided albeit not a whitewash. If the truth be known, however, the turbulent, fragmented disorders that took place in Los Angeles in 1992 were probably no more chaotic than those in earlier riots for which more sporadic records exist. The apparent coherence of narratives and "agreement" on when and where what happened in other riots are to some extent artifacts of ignorance and the frameworks adopted by postriot committees of inquiry. In contrast, the multiplicity of sources on Los Angeles in 1992 yields disagreements and contradictions that arise not only from different perspectives and ideological frames but from the very surfeit of undigested information on which different analysts have selectively drawn. (Figures on deaths for example, range between 45 and 54.)

It may be significant that no official inquiry into the riot itself was ever conducted. The Webster Report focused on how the Los Angeles Police Department should be reformed. And since the Christopher Commission had already skewered the Los Angeles Police Department and condemned its police chief Gates for his handling of the King beating, the impulse may have been to bury the riot itself as "past history"—much too complicated to untangle.

There is, for example, no agreement even as to the length of the riot—variously given as three, five, or even six days! The shorter time span is given in a very brief section of Morrison and Lowry's deceptively titled subheading "Chronology of the Riot,"[35] for which they cite as their chief source the *Los Angeles Times*'s collection of articles *Understanding the Riots*.[36] Lou Cannon counts the riot as lasting five days between the afternoon of April 29 and the lifting of the curfew the afternoon of May 4, as do most other writers, but even this detail-addicted journalist does not attempt a chronology. The collective volume produced by the Institute for Alternative Journalism, *Inside the L.A. Riots*,[37] follows the *Los Angeles Times*'s format by bringing together brief "essays and articles by more than 60 of America's leading independent writers and journalists" (of more progressive orientation). It excerpts a five-page chronology of the five-day uprising, collated from items published in the *Los Angeles Weekly*, which is consistent with its more radical point of view. In contrast, the Webster Report on police and armed force actions covers the entire period up to midnight, May 10, when federalization was lifted, and 6 a.m., when the troops were finally demobilized.[38] And that is about the total of "chronologies" that I have found.

In lieu of a linear account, some analysts have used metaphors that describe the event as a postmodern kaleidoscope that defies simple narrative.[39]

Such analysts are more interested, and I think rightly so, in exploring the causes and explanations for the uprising than in developing theories based on the well-documented and spatially specific results of the riots themselves. Before turning to these analyses, however, it is necessary to describe the spatial and demographic changes that had taken place in Los Angeles County and, more specifically, in South Central between the 1965 riots and those of 1992. Without this information, one is tempted to overemphasize the parallels between the two riots, ignoring the real changes that had occurred in Los Angeles's population, economy, and politics in the interim. But perhaps the more things change, the more they remain the same—at least in their outcomes.

DÉJÀ VU? BUT WITH A DIFFERENCE: COMPARING 1965 AND 1992

The prophetic question in the subtitle of the McCone Report (an end or a beginning?) was thus answered on April 1992 with another "riot" that began in roughly the same curfew zone of 46 and a half square miles but expanded more widely, eventually causing the "curfew zone" to be extended to almost the entire city at the peak of the explosion. (See maps 7.1 and 7.2 above showing how quickly and how far hostilities spread.)

This new uprising not only matched but actually exceeded the violence of 1965.

> Many more were arrested in 1992—16,291—and a larger number were injured, 2,383. In 1992 at least 52 were killed[40] ... and estimates for property damage ranged as high as $1 billion. This time it took approximately 20,000 LAPD, CHP, national guard, and seven related military forces to subdue those who were "looting" and burning.[41]

The immediate trigger also involved police brutality, but ignited only after a year's delay, revealing that the riot initially was a frustrated response to injustice, not just a reaction to ongoing brutality. It represented outrage over the court decision, whose legitimacy was deeply questioned, if not completely rejected. The media announcement of the verdict simply served as an accelerant to the "fire this [second] time." Sadly, it was a sign that little had improved for the residents of South Central Los Angeles in the intervening 27 years.

There were differences, however. Many of South Central's residents had changed, as had the demographic configuration of the city, county, and even nation. The census of 1990 revealed an enormous transformation in the ethnic/

racial composition of the city and county's population and their distribution in space. This fluidity, attributable to both local and international causes, resulted in some important and disastrous consequences for the deteriorating zone of South Central.

LOS ANGELES COUNTY'S RACIAL/ETHNIC COMPOSITION AND DISTRIBUTION IN SPACE

Changes in South Central must be placed in the wider context of the transformations in the racial/ethnic composition of Los Angeles County's population and its redistribution in space between 1960/1970 and 1990.[42] Although the county's total population continued to grow, from about 7 million in 1970 to almost 7.5 million in 1980 and over 8.8 million in 1990, this growth came almost exclusively from an increase in the number of Hispanics, primarily immigrants from Mexico, and from smaller increases in the Asian population, again due primarily to immigration from abroad.

The white non-Hispanic population had stabilized or declined slightly, making it a smaller portion of the total. Whereas as late as 1960, non-Hispanic whites had constituted over 80 percent of the county's population, this proportion had declined to 67 percent by 1970 and had fallen to only 53 percent by 1980. By 1990 it stood at less than 41 percent. Over the same 30-year period, the proportion of African Americans had increased from 7.6 percent in 1960 to about 11 percent in 1970, peaking at 12.6 percent in 1980, before declining to only 11.2 percent by 1990. The differences in racial/ethnic identity were made up for by a dramatic increase in the percentage of Hispanics, rising from about 9.6 percent in 1960 to 18.3 percent in 1970, 27.4 percent in 1980, and 36.4 percent by 1990.

My own calculations (see table 7.1) give somewhat different totals for Los Angeles County in 1990, indicating how more complicated the county's ethnic composition had become. I have been reluctant to interpolate the same definitions back into earlier census returns because of changes and expansions in census categories.[43] But others have found it equally difficult.[44] I include here an excellent chart that appears in *Prismatic Metropolis*, by Lawrence Bobo and his colleagues, which clarifies many of the changes that occurred between 1970 and 1990 (see fig. 7.1).[45]

By 1990, the distributions in space of these racially and ethnically identified "groups" had also shifted from earlier decades, although given the changing category definition of Latinos/Hispanics, it is difficult to make comparisons to earlier years. However, we do have excellent computer-generated

Table 7.1 The Racial/Ethnic Composition of the Population of Los Angeles
County (PSMA), 1990 (%).

White non-Hispanic	40.8
Black non-Hispanic	10.5
Asian non-Hispanic	10.2
Amerindian non-Hispanic	0.3
Other non-Hispanic	0.2
Hispanic	37.8
Unknown or due to rounding	0.2
Total	100

Source: Abu-Lughod, *New York, Chicago, Los Angeles*, p. 377, table 12.6.

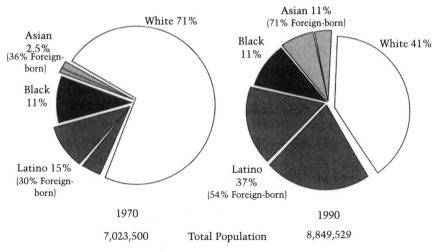

Figure 7.1.   Percentages of Population in Los Angeles County by Major Racial/Ethnic
Groups, 1970 and 1990.

Source: David Grant, in *Prismatic Metropolis: Inequality in Los Angeles*, Edited by Lawrence
Bobo, Melvin Oliver, James Johnson, Jr., and Abel Valenzuela, Jr. Copyright: Russell Sage
Foundation, 2002.

maps covering the Los Angeles County (PMSA) area by census tracts, showing the
areas of the county that were predominantly occupied by blacks and Hispanics in
1990 (see maps 7.3–7.4.) These clearly show their differential degrees of segregation
and the continued virtual isolation of Los Angeles's black population.[46]

Map 7.3.   Distribution of the Black Population of Los Angeles County, 1990.
Source: Courtesy of Dr. William A. Bowen, California Geographical Survey.

Map 7.4.   Distribution of the Hispanic Population of Los Angeles County, 1990.
Source: Courtesy of Dr. William A. Bowen, California Geographical Survey.

ETHNIC CHANGE IN SOUTH CENTRAL BETWEEN 1965 AND 1990

In 1965, according to the special census taken after the Watts riot in the zone bounded roughly by Pico Boulevard on the north, Rosencrans Avenue on the south, Van Ness Avenue on the west and Alameda Street on the east,[47] some 81 percent of the residents were African Americans. (The remaining 17-plus percent were reported as "white," possibly including some with Spanish surnames, and 2 percent were Asian.) By 1990, of the 672,416 residents living in the zone, few whites remained (under 3 percent), the percentage of blacks had dropped to under 45, and the proportion of Latinos had climbed to 50 percent. Asians comprised the rest.

In the interim, therefore, the area had become a "port of entry" primarily for immigrants from Mexico and Central America—those seeking a purchase on the lowest rung of the ladder of American society. By 1990, one in three residents had been born abroad, and of these, 60 percent had immigrated within the preceding decade. Despite the extensive loss of housing stock, destroyed in the earlier riot and never replaced, the total population in the zone had increased substantially, as immigrants doubled and even tripled up in existing dwellings or took up residence in garages or other nonlegal spaces.[48]

It is clear that the riot zone of 1965 had also undergone a significant decline in socioeconomic status relative to other parts of the metropolitan region, thus reflecting the growing disparities in income that characterized the decade of the 1980s. This was the joint product of the exodus of whites and better-off blacks (who tended to move westward into adjacent areas) and their replacement by a highly marginalized population of (primarily) political refugees from Central America (notably from El Salvador), as well as economic refugees (many undocumented) from Mexico. In a classic pattern of succession, they crowded into the most deteriorated eastern half of the district, sometimes replacing more successful African Americans who had moved into adjacent quarters vacated by the declining number of whites in the city and county, but mostly joining the increasingly marginalized and poorest African Americans left behind in the most deteriorated section of the city south of downtown.

Many had incomes far below the poverty line, and unemployment rates remained high. By 1990, 30 percent of families were living below the poverty line, as compared to some 27 percent in 1965. The unemployment rate had increased from 5.6 percent in 1965 to 8.6 in 1990.[49] But by then, South Central had virtually bifurcated into a predominately Hispanic section east of Vernon and a predominantly African American area west of that street.

In contrast to the exponential growth of the Latino population attributable to immigration, the number of African Americans in all of South Central had increased by only 1 percent between 1980 and 1990, perhaps reflecting disillusionment

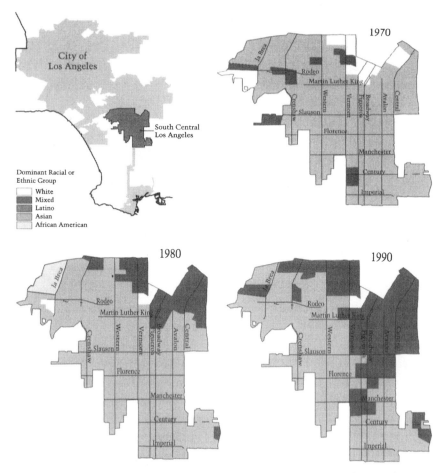

Map 7.5.   Changing Distribution of Dominant Ethnic Groups in South Central Los Angeles, 1970, 1980, and 1990.

Source: Lawrence Bobo, Melvin Oliver, James Johnson, Jr., and Abel Valenzuela, Jr., Eds., *Prismatic Metropolis: Inequality in Los Angeles.* Copyright: Russell Sage Foundation, 2002.

with the "new promised land" lauded by W. E. B. Du Bois decades before (and more recent disempowerment in the political arena) but also signaling some upward and outward mobility. Blacks and Latinos, while not completely segregated from one another, tended to dominate different subzones of South Central.

One can trace these geographic changes clearly from the sequence of maps illustrating the distribution of dominant ethnic groups in South Central Los Angeles between 1970 and 1990. As early as 1970, the entire area was predominately black, with only the northern fringe occupied chiefly by a mix of Hispanics and others. Ten years later, Hispanics had made deeper inroads all along the northern edge and had moved south and west, taking over much of the zone east of Vernon as far south as Florence and beyond. By 1990, the zone had been split in two. (See map 7.5.)

This cleavage is confirmed in a series of colored maps that trace the changes in the distribution of African Americans and Latinos between 1980 and 1990 in South Central, demonstrating how the relative socioeconomic situation of Latinos declined precipitously in the ten years before the riot, in comparison to that of African Americans.[50] Between 1980 and 1990, the proportion of African Americans on the eastern half declined, while that of Latinos increased. This cleavage also intensified a break in the distribution of social capital, with eastern areas exhibiting lower levels of per capita income and household income than areas to the west, and with the lowest housing values found in heaviest concentration in the eastern half.

Given this distribution, it should come as no surprise that participants in the riot included members of both communities and that destruction, injuries, and fatalities were concentrated along the major commercial avenues, which both

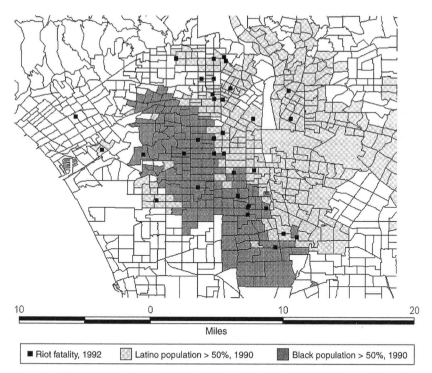

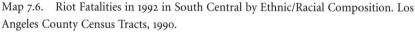

Map 7.6.   Riot Fatalities in 1992 in South Central by Ethnic/Racial Composition. Los Angeles County Census Tracts, 1990.

Source: Albert Bergeson and Max Herman, "Immigration, Race, and Riot: The 1992 Los Angeles Uprising," *American Sociological Review* 63, No. 1 (February 1998). Used with permission from the American Sociological Association and the authors.

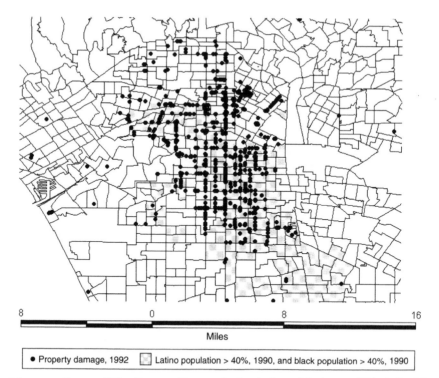

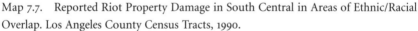

Miles

• Property damage, 1992   ▢ Latino population > 40%, 1990, and black population > 40%, 1990

Map 7.7.   Reported Riot Property Damage in South Central in Areas of Ethnic/Racial Overlap. Los Angeles County Census Tracts, 1990.

Source: Albert Bergeson and Max Herman, "Immigration, Race, and Riot: The 1992 Los Angeles Uprising," *American Sociological Review* 63, No. 1 (February 1998). Used with permission from the American Sociological Association and the authors.

communities shared and which were therefore most heavily policed.[51] It is also not surprising that arrests were evenly divided between the two communities, with a slight plurality among less urban-savvy Latinos, who may even have been selectively targeted for their immigration status (see maps 7.6 and 7.7).

Thus, the "breeding grounds" for civil strife may have been similar and the generally appalling economic conditions unchanged since 1965, but the potential participants were certainly different. Widespread resentment over the acquittal of the four offending police officers in the first Rodney King trial was certainly the match that ignited the South Central uprising, but underlying this were poverty and fear, as well as resentment of the treatment Latino immigrants received from the "Migra." New also was the hostility of both Latinos and blacks toward the Korean shopkeepers who had largely replaced the white (mostly Jewish) merchants in the zone since 1965. At least, a census of the properties intentionally destroyed in the riot suggests a special animosity toward this group.[52] In turn, Koreans accused the police of deserting them in their "hour of need," leaving them to fight off "invaders" with their own weapons. The pictures of armed Koreans on the rooftops of their stores, aiming at would-be looters, thus joined the images of the King and Denny beatings as the third icon of the riots.

NEW INTERETHNIC TENSIONS: THE CASE OF THE KOREANS

After the Korean War, small numbers of Korean immigrants joined a tiny existing Los Angeles community—their numbers increasing substantially after the changes in U.S. immigration law in 1965. Some were educated professionals; others were of less sophisticated but no less ambitious backgrounds. A niche in small grocery and liquor stores had just been vacated in South Central in the wake of the 1965 riot. Some Korean immigrants, lacking moveable cultural capital, entered the area with little foreknowledge of how they would be received and little sensitivity to the cultural differences between their ways of doing business and the expectations of their customers. Since many small operations used family labor exclusively, they provided few jobs to local residents, and almost all owners lived outside the area. By the beginning of the 1990s, Koreans owned some 350 small stores in South Central, many of them abandoned by Jewish owners after 1965.[53] If anything, relations between these new absentee proprietors and their customers were even tenser than in 1965.

It was the shooting death of Latasha Harlins by Soon Ja Du, a middle-aged Korean shopkeeper of the Empire Liquor Market Deli on Figueroa Street only 13 days after the Rodney King beating that further inflamed the simmering animosities between South Central African Americans and Koreans.[54] On March 16, 1991, Harlins, a 15-year-old black girl, entered the store to buy a plastic container of orange juice priced at $1.79; she put it partway into her backpack and approached the counter with two dollars in her hand.[55] Du accused Harlins of shoplifting. Harsh words and a physical struggle followed. Outweighed, tiny Mrs. Du

> reached beneath the counter and pulled a revolver from a brown holster.... When [Harlins] saw the gun in Du's hand, she turned and began to walk away. Bracing herself on the counter and using both hands on the gun, Du fired a single shot at the retreating girl. The bullet, fired from a distance of less than four feet, struck Harlins in the back of the head.... She died instantly.[56]

The facts in the case were not disputed. The victim was dead and unable to testify. The only witness testifying at the trial was a 12-year-old black girl who had been present in the store; she confirmed that Latasha had been shot as she was leaving.[57]

Du's husband, who had called the police to report a robbery in progress, did not deny that his wife had fired the shot. Taken to a local hospital where she was treated for minor injuries, Soon Ja Du was arrested and charged with first-degree murder.[58]

The case came to trial six months later before Judge Joyce Ann Karlin, a young and inexperienced judge who had never before presided over a jury trial.[59] The trial was relatively short. Jury deliberation began on October 8, and four days later the split jury returned a compromise verdict: guilty of voluntary manslaughter. There was some anger over the racist comments from the accused Korean, but also begrudging acceptance of the verdict on the part of concerned black leaders.[60] The outrage did not begin until the judge's sentence!

> Karlin imposed and immediately suspended a ten-year prison sentence. Soon
> Ja Du was placed on probation for five years on the condition that she perform
> four hundred hours of community service, pay a $500 fine, and "pay full
> restitution to the victim's immediate family for the out-of-pocket expenses
> related to Latasha's funeral and any medical expenses if there were any."[61]

The black community was outraged at what they considered a flagrant miscarriage of justice, which essentially freed a killer in return for a small amount of "blood money." This anger against Korean "privilege" would be revived, especially when compared to the not-guilty verdict for the four police officers accused of beating Rodney King. It added to the ongoing resentment between South Central customers and Korean shopkeepers, not only in the neighborhood but in adjacent Koreatown to its north, where there were more tempting consumer goods.

Koreatown

By 1990, there were 145,000 Koreans living in Los Angeles County, more than in any city other than Seoul.[62] Varying in socioeconomic status and not subject to rigid residential exclusion, they lived in neighborhoods that were more segregated by income than by ethnicity, although often clustered near their Korean Presbyterian churches. The rapid growth of the Korean community in southern California since 1965 was, however, not matched by the availability of ethnic-specific stores, restaurants, and services in a central place. As Abelmann and Lie tell us:

> The symbolic beginning of Koreatown in Los Angeles was the opening of the
> Olympic Market in 1971. Coming to Los Angeles from West Germany, where
> he worked as a miner, Hi Duk Lee bought the Olympic Market at 3122
> Olympic Boulevard, which attracted many Korean Americans throughout
> the region.... Korean businesses clustered around the food empori-

um.... By the mid-1970s, Korean-American-owned businesses expanded in all directions... [and] the area was... dotted with Korean-language signs.[63]

By 1980, this thriving linear commercial district contained so many specialty stores that it was officially designated Koreatown by the city.[64] Its prosperity benefited not only from its commercial and symbolic attractions but also from foreign investments. "In addition to individual investors, South Korean banks and corporations established offices in Koreatown.... This transnational business investment contributed to Koreatown's growth."[65] Both its prosperity and its symbolic meaning were to prove targets for looting in 1992.

Koreatown was very different from a traditional ethnic enclave, however. In 1990, only 40 percent of its businesses were Korean owned, and only 10 percent of its residents were Korean American. Latinos constituted the overwhelming majority of its residents (68 percent), often paying high rents for inferior apartments owned by Koreans. Abelmann and Lie suggest that the large number of Latinos living in or near Koreatown accounted in part for the large number of Latino looters involved in the riots.[66] Korean store owners paid their Latino workers poorly, as did Korean employers in the garment district, located between downtown and South Central. The Latino population may not have shared with African Americans the same degree of anger over the miscarriages of justice in the death of Latasha Harlins and the beating of Rodney King, but they had their own legitimate grievances.

THE KOREAN RESPONSE TO THE RIOTS

A college-educated Korean man interviewed by Abelmann and Lie reported:

> The greatest shock to me was the Hispanic looting of Koreatown.... They were the same people that I live with, drive by, walk by, talk to, the very same ones who were looting the stores. And here they were, a baby carriage full of looted goods in one arm and a baby in the other.... [I saw] the fortresses of Korean-American middle-aged men, [with] "cars, guns, bats, sticks, knives, whatever" at the main entrance to Koreatown.... Make no mistake, they really knew what they doing [suggesting that they had experience as soldiers in the Korean War].... What's worse, the looters were arrogant, laughing as they went.[67]

Less-organized defenses of the smaller shops in South Central were also mounted, but less effectively.

Collectively, the Korean American community felt betrayed. They accused the Los Angeles Police Department of abandoning them while retreating to defend white-owned stores in fancier neighborhoods. They claimed that instead of supporting the defenders, the police arrested them for carrying arms. They claimed they had suffered excessive losses and complained about the red tape involved in obtaining insurance settlements. Not only did Koreatown's prosperity decline in the wake of the riots, but the area's reputation suffered, since many Koreans feared to go there. The situation was worse in South Central. Very few of the small shops outside Koreatown ever received compensation. They could not rebuild, nor did they wish to return. Nothing could heal the rift. The only positive consequence was the beginning of political organization of the community.[68]

SOCIAL SCIENTISTS' DIAGNOSES AND AUTOPSIES

As in 1965, there was one expanding industry that was stimulated by the riots of 1992: a virtual outpouring of articles and book collections dissecting the causes and consequences of the disaster. The police may have been unprepared and the media deficient in interpreting the meaning of the events, but social scientists, who had been following the sidewise rather than upward changes in South Central since 1965, were not surprised, since they had been noting, with depressing regularity, the continued neglect of Los Angeles's poorest minority area.

The most noteworthy change between 1965 and 1992, however, was in the racial and ethnic identities of the prominent commentators and scholars whose analyses dominate the post-1992 autopsies. Just as white psychologists and political scientists, such as Cohen and Sears and their associates at UCLA, dominated the field in 1965, black scholars and commentators, with few exceptions, have been the most prominent analysts/interpreters of the 1992 "riot."

They are, of course, not the first African American scholars to study race riots. It will be recalled that prominent black analysts had played crucial roles in earlier postriot explanations. Charles S. Johnson, the unacknowledged author of the text issued by the interracial commission charged with investigating the 1919 Chicago race riot, was the first. But despite his pessimistic descriptions, he tended to follow the more optimistic view of his mentor, Robert Park, who had faith in the future when he argued that through assimilation and closer contacts, race relations would undergo a "cycle" resolving the tensions. Kenneth Clark analyzed the 1964 New York riot, attributing what he considered a "frightening and senseless outbreak" to the alienation of its participants, and, through his work with HARYOU, hoped to offer positive outlets for black achievement and easier integration. But neither had the institutional backing or the technical skills to carry out systematic inquiries on racial inequalities. This time, members of the UCLA Center for the Study of Urban Poverty were the leaders in redefining the causes and consequences of the riot.

Table 7.2 Terms Used by Analysts of 1992 Events by Ideological Position

Category 1: Riot/Riots[a]	Category 2: Mixed Terms[a] (Riot/Uprising, Riot/ Rebellion, Riot/Protest)	Category 3: Conflict/Discontent/Civil Disturbance/Civil Unrest/Competition[b]	Category 4: Rebellion/ Uprising/Intifadab[b]
Mark Baldassare, ed., *The Los Angeles Riots: Lessons for the Urban Future*	Albert Bergesen and Max A. Herman, "Immigration, Race and Riot: The 1992 Los Angeles Uprising"	L. Bobo et al., "Public Opinion before and after a Spring of Discontent"	Mike Davis, interview with Cindi Katz and Neil Smith, "L.A. Intifada: Interview with Mike Davis"
Lou Cannon, *Official Negligence: How Rodney King and the Riots Changed Los Angeles and the LAPD*	Burt Useem, "The State and Collective Disorders: The Los Angeles Riot/Protest of April 1992"	Maria-Rosario Jackson, James Johnson, Jr., and Walter C. Farrell, Jr., "After the Smoke Has Cleared: An Analysis of Selected Responses to the Los Angeles Civil Unrest of 1992"	Robert Gooding-Williams, ed., *Reading Rodney King/ Reading Urban Uprising*
D. DiPasquale and E. L. Glaeser, "The Los Angeles Riot and the Economics of Urban Unrest"	Paul Ong and Suzanne Hee, *Losses in the Los Angeles Civil Unrest, April 29–May 1, 1992: Lists of Damaged Properties and the L.A. Riot/Rebellion and Korean Merchants*	J. Johnson, Jr., et al., *First Status Report on the Center for the Study of Urban Poverty's Evaluation of Responses to the Los Angeles Civil Unrest of 1992*	J. H. Johnson, Jr., and W. C. Farrell, Jr., "The Fire This Time: The Genesis of the Los Angeles Rebellion of 1992"[c]

(Continued)

Table 7.2 (Continued)

Don Hazen, ed., *Inside the L.A. Riots: What Really Happened, and Why It Will Happen Again*	Melvin L. Oliver and James H. Johnson, Jr., "Inter-ethnic Conflict in an Urban Ghetto: the Case of Blacks and Latinos in Los Angeles"
	J. H. Johnson, Jr., W. C. Farrell, Jr, and M. L. Oliver, "Seeds of the Los Angeles Rebellion of 1992"[c]
J. Kotkin and D. Friedman, *The Los Angeles Riots: Causes, Myths and Solutions*	Karen Parkers, Patricia McCall, and Jodi Lane, "Exploring Racial Discrimination and Competition Processes of Race-Specific Violence in Urban Context"
	J. H. Johnson, Jr., et al., "The Los Angeles Rebellion of 1992: A Retrospective View"[c]
Staff of the *Los Angeles Times*, *Understanding the Riots: Los Angeles before and after the Rodney King Case*	Haki R. Madhubuti, ed., *Why L.A. Happened: Implications of the '92 Los Angeles Rebellion*

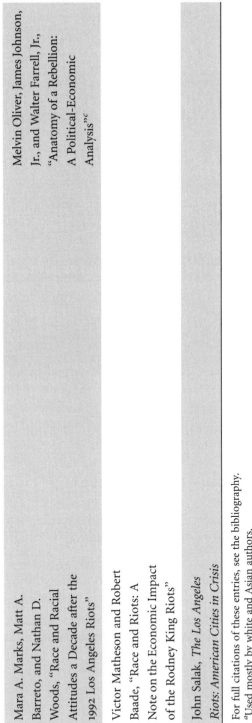

Mara A. Marks, Matt A. Barreto, and Nathan D. Woods, "Race and Racial Attitudes a Decade after the 1992 Los Angeles Riots"

Melvin Oliver, James Johnson, Jr., and Walter Farrell, Jr., "Anatomy of a Rebellion: A Political-Economic Analysis"[c]

Victor Matheson and Robert Baade, "Race and Riots: A Note on the Economic Impact of the Rodney King Riots"

John Salak, *The Los Angeles Riots: American Cities in Crisis*

For full citations of these entries, see the bibliography.
[a]Used mostly by white and Asian authors.
[b]Used mostly by minority authors.
[c]It is interesting to note the repositioning, between 1992 and 1993, of Johnson, Farrell, and Oliver from category 3 to category 4.

What difference did this make? For one, the different analytical frame they initiated is reflected in a new set of preferred terms. Before proceeding to the findings of these and other investigators, we might consider how the term one uses for "the riot" reveals the position one takes toward it. I have done a simple sort of the terms adopted by authors in the major titles of articles and books produced in the wake of the event (see table 7.2). The terms used range from the unambiguously negative term "riot"[69] to "rebellion," "uprising," even "intifada," passing through such more neutral usages as "civil unrest," "minority conflict," "discontent," and "competition."

While it would be illegitimate to infer from this list the political positions of authors, the fit is fairly consistent. Each set of authors defines and frames the event differently. The first accepts, however critically, the definition of events as violations of law and order and places the onus on the actors themselves. The second set is clearly ambivalent, employing mixed terms. The third set uses more neutral distancing terms, as a claim to greater "scientific objectivity." And the final set defends militancy as a "legitimate" means of last resort to achieve necessary deep structural changes.

One must ask, therefore, how these frames of analysis are used by interested parties, participants, and observers, and with what consequences. We can dismiss the police obsession with more and better control of riots, despite their lip service to "social problems." That is their "work," their mission. The case of social analysts and commentators is more complicated. The frame of the first two sets is to interpret race riots as explosive moments of discontent—often exacerbated by "gangs," hot weather, economic downturns, and media-spread infections—that "bubble up" periodically from ongoing inequalities in "the system," which, though flawed, is basically legitimate. Implicit in the third set is the acknowledgment that there are serious faults in "the system" but the hope that they can be "fixed" by institutional reforms and a more open class/race/gender opportunity structure. The final set stresses the oppressive domination of the disenfranchised by powerful agents who benefit from their ability to ignore or suppress their victims. The latter approach tends to draw parallels between the colonizers and the colonized that can only be rectified, in the long run, by fundamental liberation.[70]

ATTITUDINAL REACTIONS TO THE RIOT/CIVIL DISTURBANCE/REBELLION

Did people in Los Angeles share in these views? It will be recalled that the retrospective data compiled by Cohen and associates after the 1965 riot revealed a wide gap between white and black perceptions of the efficacy of protest. In general, black respondents were hopeful that the riot would help to improve race relations by calling the attention of whites to their difficulties and pains. In actual fact, however, white attitudes became more negative, thus disappointing those expectations. The gap between the responses suggested an increased polarization. Would similar results be found in the post-1992 period?

Unfortunately, the methods of that enormous study could not be replicated in the post-1992 period. However, there are some serendipitous findings from an ongoing attitudinal survey of racial attitudes whose researchers, in an unanticipated "experiment," had completed about half of their interviews before the riot and went on to complete the remaining half in its aftermath. Between the two sets of interviews there was an opportunity to add four questions about the riots themselves.[71]

The annual Los Angeles County Social Survey done by UCLA for 1992 had as its focus "Ethnic Antagonisms in Los Angeles." This was a random-digit-dialing telephone survey that had oversampled black and Asian households and was available in English or Spanish to Hispanic respondents. The survey questions were designed, among other things, to elicit the stereotypes that each of the four subgroups held about the others and to assess the relative social distances between racial/ethnic groups. Because of the fortuitous timing, it also became possible to infer what changes, if any, had resulted from the riots themselves.

On a number of questions, little change was registered. When asked whether they felt that Los Angeles had become a better or worse place in which to live over the past five years, the responses in each group were consistently negative: "70% or greater of each of the four major ethnic groups felt that LA had become a 'worse' place." The riots did not change this except marginally, possibly because "opinions... were already so negative that there was little room for the verdict/rebellion to further shift opinion in a negative direction."[72] Nor did the riots increase anxieties about job losses, although Hispanics (who had the lowest household incomes of any group) were more concerned about this than were Asians, blacks, or whites (in descending order). The riot also did not seem to affect the degree to which respondents in each group had confidence in the local government. Both before and after, blacks expressed the least confidence, "followed by Hispanics, whites, and, lastly, Asians." Confidence in the police also remained fairly constant, in roughly the same order. "Fifty-six percent of blacks expressed 'not much' confidence in the local police as compared to 31.1% of Hispanics, and 26.3% of Asians." Only white attitudes seem to have been affected by the riot, since the percentage expressing "not much confidence" rose from 13 to over 20 percent.[73]

The four questions added to the study after the riot elicited responses to the precipitating verdicts, asked how fairly the criminal justice system treats African Americans, whether they supported the proposed amendment to limit the term of police chiefs, and, most important, "whether the violence following the verdicts was mainly legitimate social protest or criminal behavior."

Here the opinions of the four groups diverged significantly. Some 96 percent of black respondents disagreed with the not-guilty verdicts, as compared to about three-quarters of Asian and Latino respondents and just under two-thirds of whites. But a full 20 percent of whites agreed with the verdicts. Support for limiting the terms of chiefs of police was similarly high, with blacks (79 percent) and Asians (76 percent) marginally more supportive than either whites (71 percent) or Hispanics (63 percent).[74]

These relatively high agreement rates were not paralleled on the other two questions. In response to the statement that blacks usually don't get fair treatment in the courts and in the criminal justice system, blacks were much more likely to agree or strongly agree (80 percent) than were Asians and Hispanics (45 percent) or whites (40 percent). The same discrepancies were found in the answers to whether the riots were mostly protests against unfair conditions or mainly a way of engaging in looting and street crime. Some 68 percent of blacks answered "mainly protest," and another 10 percent said it was mixed with looting. Only 23 percent of blacks dismissed it as simply looting and street crime. In contrast, 56 percent of whites labeled it looting and street crime, followed by 52 percent of Latinos and 51 percent of Asians.[75] The authors suggest that on all these questions,

> a particularly sharp contrast [emerged] . . . between the views of blacks and whites. On the whole, blacks appear to be strongly inclined to see the verdict as part of an on-going and systematic pattern of injustice that blacks face when dealing with the criminal justice system. Whites, and to a considerable degree Asians and Hispanics, see the verdict as wrong but also exceptional.[76]

The gap between these "definitions of the situation" reveals an increased isolation of blacks that parallels their relative wide social distance from the three other ethnic groups. It also accounts for their greater feelings of alienation in the wake of the riots. No longer expecting, as they had in 1965, that their protests might make a difference by sending whites a message of their frustration and possibly inviting better understanding, they had become more pessimistic about overcoming the barriers of racial discrimination, to which they increasingly attributed black/white inequality.[77] The authors reached a discouraging conclusion.

> This strong and uniform rise in black alienation from American social institutions is the single clearest and most consistent change for any of the items we have examined. . . . This rising discontent occurred among black men and women, as well as across educational and income levels. . . . [T]he

rise in discontent was strongest among black households whose incomes were $50,000 or higher. Mean alienation scores rose after the verdict/ rebellion for all income groups, but *the increase was greatest among blacks in the highest income category. The magnitude of the change among the high income category is very nearly a full standard deviation unit increase.*[78]

The only other significant change in intergroup relations was, as might have been anticipated, an increase in Asian prejudice and fear of blacks. I have not reported the survey's findings on social distance, since I have major doubts about whether respondents answer honestly to the kinds of hypothetical questions that are asked. Far more significant is the objectively noted greater isolation of blacks in the city in the postriot period, as contrasted with the greater diffusion of Asians and Hispanics, and the equally objective betrayal of promises to rebuild South Central.

In the years since the riot/rebellion, blacks have lost some measure of the political visibility they had gained under Bradley's coalition. As I argue at the end of this chapter, there has been a slow movement of ethnic tectonic plates, as the increasing Latino population has gradually won a place for its new citizens. This has been altering the balance of power in the city, to the detriment of Los Angeles's declining black population.

AFTER THE RIOTS—NO BETTER THAN BEFORE

Given the rather dramatic changes in South Central between 1965 and 1992, one might have expected the city's responses during and after the 1992 uprising to have been different, if not better. Changes in the cast of players, however, seem to have made little difference in outcomes. True, South Central's residents had changed from almost exclusively African American poor people to an even mix with equally vulnerable Spanish-speaking recent immigrants, primarily from Central America; but the disappearance of industrial jobs in the area had turned into a rout, and the two groups were potentially competitive in a race to the bottom. Absentee Korean shopkeepers had replaced Jewish merchants in similarly modest stores, but they seemed even less empathetic than their predecessors. And now they were gone as well.

The city's leaders had also changed. Police Chief Parker had been replaced by an equally insensitive Daryl Gates, who had come under attack for perpetuating the Los Angeles tradition of a militarized police force, albeit by then leavened with some newly appointed but similarly trained Hispanics and blacks. Thanks to the passage of Proposition F, Gates was finally removed, and Willi Williams, Philadelphia's black chief of police, was recruited to replace him; but a demoralized police department could neither be restored to its former cockiness nor embrace a new program of greater enlightenment. Williams proved a disappointing choice, and his contract was not renewed for a second five-year term. The department continued to seek leadership.

A clueless white mayor, Sam Yorty, had been replaced by Tom Bradley, a black former football star and police captain, who had parlayed his success on the city council to becoming elected as mayor in 1973. By 1992, however, he had adapted to his role as helpmate to downtown commercial interests, and although he had shared with his supporters some of the emotional outrage over the beating and verdict, he failed to exercise a more forceful response, even though he had little to lose, since he was close to completing his 20-year reign. In 1993, in a backlash attributed to the riots, Bradley was replaced by a wealthy white businessman, Richard Riordan, the first Republican mayor in 30 years, who defeated his Chinese American Democratic opponent by garnering support from an overwhelming plurality of white voters. He achieved this victory with practically no support from the black community and with few votes from Hispanic citizens, who mostly stayed away from the polls.[79] Riordan hoped to combine his loyalties to downtown interests with his dedication to reforming the school system, as well as to repairing South Central. In the latter attempt, he failed miserably to entice the business community to invest in creating new employment opportunities for South Central's needy residents. In short, the cast had changed, but the roles they assumed in the crisis were patterned on a discredited mold.

It should therefore not be surprising that the responsiveness in the aftermath of the crisis was substantially no more effective. Promises to rebuild, broken in 1965, were similarly disappointing in 1992. At first, extravagant hopes were invested in Rebuild L.A., headed by Peter Uberroth, former head of the 1964 Olympics, whom Bradley appointed to coordinate the efforts of a coalition of public and private investments in repairing the ravages of the riot. But this was not even Johnson's truncated War on Poverty. Public funds had since dried up, as supports were slashed under the elder Bush administration. With no funds forthcoming from Washington or even Sacramento, the strategy devolved to raising pledges from corporate sponsors, who not only failed to meet them but even denied having made such pledges. In the view of critic Mike Davis, "in the eyes of many, R[ebuild] LA was therefore . . . exposed as the philanthropic equivalent of the classic Ponzi scheme: mendaciously pyramiding false promises into purely fictitious community 'rebuilding.'"[80]

If Davis describes the autopsy, the journalist James Stern details the burial of the rebuilding plan a few years later.

> Four and a half years after an ambitious campaign was launched to revitalize
> the neighborhoods left smoldering by a three-day spasm of rioting here, the

effort seemed last week to have come down to little more than a couple of sound bites in the Vice Presidential debate.... The history of the efforts to rebuild the afflicted neighborhoods has been filled with frustration, symbolized by the announcement last Wednesday that Rebuild L.A., the organization hastily formed to bring jobs and hope to the city's poor areas after the riots in April 1992, would shut down.[81]

It was being shut down after the abysmal failure of the business community to invest in rebuilding the area and to provide opportunities for employment for its residents. "Some 40 percent of young blacks in the hardest-hit areas are still without jobs." A consultant company estimated that an investment of $6 billion would have been "required to create the 90,000 [jobs] needed by residents in the neighborhoods." Firms involved in Rebuild L.A. "had pledged $580 [million] in a well-attended news conference, but of these, only $380 million have materialized [and may have been used toward covering administrative costs of the program].... And only half of the 32 supermarkets that were supposed to bring convenience, lower prices and jobs to the area have been built."[82]

> Most experts now agree that the original approach of Rebuild L.A., while well-intentioned, was misguided because of ignorance about the local economy. The first chairman, [former] ... baseball commissioner Peter Ueberroth, who quit after a year of criticism over a lack of results, was brought in partly because of his business connections. He lined up commitments from big corporations like I.B.M. and Hughes Aircraft on the assumption that only major private investment from outside could transform the area.... Some of those investments were quite successful in providing jobs and training, but within a year, some of the other companies denied ever making the commitments.[83]

Measures of "success" were being doctored by surveys that covered not only South Central but Pico Union and other areas south of downtown where garment sweatshops prevail. Between 1994 and 1996, surveys were conducted that counted some 87,000 manufacturing jobs, "mostly in shops with 50 or fewer employees. Nearly half are in the garment industry, while many others are in [poorly paid] ... furniture, retail and metal fabrication industries," no match for the disappeared heavy industries that formerly offered union pay. Only about two-thirds are held by local residents of the expanded survey zone.[84] "There are still grave concerns about the poverty and hopelessness of these neighborhoods... and [some] think rioting could break out again, given the right spark."[85]

To put a more charitable interpretation on these failures, one must acknowledge that efforts to help South Central were deflected by a new and massive crisis that affected many more and diverse victims in Los Angeles and demanded the full attention of its mayor. On January 17, 1994, the city was struck by an earthquake (calibrated at more than 6.6) that was "more destructive than any other in the modern history of the city." Fifty-seven died, thousands were injured, and thousands more became homeless. Destruction, which concentrated in the San Fernando Valley section of the city far from South Central, was widespread through downtown and Hollywood as well. Martial law had to be imposed. "For the first time in history, virtually all of Los Angeles was blacked out. But the effects were also felt as far away as rural Idaho, where 150,000 customers lost power."[86] Highways and bridges crumbled, streets became impassable, and the costs of rescue, maintaining order, and recovering from public and private property damage soared to the billions.

But even without this competing distraction, it is unlikely that South Central would have received more attention. The saddest words were spoken by Celes King III, chairman of CORE, on April 29, 1997, on the fifth anniversary of the Los Angeles riots. "*The big lesson that has been learned is that no one really cares.*"[87]

Ten Years after the Second Uprising

Was Celes King's despair mirrored by an expectation that future riots might recur on the unreconstructed site of the earlier two? The fears of such a recurrence were on the minds of at least half of Los Angeles residents questioned a decade after the 1992 riot. Half of the respondents reported that they anticipated another riot. Their fears were associated with "negative assessments of life in Los Angeles," and especially with pessimism over racial issues. Although there were variations in expectations based on income, educational attainment, and duration of residency in Los Angeles, the surprising finding was that racial and ethnic identity per se had "no appreciable direct or mediating impact on expectations of future riots, a striking finding in light of the central place race occupies in social science research and public discourse."[88]

Long-Term Political Consequence of the Riots

The period between 1965 and 1992 had recorded a dismal history of halfhearted reforms in the political regime and virtually none in the all-important police department, which Horne singled out as "the constant that linked 1965 and 1992."[89] In contrast, the post-1992 period has seen greater attempts to change the distribution of power and to rein in the autonomy of the police. Admittedly, progress has been slow and erratic. But in the dozen or so years since 1992, fundamental changes appear to be taking place in Los Angeles, although it is still too early to assess their staying power. Whether these changes will be sufficient to moderate the intractable inequalities generated by international and national forces and to bridge the gap between the police and those they are supposed to protect and serve remains to be seen. As in all cases, some will benefit more than others. If Latino voters use their new political strength to the detriment of the interests of blacks and new immigrants, there is no guarantee that future uprisings will not recur. And the great unknown is the future shape of the California economy.

EPILOGUE

The most striking change in the recent period was the election in 2005 of the Democratic mayoral candidate Antonio Villaraigosa, the first Mexican American to hold that office since the 1870s. But this victory was more than a token gift to the Latino community, even though their voting strength had increased over the past decades as new immigrants were naturalized. To many of all ethnicities, the victory represented a new rainbow coalition, under the leadership of a charismatic politician who had both impeccable liberal credentials and a successful career in state and local politics.[90]

The son of a Mexican immigrant father and a California-born mother of Mexican descent, by age 15 Villaraigosa had earned his civil rights/union stripes as a volunteer in Cesar Chavez's first grape boycott. In the early 1980s, Villaraigosa was a community organizer who collaborated with an equally young and active African American leader to form the African-Latino roundtable to bridge the differences between Los Angeles's two largest ethnic groups. By the mid-1980s he had worked himself up to become a prominent organizer for the Los Angeles United Teachers' Union. He was also rising in local politics, serving between 1990 and 1994 on the Los Angeles Metropolitan Transportation Board as an advocate for improved public transport. In 1994 he ran successfully for his first elected office, a seat on the California State Assembly, becoming Democratic whip and Assembly majority leader. Four years later he was chosen as speaker of the Assembly, the first from Los Angeles in 25 years. Because of term limit restrictions, he left state office in 2000 and in 2001 ran for mayor of Los Angeles to replace Riordan, who was completing his second term. Villaraigosa was narrowly defeated in a runoff contest against James Hahn, the son of an old party boss who had black support. In 2005, Villaraigosa won a resounding endorsement in the mayoral election, receiving support not only from the increased Latino electorate but from African American, Asian, and liberal white voters. He assumed office in January 2006.

The faltering search for new leadership in the police department followed a similar tentative path. The preferred solution to achieving a more racially sensitive police force was initially believed to lie in selecting an African American as chief, but none lasted long enough to have their five-year contract renewed for a second (and last) term.[91] Finally, ignoring skin color, the city turned to William Bratton, former police chief in Boston and in New York City, who was appointed by James Hahn in 2002 and welcomed enthusiastically by the new mayor. It remains to be seen whether Bratton can succeed in both disciplining his force and encouraging them to follow his plans for greater community policing.

DOES THE ELECTION MEAN REAL CHANGE IN LOS ANGELES?

The shift in the demographic tectonic plates alluded to earlier has been long overdue. Mexicans, for some time the largest single ethnic group in the city, have hitherto failed to translate their numbers into political power. But as more immigrants and their children qualify for citizenship and the franchise, the composition of an energized electorate has begun to resemble that of its population. This may not automatically lead to improvements in South Central. The sanguine hope that the more established Chicano residents in the oldest "barrios," such as Boyle Heights, who never joined the 1992 rebellion and who harbor ambivalence, if not reserved animosity, toward both the blacks and the undocumented Latinos of South Central, will be more supportive of their needs may be too naïve.

Long dominated by Anglos, the political terrain has shifted, not only ethnically but ideologically. A new coalition between blacks and Latinos may develop policies aimed at greater equality, more investments in socially distributed amenities, and greater assistance to the poor.[92] Can this apparent commitment—so deviant from the current mood of middle America and so lacking in federal support—be sustained (and funded) in the face of the persistent underlying power structure of big business and the military-industrial complex that dominates southern California? I have elsewhere described the restructuring of Los Angeles's economy under the impact, *inter alia,* of globalization. In recent years there has been an irreversible bifurcation of the region's labor force into high and low wage segments associated with race and ethnicity, often in the same plants, and an irreversible movement of factories from derelict, old-style industrial districts accessible to South Central to peripheral (and whiter) regions.

The same has been true in the so-called service sector, with its bifurcation into high-tech professionals and "lowly servants."[93]

Given these trends, will the promises to rebuild South Central have any greater chance under the new political regime? Where will the needed funds be found, especially given cutbacks in federal and state subventions for social services, education, and health? Unless California voters rescind Proposition 13, which places a tight ceiling on increases in real estate taxes, cities in the state will continue to come up empty. Despite the superficial glow of health on the economy, at least some scholars have argued that the shortfalls caused by the 1992 riots have still left their mark on the city's economy[94]—and, we might add, on the psyche of its residents.

What are the possibilities that the new political coalition between Latinos and African Americans can be sustained? One recalls the jubilation that both of these excluded communities felt when Harold Washington won the mayor's office in Chicago, an alliance that soon broke down over complaints that he favored blacks over his Puerto Rican allies. One wonders also about a possible backlash as African Americans lose some of their past political influence to upcoming Latino politicians and begin to accuse the white-led police force of perpetuating the same oppression as before. The better-off blacks who reacted, in the post-1992 survey, with depression and alienation may follow the many disillusioned whites who left Los Angeles for distant suburbs or even other states,[95] ceding the ground to Mexican irredentism. The land base for rebellion is shrinking, and the geographic and social isolation of the poor black community continues to increase. Will Los Angeles's first multiethnic riot be its last?

Most important for the future of race relations in Los Angeles, given the zero-sum struggle between poor Latinos and poor blacks for bad jobs in the service sector, can any lasting alliance be forged between them? The somber conclusion of Michael Lichter and Melvin Oliver is that poorly educated black males "are being squeezed out of the labor force by whites and Asians from 'above' and Latino immigrants from 'below.'"[96]

The situation may even be more alarming than this. Both poor Latinos and poor blacks may constitute a redundant labor pool that can never be absorbed by the civilian economy and that therefore may pose a threat to domestic peace.[97] It is a well-accepted truism that young males living in poor minority neighborhoods, especially if they are neither in school nor the legal labor force, are the most enthusiastic participants in urban riots.[98] These men are especially unlikely to find jobs in the civilian economy if they have ever come into contact with the criminal justice system.[99] Unfortunately, what a telephone survey of residences, no matter how carefully conducted and analyzed, can never measure is the disappearance of vulnerable males into the expanding maws of what some have called the prison industrial system into which offenders have been sucked in increasing numbers in recent decades. Among the critics of this system have been Loic Wacquant and Mike Davis.[100] Both recognize that prisons remove young black males from the streets, but they fail to stress the equal toll of this system on Hispanics in California, and they do not fully appreciate how the incarceration of young men can also serve as a deterrent to riots.[101]

As I write this in mid-February 2006, news reports have been coming from southern California about "race riots" between hundreds of African American and Hispanic prisoners that began on February 4 in a Los Angeles County maximum security jail, spread to other county detention centers, including a Los Angeles County jail dorm, and even to buses transporting prisoners from a detention center to the courts in San Bernardino County. The explanations of law officials were that the riots involved rival gangs that could not be legally separated into segregated lockdowns. We may now be seeing a new strategy for diverting rebellions and civil strife from city streets into the penal system itself. I turn to these themes in chapter 8.

NOTES

1. Missing from his tape were the preceding few minutes during which King evidently resisted arrest.
2. Their hands were tied; he could not be fired, due to a well-intentioned regulation originally designed to insulate the position from arbitrary, politically inspired power—an ironic turn of events.
3. Lou Cannon, *Official Negligence: How Rodney King and the Riots Changed Los Angeles and the LAPD* (New York: Times Books, 1997), pp. 122–23. This almost-700-page source is the most detailed and balanced account I have found of the events surrounding the riot and the politics of policing in Los Angeles.
4. Ibid., p. 129.
5. See Independent Commission on the Los Angeles Police Department, Christopher Commission Report, issued July 1991.
6. Raphael Sonenshein, *Politics in Black and White* (Princeton, N.J.: Princeton University Press, 1993), quotation from pp. 218–19. Sonenshein cites the Christopher Commission Report, pp. 71–74. Details on how this quotation was obtained have been provided by Cannon, *Official Negligence*, p. 79. The remark about "gorillas in the mist" was traced to Officer Lawrence Powell, one of the two officers later found guilty in the second (federal) trial for violating King's civil rights (i.e., being racist). Immediately after the beating, Powell had sent a computer message to a fellow officer on his MDT that included the phrases "I haven't beaten anyone this bad for some time," and "It was right out of gorillas in the mist," a clearly racist remark. Transcripts of these MDTs were finally released on March 18 and quoted on television that night. A random sample of

16 months of MDTs had been reviewed in preparation for the Christopher Commission Report. Although most were routine, there were hundreds that contained derogatory comments about racial and ethnic minorities, women, and gays—certain of them "patently offensive" (p. 137).

7. Quoted from Hiroshi Fukurai, Richard Krooth, and Edgar W. Butler, "The Rodney King Beating Verdicts," in Mark Baldassare, ed., *The Los Angeles Riots: Lessons for the Urban Future* (Boulder, Colo.: Westview Press, 1994), p. 79.

8. Sonenshein, *Politics in Black and White*, p. 225.

9. A detailed account of the trial, its change of venue to Simi Valley, and its unexpected denouement can be found in Fukurai et al., "The Rodney King Beating Verdicts," pp. 73–102. See also the detailed account in "Judicial Negligence," chap. 8 in Cannon, *Official Negligence*, pp. 174–92.

10. Fukurai et al, "The Rodney King Beating Verdicts," p. 81.

11. Ibid., p. 82.

12. Ibid., pp. 85–86.

13. Quoted in ibid., p. 87.

14. The most easily accessible account of the sequence and spread of the riot is "Nightmare City," chap. 12 in Cannon, *Official Negligence*, pp. 303–46, which is based largely on the Webster Report (see William H. Webster and Hubert Williams, *The City in Crisis: A Report by the Special Advisor to the Board of Police Commissioners on the Civil Disorder in Los Angeles*, submitted October 21, 1992). This is a two-volume, 450-page report (vol. 1, text; vol. 2, appendices and maps). The reader is referred to both these sources for fuller details. Satellite images of the average of three new fires per minute, taken during an early three-hour period (probably between 12 and 3 a.m.), clearly revealed the scope of the social explosion on a thermal map. This point was noted by Ando Arike, "Owning the Weather," *Harper's*, January 2006, p. 73.

15. See Darnell M. Hunt, *Screening the Los Angeles "Riots": Race, Seeing and Resistance* (Cambridge: Cambridge University Press, 1996).

16. Webster Report, 1:11–12. Unaccountably, almost no secondary sources except Cannon seem to have consulted this report, which contains the fullest time line of developments over the entire period between April 29 and May 10.

17. Ibid., 1:85.

18. Cannon, *Official Negligence*, p. 265.

19. Ibid., p. 281; Webster Report, 1:13.

20. Time line, Webster Report, 1:1–19. As noted, the Webster Report contains the only complete chronology of the riot from its outbreak after the verdict on the afternoon of April 29 to 6 a.m. on May 10, when the city-wide mobilization was lifted. Unless otherwise noted, I depend on this definitive source.

21. Cannon, *Official Negligence*, pp. 285–87, 298.

22. Ibid., pp. 304–7.

23. Ibid., p. 298. Details on pp. 313–14.

24. Time line, Webster Report, 1:13.

25. Cannon, *Official Negligence*, p. 323. Swap meets were Asian-style open-air markets common in South Central.

26. Cannon, *Offiicial Negligence*, pp. 332–33. This points to the ongoing enmity between the projects, presumably hotbeds of gang organization who kept some order, and the police. Nickerson Gardens, Los Angeles's largest public housing project, was home to some 3,700 black and Latino residents—the very poorest and most dependent populations in the city. The Webster Report does not mention this shoot-out.

27. Time line, Webster Report, 1:13.

28. Cannon, *Official Negligence*, p. 325.

29. The *Los Angeles Weekly* devoted its entire issue of May 8–14, 1992, to chronicling the riot. Jim Crogan, a reporter, observed the first arrival of the guard, p. 21.

30. Cannon, *Official Negligence*, p. 328.

31. Webster Report, p. 14. There were several attempts to declare a nighttime curfew and to extend its range, but its boundaries kept changing, and it could not be enforced uniformly. The curfew was not lifted until 5:15 p.m. on May 4, which marked the "end" of the riot, although troops were not withdrawn until May 10.

32. Ibid., 1:14.

33. Ibid., 1:15.

34. Webster Report, 1:17–19, for May 1 and subsequent days.

35. See Peter A. Morrison and Ira S. Lowry, "A Riot of Color: The Demographic Setting," in Baldassare, *The Los Angeles Riots*, pp. 19–46, but only pp. 20 and 22–23 actually cover the chronology.

36. Staff of the *Los Angeles Times, Understanding the Riots: Los Angeles before and after the Rodney King Case* (Los Angeles: Los Angeles Times, 1992). This source itself is quite thin and covers only the first three days. April 29 is covered in chap. 4, which presents hourly and disconnected vignettes (see pp. 45–65). The April 30 account appears in similar format as chap. 5, pp. 67–95, followed by an equally fragmented and anecdotal coverage of May 1.

37. Don Hazen, ed., *Inside the L.A. Riots: What Really Happened—and Why It Will Happen Again* (New York: Institute for Alternative Journalism, 1992).

38. Time line, Webster Report, 1:19.

39. The most remarkable attempt to capture the conflicting "voices" of participants in and reactors to the riots is, of course, the work of the brilliant monologist Anna Deavere Smith, in her *Twilight Los Angeles* (1992). I was privileged to attend two performances (in New York and Princeton). A transcript is available, but it fails to convey the impact of her delivery. A performance is available on video cassette (New York: Twilight 1992, distributed by PBS [Alexandria, Va.]).

40. The final count of fatalities turned out to be 54, of whom 26 were black, 14 Latino, 9 non-Hispanic white, 2 Asian, and 3 so badly burned that their race could not be determined. Cannon, *Official Negligence*, p. 347. Webster Report, 2: 9–12, lists 42 dead.

41. Gerald Horne, "Epilogue: The 1990s," in *Fire This Time: The Watts Uprising and the 1960s* (originally published Charlottesville, Va.: University Press of Virginia, 1975; reprinted, New York: Da Capo Press, 1997), pp. 355–56.

42. The Los Angeles Primary Metropolitan Statistical Area (PMSA) is coterminous with Los Angeles County, which is why I have chosen to use the unit of the county here. The figures in this section depend on several sources, including my own calculations from

the U.S. census of 1990, volume for the Los Angeles Consolidated Metropolitan Statistical Area (CMSA). I have subtracted data for the four counties adjacent to Los Angeles County. I also depend on the calculations of others that deviate slightly from my own (see table 7.1 and fig. 7.1 below).

43. See my *New York, Chicago, Los Angeles: America's Global Cities* (University of Minnesota Press, 1999), pp. 376, 377, tables 12.5 and 12.6, with notes. One must exercise extreme caution in attempting to estimate the number of "Hispanics" counted as such in successive censuses, since definitions of Hispanics have changed over time and by race, and different categories existed in the 1970 census. I have taken these estimates from unpublished sources prepared by Georges Sabbagh and others.

44. For example, see the complicated estimates of ethnic and racial composition in the excellent collection edited by Roger Waldinger and Mehdi Bozorgmehr, *Ethnic Los Angeles* (New York: Russell Sage Foundation, 1996), which I adapted to produce my table 12.4, p. 373, in *New York, Chicago, Los Angeles*.

45. Lawrence Bobo, Melvin Oliver, James Johnson, Jr., and Abel Valenzuela, Jr., *Prismatic Metropolis: Inequality in Los Angeles* (New York: Russell Sage Foundation, 2000). This is one of the most important investigations of the character and causes of inequality in the city. It grew out of the work of the UCLA Center for the Study of Urban Poverty, which was founded by and/or participated in by the authors/editors. All, except Valenzuela, have left to accept other distinguished appointments: Bobo to chairs at Harvard and then Stanford; Johnson to a chair at the University of North Carolina at Chapel Hill; and Oliver to a vice presidency at the Ford Foundation and, most recently, to become dean at the University of California at Santa Barbara. During my residence at UCLA in 1993–94, I was fortunate to benefit from their remarkably synergistic collaboration.

46. William Bowen, Department of Geography, California State University at Northridge. (Northridge was at the epicenter of the Los Angeles earthquake of 1992.) See also the work of his colleagues, whose maps are in color, which makes it impossible to reproduce them here. Eugene Turner and James Allen, *An Atlas of Population Patterns in Metropolitan Los Angeles and Orange Counties 1990* (Northridge, Calif.: Department of Geography, California State University, 1991).

47. U.S. Department of Commerce, Bureau of the Census, *Special Survey of the South and East Los Angeles Areas, November 1965* (Washington, D.C.: Government Printing Office, 1965).

48. Shawn Hubler, "South L.A.'s Poverty Rate Worse than '65," *Los Angeles Times*, May 11, 1992, pp. A1, A22.

49. *Los Angeles Times*, May 11, 1992, p. A23, boxed data table. Real unemployment was higher, because it did not include those who had given up and no longer sought a job.

50. Stuart Anderson et al., *An Atlas of South Central Los Angeles* (Claremont, Calif.: Rose Institute of State and Local Government, Claremont McKenna College, 1992). The maps in this work are remarkable; unfortunately, their color makes it impossible to reproduce them here.

51. In their excellent analysis of the 1992 riots, Albert Bergesen and Max A. Herman present data identifying this zone of contact between the two communities as the core of hostilities between them. They also propose a theory that posits prior rapid demographic change as a common factor in all riots. See their "Immigration, Race, and Riot:

The 1992 Los Angeles Uprising," *American Sociological Review* 63, no. 1 (February 1998), 39–54. Herman makes this theory even more explicit in his *Fighting in the Streets: Ethnic Succession and Urban Unrest in Twentieth-Century America* (New York: Peter Lang, 2005). Herman, through a series of sophisticated statistical measures, is able to test this hypothesis with data from Chicago, Detroit, Newark, Miami, and Los Angeles. He finds some spatial correlation between substantial demographic change prior to a given riot and the severity of the ensuing riot as measured by fatalities. His approach is promising, albeit very different from my own.

52. Paul Ong and Suzanne Hee, *Losses in the Los Angeles Civil Unrest, April 29–May 1, 1992: Lists of Damaged Properties and the L.A. Riot/Rebellion and Korean Merchants* (Los Angeles: UCLA Center for Pacific Rim Studies, 1993).

53. Cannon, *Official Negligence*, p. 114. It has been estimated that almost 50 percent of the small businesses in South Central were Korean owned. See also Regina Freer, "Black-Korean Conflict," in Baldassare, *The Los Angeles Riots*, p. 183.

54. A second shooting death of a black male in June 1991 by the Korean owner of John's Liquor Store, while judged a justifiable homicide, resulted in a prolonged black boycott of that store. On the boycott and negotiations to resolve it, which widened to involve the mayor, see, among others, Freer, "Black-Korean Conflict," pp. 188–96.

55. I base this account on Cannon's narrative, *Official Negligence*, chap. 5, pp. 108–20.

56. Ibid., p. 109.

57. Ibid., p. 152.

58. Ibid., p. 113.

59. The following account is based largely on ibid., chap. 7, pp. 148–73.

60. Ibid., p. 159.

61. Ibid., p. 169.

62. Ibid., p. 113.

63. Nancy Abelmann and John Lie, *Blue Dreams: Korean Americans and the Los Angeles Riots* (Cambridge, Mass.: Harvard University Press, 1995), p. 100.

64. This was done in 1980, and street signs were posted to recognize its identity. Ibid., p. 101.

65. Ibid., p. 101.

66. Ibid., pp. 104–5.

67. Interview reported in ibid., p. 41.

68. Ibid., esp. pp. 184–87.

69. In chapter 1, I expressed my discomfort with this term, while explaining my reason for using it.

70. The most explicit statements of this type are to be found in the essays included in Haki R. Madhubuti, ed., *Why L.A. Happened: Implications of the '92 Los Angeles Rebellion* (Chicago: Third World Press, 1993), and in Robert Gooding-Williams, ed., *Reading Rodney King/Reading Urban Uprising* (New York: Routledge, 1993). Both derive some their assumptions from works such as Robert Staples, *The Urban Plantation: Racism and Colonialism in the Post-Civil Rights Era* (Oakland, Calif.: Black Scholar Press, 1987). Much earlier, a white sociologist, Robert Blauner, writing in the wake of the 1960s riots, had drawn the same analogy, which was generally accepted by many of us who studied

the Third World. See his "Internal Colonialism and Ghetto Revolt," *Social Problems* 16, no. 4 (spring 1969): pp. 393–408.

71. See Lawrence Bobo, Camille L. Zubrinsky, James Johnson, Jr., and Melvin Oliver, "Public Opinion before and after a Spring of Discontent," in Baldassare, *The Los Angeles Riots*, pp. 103–33.

72. Ibid., p. 108.

73. Ibid., p. 109.

74. Ibid., p. 110.

75. Generalized from entries in ibid., p. 111, table 5.1.

76. Ibid., p. 112.

77. Ibid., pp. 112–16, esp. p. 115, table 5.2.

78. Ibid., p. 116 (italics added).

79. Riordan was reelected in 1997 for a second four-year term, this time with wider pluralities among Latino voters, whose 60 percent vote in support tracked the white vote almost exactly.

80. Mike Davis, "Who Killed LA? A Political Autopsy," *New Left Review* 197 (January/February 1993), quotation p. 5.

81. See James Stern, "What Is Made of Broken Promises," *New York Times*, October 13, 1996, sec. 4, pp. 1, 5.

82. Ibid. In fieldwork I undertook in 1994, I could find little evidence of supermarkets. The so-called roach mobiles (trucks circulating with bare necessities) were very much in evidence, as were a few Mexican restaurants and bakeries. In contrast, empty lots alternated with churches, also in abundance.

83. Ibid., p. 5.

84. Ibid. I am clearly less enthusiastic than the authors of the survey reported by Stern.

85. Ibid. I am one of them.

86. J. Michael Kennedy, "Overview," in *Images of the 1994 Los Angeles Earthquake by the Staff of the Los Angeles Times* (Los Angeles: Times Mirror, 1994), p. 7.

87. Quoted in Cannon, *Official Negligence*, p. 584.

88. See Mara A. Marks, Matt A. Barreto, and Nathan D. Woods, "Race and Racial Attitudes a Decade after the 1992 Los Angeles Riots," *Urban Affairs Review* 40, no. 1 (2004), pp. 3–18. The anxieties of Angelenos have been captured in dramatic fashion by Mike Davis. See his *The Ecology of Fear: Los Angeles and the Imagination of Disaster* (New York: Holt, 1998).

89. Horne, *Fire This Time*, p. 359.

90. The following biographical information has been extracted from his official website, www.lacity.org/mayor/bio.htm. But see a move critical view: Connie Bruck, "Fault Lines," *The New Yorker*, May 21, 2007, pp. 44–55.

91. Willi Williams, African American chief of police of Philadelphia, was recruited in 1992 but not kept on. He was replaced by Bernard Parks, a respected longtime officer of the Los Angeles Police Department who had often been second in command. After serving from 1997 to 2002, Parks left the police force to run for a seat on the Los Angeles city council.

92. Unreserved confidence is expressed in the headline of John M. Broder, "A Black-Latino Coalition Emerges in Los Angeles," *New York Times*, April 24, 2005, p. 24.

93. See "The Los Angeles Region Transformed" in my *New York, Chicago, Los Angeles*, esp. pp. 362–67.

94. Victor Matheson and Robert Baade, "Race and Riots: A Note on the Economic Impact of the Rodney King Riots," *Urban Studies* 41, no. 13 (December 2004), pp. 2691–96.

95. See the data on interstate transfers of drivers' licenses reported in my *New York, Chicago, Los Angeles*, pp. 376–78.

96. See Michael Lichter and Melvin Oliver, "Racial Differences in Labor Force Participation and Long-Term Joblessness among Less-Educated Men," in Bobo, Oliver, Johnson, and Valenzuela, *Prismatic Metropolis*, quotation pp. 240–41.

97. Marx's reserve labor army?

98. The temptation is to assume that gang membership is responsible for the threat they pose, but gangs may serve to organize an otherwise anomic situation. In the aftermath of the Los Angeles riot, for example, the Crips and the Bloods seem to have cooperated, albeit in a temporary truce.

99. See, among others, James H. Johnson, Jr., Walter C. Farrell, Jr., and Jennifer A. Stoloff, "African American Males in Decline: A Los Angeles Case Study," in Bobo et al., *Prismatic Metropolis*, esp. pp. 328–34, where they argue that rather than explaining disabilities in the labor force by criminal activity, such disabilities are intensified, if not initially created, by the systematic and selective targeting of such individuals by the police. I return to this theme in chap. 8

100. In a brilliantly prescient choice, the attractive paperback cover of Davis's preriot *City of Quartz: Excavating the Future in Los Angeles* (New York: Vintage Books, 1992) is a photograph by Robert Morrow of the Metropolitan Detention Center in downtown Los Angeles—a theme Davis has pursued under the term "the carceral society."

101. The deficit in the number of young minority males in urban America due to their recruitment to the voluntary army remains uncalculated. Certainly, the invasion of Iraq has intensified recruitment activity in poor minority areas.

8

Explaining Differences

Predicting Convergence?

> The wonder is that there have been so few riots.
>> *Kenneth Clark, 1965*

W hen I began researching this book, I had not anticipated that I would
concur with this shocking statement. Given the obdurate persistence of
racism in American culture, and the widening divides in the racial/ethnic/class
system over the past three decades (attributable to changes in the international
division of labor that have reshaped labor demands in the United States, coupled
with massive immigration and a generation of neoliberal national policies that
have shred the welfare safety net woven in the Great Depression), I am amazed
that major urban rebellions have thus far been so constrained. Pondering the
conditions that have previously been associated with race-related violence (wars,
economic downturns, interethnic competition, spatial apartheid, blocked social
mobility, resentments over provocative police behavior and the unjust administration of the criminal justice system), one might have expected more collective
responses, especially in the major cities of the nation, where their effects are felt
most profoundly.

This book's case studies of major race riots in the three largest urban areas
of the United States over the past century, however, reveal that although general

underlying causes of discontent may be similar in their character and roughly congruent in their timing, there are sufficient and relatively consistent variations among them to warrant closer examination of the specific ways that economic, demographic, spatial, and political factors have come together in each city to shape the form and virulence of their race riots. Indeed, if one views riots and their outcomes as an interactional arena in which protesters with real grievances come into open and direct conflict with the larger system of political power, we can identify several dimensions of increasingly broad and fundamental character that affect the frequency, duration, and degree of violence of riots in specific places.

At the most proximate level is the ongoing relationship between potential protesters and the forces of law and order that are charged with restoring peace and disciplining and punishing participants. In cases where local police forces are trained to respond with restraint, where there is greater familiarity and less underlying animosity between protesters and the police, and where careful planning and disciplined responses by the police are able to avert or defuse lethal confrontations, the chances for minimizing the duration and costs of any riot are enhanced. In contrast, the wider the social and ethnic gap between the police and the protesters, the more haphazard the planning, the more panicky and unrestrained the police, and the greater the dependence on imported and untrained armed members of the national guard to handle the emergency, the more prolonged the riot and the greater its destructive results.

At the more general but fundamental level is the ongoing relationship between the protesting community and the local government. Where there is ongoing interaction between well-organized protest movements, with leaders capable of articulating specific demands for change, and a responsive local government, the more quickly hostilities can be brought to an end. Responsiveness is greater when the local power structure actually includes representatives of the dissatisfied minority group and can acknowledge the frustrations underlying the explosion and the legitimacy of the grievances being expressed. Without such ongoing interactions, protests more readily turn into street wars between two parties, each of which denies the legitimate claims of the other. Under those circumstances, conflicts can escalate to brute but often random shows of force, until protesters are defeated. Under these conditions, few positive adjustments are likely.

These possibilities for positive interactions are in turn mediated by such variables as the characteristics of minority groups on the one hand (i.e., their proportions in the population, their diversity, the degree to which their locations are concentrated and their alternate opportunities are constrained by conditions of exclusion) and, on the other hand, the degree to which enhanced paths to political representation and power in a competitive political system exist and can therefore offer constructive ways to bring about desired reforms in local policies without recourse to street violence.

Conditioning both of these are the relative opportunities for greater progress and equality afforded by the structures of the local economy. To what degree is the local job structure able to absorb minority workers with little education? How prevalent and tolerated are discriminatory hiring practices? To what extent can well-prepared minority members gain access to jobs (and respect) commensurate with their training and skills?

On all these levels, there is no city with a perfect record, and it is clear that not all the factors that could yield greater racial peace are within the control of local governments. In the comparisons that follow, I examine the relative histories of race riots in the three cities and the roles that these variables have played in either exacerbating racial tensions and riots or containing them by ameliorating the conditions that give rise to them.

NEW YORK

My first conclusion is that, for many reasons, major race riots in New York have been shorter in duration, more spatially confined, less destructive of buildings if not moveable property, and less lethal to their participants than race riots in Chicago and Los Angeles. With the exception of those in the late nineteenth century and the opening decade of the twentieth century, interracial conflict in New York has been largely between African American protesters and a still primarily white (and Irish) police force. Almost always, the trigger has been the actual or rumored harassment or killing of a black male by a member of the police,[1] but this is symptomatic of underlying grievances: the selective and discriminatory application of excessive force (police brutality) against nonwhites.

Such complaints are widely shared by nonwhites, regardless of their place of birth, national origin, and subculture. Whether different oppressed groups recognize their common cause affects how powerfully they can claim rectification. This is particularly important in the post-1965 era, as ethnic and linguistic diversity has accelerated in New York. Despite the varied backgrounds of its minority populations, and despite some tensions between blacks and Hispanics (largely Puerto Rican but now Mexican), the two largest minority communities have managed to coexist. They share close or even overlapping territories, some political leadership (albeit highly competitive), and often, common grievances such as resentment of police harassment and brutality and dissatisfaction with inferior schools, poor housing conditions, and blocked and declining job opportunities.

These issues were all clearly articulated by African American community leaders in the earliest Harlem protest riots of 1935 and 1943, were explicitly acknowledged in official postriot investigations, and have been embraced by successive waves of black immigrants from Jamaica, Haiti, the Dominican Republic, and even Africa, despite their different linguistic and cultural backgrounds. An identity of interest seems to have been sufficiently forged—despite their now scattered and often specialized neighborhoods of residence in Manhattan and three of the outer boroughs[2]—to constitute a political constituency that cannot be ignored by the local political system, characterized since the consolidation of the five boroughs in 1898 by multiple paths to political office and multiple opportunities for representation on "balanced" ethnic tickets.[3]

To be sure, an alliance between blacks and Latinos is not guaranteed.[4] Reverend Sharpton endorsed the reelection of Republican incumbent Michael Bloomberg against his Democratic Puerto Rican challenger, Bronx borough president Fernando Ferrer. Recent protest marches by Latinos (and other vulnerable immigrant groups) in response to congressional threats to criminalize undocumented immigrants and those who help them, point to a possible split. The massive protest marches in early April 2006 by New York's Latinos were not joined by African Americans, and only a few black leaders expressed guarded sympathy.[5] At the national level, members of the congressional Black Caucus have also been ambivalent about how to avoid zero-sum competition between the two groups.

This potential rift aside, there is, nevertheless, a distinctive characteristic of New Yorkers: their greater acceptance of, if not universal enthusiasm for, social diversity. To a limited extent, this may be attributable to the city's fragmented and fine-grained spatial pattern, knitted together by, and dependent on, a mass transit system that throws together a wide range of people of varied appearances and behavior patterns who are inadvertently exposed, at least visually, to one another and have thus developed unique forms of, if not tolerance, studied social nonobservance of one another.[6] (This accommodation is not without its occasional frictions and even dangers.) These daily reminders of diversity are also replicated, at lesser scales, in the juxtaposing or overlapping divisions in both public and private space and along shared major pedestrian pathways. This is true not only on the island of Manhattan but also in denser parts of the outer boroughs. The mass transit system also makes it possible for minority workers to reach jobs distant from their residences, thus importing diversity into the workplace, even when residences may be segregated.

The other side of fragmentation is that it applies to all neighborhoods, regardless of whether they are predominantly occupied by native-born whites of various extractions, by native-born blacks, and/or by immigrants from different continents.[7] This is not to deny the existence of segregation by race, ethnicity and class, but the fine-grained spatial patterns of the city's racial, ethnic, and class "mosaic" are complex, often broken up into multiple same-race/same-ethnic-origin zones that are not necessarily contiguous.[8] On the other hand, the scattered patterns of black and Hispanic segregation throughout at least four of the five boroughs also reduce the probability of a concerted simultaneous rebellion.

Another deterrent to massive racial/ethnic explosions has been the relative responsiveness of the political system to grievances.[9] This was evident even when African Americans were proportionately less numerous than they are now. Although the areas of protest in Harlem in 1935 and 1943 were cordoned off, the police were cautioned against provocative attacks, the state and national guards were not deployed, the mayor resisted condemnation in his appeals for peace, and immediate relief was provided. In contrast to the police-dominated postriot committees of investigation that followed the 1965 and 1992 riots in Los Angeles and the 1968 riots in Chicago, the biracial committee appointed by Mayor La Guardia in 1935 articulated the major grievances of the Harlem community and made serious recommendations for reform. Although not fully implemented (to this day), they gave voice to legitimate complaints, at least some of which were addressed, albeit within the limitations of Depression-reduced finances (i.e., public housing, school construction, hospital reforms, and enhanced recreational facilities). Again, in 1943, the city, at La Guardia's initiative (albeit responding to well-organized African American pressures), passed the Fair Employment regulations that were later incorporated into national laws, and averted rent gouging in a dual housing market through its (now much-maligned) rent control/regulation laws, which, for all their flaws, slowed down—although they did not prevent—white flight to the suburbs in the postwar era.

When this pattern of sympathetic response was violated in 1964, the result was a more prolonged and destructive riot. Mayor Wagner attempted, albeit belatedly and with less success, to follow La Guardia's model to tamp down the flames of rebellion and to avoid punitive measures. But his initial absence from the scene, his failure to discipline his police commissioner's insensitivity and incompetence, and his unwillingness to confront police resistance to the greater civilian control demanded by minority leaders was disappointing;[10] and it was short-sighted. It was not reversed until two years later—by John Lindsay, the same mayor who, in 1968, allegedly averted the spread to New York of riots from Chicago and other cities that were responding to the assassination of Martin Luther King, Jr. Recall, also, Lindsay's vigorous castigation of Mayor Daley's demand that arsonists be killed and looters maimed.

Whatever the full explanation may be, the fact is that whereas there have been numerous localized protests tied to specific incidents/grievances, there has been no major race riot/uprising in New York for more than four decades, even in reaction to the 1992 Los Angeles riot. I think this cannot simply be attributed to the cautious and conciliatory policies of mayors, or even to the sophisticated level of organization within the African American community, although there is clear interaction between these two factors. I posit a political culture in the city that has evolved from social learning and from the unique history of the city as a port of entry for diverse immigrant groups.

One could describe this political culture as a constant jockeying for position in a negotiated order of competitive coexistence, necessitated more by the inability of any one group to establish stable dominance than facilitated by the much-vaunted tolerance admired by James Weldon Johnson in his early book on Harlem. This pattern of negotiated order occurs in spite of, or possibly because of, the fact that no political party or ethnic group has had a permanent lock on local power. Even though New Yorkers tend to vote overwhelmingly for the Democratic Party's candidates at the national level, mayors have been drawn from diverse sources: Patricians, Whigs, Tammany Hall "Boss Tweed" types, Republicans,[11] Fusion tickets, Democratic-machine bosses, and even some—like Michael Bloomberg, the present mayor—who are Democrats posing as Republicans. Mayors have been Protestant, Catholic, and Jewish. Each has come to power through changing coalitions in an electorate whose fragmentation mirrors, but not exactly, the city's racial and ethnic diversity and its diffused spatial distribution.

One downside of this fluidity is that few reforms introduced by one set of "incumbents" are guaranteed to last, so reforms must constantly be renegotiated. This has been especially the case with imposing permanent constraints on provocative police behavior. Enforcement tightens and loosens at the discretion of the mayor and his police chief.[12] Therefore, although some have claimed that New York's "success" in reducing the probability of wide-scale civil unrest has been the more restrained behavior of its police force and its greater accountability,[13] this continues to be a contested issue, most recently tested in the shooting death in Queens of an unarmed young black man, Sean Bell, on the morning of his planned wedding, when plainclothes police fired 50 bullets at him. The mayor deplored this excess, and significant protests were immediately mounted, including some by resurgent Black Power militants.

Comparing Police Behavior in the Three Cities: Space Matters

Throughout the cases discussed in this book, I have pointed to the role that provocative police acts routinely play in inflaming protests. I have come across only one systematic attempt to compare police traditions in New York as contrasted with those in Los Angeles: Paul Chevigny's *Edge of the Knife*. He has summarized what he sees as the main contrasts as follows.[14]

> The governments of New York City and Los Angeles...have taken almost opposite approaches to policing. The Los Angeles police...have had a reputation as the quintessential anticrime force, with a semimilitary attitude both to the job and the public. There have been no major corruption scandals for decades, and morale has been good...at least until the Rodney King scandal. In contrast, the...NYPD...has been concerned with controlling the discretion of its officers and maintaining good relations with the public and political forces. In the 1990s, the NYPD embraced a philosophy of community policing.... The reason for the divergence in the styles of policing in the two urban areas has been that, while each of the cities has had endemic problems with the abuse of non-deadly force—police brutality—...Los Angeles made no serious attempt to control such violence before 1991 [whereas]...New York long ago took the lead in the nation in trying to make officers accountable and reduce the use of deadly force...while the police in Los Angeles have continued to shoot more people than any other police department in the largest U.S. cities.[15]

The two cities' forms of municipal governance and the historically evolved cultures of their politics and police forces may explain some of these differences. But such policies can be changed, although with difficulty. It will be recalled that in its evaluation of the Los Angeles Police Department's response to the city's 1992 riots, the Webster Report came out strongly in favor of term limitations for police chiefs, greater civilian supervision, and community policing—policies that the Police Foundation's "National Center for the Study of Police and Civil Disorders" has been promoting.[16]

Community policing, however, depends heavily on street foot patrols and the development of sympathetic relations between the officers and the communities to which they are assigned.[17] Its feasibility, therefore, depends not only on procedures but also on spatial factors. The spatial density of New York facilitates street monitoring by foot patrols, as does the size and composition of the force— three times larger than that of Los Angeles, as well as more ethnically diverse.[18] Locality-based decentralization is still feasible in Chicago's moderately dense setting, where it was introduced experimentally in 1993 in five districts; it has subsequently been expanded citywide. Its results are being monitored annually.[19] However, at least some Chicago studies suggest that whereas community policing may make residents less fearful and more satisfied with police services, it alone does not necessarily reduce crime.[20] And without some assurance that this more personalized contact will not simply permit the freer exercise of racism and discriminatory targeting, the attitudes of police officers must be "reeducated"—a policy also advocated by the Police Foundation.

Ethnic Mix in the Three Cities

Differences in ethnic diversity between New York and the other two cities in this study, although important, are insufficient to explain their differences in racial tensions, riots, and uprisings. Chicago and Los Angeles have also been cities of immigrants, so that cannot be the simple explanation. The history of their settlements and the specific racial and ethnic compositions of their populations, as well as the historic ways that race and ethnicity have intersected with each city's unique economic base, have left lasting marks on their political cultures. Their demographic compositions, spatial arrangements, and politics have evolved from different beginnings and within different institutional structures.

CHICAGO

Chicago is a case in point. As I have argued, racial/ethnic animosities were inscribed, early on, in Chicago's class system and its spatial organization—long before African Americans came to constitute a noticeable fraction of its population. Racial apartheid has persisted to the present, albeit on shifting and contested terrains. It seems no accident that two of the most serious race riots of the twentieth century have taken place in that city.[21]

The nascent Fordism of Chicago's powerful industrial base toward the end of the nineteenth century pitted *nouveaux riches* capitalists not against African Americans but against their white immigrant workers, drawn sequentially from Germany and Ireland and later from eastern and southern Europe. The barons of the Lake Shore façade did not need to become politicians: they only needed to control them. In the ward system of the large city council, zones occupied by the immigrant workers and their families held the numerical plurality, and the leaders of Chicago's thriving vice industries were aligned with them.[22] Reforms to clean up the system failed, but by the opening decades of the twentieth century, the two contenders had granted each other a fair amount of autonomy, especially after the capitalist moguls of the Commercial Club of Chicago got their lakefront plan (by Daniel Burnham in the first decade of the twentieth century), which served to insulate them from the masses.[23]

A turning point in ethnic power came around the World War I, when in a campaign that played on anti-Catholic (anti-Irish) feelings, "Big Bill" Thompson was elected mayor on the Republican ticket in 1915, receiving support from Chicago's black (Protestant) voters, who retained their traditional loyalty to the party of Lincoln.[24] This may have enraged Irish Democrats, including Ragen's Colts, who, in 1919, initiated the invasion across the "dead-line" into the expanding black "ghetto" east of Wentworth. This was the political setting for the riot of 1919, in which Thompson deployed his local police to defend the black community. He remained in office, with one interruption, until 1931, when the Democrats retook city government—and never let it go.[25]

The Democratic Party machine, under Irish hegemony, has governed Chicago, with rare exceptions, into the present. As the African American community grew in numbers and geographic extent of segregation, African American politicians eventually surfaced (for example, in the West Side's "plantation" wards, as well as Dawson's more autonomous South Side wards), but they had little bargaining power in city government. There was no counter-power or viable opposition political party they could appeal to or work through. By the 1930s, and even more in the 1940s, the Democratic Party, with greater black support, consolidated its lock on city government, which it has never really relinquished.

It was within this monolithic political culture that Richard J. Daley asserted his control over the party and the city in the mayoral race of 1955, which he won with strong support from black politicians from the South Side. For over 20 years he ruled with such a strong hand that he was known as "The Boss" until his death in 1976.[26] The overwhelming vote he received for his reelection in 1967, albeit with declining black support,[27] may have emboldened him during his subsequent struggles with Martin Luther King, Jr., and encouraged his draconian response to the riot of April 1968, for which he suffered no adverse consequences.

His dynasty reestablished itself after a dozen years of inconclusive interregnums,[28] when his son, Richard M. Daley, was elected mayor in 1989 in the most racially polarized vote in the city's history.[29] Daley has subsequently been reelected (five terms and counting), although with declining turnouts that are symptomatic of the degree to which potential opponents have capitulated, resigning themselves to cooperating with his powerful machine, or have withdrawn from the struggle.

Daley has tried to undo the "dis-reputation" his father earned during the 1968 race riot/rebellion, largely through coopting some black leaders who place peace, personal power, and potential profits above deep transformation. He has had little choice of strategy, given the underbounded borders of his city in relation to the metropolitan region and the pluralities of racial minorities within these constrained city limits. Doing business with Daley promises to preserve Chicago from the fate of economic blowout suffered by Gary, Indiana, and

Detroit, among others. (Interestingly enough, Daley's success in getting wealthy Chicagoans to fund the new and impressive Millennium Park at the lake front recapitulates and expands the Burnham Plan that was used almost a century ago to separate the classes.)[30] Reforms of the police and greater local controls over the failing school system have also made Daley Jr. the "least bad" alternative.

Even though their numbers are declining slightly, African Americans remain the largest potential voting bloc in the city and therefore could have a powerful voice in Chicago's politics, despite increases in the proportion of other minorities (Puerto Ricans, Mexicans, and Asians). Short of taking over control of the Democratic Party, however, they are unlikely to radically alter Chicago's political culture.[31]

In the meantime, the destruction of the "projects"offers a selective depopulation of the "ghettos,"[32] and HOPE[33] holds out the promise that black entrepreneurs can make healthy real estate profits by redeveloping the Near South Side at much lower densities. To this must be added the increased incarceration of young black and Latino males, a strategy that not only removes them from the scene but, when they return, removes them from the voter rolls as well. I return to this discussion below, which has implications for potential riot "prevention" in all three cities.

LOS ANGELES

Despite the similarities between the Los Angeles riots of 1965 and 1992, it is difficult to infer that a consistent long-term political culture accounts for them. This is because, more than New York and Chicago, Los Angeles's relatively newer existence as an American city demonstrates significant discontinuities in its social, economic, and spatial structures. To understand these discontinuities, one must go farther back in history. At least three major phases must be distinguished in its racial and ethnic relations as conditioned by changes in the city's governance, economic base, and demographic composition.[34] A fourth stage is apparently now beginning—what some are calling the *reconquista* by Mexican immigrants. Los Angeles's narrowly based structure of local government, set during the Progressive Era, has made it sluggish in responding to these changes.

Phase 1

The first phase in Los Angeles's existence as an American city began in the mid–nineteenth century, precipitated by the Gold Rush in northern California, which redoubled the urgency of adding California to the United States. In 1846 the

United States declared war on Mexico, and after seesaw battles in which Los Angeles changed hands several times, the city came under the control of American forces by 1847; this new "ownership" was regularized two years later. A census conducted in 1850 revealed the preponderance of the town's Mexican residents. Only 300 residents were of American ancestry, with men outnumbering women three to one. The region around the small town was certainly not empty. It was already divided up into sizeable ranches, owned by a quasi-feudal hierarchy of "lords" (the *gente de razon*) and populated by their serf-like workers.[35] This set in motion the first phase of the relationship between Mexicans and Anglos, in which the basic racial fault lines were laid down.

> California's State Constitutional Convention of 1849 fiercely debated how...racial lines were to be drawn and, consequently, who would and would not be extended the franchise and other important citizenship rights. In the final analysis, Mexicans were socially defined as "white" and extended citizenship while the California Indians...were deemed "nonwhite" and ineligible for citizenship.[36]

This not only encouraged intermarriage between ambitious Anglo men (seeking acceptance, money, and access to land ownership) and the daughters of the wealthy ranch owners but also served as grounds for denying citizenship to Chinese and Japanese newcomers, whose racial status was elided with that of Indians. After whites from the Midwest flooded into Los Angeles from the 1870s on, thanks to the completion of cross-continental railroads and a partial solution to Los Angeles's water shortage, a racialized hierarchy was solidified that "clearly privileged and elevated the status of white immigrants...and placed below them, in descending order, the Mexican, black, Asian and Indian populations."[37] This ushered in the second phase.

Phase 2

The story of this transformation—its causes and consequences—has been told by others and in great detail; it is not necessary to retell it here.[38] But by the opening decades of the twentieth century, Los Angeles had solidified characteristics that distinguished it from Chicago and New York.

First, the city's population had become overwhelmingly "Anglo." Only 10 percent were Mexicans in 1930, when the census counted them separately instead of including them in the "white" category,[39] and an even smaller percentage were black. Second, the vast fortunes of the city's leading citizens had been created chiefly through expanding the transportation lines and developing the ports (both with help from Washington), which yielded related and commensurate gains in booming real estate values. The social values of the elite, expressed in Chandler's powerful newspaper, were far from progressive: they favored unfettered capitalism, albeit with state subsidies, suppressed progressive movements (deemed communist in the "Red Scare" of 1911), and fought unionization, which threatened to undermine their treasured "open shop" for labor. Their racism, if not their conservative economic philosophy, was shared by most "Anglos," as evidenced by their general satisfaction when, at the beginning of the Depression, 80,000 Mexicans were deported.[40] Nor did they protest the removal and internment of the Japanese in 1943. In both cases, no distinctions were made between native-born citizens and "foreigners."

The entrepreneurial self-styled patriciate controlled a pliant political system that did not interfere with either its corporate interests or its links to federal authorities.[41] The structure of local government for both Los Angeles city and county was lean indeed, based on the philosophy of the Progressive Era that favored an apolitical managerial system of government based on civil service, limited size and even less power vested in a representative city council, and dependence on citizen referenda for major policy changes. This structure explains how, in the third phase of Los Angeles's history, during which the two race riots occurred, the city's small but highly concentrated black population was able to gain more power than the more numerous but more geographically dispersed Chicano population. It also explains why the police department was insulated from civilian control and why its chief was protected for so long from politically motivated dismissal.

Phase 3

The third phase, which began with World War II, saw the growth of heavy industries and the economic, but not political, integration of the metropolis's sprawling region. The rapidly increasing demands for labor attracted significant numbers of African American migrants, especially since immigration of Mexicans was restricted solely to meeting the shortage of farm laborers, under the federal bracero program.[42] The black population increased from under 39,000 in 1940 to more than 113,000 by 1945–46 and 171,300 by 1950.

Given the pattern of racial segregation in the city, African Americans were virtually confined to the small area known as South Central. Despite this, the city council contained no black member. Thanks to gerrymandering of ward boundaries and the expansion of the number of wards from 12 to 15, the black vote was intentionally split into three of the city's wards (the eighth, ninth, and tenth). In only one of these, the eighth, did African Americans constitute even a bare majority. This was to change in 1963, when astute political organizing gained all three seats for black representatives. That year marked Tom Bradley's first entry into coalition politics,[43] an entry that 10 years later would lead him to the mayor's office, again through coalition support from the black-dominated wards and that of the white so-called liberal West Side.[44] Some attributed his attractiveness to backlash from the 1965 riots, when it was hoped that his pigment would placate racial dissent. But only his skill as a cooperative coalition player with the big business leaders, who always operated behind the scenes of elected government, and the managerial bureaucracy, could have guaranteed his 20-year survival.

The absence of Mexican Americans from the small city council remained conspicuous. Given their wider distribution in the city and their scattering throughout the county, they stood a greater chance of success in countywide contests, but there, the openings were even fewer. The county was governed by a board of commissioners with only five members. (For many years the popular politician Edward Roybal was the sole Hispanic member.)

The second half of this third phase began slowly after 1965, affected more by changes in U.S. immigration laws than by the recent riot. The new laws liberalized the entry of special classes of immigrants, including those from Latin America and selected Asian countries, and provided a cover for entrants of similar appearance to join them without proper documentation. We have seen some of the results in the uprising of 1992, and most dramatically in the 2006 election of Los Angeles's first mayor of Mexican descent in more than a century.

Phase 4

This marks the possible beginning of a fourth phase in Los Angeles history. Although Villaraigosa was swept to power on the wave of multiracial support, it still remains to be seen whether this new coalition will survive. The great unknown is whether African Americans will benefit from Villaraigosa's triumph or latent tensions between blacks and Latinos will erupt into conflict and/or further marginalization of disaffected African Americans in response to what I have termed this tectonic shift.

I noted earlier that immigrants, both documented and undocumented, participated in massive and well-orchestrated protests in many cities throughout the nation in March/April 2006 opposing a congressional threat to define illegal entry as a felonious crime. The large demonstration in New York was given police protection but was neither joined by African Americans nor acknowledged by the city's political leaders. A march of perhaps as many as 300,000 that took place in Chicago was reported as including not only Latinos but Irish, Vietnamese, Chinese, eastern Europeans, and other nationalities that have provided undocumented immigrants to the city. The line of march stayed clear of African American neighborhoods, and Mayor Daley did not attend.

The situation was very different in Los Angeles, where an estimated 500,000 marched, in a city dominated by Hispanics, who now constitute an estimated 47 percent of the population, their numbers having increased considerably in the near decade and a half since the 1992 multiethnic uprising. The march was attended by Mayor Villaraigosa, who briefly addressed the crowd, and he was accompanied by Bratton, his white police chief. The city council of Los Angeles passed a resolution condemning the proposed congressional legislation. In addition, there were selective but major walkouts by Hispanic students from high schools in the Los Angeles Unified School District (which covers the city and the county), where some scuffles with black classmates were reported. In an odd turnabout, in light of the 1992 riot, Korean merchants supported the march, in part because they feared the loss of their cheap workers. If Los Angeles ever experiences another race/ethnic riot, it is likely to deviate significantly from the two prior ones described in this book.

I have argued throughout that, despite their common underlying causes and their superficial similarities, there are major differences between riot events in the three cities, as well as continuities in each city's successive events. Is my analysis of the differences overly determined? Is heredity destiny? I turn now to certain convergent trends taking shape in the twenty-first century, albeit to be played out somewhat differently in each of the three cities.

THE DECLINING VOICE OF BLACK CITIZENS IN CENTER CITIES

One of these convergent trends, ironically, is the declining voice of African Americans, weakened not only by their numerical displacement by Latinos as America's largest "minority" group at a time when Hispanics are increasing rapidly, through both immigration and high rates of natural increase, but also by the Latinos' ideological and media visibility. (Some pundits are suggesting that immigrant rights have displaced the older civil rights movement.) This shift, in itself, poses no short-term political threat to African American voters, given the broad-based age structure of Latinos, with many offspring below voting age, and the gap between sheer numbers and enfranchised voters. Rather, it is in many ways a testament to the uneven fruits of civil rights achievements, which have enhanced the opportunities for education and advancement for some African Americans, while leaving others farther behind.

Demographically, the sheer size of the non-immigrant black population in all three cities has been declining, due to lower rates of natural increase, somewhat expanded options for intermarriage and identity change, disillusionment with life chances in northern cities, and voluntary moves to segregated suburban communities[45] and even to southern cities that now offer expanding openings for advancement. This has recently been compounded in negative fashion by involuntary displacements into the expanding carceral system, where rates of imprisonment are considerably higher for blacks than Hispanics, and many times higher for both than for whites.

These two trends, which we may call the virtuous and vicious circles, reflect the bimodal effects of greater class differentiation within the black community— between those who have benefited from the civil rights movement, increased access to higher education and commensurate jobs, and greater acceptance by whites[46] and those left behind in what Wacquant has called the more isolated and vulnerable hyperghettos. Whether they are doing well or poorly, however, many African Americans feel alienated from the American system of white domination, which has stigmatized no other ethnic group as permanently as blacks.

THE STILL-PERSISTING VICIOUS CIRCLE

This phrase has been applied so frequently and powerfully in race relations literature that I have tried to trace when it was first used. The earliest succinct description I have found is in a book by Edwin R. Embree, *Brown Americans: The Story of a Tenth of the Nation.* In 1931, he wrote:

> There is a vicious circle in caste. At the outset, the despised group is usually inferior in certain of the accepted standards of the controlling class. Being inferior, members of the degraded caste are denied the privileges and opportunities of their fellows and so are pushed still further down and then are regarded with that much less respect, and therefore are more rigorously denied advantages, and so around and around the vicious circle. Even when the movement starts to reverse itself—as it most certainly has in the case of the Negro—there is a desperately long unwinding as a slight increase in good will gives a little greater chance and this leads to a little higher accomplishment and that to increased respect and so slowly upward toward equality of opportunity, of regard, and of status.[47]

Despite the optimistic tone of the second part of the quotation, its positive reversal is not guaranteed, even though it has been occurring for a highly selected subset of younger and better educated African Americans, especially in the post–civil rights/riots period.

At the present moment, however, when the police state is being substituted for the welfare state as the preferred mechanism for regulating the poor,[48] we can observe a renewed intensification of the vicious circle. This is not unrelated to an expansion of the prison system, which is multiplying the disabilities not only of those caught in its trap but inflicting collateral damage on their relatives, friends, and neighborhoods as well. Prisoners and ex-felons are denied voting rights, find it almost impossible to gain legitimate employment after their release, and cannot qualify for food stamps, subsidized housing, health care, government loans for education, and other benefits. This creates a spiraling vicious circle that has its greatest impact on poor minorities and the communities in which they are disproportionately targeted and to which they return. The authors and editors of an outstanding collection, *Civil Penalties, Social Consequences,* point to what they call "collateral civil penalties" that not only extend temporally far beyond the prison terms of released prisoners but extend laterally to punish their friends, relatives, wives, and children, that is, innocent members of the communities from which they are drawn.[49] Prisons themselves also serve as schools for crime, as well as foyers for infections such as tuberculosis and HIV. Blacks have been the "caste" most affected by the unequal criminal justice system.

The Unequal Criminal Justice System

David Cole has carefully laid out the sequential steps in the criminal justice system that disproportionately victimize minorities, including all African Americans to some extent, but especially poor ones.[50] The inequalities begin with discriminatory violations of reasonable search and seizure, when police routinely use racial profiling to stop and search drivers and persons in targeted neighborhoods and public places, based on the ambiguous grounds of "probable cause."[51] White violators of minor regulations are often let go with warnings, whereas the same infractions by darker persons meet with police intimidation and more often result in arrest. Once arrested, wealthier and more knowledgeable victims of arrest have immediate access, even before charges are made, to legal advice and bail, whereas poorer ones stay in jail and are defended in court by overworked and often incompetent public defenders, or agree to plea bargains without understanding their implications. Trials by jury are distorted by venue changes, incomplete and often unrepresentative lists of eligible jurors, and peremptory challenges, obviating proportional or even mixed-race juries.[52] Sentences for minority perpetrators are harsher than those for whites committing similar offenses.[53] Death penalties are more likely to be imposed on blacks who kill whites than those whose victims are black. These long-acknowledged inequities in the criminal justice system not only undermine the legitimacy accorded to it in minority communities but also intensify the fears of police oppression/

brutality that often lead to flight or resisting arrest, acts that guarantee further punishment.[54]

The Recent Increase in Imprisonment Rates

Beginning some three decades ago, a number of changes in the criminal justice system at the federal and state levels were introduced that have, through their selective enforcement, increased inequities of class and race. The federal "war on drugs," with its mandatory minimum and maximum sentences, gives judges some latitude to discriminate between offenders, choosing minimum for the favored, maximum for others. The "three strikes and you're out" laws adopted by many states lead to mandatory long-term incarceration for individuals whose third arrest even may be for a very minor infraction. These have all opened the door to further inequalities in a system where minorities are consistently more likely to be targeted, arrested, and found guilty. As a result, the prison population in the United States has been skyrocketing upward and has become even more skewed racially.

According to recent available figures released by the United States Bureau of Justice Statistics, as of the end of 2005, some 2.2 million persons were in prison in the United States—most in state prisons, lesser numbers in federal custody, a large number awaiting trial or serving a sentence in local jails, and an additional but smaller number under local jail supervision doing community service.[55] In all, more than seven million, or 1 out of every 32 U.S. adult residents, were in jail or prison, on probation or on parole; two million of these were guilty of drug crimes. The United States, with 5 percent of the world's population, accounts for fully one-quarter of the world's incarcerated population. Despite little change in the actual crime rate, the rate of incarceration more than quadrupled between the early 1970s and 2000. By 2000, the rate stood at more than 600 persons per 100,000. Five years later, it had risen to 737 per 100,000, making it by far the highest in the world.[56]

In the decade between 1990 and 2000 alone, the number of male inmates increased by 77 percent, and the number of females by 108 percent. Black ratios of imprisonment were disproportionate. By the end of 2000, there were 3,457 black male inmates per 100,000 black male adults in the United States, 1,220 sentenced Hispanic male inmates per 100,000 Hispanic males, and only 449 white male inmates per 100,000 white males. At year's end, almost 1 in 10 black males between the ages of 20 and 30 were in prison. Among the more than 1.3 million sentenced inmates (not including those in jail custody), an estimated 428,300 were black males between the ages of 20 and 39.[57] A recent Bureau of Justice Statistics study predicts that if current rates continue, a black male now 16 years old has a 29 percent chance of spending time in prison during his lifetime.

One of the effects of this burgeoning demand for incarceration facilities has been a boom in prison construction and, with it, generous profits to private firms to which the government has outsourced the supply and management of prisons. The locations of these new facilities have implications for reducing black representation in cities. Although arrests occur disproportionately in the central ghettos of major cities, the new prisons in which the (mostly minority) prisoners are warehoused are primarily located in declining small (white) towns. Changes in the way the census records the place of residence of prison inmates (from the prior system of their "normal" residence to counting them as residents of the place in which they are incarcerated) shift per capita federal allocations and the weight of electoral representation from center cities to more rural zones and even to other states.[58]

But the most dramatic consequence of the racialization of imprisonment is felt in the poorest ghettos of our major cities. After pointing out that, according to Bureau of Justice Statistics, some 30 percent of African American men between the ages of 20 and 29 are either in jail, in prison, on probation, or on parole, Paul Street explored its implications for Chicago and its neighborhoods:

> Two-thirds of [the] state [of Illinois]'s more than 44,000 prisoners are African-American. According to the *Chicago Reporter*, 1 in 5 Black Cook County...men in their 20s are either in prison or jail or on parole....In some inner-city neighborhoods, a preponderant majority of Black males now possess criminal records. According to Congressperson Danny Davis, fully 70 percent of men between ages 18 and 45 in the impoverished North Lawndale neighborhood on Chicago's West Side are ex-offenders. The rates are similar in two high poverty neighborhoods on the south side.[59]

As Street concludes, for poor black men living in big-city ghettos, going to prison has become so common that it is an "almost normative life experience." A record initiates a downward spiral: once they have a record, it is almost impossible for those with low marketable skills to get a legal job, which creates "irresistible incentives for parolees to engage in precisely the sort of income-generating conduct that leads back to prison. In Illinois today, 36 percent of ex-offenders and a staggering 48 percent of Black ex-offenders return to prison within three years."[60] And once released back into the small number of poor hyperghettos segregated by race and class, they have little chance to escape. Nor have those who maintain contact with them, because of the social collateral damage.[61]

By far the most methodologically sophisticated analysis of how the absolute increase in incarceration rates in recent years has disproportionately affected the life chances of poorly educated African Americans has been done by the sociologists Becky Pettit and Bruce Western.[62] Their findings confirm an intensified vicious circle. Poorly educated African Americans who reached adulthood during the most recent period of heightened imprisonment now run a much higher risk of going to prison than educationally disadvantaged blacks who reached adulthood in the 1970s, when incarceration rates were lower. The gap between incarceration rates for African Americans and whites of similar education has actually widened, except for the college educated.[63]

Using an ingenious methodology based partially on life tables, Pettit and Western calculated the cumulative risks of imprisonment for two successive birth cohorts (those born in 1945–49 and those born in 1965–69)[64] and compared the relative "risk trajectories" of white and black males in each cohort by level of education.[65]

First, they note that the incarceration rate for blacks is now about eight times higher than for whites.[66]

> Although crime rates may explain as much as 80 percent of the disparity in imprisonment...a significant residual suggests that blacks are punitively policed, prosecuted, and sentenced....A large residual racial disparity appears due to the differential treatment of African Americans by police and the courts....Thus, imprisonment may be more common among low-education men because they are the focus of the social control efforts of criminal justice authorities.[67]

Some of this increase is clearly attributable to the war on drugs, but "if poor black men...[have been] attracted to the illegal drug trade in response to the collapse of low-skill labor markets, the drug war raised the risks that they would be caught, convicted and incarcerated."[68] Once imprisoned, having a record in itself "confers an enduring stigma" that further diminishes their life chances.[69]

Turning to the specific results of their analysis, we can single out some noteworthy comparisons: black men born 1945–49 had a 10.6 percent chance of spending time in state or federal prison by their early thirties. This cumulative risk had climbed to over 20 percent for black men born 1965–69. In contrast, the comparable rates for white men dropped from close to 3 percent in the earlier cohort to only 1.4 percent in the later cohort. In short, black risk rates increased with time, and the gap between whites and blacks grew even greater. Most at risk were high school dropouts, but even here, the racial discrepancies were very large.

By the end of the 1990s, 21 percent of young black poorly-educated men were in state or federal prison compared to an imprisonment rate of 2.9 percent for young white male dropouts.... Incredibly, a black male dropout, born 1965–69, had nearly a 60 percent chance of serving time in prison by the end of the 1990s. At the close of the decade, prison time had indeed become modal for young black males who failed to graduate from high school.[70]

Even completing high school did not protect black males from prison, since some 20 percent of high school graduates had served a prison term by their early thirties. These rates were considerably higher than for the earlier cohort. "When figures for dropouts and high school graduates are pooled together, the risk of imprisonment for non-college black men aged 30–34 in 1999 is 30.2 percent compared to 12.0 percent in 1979. Prison time has only recently become a common life event for black men." [71]

IS THERE EVIDENCE OF A VIRTUOUS CIRCLE?

Embree suggested that a reduction in stigma, brought about chiefly by attitude changes in the dominant race, would gradually allow greater access to improved conditions (i.e., enhance the human capital of African Americans) and that this would gradually result in greater social mobility and acceptance. This has certainly been occurring for the post–civil rights cohort born after the major race riots of the 1960s—suggesting that for some African Americans, the riots may have had some positive effects in opening opportunities for advancement, and may have led some whites to recognize the aspirations of at least some "acceptable" African Americans as legitimate.

Today, even though the number of young black males enrolled in college is still exceeded by the number in prisons, African Americans (and especially black women) have made enormous strides in education and employment. The result is a widening gap between college-educated African Americans and what Wilson, in an unfortunate term, called "the underclass." In the absence of fundamental changes in the society itself, however, the deplorable situation of black men and women trapped in the vicious downward cycle is not likely to improve by simply advising them to change their "self-destructive culture," as the suave Harvard professor Orlando Patterson did, in a recent op-ed piece in the *New York Times*, a paper they are unlikely to read.[72]

Note that in the Pettit and Western cohort analysis, the only subgroup of blacks to have escaped the rising risk of imprisonment was comprised of college-educated members of the cohort born in 1965 or later. We can only presume that their opportunities were expanded by the relative success of the civil rights movement (possibly reinforced by the riots themselves), which resulted in greater access to better (nonghetto) schools, greater acceptance in less racially segregated workplaces, and less prejudice based on abstract stereotypes. These expanded opportunities are being gradually translated into more and better jobs in the upper service sector, leading to greater exposure and visibility in offices and the media, and yielding easier access to middle-class activities, where expressions of culture more closely approach the standards of "white" America.

However, while it is true that blacks have become more visible in the national media as newscasters, talk show hosts, and pundits, that members of both the "old black bourgeoisie" (Condoleezza Rice) and the "new" (Colin Powell) rose to prominent positions in the Bush administration, and that highly respected black scholars and writers now teach in leading universities, theirs is still a "marked" presence. Their recognition depends not only on their talents, but on adopting attributes of white culture in speech patterns and grooming, if not in message. Rival counter-cultural black models innovating popular protest art forms (despite their white imitators) have yet to receive the respect they demand.

William Julius Wilson has argued that structural changes in the postmodern economy have opened these new chances for black mobility.[73] The situation, however, is far more complex than macroeconomic changes in the occupational structure of the United States and its expanded demand for professional and technical services. Without changes both in laws and the attitudes of whites, the expanding job opportunities so created at the top need not have been filled by blacks, no matter how much better prepared they became. Furthermore, the expansion of a new young black professional middle class has erased neither the disabilities of being black in America nor the economic differences between blacks and whites, even at the same levels of individual pay scales.

To achieve middle-class incomes and lifestyles, black families are more likely to require more wage earners than whites of equal family income. In addition, as Oliver and Shapiro have pointed out, members of the white middle class are more likely to have benefited from inherited wealth, whereas their black counterparts not only lack this advantage but often achieve their lifestyles by going deeper into debt.[74] Despite the proliferation of self-segregated black suburbs, most middle-class black families still live in same-race urban communities where their children are exposed to enough coresidents of lesser income and ambition to make it a struggle to insulate them from such influences.[75] The health of middle-class blacks suffers, in comparison to whites, not only because of inferior medical care but also from hypertension exacerbated by suppressed anger, and by poor dietary habits learned in childhoods spent in poverty.[76] In short, the virtuous circle is operating, but only incompletely and for a limited set of African Americans who have escaped the intensified vicious circle.

WHITE PREJUDICE AND/OR INDIFFERENCE—BLACK INVISIBILITY

While there may be a slow dialectical process in race relations that makes fundamental change dependent on the reactions of both whites and blacks,[77] white attitudes remain, as Embree suggested, the most crucial part of the equation. Some of the multiple authors who contributed (anonymously) to Myrdal's book *An American Dilemma* refused to use an older term, "The Negro Problem," instead preferring to call it either "The White Problem" or the "Problem of American Society's Contradiction."

In a wonderful play on W. E. B. Du Bois's title *The Souls of Black Folk,* Joe E. Feagin and Hernán Vera devote a chapter of their book, *White Racism: The Basics,* to "The Souls of White Folk."[78] In it they document, through successive public opinion polls and their own studies, the obdurate persistence of white negative stereotypes of blacks. The authors acknowledge that, when asked directly for their attitudes toward blacks, "in recent decades whites as a group have become less negative in assessments of civil rights or of African Americans.... [But] on the basis of survey data and our own in-depth interviews... many whites still hold negative images of and stereotypes about African Americans."[79]

More intriguingly, they note that few whites ever give much thought to the advantages they enjoy as "whites," and that their lack of daily reflection on whiteness appears to come from social isolation, what Feagin and Vera refer to as "living in a white bubble." This attitude "contrasts sharply with the reports of many African Americans that their blackness is forced into their consciousness virtually every day by contacts with white Americans."[80] Here the vicious circle of physical segregation combines with selective media treatments to permit the experiential vacuum of the "invisible man" to be filled by fear-driven fictions.[81]

In an earlier (1963) sophisticated study of black and white public opinions on race, which found levels of white prejudice much higher than today, there was one interesting finding: negative stereotypes about Negroes were systematically lowest among a special group of white respondents: the 25 percent of the total sample who "had had social contact with Negroes."[82] In short, the invisible has to be seen to affect white attitudes. Merely being seen, however, is no guarantee that black alienation will disappear.

Invisibility, Alienation, Anomie

Two powerful books by African American writers, *inter alia,* have addressed the issue of invisibility: Ralph Ellison's masterful novel *Invisible Man* and Du Bois's somber *Dusk of Dawn.* Neither man was himself "invisible," but in combination they captured the dual character of invisibility.[83]

Du Bois wrote the following devastating description of caste invisibility, defining it unequivocally as white rejection; it can serve as a reminder of both the futility of the race riots in Chicago and Los Angeles and a foreshadowing of the current strategy of imprisonment, as his metaphor of the plate-glass barrier is being transmuted into real prison bars.

> It is difficult to let others see the full psychological meaning of caste segregation. It is as though one, looking out from a dark cave..., sees the world passing and speaks to it: speaks courteously and persuasively, showing how these entombed souls are hindered in their natural movement, expression, and development; and how their loosening from prison would be a matter not simply of courtesy, sympathy, and help to them, but aid to all the world. One talks on evenly and logically in this way but notices that the passing throng does not even turn its head, or if it does, glances curiously and walks on. It gradually penetrates the minds of the prisoners that the people passing do not hear; that some thick sheet of invisible but horribly tangible plate glass is between them and the world. They get excited; they talk louder; they gesticulate. Some of the passing world stop in curiosity; these gesticulations seem so pointless; they laugh and pass on.... Then the people within may become hysterical. They may scream and hurl themselves against the barriers, hardly realizing in their bewilderment that they are screaming in a vacuum unheard.... They may even, here and there, break through in blood and disfigurement, and find themselves faced by a horrified, implacable, and quite overwhelming mob of people frightened for their own very existence.[84]

It is as if Du Bois were describing both the causes of ghetto revolts and the current "solution" to them—reimprisoning rather than helping those most likely to participate in riots, namely, young black males. But one can also think of the demand for visibility in its more benign and sublimated forms: in graffiti, hip-hop, rap protest, break-dancing, and other public displays.

The other response to invisibility, withdrawal in disillusionment, is illustrated by Ellison's fictional hero, who finally elects to become invisible in his secret basement hiding place, illuminated by thousands of light bulbs powered by "stolen" electricity. This, indeed, is sadder for its waste. Betrayed first by the duplicity of the black president and white members of the board of trustees of his southern black college, and then by his employers in the interracial "Brotherhood Society" in New York City who exploit his idealistic commitment to racial justice and his oratorical skills for their own dubious ends, he withdraws in isolation, after the race riot of 1943, to a place where he can experience his "whole humanity." His alienation from an unjust society is complete.

In the face of such alienation, which can be experienced in various ways even by those, like Du Bois and Ellison, who presumably have escaped from the cave, much remains to be done. Many years ago, Robert Merton defined "anomie" as a condition of strain/distress brought about by a discrepancy between the shared cultural goals and ideals of American society and the lack of institutional means to achieve them.[85] Although his reference was chiefly to material success, it can apply equally, and perhaps more poignantly, to the gap between true human dignity/ personhood, and the subtle disrespect even the most accomplished African Americans are sometimes accorded. Merton posited five possible responses to the strain:[86] conformity (acting "white"), innovation (the "use of institutionally proscribed [illegal] means"), ritualism ("adapting to failure by scaling down hopes"), retreatism (the rejection of both goals and institutional means, as in Ellison's novel), and finally rebellion, which, "although distinctive from ressentiment, may draw upon a vast reservoir of the resentful and disoriented as institutional dislocations become acute."[87] The last is a good explanation of periodic race uprisings. Clearly, curing the objective roots of anomie itself must be the real goal.

THE FUTURE OF RACE RIOTS

In comparison to this fundamental diagnosis, recommendations for reducing the likelihood of future riots seem paltry and inadequate. In any model of riot reduction, one needs to distinguish between deep underlying sources of tension and more superficial and even counter-productive policies that simply offload the "riot-prone" populations into the carceral system or displace them to other localities. In between are techniques for reforming police behavior, decentralizing and improving relations between the police and local neighborhoods through such mechanisms as community policing, hiring more minorities on the police forces, reeducating police to reduce provocative behavior and the excessive use of force, and avoiding differential treatment of minorities based on racist stereotypes and prejudiced attitudes.

But the deepest levels remain: correcting the injustices inherent in unequal opportunities for advancement (rewards) on the one hand and unequal punishments in the criminal justice system on the other. Here, changing not only the attitudes of whites but their actions will be necessary. Such attitudes are reflected in and given objective form not only in individual behavior but, more fundamentally, in public policies adopted by law and funded by the public purse. Therefore, our most basic critique is that political priorities have been callously inverted. Present policies of selective imprisonment are not only the most expensive solutions but also the most counterproductive in the long run.[88]

If indeed the disappearance of legitimate jobs paying a living wage—jobs that could be filled by less-educated African Americans living in center cities—is recognized as the root cause of many problems, then the solution must be sought not in the very costly policy of building and maintaining an ever larger supply of prisons to make the offenders disappear (to render them invisible) but massive investments in more functional schools and even offering attractive incentives/rewards (including stipends) so that students will remain in them.[89] The major incentive, however, would have to be not only the promise of, but a real chance for, a decent future job.

Some economists blame the changing international division of labor as it is currently unfolding—the relatively unimpeded mobility of capital to poorer countries to maximize profits by exploiting wage differentials, to the detriment of local labor, white, black, and Hispanic—considering it a force beyond our ultimate control. The disappearance of "good" jobs, however, is not due solely to global restructuring, nor can unfair competition from undocumented immigrants be blamed for poorly paid ones. Not all labor demands are exportable, and legal means exist to enforce and, we must hope, even to increase minimum wages.

The neglect of our cities over decades has generated enormous current deficiencies in urban infrastructures (lack of affordable housing, deteriorated roads and transportation systems, aging utilities, schools, hospitals and other public buildings needing repairs) that, if nationally funded, could provide preferential jobs to American citizens from low-income neighborhoods. Local governments can scarcely be expected to bear this burden; massive federal subsidies would be required. Reducing the incentives and increasing the penalties to local employers who seek to cut their costs by exploiting vulnerable immigrant workers might help to level the playing field and thus avert the acknowledged zero-sum competition between African American and immigrant labor at the lowest skill levels. And if unstable family structures are diagnosed as deterrents to the secure and healthy development of children and youth, then workfare's insistence on low-paid jobs for mothers, without the provision of safe, subsidized, and educational childcare, can only intensify this handicap.

In short, we have not progressed beyond the pious recommendations for job creation, income supports, better schools, and reduced segregation and discrimination that were set forth in the Kerner Report almost four decades ago. Now, as then, the issue is certainly not lack of knowledge but lack of will and commitment. It is instructive, albeit sad, to read the concluding humble sentences of that report.

> We have provided an honest beginning. We have learned much. But we have uncovered no startling truths, no unique insights, no simple solutions. The destruction and the bitterness of racial disorder, the harsh polemics of black revolt and white repression have been seen and heard before in this country. It is time now to end the destruction and the violence, not only in the streets of the ghetto but in the lives of people.[90]

To do this, now as then, requires firm commitment to a different set of social and political priorities, and a willingness to devote sufficient resources in line with those priorities. This requires some unpalatable reforms in the distribution of income, as recent changes in the tax law and deregulation of corporation governance have redistributed wealth in favor of the already rich at the expense of the middle and lower classes. And above all, this requires an end to the squandering of human lives and the public purse on an ill-conceived (and interminable) war that, like failed and provocative repressive police tactics, seeks submission rather than equality and justice among nations. Now, as then, fundamental reforms are unlikely to materialize, because the political power that goes with money power will resist them, even if a substantive restoration of the two-party system occurs, as seems to be happening. Note the parallels between Johnson's ill-starred campaigns against Vietnam and Bush's quagmire in Iraq. Both direct attention away from domestic needs for justice and deprive the domestic economy of the means to achieve it.

In all of this, there is only one possibly hopeful sign. It is that white America's historic obsession with the "color line" may finally be subverted by becoming hopelessly blurred. Two factors can contribute to their cognitive dissonance. First, "whites" may be forced from their "bubble" of indifference by greater exposure to immigrants from societies whose wider range of skin pigmentation provides intermediate tones between black and white. Second, the presumed easy correlation between skin pigmentation and social stigma may gradually be undermined, as socially mobile African Americans become increasingly visible and taken for granted. Only then will society fulfill Wilson's hope for a declining significance of race. That does not guarantee that the neglect of the poor and disenfranchised will end. Only a common commitment to American ideals of equality and social justice can accomplish this task.

The great unknown is how the tectonic shift will play out in American politics. The black-white dichotomy is no longer the sole issue, even though it remains the one with the longest and most intractable roots. The current conflicts over Hispanic (mostly Mexican) immigration complicate the picture and, depending on how they are resolved, could potentially inflame Latino-black hostilities. *Tertius gaudens* has not worked well in Los Angeles and remains only latent in Chicago. As Latinos increasingly come to outnumber blacks,[91] they are developing greater sophistication in playing the protest game and, with naturalization, will soon be stronger in the political enfranchisement game as well. Much depends on whether more open and representative governmental structures, nationally and locally, can nurture productive and shifting coalitions, rather than a zero-sum game. In this, perhaps New York's experience, although "deviant," may yet provide some guidance. But that would be a topic for a different book.

NOTES

1. The Crown Heights intercommunal "riot" between Hasidic Jews and Jamaicans deviated from this pattern. That the Hasidim seem subsequently to have internalized the New York repertoire of street protest against alleged police mistreatment surfaced in Borough Park in early April 2006 in a brief explosion that was handled with extreme caution by the police.
2. The exception is the smallest and whitest borough, Staten Island, which periodically discusses secession.
3. Each borough elects its own president. The mayor, comptroller, and some judges are elected city-wide. Aldermen (members of the city council) are each elected from local wards. A higher body, the Board of Estimate and Appropriations, consisting of the mayor, the borough presidents, and the comptroller, formerly coordinated/adjudicated the distribution of appropriations, until a charter revision did away with it in 1989.
4. Puerto Ricans, who still constitute a declining majority of Latinos in New York City, do not face the same threats from the proposals to penalize undocumented immigrants, since they have long been accorded quasi-citizenship rights. It is difficult to determine how many of them participated in recent marches against immigration restrictions, or how many dark-skinned African American marchers were recent immigrants from the Caribbean or Africa. Pigmentation is never a very reliable guide to cultural ethnicity, but especially so in New York City.
5. The evidence that the greater availability of Mexican/Central American labor has depressed the wages and job opportunities of poorly educated African American (and even Puerto Rican) males is now quite conclusive. Jesse Jackson, among others, believes the solution lies in raising the wages of immigrant workers.

6. Massive and diverse immigration has helped to sustain the city's population growth in recent decades, and the proportion of foreign born now rivals the situation that obtained at the turn of the last century. For information on the numbers and diverse origins of immigrants, see, *inter alia,* New York City Department of City Planning, *The Newest New Yorkers 1990–1994: An Analysis of Immigration to New York City in the Early 1990s* (New York: New York City Department of City Planning, 1997), which updated their two-volume edition, *The Newest New Yorkers: An Analysis of Immigration into New York City during the 1980s* (New York: New York City Department of City Planning, 1992).

7. This is not to deny that there have been numerous ethnic-specific territorial conflicts, as well as individual attacks on blacks viewed as "invaders," as in the Howard Beach case, or, more collectively, in portions of Brooklyn; see, for example, Jonathan Rieder, *Canarsie: The Jews and Italians of Brooklyn against Liberalism* (Cambridge, Mass.: Harvard University Press, 1985). Such tensions provided the theme for Spike Lee's film *Do the Right Thing.*

8. Conspicuously absent in this book is a single map of the city depicting the complex distribution of racial/ethnic groups in overlapping and multiple spaces. See William Bowen, "Atlas of New York City" for 2000, map series, available at http://130.166.124.2/atlas.nyc/ny6_20.gif. Separate maps show the percentage distribution of blacks in the five boroughs and the size distributions of blacks of various ancestries, but these maps cannot be combined except by inspection and verbal descriptions. One cannot print out even individual maps from the website. All attempts to locate appropriate (non-interactive) maps have failed.

9. A dissenting note, however, was struck by Charles Green and Basil Wilson, in *The Struggle for Black Empowerment in New York City: Beyond the Politics of Pigmentation* (New York: Praeger, 1980).

10. Marilynn Johnson, *Street Justice: A History of Police Violence in New York City* (Boston: Beacon Press, 2003), p. 238.

11. Both La Guardia (Fusion) and Lindsay (Republican) were liberals. In New York, given its historical association between the Democratic Party and corruption, "reform"candidates have often been not so much Republican as antimachine.

12. Rudolph Giuliani favored the police over citizen rights and established the notorious street crime control units whose commando tactics resulted in several unprovoked shootings of innocent men, whereas Michael Bloomberg has opposed the *modus operandi* of police out of uniform.

13. The importance of accountability is central to arguments made in Leonard I. Ruchelman's edited volume *Who Rules the Police?* (New York: New York University Press, 1973). As early as 1972, a blue-ribbon panel recommended that the Chicago police department should "Follow the Example of the New York Police Department by Opening the Entire Range of Police Activities to Public Inquiry and Research." See *The Misuse of Police Authority in Chicago A Report and Recommendations Based on Hearings... Convened by the Honorable Ralph H. Metcalfe* (1972), pp. 76–77.

14. Paul Chevigny, *The Edge of the Knife: Police Violence in the Americas* (New York: New Press, 1995); quotation from the "prelude" and pp. 1–2.

15. This may no longer be accurate. According to data presented in a boxed item in the *Los Angeles Times* sometime in the spring of 1995, Washington, D.C., had the highest rate: 2.9 officer-caused deaths per 1,000 police officers. Los Angeles was second, with 2.7 police-caused fatalities. Chicago and New York followed, with one police-caused shooting death per 1,000 officers. Data came from the Justice Department's Uniform Crime Reports.

16. Webster Report, *Crisis in the City*. See also the website of the Police Foundation, www.policefoundation.org/docs/commun_police.html.

17. One unintended consequence in New York has been the facilitation of corruption (deals and payoffs to officers walking the same beat over time), which has sometimes required regular reassignments. This contrast may no longer be valid. In 1999, a Los Angeles Police Department scandal erupted in the Rampart district, where "as many as seventy members... [of the force] had been robbing, murdering and framing gang members for many years." David Halle, ed., *New York and Los Angeles: Politics, Society, and Culture, A Comparative View* (Chicago: University of Chicago Press, 2003), pp. 39–40.

18. Size matters. Up to now, Los Angeles has depended on vehicular mobility and helicopter surveillance. See, for example, Sewell Chan, "Counting Heads along the Thin Blue Line," *New York Times*, March 26, 2006, Week in Review, p. 4, on plans to increase New York's police force by 1,200, even though the city already has 4.5 officers for every thousand residents (or 118 per square mile), as contrasted with Los Angeles' 2.4 officers per 1,000 residents (only 20 per square mile). The new mayor of Los Angeles and Bratton, his police chief, are seeking to increase the Los Angeles Police Department force by 1,000 officers, but "so far there has been little action." See also Jennifer Steinhauer, "A Tough East Coast Cop in Laid-Back Los Angeles: Bratton Poised for Second Term as Chief," *New York Times*, September 3, 2006, p. 14, where the Ramparts scandal is mentioned.

19. Wesley Skogan has been evaluating this innovation and has written several accounts of its progress. See, for example, Wesley G. Skogan and Susan M. Harnett, *Community Policing Chicago Style* (New York: Oxford University Press, 1997); Wesley G. Skogan, *On the Beat: Police and Community Problem Solving* (Boulder, Colo.: Westview Press, 1999), and most recently, *Police and Community in Chicago: A Tale of Three Cities* (New York: Oxford University Press, 2006).

20. In Skogan and Harnett, *Community Policing Chicago Style,* the authors suggest that the experimental program was least successful in Hispanic areas, a finding confirmed in Skogan, *Police and Community.* For an earlier study of the relationship between perceived fear of crime and racial tipping points in Chicago, see Richard P. Taub, D. Garth Taylor, and Jan D. Dunham, *Paths of Neighborhood Change: Race and Crime in Urban America* (Chicago: University of Chicago Press, 1984). This empirical study of racial transition in selected Chicago neighborhoods found a relationship between racial stereotyping of criminals and the propensity of whites to move but, interestingly enough, little direct relationship between actual crime rates and feelings of safety. Community policing seems to lower feelings of threat, even in the absence of actual crime reduction.

21. There are structural similarities between the economies and spatial patterns of Chicago and Detroit that make these cities stand out in their degrees of racial animosity.

22. For fuller details, see "Chicago Becomes Fordist," in my *New York, Chicago, Los Angeles: America's Global Cities* (Minneapolis: University of Minnesota Press, 1999), pp. 100–32.

23. The roster of backers of this plan to create a lakefront façade included the owners of major meat-packing firms, the manufacturers of heavy machinery, heads of railroads, and so forth. They are listed in the *Plan of Chicago Prepared under the Direction of the Commercial Club during the Years 1906, 1907, 1908* (reprinted New York: Da Capo Press, 1970). This is always referred to as "the Burnham Plan."

24. Black voters did not begin to shift party affiliations to the Democrats until the Depression.

25. In 1931, Democrat Anton Cermak (of Bohemian descent) won the mayor's race with strong Irish backing. When he was killed in an early assassination attempt on Franklin Roosevelt's life, the Irish politicos stepped out from behind to take over the party.

26. The classic study remains newspaper columnist Mike Royko's ruthlessly critical but awed political biography, simply titled *The Boss*. "This man was the closest thing you could get to a king," said the actor who plays Daley in a recently opened play in Chicago, *Hizzoner*. Quoted in Micheline Maynard, "The Mayor for Life Packs the House, Posthumously," *New York Times*, March 26, 2006, entertainment sec., p. 4. A recent book by Adam Cohen and Elizabeth Taylor elevated the metaphor further— from Boss and king to *American Pharaoh: Mayor Richard J. Daley: His Battle for Chicago and the Nation* (Boston: Little Brown, 2000).

27. See ward-specific votes for that year reproduced in Len O'Connor, *Clout: Mayor Daley and His City* (Chicago: Regnery, 1975), pp. 192–93.

28. These interregnums were achieved through Democratic primary elections, including the three-way contest (that included Daley Jr.) won by Harold Washington, making him Chicago's first and thus far only black mayor. Reelected to a second term, Washington died of a heart attack in the first year of the new term. This proved to be only a brief interruption of Irish dominance.

29. Significantly, Skogan and Harnett, *Community Policing Chicago Style*, suggest that the younger Daley's initial interest in the community policing experiment was motivated by his search for a reform issue that could unite all races, especially the overly victimized and underprotected black community: namely, crime reduction. Daley engaged the services of the consultants Booz-Allen, whose findings were incorporated in Illinois Advisory Committee to the United States Commission on Civil Rights, *Police Protection of the African American Community in Chicago* (Chicago: Illinois Advisory Committee to the United States Commission on Civil Rights, September 1993). This report included the astounding information that "an African American living in the city of Chicago is now seven times more likely to be murdered than a white" (p. 11). It seems to me, however, that extending the responsibilities of "beat" patrolmen to encompass broader activities, such as calling for improved city services in response to expressed complaints from neighborhood residents, begins to approximate the old role played by precinct captains.

30. See Timothy Gilfoyle, *Millennium Park: Creating a Chicago Landmark* (Chicago: University of Chicago Press, 2006).

31. There is a good chance for a black mayor, but only in the unlikely event that Illinois's popular senator, Barack Obama, foregoes wider ambitions.

32. According to Chicago Housing Authority reports, before their destruction, over 90 percent of their non-senior project units were occupied by African Americans.

33. HOPE is the new federal program discussed in chap. 3.

34. In this and the following narrative I have drawn heavily on my *New York, Chicago, Los Angeles*, chiefly chap. 3, "Developments between 1820 and 1870," pp. 54–58, for phase 1; chap. 6, "Los Angeles Becomes "Anglo," pp. 133–64, for phase 2; and chap. 9, "Los Angeles Becomes Industrial," pp. 237-68, for phase 3.

35. The best introduction to the class/ethnic structure of early California remains Carey McWilliams, *Southern California: An Island on the Land* (1946; reprint, Salt Lake City: Peregrine Smith, 1990). He paraphrased Charles Dwight Willard, who described the pre-American social structure of southern California as "not unlike that of the Deep South: the Indians were the slaves, the *gente de razon* were the plantation owners or "whites," and the Mexicans were the "poor whites"; quoted in my *New York, Chicago, Los Angeles*, p. 57. The ranchers had recently benefited from increased demands for meat from San Francisco's gold rush.

36. See Tomás Almaguer's remarkably nuanced account of *Racial Fault Lines: The Historical Origins of White Supremacy in California* (Berkeley: University of California Press, 1994), which focuses on the nineteenth century. Quotation from p. 9.

37. Ibid., pp. 8–9.

38. See the best single-volume history of the city during this period: Robert Fogelson, *The Fragmented Metropolis* (Cambridge, Mass.: Harvard University Press, 1967); the more complimentary multivolume works by the great historian of California Kevin Starr, especially his *Material Dreams: Southern California through the 1920's* (New York: Oxford University Press, 1990); and the hard-hitting muckraker account in Mike Davis, *City of Quartz* (New York: Vintage Books, 1992). They agree on the main lines of development, although they clearly differ in their interpretations.

39. See my *New York, Chicago, Los Angeles*, p. 141, table 6.1.

40. Figures from Armando Morales, *Ando Sangrando! (I am Bleeding): A Study of Mexican American–Police Conflict* (La Puente, Calif.: Perspectiva, 1972). For a broader treatment of this nationally, see Abraham Hoffman, *Unwanted Mexican Americans in the Great Depression: Repatriation Pressures, 1929–1939* (Tucson: Arizona University Press, 1974). Mexicans had already found their way to the Chicago region to work on the railroads and as migrant farm workers. Their settlements were also emptied out, at least temporarily.

41. For a fine-tuned analysis of the evolution of Los Angeles's political culture between 1880 and 1932, see Steven Erie, "The Local State and Economic Growth in Los Angeles, 1880–1932," *Urban Affairs Quarterly* 27, no. 4 (1992), 519–54.

42. This emergency "temporary" labor program was not dissimilar from President Bush's proposal to limit Mexican immigrants to temporary contracts carrying no rights to remain beyond the contracted period, although Bush's plan was no longer restricted to farm laborers.

43. The best explication of this system I have found is Raphael J. Sonenshein, *Politics in Black and White: Race and Power in Los Angeles* (Princeton, N.J.: Princeton University

Press, 1993): see esp. pp. 15–17, map series of city council districts; see pp. 36–48 for details on the 1963 city council elections.

44. Note the parallel to the Chicago coalition between blacks and "lake front liberals" that would elect Harold Washington 15 years later.

45. David J. Dent, "The New Black Suburbs," *New York Times Magazine,* June 14, 1992, pp. 18–23, 25. Towns like these offer middle-class amenities as well as same-race and same-class neighbors. In Los Angeles, given the peculiar shape of the city, even a relatively short move westward from South Central places African Americans beyond the city limits and therefore deprives them of their franchise in city elections.

46. William J. Wilson, in his *The Declining Significance of Race* (Chicago: University of Chicago Press, 1978; 2nd ed. 1980 [see esp. 1980 ed.]), attributes this newer class mobility largely to macro changes in the economy, whereas I see it as the delayed fruits of both the riots and the civil rights movement that privileged greater acceptance of blacks with credentials. I return to this subject below.

47. Edwin Embree, *Brown Americans: The Story of a Tenth of a Nation* (New York: Viking Press, 1931; reprinted 1943). Quotation on p. 200. A longtime friend of Charles S. Johnson, with whom he coauthored *The Collapse of Cotton Tenancy,* Embree chose action over teaching, and spent the rest of his life guiding the ambitious investment program of social reform undertaken by the Julius Rosenwald Fund, of which he was president from its founding in 1928 to its closing in 1948. The living endowment of the fund, financed by the Jewish philanthropist founder of Sears Roebuck, counted among its many accomplishments the establishment of more than 5,000 rural schools for blacks in 15 states.

48. The vicious circle of joblessness was noted in Sidney M. Willhelm's classic *Who Needs the Negro?* (New York: Silver Burdett Press, 1970). See also Frances Fox Piven and Richard A. Cloward, *Regulating the Poor: The Functions of Public Welfare* (New York: Pantheon, 1971; reprint, New York: Vintage Books, 1993), on this early period. We may look back with nostalgia to this "more benign" form of control.

49. See Christopher Mele and Teresa A. Miller, eds., *Civil Penalties, Social Consequences* (New York: Routledge, 2005).

50. David Cole, *No Equal Justice: Race and Class in the American Criminal Justice System* (New York: New Press, 1999).

51. "As Charles Ogletree, a black professor at Harvard Law School, summed it up, 'If I'm dressed in a knit cap and hooded jacket, I'm probable cause.' " Quoted in ibid., p. 47.

52. The Los Angeles riot of 1992 has been directly attributed to such a breach of justice.

53. The most notorious of these differences is the light penalty for cocaine possession (more common among whites) and the heavy mandatory penalty for crack possession (more common among blacks).

54. These inequities are hardly a new discovery. They occupy a chapter in Gunnar Myrdal's neglected collective masterpiece *An American Dilemma: The Negro Problem and Modern Democracy* (New York: Harper, 1944). See esp. chap. 24, "Inequality of Justice," pp. 523–69, although at that time white political control of the courts, especially in the South, was the main focus. But each of the steps is acknowledged.

55. Periodic censuses are conducted by the Department of Justice and reported, along with sophisticated analyses, by the Bureau of Justice Statistics. Summary data are made

available on their web pages. Unless otherwise noted, I have used data for the end of 2005, available as of November 2006, from the website of the Bureau of Justice Statistics, http://www.ojp.usdoj.gov/bjs/correct.htm. I have not updated these to the end of 2006. Summary data, as of the end of 2005, can also be found in a recent press release, available at http://www.ojp.usdoj.gov/bjs/pub/press/pripropr.htm. The successive figures show a steady increase over the past five years. "'The racial makeup of inmates changed little in recent years,' said Allen Beck, the bureau's chief of corrections statistics. 'In the 25–29 age group, an estimated 11.9 percent of black men were in prison or jails, compared with 3.9 percent of Hispanic males and 1.7 percent of white males' "; quoted in Elizabeth Write, "Number of U.S. Inmates Rises Two Percent," Associated Press, May 22, 2006.

56. Bureau of Justice Statistics, 2006 website. Graphs of the astronomical growth in number of incarcerated adults under correctional surveillance in state and federal institutions between 1980 and the end of 2004 show an exponential increase in both. The year 2005 continued this upward trajectory.

57. "Prison Statistics, 1990–2000," *Bureau of Justice Statistics Bulletin*, as reproduced at http://wrongfuldeathinstitute.com/links/prison/prisonstats.htm.

    It is difficult to compare these numbers to earlier times, but they seem to be much higher and more racially skewed than the ones presented in Myrdal, *An American Dilemma*, in the following tables: "Prisoners Received from Courts by State and Federal Prisons and Reformatories, by Sex, Race and Nativity," chap. 44, p. 971, table 1, and "Prisoners Received from Courts by State and Federal Prisons and Reformatories, by Geographic Areas and by Race and Nativity: 1939" (per 100,000), according to the U.S. Census of 1940, as shown in chap. 44, p. 971, table 2. Table 2 revealed that the difference between Negroes and whites was much larger in the North than in the South.

58. For example, a 2002 study by Peter Wagner, "Importing Constituents: Prisoners and Political Clout in New York: A Prison Policy Initiative Report," available at www.prisonpolicy.org/importing/importing.shtml, asserts that although 66 percent of New York state's prisoners are from New York City, all new prisons built since 1980, when the rate of incarceration more than tripled, have been located upstate. By state constitutions and U.S. Supreme Court precedent, all states are required to redraw state legislative district lines every 10 years. Counting prisoners in the locality of their incarceration deprives New York City of close to 44,000 persons normally residing in the city but held in prisons outside the city. This violates the principle of equal-size districts (including all persons, i.e. children, noncitizens and other nonvoters), enhances the proportionate state senate representation of voters in small white rural areas containing prisons and their population-based share of federal funds, while reducing the clout and distribution of federal funds to New York City. The same distortion occurs in Chicago and Los Angeles.

59. Paul Street, "Race, Prison, and Poverty: The Race to Incarcerate in the Age of Correctional Keynesianism," *Z Magazine* (May 2001) has been made available at www:thirdworldtraveler.com/prisonsystem/race_prison_poverty.html. Paul Street was the vice-president and research director of the Chicago Urban League. The magazine article was based on his report, *The Vicious Circle: Race, Prison, Jobs and*

Community in Chicago, Illinois and the Nation (Chicago: Chicago Urban League, 2001). The quotation has been taken primarily from pp. 1–2 on the website given above. His findings have also been summarized in Bruce Dixon, "Ten Worst Places to Be," *Black Commentator* (issue 146), available at www.blackcommentator.com/146/146_cover _dixon_ten_worst.html.

60. Street, "Race, Prison, and Poverty," n.p.

61. The collateral damage suffered by the children of the rising number of women in prison and the spouses, mates, and mothers attached to released prisoners has expanded the circle of those punished by a system that offers no way out, even in the long run.

62. Becky Pettit and Bruce Western, "Mass Imprisonment and the Life Course: Race and Class Inequality in U.S. Incarceration," *American Sociological Review* 69 (April 2004), 151-69. They combine data sources from the census, the Bureau of Justice Statistics, and the National Survey of Youth in ingenious ways.

63. Their findings also hint at the recent appearance of a "virtuous" circle for African Americans with a college education, a topic I turn to in the next section.

64. The first cohort would have reached adulthood by the early 1970s, when incarceration rates were low, whereas the second cohort would have reached adulthood during the later period, when incarceration rates went through the roof—having increased about five- or sixfold in the interim.

65. The authors actually underestimate prison risk rates because their populations in prison include only those in state and federal lockups, not in local jails.

66. Pettit and Western, "Mass Imprisonment and the Life Course," p. 152.

67. Ibid., p. 153.

68. Ibid., p. 154.

69. Ibid., p. 155.

70. Ibid., pp. 168–69.

71. Ibid., p. 161.

72. See Orlando Patterson, "A Poverty of Mind," *New York Times,* March 26, 2006, op-ed sec., p. 13. In all fairness, Patterson stresses the need to build stronger communities that can offer positive alternatives to reward good behavior rather than punish "deviance," but he is addressing the wrong audience for that. There is certainly something valuable about voluntary mentoring, which is occurring beneath the radar, but it cannot substitute for improved conditions.

73. See especially the second edition of Wilson, *The Declining Significance of Race* (1980).

74. Melvin Oliver and Thomas Shapiro, *Black Wealth/White Wealth: A New Perspective on Racial Inequality* (New York: Routledge, 1995).

75. See the careful and qualified discussion of this dilemma in Mary Pattillo-McCoy, *Black Picket Fences: Privilege and Peril among the Black Middle Class* (Chicago: University of Chicago Press, 1999). Through her participant observation study of a generally middle-class district in Chicago, where middle-class blacks are not only segregated from whites but mingle with others who have fewer human capital attributes, there are dangers in the conflicting messages their children receive from those around them.

76. Thomas M. Shapiro, *The Hidden Cost of Being African American: How Wealth Perpetuates Inequality* (New York: Oxford University Press, 2004).

77. P. L. Wachtel, *Race in the Mind of America: Breaking the Vicious Cycle between Blacks and Whites* (New York: Routledge, 1999).

78. See Joe E. Feagin and Hernán Vera, "The Souls of White Folk," in Feagin and Vera, *White Racism: The Basics* (New York: Routledge, 1995), chap. 7, pp. 135–61.

79. Ibid., p. 136.

80. Ibid., p. 139.

81. What one might call the "Willie Horton effect."

82. William Brink and Louis Harris, *The Negro Revolution in America: What Negroes Want? Why and How They are Fighting; What They Support; What Whites Think of Them and Their Demands* (New York: Simon and Schuster, 1963), pp. 140–41, unnumbered table.

83. Ralph Ellison, *Invisible Man* (New York: Random House, 1952; reprint, Vintage Books, 1989); W. E. B. Du Bois, *Dusk of Dawn* (New York: Harcourt, Brace, 1940). Du Bois was of course raised in a white New England town, received a Ph.D. from Harvard, became the leading black sociologist in the United States, and founded and edited the NAACP's journal, *The Crisis*, the most important black periodical of its day. Nevertheless, he, too, finally withdrew in disappointment, moving to Ghana, where he later died. Ralph Waldo Ellison, Oklahoma born, well-educated, and a belated member of the Harlem Renaissance, acknowledges the help and encouragement he received not only from Richard Wright and Langston Hughes but also from white friends in Vermont and New York. He later held a chair in literature at New York University. (Although he did not witness the Harlem riot of 1943, his novel includes the most graphic fictional account of it I have ever read.)

84. I have taken this long quotation from its reproduction in Myrdal, *An American Dilemma*, p. 680; it references Du Bois, *Dusk of Dawn*, pp. 130–31.

85. Robert Merton, "Social Structure and Anomie," in Merton, *Social Theory and Social Structure* (Glencoe, Ill.: Free Press, 1949), pp. 125-49. He proposed a theory to analyze the "social and cultural sources of deviant behavior." Leaving aside his assumptions of "deviance" that ignore subcultural variations, he stresses the discrepancy in American society between its "great emphasis upon certain success-goals," chiefly monetary, "without equivalent emphasis upon institutional means" (p. 129).

86. Ibid., p. 133.

87. Ibid., p. 145. These alternative reactions are described for poorer African Americans in successive chapters in William McCord, John Howard, Bernard Friedberg, and Edwin Howard, *Life Styles in the Black Ghetto* (New York: Dutton, 1969), but can be applied more broadly. (This source includes excellent chapters such as McCord's "The Defeated," "The Achiever," "The Exploiter," "The 'Rebel without a Cause,'" John Howard and William McCord's "Watts: The Revolt and After," and John Howard's "The Activist" and "The Revolutionary.")

88. It is estimated that the annual cost of keeping a prisoner in jail is $60,000.

89. A solution similar to this has recently been suggested by James Traub, "Paying for Good Behavior?" *New York Times Magazine*, October 8, 2006, pp. 15–16.

90. Kerner Report, p. 483. Ironically, it is followed by a lengthy "Supplement and Appendices" devoted to "better control of riots."

91. See, inter alia, Dale Maharidge, *The Coming White Minority: California's Eruptions and the Nation's Future* (New York: Times Books, 1996).

Bibliography

ABBREVIATED TITLES OF OFFICIAL REPORTS

General

Kerner Report:
U. S. Riot Commission, *Report of the National Advisory Commission on Civil Disorders.* New York: New York Times, 1968; reprint, Pantheon Books, 1988.

Chicago

Johnson, *The Negro in Chicago:*
Charles S. Johnson. *The Negro in Chicago: A Study of Race Relations and a Race Riot.* Author for the Chicago Commission on Race Relations. Chicago: University of Chicago Press, 1922. Reprint, New York: Arno Press, 1968.
Mayor's Riot Committee report:
Mayor's Committee. *Report of the Chicago Riot Study Committee to the Hon. Richard J. Daley.* Chicago: Mayor's Committee, August 1, 1968.
Walker Report:
Rights in Conflict: The Violent Confrontation of Demonstrators and Police in the Parks and Streets of Chicago during the Week of the Democratic National Convention. The Walker Report to the National Commission on the Causes and Prevention of Violence. New York: Bantam Books, 1968.

New York

Mayor's Commission report:
Mayor La Guardia's Commission. *The Complete Report of Mayor La Guardia's Commission on the Harlem Riot of March 19, 1935.* (Transcript of unreleased full version, published in the *Amsterdam News,* July 1935.) Mass Violence in America series. New York: Arno Press, 1969. Page references are to this reprint.

Los Angeles

Christopher Commission Report:
Independent Commission on the Los Angeles Police Department. Los Angeles: Independent Commission on the Los Angeles Police Department, July 1991.
McCone Report:
California Governor's Commission on the Los Angeles Riots, *Violence in the City—An End or a Beginning? A Report by the Governor's Commission on the Los Angeles Riots.* Los Angeles, December 2, 1965. Reprinted in Robert M. Fogelson, comp. *Violence in the City—An End or a Beginning? The Los Angeles Riots.* Mass Violence in America series. New York: Arno Press, 1969. Page references same in original and in the 1969 reprint.
Webster Report:
William H. Webster and Hubert Williams. *The City in Crisis: A Report by the Special Advisor to the Board of Police Commissioners on the Civil Disorder in Los Angeles.* 2 vols. Vol. 1, text. Vol. 2, apps. and maps. Submitted October 21, 1992. Los Angeles: n.p.

General and Comparative Bibliography

Abu-Lughod, Janet. *New York, Chicago, Los Angeles: America's Global Cities.* University of Minnesota Press, 1999.

Abu-Lughod, Janet. *Changing Cities.* New York: HarperCollins, 1991.

Abu-Lughod, Janet. "Comparing Chicago, New York and Los Angeles." In *World Cities in a World System,* edited by Peter Taylor and Paul Knox. Cambridge: Cambridge University Press, 1995.

Almaguer, Tomás, and Moon-Kei Jung. "The Enduring Ambiguities of Race in the United States." In *Sociology for the Twenty-First Century: Continuities and Cutting Edges,* edited by Janet Abu-Lughod. Chicago: University of Chicago Press, 1999, pp. 213–37.

Balbus, Isaac. *The Dialectics of Legal Repression: Black Rebels Before the American Criminal Courts.* New Brunswick, N.J.: Transaction Books, 1973.

Banfield, Edward. "Rioting for Fun and Profit." In *The Unheavenly City: The Nature and Future of Our Urban Crisis.* Boston: Little, Brown, 1968, pp. 185–209. (Reproduced without change in Banfield, *The Unheavenly City Revisited* [Boston: Little, Brown, 1978].)

Bayor, Ronald. "Reform Mayors and Urban Politics: New York and Chicago." *Journal of Urban History* 18, no. 1 (November 1991): 93–98.

Bennett, Lerone, Jr. *Confrontation: Black and White.* Baltimore: Penguin, 1968. Originally published 1965.

Blauner, Robert. "Internal Colonialism and Ghetto Revolt." *Social Problems* 16, no. 4 (spring 1969): 393–408.

Boskin, Joseph, ed. *Urban Racial Violence in the Twentieth Century.* Beverly Hills, Calif.: Glencoe Press, 1969.

Bracey, John Jr., August Meier, and Elliot Rudwick., eds. *The Black Sociologists: The First Half Century.* Belmont, Calif.: Wadsworth, 1971.

Bracey, John Jr., August Meier, and Elliot Rudwick, eds. *The Rise of the Ghetto.* Belmont, Calif.: Wadsworth, 1971.

Brink, William, and Louis Harris. *The Negro Revolution in American: What Negroes Want and Why They Are Fighting: Whom They Support: What Whites Think of Them and Their Demands.* New York: Simon and Schuster, 1964.

Bullard, Robert D., et al. *Residential Apartheid: The American Legacy.* Los Angeles: UCLA Center for Afro-American Studies, 1994.

Chan, Sewell. "Counting Heads along the Thin Blue Line." *New York Times,* March 26, 2006, week in review sec., p. 4.

Chevigny, Paul. *The Edge of the Knife: Police Violence in the Americas.* New York: New Press, 1995.

Clark, Kenneth. "The Wonder Is That There Have Been so Few Race Riots." *New York Times Magazine,* September 5, 1965. Excerpt reprinted in *Black Protest in the Sixties: Articles from the New York Times,* edited by August Meier, Elliot Rudwick, and John Bracey. New York: Markus Wiener, 1991, pp. 107–15.

Clarke, Susan E., and Jeffrey L. Obler, eds. *Urban Ethnic Conflict: A Comparative Perspective.* Chapel Hill: University of North Carolina Institute for Research in Social Science, 1976.

Cole, David. *No Equal Justice: Race and Class in the American Criminal Justice System.* New York: New Press, 1999.

Cople, Frederic C. *The Urban Establishment: Upper Strata in Boston, New York, Charleston, Chicago and Los Angeles.* Urbana: University of Illinois Press, 1982.

Cottingham, Clement, ed. *Race, Poverty, and the Urban Underclass.* Lexington, Mass.: Lexington Books, 1982.

Danziger, Sheldon, and Peter Gottschalk, eds. *Uneven Tides: Rising Inequality in America.* New York: Russell Sage Foundation, 1993.

Darity, William, Jr., and Samuel Myers, Jr. "Changes in Black-White Income Inequality, 1968–1978: A Decade of Progress?" *Review of Black Political Economy* 10 (Summer 1980).

Davis, Angela Y. *Are Prisons Obsolete?* New York: Seven Stories Press, 2003.

Dent, David J. "The New Black Suburbs." *New York Times Magazine,* June 14, 1992, pp. 18–23, 25.

Du Bois, W. E. B. *Dusk of Dawn.* New York: Harcourt, Brace, 1940.

Ellison, Ralph. *Invisible Man.* New York: Random House, 1952. Reprint, New York: Vintage Books, 1989.

Embree, Edwin R. *Brown Americans: The Story of a Tenth of the Nation.* New York: Viking Press, 1931. Reprint, with update, 1943.

Fainstein, Susan, Ian Gordon, and Michael Harloe. *Divided Cities: New York and London in the Contemporary World.* Oxford: Blackwell, 1992.

Farley, Reynolds. *Blacks and Whites: Narrowing the Gap?* Cambridge, Mass.: Harvard University Press, 1984.

Feagin, Joe R., and Harlan Hahn. *Ghetto Revolts: The Politics of Violence in American Cities.* New York: Macmillan, 1973.

Feagin, Joe R., and Hernán Vera. *White Racism: The Basics.* New York: Routledge, 1995.

Foner, P. *Organized Labor and the Black Worker, 1619–1981.* New York: International, 1982.

Fox, Geoffrey. *Hispanic Nation: Culture, Politics, and the Constructing of Identity.* Secaucus, N.J.: Carol, 1996.

Fusfield, Daniel R., and Timothy Bates. *The Political Economy of the Urban Ghetto.* Carbondale: Southern Illinois University Press, 1984.

Gilje, Paul A. *Rioting in America.* Bloomington: University of Indiana Press, 1996.

Gonzalez, Juan, Jr. *Racial and Ethnic Groups in America.* Dubuque, Iowa: Kendall Hunt, 1990.

Goodwin, E. Marvin. *Black Migration in America from 1915 to 1960: An Uneasy Exodus.* Lewiston, N.Y.: Mellen Press, 1990.

Grimshaw, Allen D. "A Study in Social Violence: Urban Race Riots in the United States." Ph.D. diss., University of Pennsylvania, 1959.

Grimshaw, Allen D. "Urban Racial Violence in the United States: Changing Ecological Considerations." Reprinted in *Racial Violence in the United States,* edited by Allen D. Grimshaw. Chicago: Aldine, 1969.

Gusfield, Joseph, ed. *Protest, Reform and Revolt: A Reader in Social Movements.* New York: Wiley, 1970.

Hacker, Andrew. *Two Nations: Black and White, Hostile, Separate, and Unequal.* New York: Simon & Schuster, 1992.

Halle, David, and Kevin Raffter. "Riots in New York and Los Angeles, 1935–2002." In *New York and Los Angeles: Politics, Society, and Culture, A Comparative View,* edited by David Halle. Chicago: University of Chicago Press, 2003, pp. 341–366.

Herman, Max Arthur. *Fighting in the Streets: Ethnic Succession and Urban Unrest in Twentieth-Century America.* New York: Peter Lang, 2005.

Hersey, John. *The Algiers Motel Incident.* New York: Knopf, 1968.

Ignatief, Noel. *How the Irish Became White.* New York: Routledge, 1995.

Jankowski, Martin Sanchez. *Islands in the Street: Gangs and American Urban Society.* Berkeley: University of California Press, 1991.

Jasso, Guillermina, and Mark Rosenzweig. *The New Chosen People: Immigrants in the United States.* New York: Russell Sage Foundation, 1990.

Katznelson, Ira. *Black Men, White Cities: Race, Politics, and Migration in the United States, 1900–30, and Britain, 1948–68.* 1973; reprint, Chicago: University of Chicago Press, 1976.

Katznelson, Ira. *City Trenches: Urban Politics and the Patterning of Class in the United States.* New York: Pantheon Books, 1981.

Katznelson, Ira, Kathleen Gille, and Margaret Weir. *Schooling for All: Class, Race, and the Decline of the Democratic Ideal.* New York: Basic Books, 1985.

Lemann, N. *The Promised Land: The Great Black Migration and How it Changed America.* New York: Knopf, 1991.

Leonard, Jonathan S. "The Interaction of Residential Segregation and Employment Discrimination." *Journal of Urban Economics* 21 (May 1987): 323–46.

Levy, R. *Dollars and Dreams: The Changing American Income Distribution.* New York: Russell Sage Foundation, 1988.

Lieberson, Stanley. *A Piece of the Pie: Blacks and White Immigrants since 1880.* Berkeley: University of California Press, 1980.

Lieberson, Stanley, and Arnold R. Silverman. "The Precipitants and Underlying Conditions of Race Riots." *American Sociological Review* 30 (December 1965): 887–98.

Lieberson, Stanley, and Mary Waters. *From Many Strands: Ethnic and Racial Groups in Contemporary America.* New York: Russell Sage Foundation, 1988.

Logan, John, and Harvey Molotch. *Urban Fortunes: The Political Economy of Place.* Berkeley: University of California Press, 1987.

Long, Herman H., and Charles S. Johnson. *People vs. Property: Race Restrictive Covenants in Housing.* Nashville: Fiske University Press, 1947.

McAdam, Douglas. *Political Process and the Development of Black Insurgency.* Chicago: University of Chicago Press, 1982.

McCall, Michael. "Some Ecological Aspects of Negro Slum Riots." In Gusfield, *Protest, Reform and Revolt,* pp. 345–62.

McCord, William, John Howard, Bernard Friedberg, and Edwin Harwood. *Life Styles in the Black Ghetto.* New York: Norton, 1969.

McGreevy, John T. *Parish Boundaries: The Catholic Encounter with Race in the Twentieth-Century Urban North.* Chicago: University of Chicago Press, 1996.

Maldonado, Lionel, and Joan Moore, eds. *Urban Ethnicity in the United States: New Immigrants and Old Minorities.* Vol. 29 of *Urban Affairs Annual Reviews.* Beverly Hills: Sage, 1985.

Massey, Douglas, and Nancy Denton. *American Apartheid: Segregation and the Making of the Underclass.* Cambridge, Mass.: Harvard University Press, 1993.

Meier, August, Elliot Rudwick, and John Bracey, Jr., eds. *Black Protest in the Sixties: Articles from the New York Times.* 2nd enl. ed. New York: Markus Wiener, 1991.

Mele, Christopher, and Teresa A. Miller, eds. *Civil Penalties, Social Consequences.* New York: Routledge, 2005.

Meredith, Robyn. "Five Days in 1967 Still Shake Detroit." *New York Times,* July 23, 1997, p. A10.

Merton, Robert. "Social Structure and Anomie." *Social Theory and Social Structure.* New York: Free Press, 1957: 131–60.

Moore, Joan, and Raquel Pinderhughes, eds. *In the Barrios: Latinos and the Underclass Debate.* New York: Russell Sage Foundation, 1993.

Morales, Rebecca, and Frank Bonilla, eds. *Latinos in a Changing U.S. Economy: Comparative Perspectives on Growing Inequality.* Newbury Park, Calif.: Sage, 1993.

Morris, Aldon. *The Origins of the Civil Rights Movement: Black Communities Organizing for Change.* New York: Free Press, 1984.

Muller, Thomas. *Immigrants and the American City.* New York: New York University Press, 1993.

Myers, Daniel J. "Racial Rioting in the 1960s: An Event History Analysis of Local Conditions." *American Sociological Review* 62 (February 1997): 94–112.

Myrdal, Gunnar. *An American Dilemma: The Negro Problem and Modern Democracy.* New York: Harper, 1944.

Oliver, Melvin, and Thomas Shapiro. *Black Wealth/White Wealth: A New Perspective on Racial Inequality.* New York: Routledge, 1995.

Olzak, Susan. *The Dynamics of Ethnic Competition.* Stanford, Calif.: Stanford University Press, 1992.

Olzak, Susan, Suzanne Shanahan, and Elizabeth McEneaney. "Poverty, Segregation, and Race Riots: 1960–1993." *American Sociological Review* 61 (August 1996): 590–613.

Park, Robert Ezra. *Race and Culture.* Glencoe, Ill.: Free Press, 1950.

Parkers, Karen, Patricia McCall, and Jodi Lane. "Exploring Racial Discrimination and Competition Processes of Race-Specific Violence in Urban Context." *Critical Sociology* 28, nos. 1–2 (April 2002): 235–54.

Patterson, Orlando. *Ethnic Chauvinism: The Reactionary Impulse*. Briarcliff Manor, N.Y.: Stein and Day, 1977.

Payne, Charles. *I've Got the Light of Freedom*. Berkeley: University of California Press, 1995.

Perea, Juan F. *Immigrants Out! The New Nativism and the Anti-immigrant Impulse in the United States*. New York: New York University Press, 1996.

Pettit, Becky, and Bruce Western. "Mass Imprisonment and the Life Course: Race and Class Inequality in U.S. Incarceration." *American Sociological Review* 69 (2004): 151–69.

Piven, Frances Fox, and Richard A. Cloward. *Regulating the Poor: The Functions of Public Welfare*. New York: Pantheon, 1971. Reprint, New York: Vintage Books, 1993.

Portes, Alejandro, and R. Bach. *Latin Journey: Cuban and Mexican Immigrants in the United States*. Berkeley: University of California Press, 1985.

Portes, Alejandro, and Ruben Rumbaut. *Immigrant America: A Portrait*. Berkeley: University of California Press, 1990.

Portes, Alejandro, and Alex Stepick. *City on the Edge: The Transformation of Miami*. Berkeley: University of California Press, 1993.

Ringer, Benjamin, and Elinor R. Lawless. *Race-Ethnicity and Society*. New York: Routledge, 1989.

Rodrigez, Clara. *The Ethnic Queue in the United States: The Case of Puerto Ricans*. San Francisco: R and E Associates, 1974.

Romo, Harriet, ed. *Latinos and Blacks in the Cities: Policies for the 1990s*. Austin: University of Texas Press, 1990.

Ruchelman, Leonard I., ed. *Who Rules the Police?* New York: New York University Press, 1973.

Rudwick, Elliot. *Race Riot at East St. Louis*. Carbondale: Southern Illinois University Press, 1964.

Sassen, Saskia. *The Global City: New York, London, Tokyo*. Princeton, N.J.: Princeton University Press, 1991.

Shapiro, Thomas. *The Hidden Cost of Being African American: How Wealth Perpetuates Inequality*. New York: Oxford University Press, 2000.

Spillerman, Seymour. "Structural Characteristics of Cities and the Severity of Racial Disorders." *American Sociological Review* 41, no. 5 (October 1976): 771–93.

Squires, Gregory D. *Capital and Communities in Black and White: The Intersection of Race, Class, and Uneven Development*. Albany: State University of New York Press, 1988.

Staples, Robert. *The Urban Plantation: Racism and Colonialism in the Post–Civil Rights Era*. Oakland, Calif.: Black Scholar Press, 1987.

Sugrue, Thomas J. *The Origins of the Urban Crisis: Race and Inequality in Postwar Detroit*. Princeton, N.J.: Princeton University Press, 1996.

Taeuber, Karl, and Alma Taeuber. *Negroes in Cities*. Chicago: Aldine, 1965.

Tobin, Gary A., ed. *Divided Neighborhoods: Changing Patterns of Racial Segregation*. Vol. 32 of *Urban Affairs Annual Reviews*. Beverly Hills, Calif.: Sage, 1987.

Traub, James. "Paying for Good Behavior?" *New York Times Magazine*. October 8, 2006, pp. 15–16.

Trotter, Joe William, Jr., ed. *The Great Migration in Historical Perspective: New Dimensions of Race, Class and Gender*. Bloomington: Indiana University Press, 1991.

U.S. Department of Justice, Bureau of Justice Statistics. 2006 website: www.ojp.usdoj.gov/bjs/correct.html.

Wachtel, P. L. *Race in the Mind of America: Breaking the Vicious Cycle between Blacks and Whites*. New York: Routledge, 1999.

Wacquant, Loic J. D. "Redrawing the Urban Color Line: The State of the Ghetto in the 1980's." In *Social Problems*, edited by Craig Calhoun and George Ritzer. New York: McGraw-Hill, 1992.

Wacquant, Loic J. D. "From Welfare State to Prison State: Imprisoning the Poor." *Le Monde Diplomatique*, July 1998, available at http://mondediplo.com/1998/07/14prison.

Wacquant, Loic J. D. "Deadly Symbiosis: When Ghetto and Prison Meet." *Punishment and Society* 3, no. 1 (2001): 95–134.

Wacquant, Loic J. D. "The Curious Eclipse of Prison Ethnography in the Age of Mass Incarceration." *Ethnography* 3, no. 4 (2002): 371–97.

Wacquant, Loic J. D. "From Slavery to Mass Incarceration." *New Left Review* 13 (January/February 2002): 41–60.

Wacquant, Loic J. D. "Race as Civic Felony." *International Social Science Journal* (UNESCO) 183 (2005): 127–42.

Ward, David. *Cities and Immigrants: A Geography of Change in Nineteenth Century America*. New York: Oxford University Press, 1972.

Ward, David. *Poverty, Ethnicity and the American City, 1840–1925: Changing Conceptions of the Slum and the Ghetto*. New York: Cambridge University Press, 1989.

Warner, Sam Bass, Jr. *The Urban Wilderness: A History of the American City*. New York: Harper and Row, 1972.

Waskow, Arthur I. *From Race Riot to Sit-in, 1919 and the 1960s: A Study in the Connection between Conflict and Violence*. Garden City, N.Y.: Doubleday, 1966.

Willie, Charles V. *Race, Ethnicity, and Socioeconomic Status: A Theoretical Analysis of their Interrelationship*. Bayside, N.Y.: General Hall, 1983.

Willhelm, Sidney M. *Who Needs the Negro?* New York: Schenkman, 1970. Reprint, Communications Systems, 1993.

Wilson, William Julius. *The Truly Disadvantaged: The Inner City, the Underclass, and Public Policy*. Chicago: University of Chicago Press, 1987.

Wilson, William Julius. *The Declining Significance of Race*. Chicago: University of Chicago Press, 1978. 2nd ed. with new final chapter published 1980. Page references are to the 1978 edition.

Wolch, Jennifer, and Michael Dear, eds. *The Power of Geography*. Boston: Unwin Hyman, 1989.

Woolbright, Louie Albert, and David Hartmann. "Hispanics and Asians: The New Segregation." Edited by Gary Tobin. In *Divided Neighborhoods: Changing Patterns of Racial Segregation*. Vol. 32 of *Urban Affairs Annual Reviews*. Beverly Hills, Calif.: Sage, 1987.

Yates, Michael D. *Longer Hours, Fewer Jobs: Employment and Unemployment in the United States*. New York: Monthly Review Press, 1994.

CHICAGO

Abu-Lughod, Janet. "Commentary: What Is Special about Chicago?" *City and Society* 17 (2005): 289–303.

Abu-Lughod, Janet. "The Specificity of the Chicago Ghetto: Comment on Wacquant's 'Three Pernicious Premises,' " *International Journal of Urban and Regional Research* 21, no. 2 (1997): 357–62.

Alkalimat, A., and D. Gills. "Chicago." In *The New Black Vote*, edited by R. Bush. San Francisco: Synthesis, 1984.

Alkalimat, A., and D. Gills. *Harold Washington and the Crisis of Black Power in Chicago.* Chicago: Twenty-First Century Books, 1989.

Allswang, John. *A House for All Peoples: Ethnic Politics in Chicago.* Lexington: University of Kentucky Press, 1971.

Anderson, Alan B., and George Pickering. *Confronting the Color Line: The Broken Promise of the Civil Rights Movement in Chicago.* Athens: University of Georgia Press, 1968.

Aschenbrenner, Joyce. *Lifelines: Black Families in Chicago.* New York: Holt, Rinehart and Winston, 1975. Reprint, Prospect Heights, Ill.: Waveland Press, 1983.

Balbus, Isaac. *The Dialectics of Legal Repression: Black Rebels Before the American Criminal Courts.* New Brunswick, N.J.: Transaction Books, 1973.

Baron, Harold M. *The Negro Worker in the Chicago Labor Market: A Case Study of Defacto Segregation.* Chicago: Chicago Urban League, 1968.

Baron, Harold M. *Building Babylon: A Case of Racial Controls in Public Housing.* Evanston, Ill.: Center for Urban Affairs, Northwestern University, 1971.

Baron, Harold M. "Black Powerlessness in Chicago." *Trans-action* 4 (1968): 27–33.

Bennett, Larry. "Challenging Chicago's Growth Machine." *International Journal of Urban and Regional Research* 11, no. 3 (1987): 351–62.

Bennett, Larry. "Harold Washington and the Black Urban Regime." *Urban Affairs Quarterly* 28 (March 1993): 423–40.

Berry, Brian. *The Open Housing Question: Race and Housing in Chicago, 1966–1976.* Cambridge, Mass.: Ballinger, 1979.

Bowen, Louise De Koven. *The Colored Population of Chicago.* Chicago: Juvenile Protective Association, 1913.

Bowly, Deveraux. *The Poorhouse: Subsidized Housing in Chicago, 1895–1976.* Carbondale: Southern Illinois University Press, 1978.

Branch, Taylor. *At Canaan's Edge: America in the King Years 1965–1968.* New York: Simon and Schuster, 2006. Selected chapters on Chicago.

Breckenridge, Sophonisba P. "The Color Line in the Housing Problem." *Survey* 40 (February 1, 1913): 575–76.

Brune, Tom, and Eduardo Camacho, et al. *Race and Poverty in Chicago: A Special Report: Analysis and Data Reflecting Race and Poverty in Chicago Based on the 1980 U.S. Census.* Chicago: Community Renewal Society, 1983.

Burgess, Ernest W. "The Growth of the City: An Introduction to a Research Project." *Proceedings of the American Sociological Society* 18 (1923): 85–97.

Burnham, Daniel H., and Edward H. Bennett. *Plan of Chicago.* Reprinted New York: Da Capo Press, 1970.

Chicago Commission on Race Relations. Study of the 1919 Chicago Riot. Cited as Johnson, Charles, *The Negro in Chicago*. Chicago: University of Chicago Press, 1922.

Chicago Committee on Urban Opportunity. *Summer in Chicago: 1968*. Chicago: Chicago Committee on Urban Opportunity, n.d.

Chicago Conference on Civic Unity. *Human Relations in Chicago, 1949, Inventory in Human Relations, 1945–1948, Recommendations for the Future: Adopted by Chicago Conference on Civic Unity, January 13, 1949*. Chicago: Mayor's Commission on Human Relations, 1949.

Chicago Conference on Home Front Unity. *Chicago Charter of Human Relations, Adopted by Chicago Conference on Home Front Unity, November 6, 1945*. Chicago: Mayor's Commission on Race Relations, 1945.

Chicago Department of Development and Planning. *Chicago's Spanish-Speaking Population: Selected Characteristics*. Chicago: Chicago Department of Development and Planning, 1973.

Chicago Fact Book Consortium, eds. *Local Community Fact Book, Chicago Metropolitan Area 1980, Based on the 1970 and 1980 Censuses*. Chicago: University of Illinois Press, 1984.

Chicago Mayor's Commission on Human Relations. *The People of Chicago: Five Year Report, 1947–1951*. Chicago: Chicago Commission on Human Relations, 1953.

Chicago Riot Study Committee. *Report of the Chicago Riot Study Committee to the Hon. Richard J. Daley*. Chicago: Chicago Riot Study Committee, 1968.

Chicago Tribune Staff. *The American Millstone: An Examination of the Nation's Permanent Underclass*. Chicago: Contemporary Books, 1986.

Chicago Urban League. *The Racial Aspects of Urban Planning*. Chicago: Chicago Urban League, 1968.

Chicago Urban League. *Blacks in Policy-Making Positions in Chicago*. Chicago: Chicago Urban League, 1980.

Christian, Charles Melvin. "The Impact of Industrial Relocations from the Black Community of Chicago upon Job Opportunities and Residential Mobility of the Central City Workforce." Ph.D diss., University of Illinois at Urbana-Champaign, 1976.

Clavel, Pierre, and Wim Weiwel, eds. *Harold Washington and the Neighborhoods: Progressive City Government in Chicago, 1983–1987*. New Brunswick, N.J.: Rutgers University Press, 1991.

Cohen, Adam, and Elizabeth Taylor. *American Pharaoh: Mayor Richard J. Daley: His Battle for Chicago and the Nation*. Boston: Little, Brown, 2000.

Collins, Dorothy. "United Gangs Patrol for Peace on City Streets." *Chicago's American*, April 8, 1968, 1, 7.

Comstock, Alzada P. "Chicago Housing Conditions." Pt. 6. "The Problem of the Negro." *American Journal of Sociology* 18 (September 1912): 241–57.

Connolly, Kathleen. "The Chicago Open-Housing Conference." In Garrow, *Chicago 1966*: 49–96.

"Daley's Dubious Order." Editorial. *Chicago Daily News*, April 16, 1968, p. 14.

Dorsey, James. *Up South: Blacks in Chicago's Suburbs, 1719–1983*. Bristol, Ind.: Wyndham Hall Press, 1986.

Drake, St. Clair, and Horace Cayton. *Black Metropolis: A Study of Negro Life in a Northern City*. New York: Harcourt Brace, 1945. Reprint with new introduction and lengthy appendix. Chicago: University of Chicago Press, 1993.

Duncan, Otis Dudley, and Beverly Duncan. *The Negro Population of Chicago: A Study of Residential Succession*. Chicago: University of Chicago Press, 1957.

Ellis, William. *White Ethnics and Black Power: The Emergence of the West Side Organization*. Chicago: Aldine, 1969.

Embree, Edwin R. Foreword to *Proceedings of the Mayor's Committee on Race Relations*. Chicago: Mayor's Committee on Race Relations, February 1944.

Finley, Mary Lou. "The Open Housing Marches: Chicago, Summer '66" In Garrow, *Chicago 1966*: 1–48.

Flannery, James A. "Chicago Newspapers' Coverage of the City's Major Civil Disorders of 1968." Ph.D. diss., Northwestern University, 1971.

Foster, Richard. "Guardsmen Patrol Disturbance Areas." *Chicago Sun-Times,* April 4, 1969, pp. 1, 6, 12, 13.

Frankel, Max. Introduction to the Walker Report.

Frazier, E. Franklin. *The Negro Family in Chicago*. Chicago: University of Chicago Press, 1932.

Garrow, David J., ed. *Chicago 1966: Open Housing Marches, Summit Negotiations, and Operation Breadbasket*. Brooklyn: Carlson, 1989. Interior title page reads: *Martin Luther King, Jr. and the Civil Rights Movement*.

Gilfoyle, Timothy. *Millennium Park: Creating a Chicago Landmark*. Chicago: University of Chicago Press, 2006.

Giloth, R. P., and J. Betancur. "Where Downtown Meets Neighborhood: Industrial Displacement in Chicago, 1978–1987." *Journal of the American Planning Association* 54 (1988): 279–90.

Giloth, R. P., and R. Mier. "Spatial Change and Social Justice: Alternative Economic Development in Chicago." In *Economic Restructuring and Political Response*, edited by Robert Beauregard. Newbury Park, Calif.: Sage, 1989, pp. 181–208.

Gordon, R. W. "The Change in the Political Alignment of Chicago's Negroes during the New Deal." *Journal of American History* 56 (1969): 584–603.

Gosnell, Harold. *Negro Politicians*. Chicago: University of Chicago Press, 1935.

Gosnell, Harold. *Machine Politics: Chicago Model*. Chicago: University of Chicago Press, 1937; reprint, 1968.

Greene, Richard. "Poverty Concentration Measures and the Urban Underclass." *Economic Geography* 67, no. 3 (July 1991): 240–53.

Grimshaw, William J. *Bitter Fruit: Black Politics and the Chicago Machine, 1931–1991*. Chicago: University of Chicago Press, 1992.

Grossman, James R. *Land of Hope: Chicago, Black Southerners, and the Great Migration*. Chicago: University of Chicago Press, 1989.

Grossman, James R. "The White Man's Union: The Great Migration and the Resonances of Race and Class in Chicago, 1916–1922." In *The Great Migration in Historical Perspective: New Dimensions of Race, Class and Gender*, edited by Joe William Trotter, Jr. Bloomington: Indiana University Press, 1991, pp. 83–105.

Hall, Peter J. "The City of Permanent Underclass." In Hall, *Cities of Tomorrow: An Intellectual History of Urban Planning and Design in the Twentieth Century.* Oxford: Blackwell, 1988.

Hartmann, David J. "Racial Change in the Chicago Area, 1980–1987." *Sociology and Social Research* 74 (April 1990): 168–73.

Herbst, Alma. *The Negro in the Slaughtering and Meat-Packing Industry in Chicago.* Boston: Houghton Mifflin, 1932. Reprint, New York: Arno Press, 1971.

Hirsch, Arnold R. *Making the Second Ghetto: Race and Housing in Chicago, 1940–1960.* Cambridge: Cambridge University Press, 1983.

Hoffman, Peter M., comp. *Official Record of the Inquests on the Victims of the Race Riots of July and August 1919.* Cook Country Coronors Report, 1918–1919, Chicago.

Holli, Melvin G., and Peter d'A. Jones, eds. *The Ethnic Frontier: Essays in the History of Group Survival in Chicago and the Midwest.* Grand Rapids, Mich.: Eerdmans, 1977.

Hurh, Won Moo. *Assimilation Patterns of Immigrants in the United States: A Case Study of Korean Immigrants in Chicago.* Washington, D.C.: University Press of America, 1979.

Illinois Advisory Committee to the United States Commission on Civil Rights. *Police Protection of the African American Community in Chicago.* Illinois Advisory Committee to the United States Commission on Civil Rights, September 1993.

Joravsky, Ben, and Eduardo Camacho. *Race and Politics in Chicago.* Chicago: Community Renewal Society, 1987.

Keiser, Richard A. "Explaining African-American Political Empowerment: Windy City Politics from 1900 to 1983." *Urban Affairs Quarterly* 29 (September 1993): 84–116.

Kelly, Thomas J. "White Press/Black Man: An Analysis of the Editorial Opinions of the Four Chicago Daily Newspapers toward the Race Problem: 1954–1968." Ph.D diss., University of Illinois at Urbana, 1971.

Kleppner, Paul. *Chicago Divided: The Making of a Black Mayor.* DeKalb: Northern Illinois University Press, 1985.

Kolkowitz, Alex. *There Are No Children Here: The Story of Two Boys Growing Up in the Other America.* New York: Doubleday, 1991.

Leonard, Jonathan S. "The Interaction of Residential Segregation and Employment Discrimination." *Journal of Urban Economics* 21 (May 1987): 323–46.

Maynard, Micheline. "The Mayor for Life Packs the House, Posthumously." *New York Times*, March 26, 2006, Entertainment sec., p. 4.

Meyerson, Martin, and Edward Banfield. *Politics, Planning, and the Public Interest: The Case of Public Housing in Chicago.* Glencoe, Ill.: Free Press, 1955.

McHugh, John. "Too Much for 4,000 Firemen." *Chicago Daily News*, April 6, 1968, p. 5.

Molotch, Harvey. *Managed Integration: Dilemmas of Doing Good in the City.* Berkeley: University of California Press, 1972.

Morris, Norval, and Hans Mattick. "Criminal Justice in Extremis: Administration of Justice during the April 1968 Chicago Disorder," *University of Chicago Law Review* 36, no. 3 (spring 1969): 455–613.

Mosby, Donald. "Threats of Violence Hit City after News." *Chicago Defender*, April 6–12, 1968, pp. 1–2.

Newman, M. W. "Behind the Rioting, a Ghetto." *Chicago Daily News,* June 18, 1966.

O'Connor, Len. *Clout: Mayor Daley and His City.* Chicago: Regnery, 1975.

Ottensmann, John R., and Michael E. Gleeson. "The Movement of Whites and Blacks into Racially Mixed Neighborhoods: Chicago, 1960–1980." *Social Science Quarterly* 73 (September 1992): 645–62.

Pacyga, Dominick A. *Polish Immigrants and Industrial Chicago: Workers on the South Side, 1880–1922.* Columbus: Ohio State University Press, 1991.

Padilla, Felix M. *Latino Ethnic Consciousness: The Case of Mexican Americans and Puerto Ricans in Chicago.* Notre Dame, Ind.: University of Notre Dame Press, 1985.

Padilla, Felix M. *Puerto Rican Chicago.* Notre Dame, Ind.: University of Notre Dame Press, 1987.

Pattillo-McCoy, Mary. *Black Picket Fences: Privilege and Peril among the Black Middle Class.* Chicago: University of Chicago Press, 1999.

Perkins, Useni Eugene. *Explosion of Chicago's Black Street Gangs 1900 to the Present.* Chicago: Third World Press, 1987.

Philpott, Thomas Lee. *The Slum and the Ghetto: Neighborhood Deterioration and Middle Class Reform, Chicago, 1880–1930.* New York: Oxford University Press, 1978.

Pinderhughes, Diane M. *Race and Ethnicity in Chicago Politics: A Reexamination of Pluralist Theory.* Urbana: University of Illinois Press, 1987.

Polikoff, Alexander. *Housing the Poor: The Case for Heroism.* Cambridge, Mass.: Ballinger, 1978.

Ralph, James R., Jr. *Northern Protest: Martin Luther King, Jr., Chicago, and the Civil Rights Movement.* Cambridge, Mass.: Harvard University Press, 1993.

Reed, Adolph, Jr. "The Black Urban Regime: Structural Origins and Constraints." In *Power, Community and the City,* edited by M. P. Smith. Special issue, *Comparative Urban and Community Research* 1 (1988): 138–59.

Reed, Christopher Robert. "A Study of Black Politics and Protest in Depression-Decade Chicago: 1930–1939." Ph.D. diss., Kent State University, 1982.

Reed, Christopher Robert. "Black Chicago Political Realignment during the Great Depression and New Deal." *Illinois Historical Journal* 78 (1985): 242–56.

Ropka, Gerald William. *The Evolving Residential Pattern of the Mexican, Puerto Rican and Cuban Population in the City of Chicago.* New York: Arno Press, 1980.

Rosenfeld, Michael J. "Celebration, Politics, Selective Looting and Riots: A Micro Level Study of the Bulls Riot of 1992 in Chicago." *Social Problems* 44, no. 4 (November 1997): 483–502.

Rossi, Peter, and Robert Dentler. *The Politics of Urban Renewal: The Chicago Findings.* Glencoe, Ill.: Free Press of Glencoe, 1961.

Royko, Mike. *Boss: Richard J. Daley of Chicago.* 1st ed. New York: Dutton, 1971.

Seligman, Amanda. *Block by Block: Neighborhoods and Public Policy on Chicago's West Side.* Chicago: University of Chicago Press, 2006.

Skogan, Wesley G. *Chicago since 1840: A Time-Series Data Handbook.* Urbana: Institute of Government and Public Affairs, University of Illinois, 1976.

Skogan, Wesley G., and Susan M. Harnett. *Community Policing Chicago Style.* New York: Oxford University Press, 1997.

Skogan, Wesley G. *On the Beat: Police and Community Problem Solving*. Boulder, Colo.: Westview Press, 1999.

Skogan, Wesley G. *Police and Community in Chicago: A Tale of Three Cities*. New York: Oxford University Press, 2006.

Smith, Janet. "Cleaning Up Public Housing by Sweeping Out the Poor." *Habitat International* 23, no. 1 (1999):49–62.

Smith, Michael. "West Side Riot Area Rubble Is Gone but Not the Scars." *Chicago Tribune*, sec.1, pp. 1, 3.

Spear, Allan H. *Black Chicago: The Making of a Negro Ghetto, 1890–1920*. Chicago: University of Chicago Press, 1967.

Squires, Gregory D., Larry Bennett, Kathleen McCourt, and Philip Nyden. *Chicago: Race, Class, and the Response to Urban Decline*. Philadelphia: Temple University Press, 1987.

Street, Paul. "Race, Prison, and Poverty: The Race to Incarceration in the Age of Correctional Keynesianism." www.zmag.org/zmag//articles/may01street.htm.

Street, Paul. "The Vicious Circle: Race, Prison, Jobs and Community in Chicago, Illinois and the Nation." Chicago: Chicago Urban League, 2001.

Strong, James. "Letters Back Daley 15 to 1, Reilly Says." *Chicago Tribune*, April 19, 1968, p. 10.

Suttles, Gerald D. *The Social Order of the Slum: Ethnicity and Territory in the Inner City*. Chicago: University of Chicago Press, 1968.

Suttles, Gerald D. *The Man-Made City: The Land-Use Confidence Game in Chicago*. Chicago: University of Chicago Press, 1990.

Taub, Richard P., D. Garth Taylor, and Jan D. Dunham. *Paths of Neighborhood Change: Race and Crime in Urban America*. Chicago: University of Chicago Press, 1984.

Terry, Don. "Chicago Neighborhood Reveals an Ugly Side: Black Youth Badly Beaten in Bridgeport." *New York Times*, March 27, 1997, A18.

Theodore, Nikolas C., and D. Garth Taylor. *The Geography of Opportunity: The Status of African Americans in the Chicago Economy*. Chicago: Chicago Urban League, 1991.

Tuttle, William M., Jr. *Race Riot: Chicago in the Red Summer of 1919*. [1970] ; Reprint, Urbana: University of Illinois Press and Chicago: Illini Books, 1996.

U.S. Department of Commerce. Bureau of the Census. *Urban Atlas, Tract Data for Standard Metropolitan Statistical Areas—Chicago, Illinois*. Washington, D.C.: Government Printing Office, 1974.

Venkatesh, Sudhir, and Isil Celimli. "Tearing Down the Community." *Shelterforce Online*, no. 138 (November/December 2004). Available at www.nhi.org/online/issues/138/chicago.html.

Wacquant, Loic J. D. "The Ghetto, the State and the New Capitalist Economy." *Dissent* (Fall 1989): 508–20.

Wacquant, Loic J. D. "Three Pernicious Premises in the Study of the Ghetto." *International Journal of Urban and Regional Planning* 21, no. 2 (1997): 341–53.

Ward, Francis. "Daley Calls Off Curfew." *Chicago Sun-Times*, April 6, 1969.

Warren, Elizabeth. *Subsidized Housing in Chicago: A Spatial Survey and Analysis*. Chicago: Center for Urban Policy, Loyola University of Chicago, 1980.

Washington, Betty. "Uproar at First Memorial Rites for King." *Chicago Defender*, April 6–12, 1968, p. 22.

Washington, Robbin E., Jr. "The *Chicago Defender* and the *Chicago Tribune*'s Coverage of the West Side Riot of April 1968." Master's thesis, Governor State University, 1980.

Wille, Lois. "Ruins of 1968 Rioting Still a No-Man's Land." *Chicago Daily News*, March 28, 1969.

Zullo, Joseph. "New York's Mayor Opposes Daley's Police Get-Tough Order." N.s., nd. Unmarked clipping, in the collection on riots. Municipal Reference Library Vertical Files, now stored in the Harold Washington Chicago Public Library.

NEW YORK

Alers-Montalvo, Manuel. *The Puerto Rican Migrants of New York City: A Study of Anomie.* New York: AMS Press, 1985.

Amnesty International [New York]. "Police Brutality and Excessive Force in the New York City Police Department." New York: Amnesty International, June 1996.

Arian, Asher, Arthur Goldberg, John Mollenkopf, and Edward Rogosky. *Changing New York City Politics.* New York: Routledge, 1991.

Asinof, Eliot. *People vs. Blutcher; Black Men and White Law in Bedford-Stuyvesant.* New York: Viking Press, 1970.

Bailey, Thomas. "Black Employment Opportunities." In *Setting Municipal Priorities 1990*, edited by Charles Brecher and Raymond D. Horton. New York: New York University Press, 1989.

Bailey, Thomas, and Roger Waldinger. "The Changing Ethnic/Racial Division of Labor." In Mollenkopf and Castells, *Dual City*, pp. 43–78.

Bailey, Thomas, and Roger Waldinger. "A Skills Mismatch in New York's Labor Market?" *New York Affairs* 8, no. 4 (1984): 3–18.

Baker, Kevin. *Paradise Alley.* New York: HarperCollins, 2002.

Belluch, Jewel, and Dick Netzer. *Urban Politics New York Style.* London: M. E. Sharpe, 1990.

Benmayor, Rina, Rosa M. Torruellas, and Ana L. Juarbe. *Responses to Poverty among Puerto Rican Women: Identity, Community, and Cultural Citizenship.* New York: Centro de Estudios Puertorriquenos, Hunter College, 1992.

Bernstein, Blanche, and Arley Bondarin. *New York City's Population—1973; Socio-Economic Characteristics from the Current Population Survey.* New York: Center for New York City Affairs, New School for Social Research, 1974.

Bernstein, Iver. *The New York City Draft Riots: The Significance for American Society and Politics in the Age of Civil War.* Oxford: Oxford University Press, 1990.

Biondi, Martha. *To Stand and Fight: The Struggle for Civil Rights in Postwar New York City.* Cambridge, Mass.: Harvard University Press, 2003.

Black, Bertram J. *Our Welfare Needs; A Study of New York City and Its Boroughs, Showing the Social and Economic Factors Affecting Relative Need for Health and Welfare Services.* New York: Greater New York Fund, 1949.

Bogen, Elizabeth. New York City Department of City Planning. *Immigration in New York.* New York: Praeger, 1987.

Boggs, Vernon, Gerald Handel, Sylvia F. Fava, and contributors. *The Apple Sliced: Sociological Studies of New York City.* New York: Praeger, 1984.

Bonilla, Frank, and Andres Torres. *Latinos in a Changing Regional Economy: New York.* Unpublished paper. Centro de Estudios Puertorriques, Hunter College, New York, June 1989.

Bowen, William. "Atlas of New York City" for 2000. Series. Available at http://130.166.124.2/atlas.nyc/ny6_20.gif.

Brecher, Charles, and Raymond Horton, with Robert Cropf and Dean Michael Mead. *Power Failure: New York City Politics and Policy since 1960.* New York: Oxford University Press, 1993.

Brown, Claude. *Manchild in the Promised Land.* New York: Macmillan, 1965.

Capeci, Dominic J., Jr. *The Harlem Riot of 1943.* Philadelphia: Temple University Press, 1977.

Caro, Robert A. *The Power Broker: Robert Moses and the Fall of New York.* New York: Knopf, 1974.

Chen, Hsiang-Shui. *Chinatown No More: Taiwan Immigrants in Contemporary New York.* Ithaca, N.Y.: Cornell University Press, 1992.

Chenault, Lawrence. *The Puerto Rican Migrant in New York City.* New York: Columbia University Press, 1938.

Clark, Kenneth Bancroft. *Dark Ghetto; Dilemmas of Social Power.* New York: Harper and Row Torchbook, 1967.

Clark, Kenneth Bancroft. "Group Violence: A Preliminary Study of the Attitudinal Patterns of Its Acceptance and Rejection: A Study of the 1943 Harlem Riot." *Journal of Social Psychology* 19 (May 1944): 319–37.

Clarke, John Hendrik, ed. *Harlem, U.S.A.* New York: Collier Books, rev. ed., 1971.

Clarke, John Hendrik, ed. *Harlem: A Community in Transition.* New York: Citadel Press, 1964.

Collins, Judith. *All Is Never Said: The Narrative of Odette Harper Hines.* Philadelphia: Temple University Press, 1995.

Connolly, Harold X. *A Ghetto Grows in Brooklyn.* New York: New York University Press, 1977.

Dugger, Celia. "City of Immigrants Becoming More So in 1990s." *New York Times,* January 9, 1997, pp. 1, B6.

Earley, Brian F. "Puerto Ricans in the New York City Labor Market, 1970: A Structural Analysis." Ph.D. diss., Fordham University, 1980.

Edwin, Ed, and Neal Hickey. *Adam Clayton Powell and the Politics of Race.* New York: Fleet, 1965.

Ellis, Arthur L. *A Mind on Harlem.* San Francisco: R and E Research Associates, 1978.

Etzkowitz, Henry, and Gerald M. Schaflander. *Ghetto Crisis: Riots or Reconciliation?* Boston: Little, Brown, 1969.

Fanelli, Vincent. *The Human Face of Poverty.* New York: Bootstrap Press, 1990.

Flamm, Michael W. "New York's Night of Birmingham Horror: The NYPD, the Harlem Riot of 1964, and the Politics of Law and Order." In *Patterns of Provocation: Police and Public Disorder,* edited by Richard Bessel and Clive Emsley. New York: Berghahn Books, 2000, pp. 81–98.

Foner, Nancy, ed. *New Immigrants in New York.* New York: Columbia University Press, 1987.

Frazier, E. Franklin. "Negro Harlem: An Ecological Study." *American Journal of Sociology* 43 (July 1937): 72–88.

Freidenberg, Judith, ed. *The Anthropology of Lower Income Urban Enclaves: The Case of East Harlem.* New York: New York Academy of Sciences, 1995.

Garrett, Charles. *The La Guardia Years: Machine and Reform Politics in New York City.* New Brunswick, N.J.: Rutgers University Press, 1961.

Gelernter, David. *1939: The Lost World Fair.* New York: Free Press, 1995.

Glazer, Nathan, and Daniel P. Moynihan. *Beyond the Melting Pot: Negroes, Puerto Ricans, Jews, Italians and Irish of New York City.* Cambridge, Mass.: MIT Press, 1963.

Green, Charles, and Basil Wilson. *The Struggle for Black Empowerment in New York City: Beyond the Politics of Pigmentation.* New York: Praeger, 1980.

Greenberg, Cheryl. "The Politics of Disorder: Reexamining Harlem's Riots of 1935 and 1943." *Journal of Urban History* 18 (August 1992): 395–440.

Gurock, Jeffrey S. *When Harlem was Jewish, 1870–1930.* New York: Columbia University Press, 1979.

Halstead, Fred, Anthony Aviles, and Don Charles. *Harlem Stirs.* New York: Marzani and Mubsell, 1966.

Handlin, Oscar. *The Newcomers: Negroes and Puerto Ricans in a Changing Metropolis.* Cambridge, Mass.: Harvard University Press, 1959.

Harlem Urban Development Corporation. *A Report to the Department of Housing and Urban Development.* New York: Harlem Urban Development Corporation, 1976.

Harlem Youth Opportunities Unlimited (HARYOU). *Youth in the Ghetto; A Study of the Consequences of Powerlessness and a Blueprint for Change.* New York: HARYOU, 1964.

Harris, Louis, and Bert Swansin. *Black-Jewish Relations in New York City.* New York: Praeger, 1970.

Jackson, Anthony. *A Place Called Home: A History of Low Cost Housing in Manhattan.* Cambridge, Mass.: MIT Press, 1976.

Jackson, Kenneth, ed. *The Encyclopedia of New York City.* New Haven: Yale University Press, 1995.

Johnson, James Weldon. *Black Manhattan.* New York: Knopf, 1930.

Johnson, Marilynn. *Street Justice: A History of Police Violence in New York City.* Boston: Beacon Press, 2003.

Jonnes, Jill. *We're Still Here: The Rise, Fall, and Resurrection of the South Bronx.* Boston: Atlantic Monthly Press, 1986.

Kantrowitz, Nathan. *Ethnic and Racial Segregation in the New York Metropolis: Residential Patterns among White Ethnic Groups, Blacks, and Puerto Ricans.* New York: Praeger, 1973.

Kasinitz, Philip. *Caribbean New York: Black Immigrants and the Politics of Race.* Ithaca, N.Y.: Cornell University Press, 1992.

Kessner, Thomas. *Fiorello H. La Guardia and the Making of Modern New York.* New York: McGraw-Hill, 1989.

Kim, Claire Jean. "Cracks in the Gorgeous Mosaic: Black-Korean Conflict and Racial Mobilization in New York City." Ph.D. diss., Yale University, 1996. Subsequently published as *Bitter Fruit: The Politics of Black-Korean Conflict in New York City.* New Haven: Yale University Press, 2000. Page references are to the dissertation unless otherwise noted.

Kim, Ilsoo. *New Urban Immigrants: The Korean Community in New York.* Princeton, N.J.: Princeton University Press, 1981.

Kinkead, Gwen. *Chinatown: A Portrait of a Closed Society.* New York: HarperCollins, 1992.

Korrol, Virginia Sanchez. *From Colonia to Community: The History of Puerto Ricans in New York City, 1917–1948.* Westport, Conn.: Greenwood Press, 1983.

Kwong, Peter. *The New Chinatown.* New York: Hill and Wang, 1987.

Lewis, David Levering. *When Harlem Was in Vogue.* Oxford: Oxford University Press, 1979.

Lewis, Oscar. *La Vida: A Puerto Rican Family in the Culture of Poverty—San Juan and New York.* New York: Random House, 1966.

Mann, Arthur. *La Guardia: A Fighter against His Times, 1882–1933.* New York: Lippincott, 1959.

Mann, Arthur. *La Guardia Comes to Power: 1933.* New York: Lippincott, 1965.

Manoni, Mary H. *Bedford-Stuyvesant: The Anatomy of a Central City Community.* New York: Quadrangle, 1973.

Marcuse, Peter. "The Beginnings of Public Housing in New York." *Journal of Urban History* 12 (August 1986): 353–90.

"Memories of My Queens." *New York Times,* September 3, 1995, pp. 1, 10.

McKay, Claude. *Harlem: Negro Metropolis.* New York: Dutton, 1940.

Mele, Christopher. "Neighborhood Burn-Out: Puerto Ricans at the End of the Queue." In *From Urban Village to East Village,* edited by Janet Abu-Lughod. Oxford: Blackwell, 1994, pp. 117–47.

Model, Suzanne. "A Comparative Perspective on the Ethnic Enclave: Blacks, Italians and Jews in New York City." *International Migration Review* 19 (1985): 64–81.

Mollenkopf, John. *New York City in the 1980s: A Social, Economic, and Political Atlas.* New York: Simon and Schuster, 1993.

Mollenkopf, John. "New York: The Great Anomaly." In *Racial Politics in American Cities,* edited by R. Browning, D. Marshall, and D. Tabb. New York: Longman, 1990.

Mollenkopf, John. *A Phoenix in the Ashes: The Rise and Fall of the Koch Coalition in New York City.* Princeton, N.J.: Princeton University Press, 1992.

Mollenkopf, John, and Manuel Castells, eds. *Dual City: Restructuring New York.* New York: Russell Sage Foundation, 1991.

Moss, Frank. *Persecution of Negroes by Roughs and Policemen, in the City of New York, August, 1900: Statement and Proofs.* New York: Citizens' Protective League, 1900.

Naison, Mark. "From Eviction Resistance to Rent Control: Tenant Activism in the Great Depression." In *The Tenant Movement in New York City, 1904–1984,* edited by Ronald Lawson. New Brunswick, N.J.: Rutgers University Press, 1986, pp. 94–133.

Nelson, Truman. *The Torture of Mothers.* With notes provided by Junius Griffin. Newburyport, Mass.: Garrison Press, 1965.

New York City Department of City Planning. *The Newest New Yorkers: An Analysis of Immigration in New York City during the 1980s.* 2 vols. New York: New York City Department of City Planning, 1992.

New York City Department of City Planning. *The Newest New Yorkers 1990–1994: An Analysis of Immigration to New York City in the Early 1990s.* New York: New York City Department of City Planning, 1997.

New York City Housing Authority. *Project Data: January 1, 1989.* New York: New York City Housing Authority, 1989.

New York City Mayor's Commission on Black New Yorkers. William R. Howard (commission chairman). *The Report of the Mayor's Commission on Black New Yorkers.* New York: New York City Mayor's Commission on Black New Yorkers, 1988.

New York City Mayor's Committee on Puerto Rican Affairs in New York City. *Interim Report of the Mayor's Committee on Puerto Rican Affairs in New York City.* New York: New York City Mayor's Committee on Puerto Rican Affairs in New York City, 1953.

New York City Youth Board, Research Department. *Indices of Social Problems: Selected Socio-Economic Characteristics of New York City by Borough and Health Area.* New York: New York City Youth Board, 1960.

Orlansky, Harold. "The Harlem Riot: A Study in Mass Frustration." Social analysis report no. 1. New York, 1943.

Osofsky, Gilbert. *Harlem: The Making of a Ghetto, Negro New York, 1890–1930.* 2nd ed. 1963; reprint, New York: Harper Torchbooks, 1971.

Osofsky, Gilbert. "The Enduring Ghetto." *Journal of American History* 55 (September 1968): 243–55.

Ottley, Roi, and William J. Weatherby, eds. *The Negro in New York: An Informal Social History.* (A WPA Writers' Project publication.) Dobbs Ferry, N.Y.: Oceana, 1967; reprint, New York: Praeger, 1969.

Ovington, Mary White. *Half a Man: The Status of the Negro in New York.* New York: Longmans, Green, 1911.

Pencak, William, Selma Berrol, and Randall M. Miller, eds. *Immigration to New York.* London: Associated University Presses, 1991.

Pinderhughes, Howard. *Race in the Hood: Conflict and Violence among Urban Youth.* Minneapolis: University of Minnesota Press, 1997.

Pinkney, Alphonso, and Roger R. Woock. *Poverty and Politics in Harlem: Report on Project Uplift 1965.* New Haven, Conn.: College and University Press, 1970.

Podair, Jerald E. *The Strike That Changed New York: Blacks, Whites, and the Ocean Hill–Brownsville Crisis.* New Haven, Conn.: Yale University Press, 2002.

Rieder, Jonathan. *Canarsie: The Jews and Italians of Brooklyn Against Liberalism.* Cambridge, Mass.: Harvard University Press, 1985.

Rosenberg, Terry J. *Residence, Employment, and Mobility of Puerto Ricans in New York City.* Research paper no. 151. Chicago: Department of Geography, University of Chicago, 1974.

Rosenberg, Terry J. *Poverty in New York City, 1993: An Update.* New York: Community Service Society, 1994.

Rosenberg, Terry J., and Robert W. Lake. "Toward a Revised Model of Residential Segregation and Succession: Puerto Ricans in New York, 1960–1970." *American Journal of Sociology* 81 (March 1976): 1142–50.

Rosenwaike, Ira. *Population History of New York City.* Syracuse, N.Y.: Syracuse University Press, 1972.

Schneider, Moses David. *The History of Public Welfare in New York State.* Chicago: University of Chicago Press, 1938–41. Reprint, Montclair, N.J.: Patterson Smith, 1969.

Schneider, Moses David, and Albert Deutsch. *The Road Upward: Three Hundred Years of Public Welfare in New York State.* Albany: New York State Department of Social Welfare, 1939.

Schwartz, Joel. *The New York Approach: Robert Moses, Urban Liberals, and Redevelopment of the Inner City.* Columbus: Ohio State University Press, 1993.

Sexton, Patricia Cayo. *Spanish Harlem: An Anatomy of Poverty.* New York: Harper and Row, 1965.

Shapiro, Fred C., and James W. Sullivan. *Race Riots: New York 1964.* New York: Crowell, 1969.

Silverstein, Barry, and Ronald Krate. *Children of the Dark Ghetto: A Developmental Psychology.* New York: Praeger, 1975.

Simon, Arthur. *Stuyvesant Town, U.S.A.: Pattern for Two Americas.* New York: New York University Press, 1970.

Sorin, Gerald. *The Nurturing Neighborhood: The Brownsville Boys Club and Jewish Community in Urban America, 1940–1990.* New York: New York University Press, 1990.

Spencer, Joseph. "New York City Tenant Organization and the Post-World War I Housing Crisis." In *The Tenant Movement in New York City, 1904–1984,* edited by Ronald Lawson. New Brunswick, N.J.: Rutgers University Press, 1986, pp. 51–93.

Sutton, Constance R., and Elsa M. Chaney, eds. *Caribbean Life in New York City: Sociocultural Dimensions.* New York: Center for Migration Studies, 1987.

Swan, L. Alex. "The Harlem and Detroit Riots of 1943: A Comparative Analysis." *Berkeley Journal of Sociology* 16 (1971–72): 75–93.

Tobier, Emanuel. *The Changing Face of Poverty: Trends in New York City's Population in Poverty, 1960–1990.* New York: Community Service Society of New York, 1984.

United States Commission on Civil Rights. New York State Advisory Committee. *Asian Americans, An Agenda for Action: A Conference Summary.* Summary report prepared by the New York State Advisory Committee to the United States Commission on Civil Rights. Washington, D.C.: United States Commission on Civil Rights, 1980.

United States Commission on Civil Rights. New York State Advisory Committee. *Documented and Undocumented Persons in New York City.* Report of the New York State Advisory Committee to the U.S. Commission on Civil Rights. Washington, D.C.: United States Commission on Civil Rights, 1982.

United States Commission on Civil Rights. *Hearing before the United States Commission on Civil Rights Held in New York, New York, February 14–15, 1972.* Washington, D.C.: Government Printing Office, 1973.

United States Commission on Civil Rights. New York State Advisory Committee. *The Forgotten Minority: Asian Americans in New York City.* Report prepared by the New York State Advisory Committee to the U.S. Commission on Civil Rights. Washington, D. C: U.S. Commission on Civil Rights, 1977.

Wagner, Peter. "Importing Constituents: Prisoners and Political Clout in New York: A Prison Policy Initiative Report." Available at www.prisonpolicy.org/importing/importing.shtml.

Wakefield, Dan. *Island in the City: The World of Spanish Harlem.* New York: Arno Press, 1975.

Waldinger, Roger. *Still the Promised Land? New Immigrants and African-Americans in New York, 1940–1990.* Cambridge, Mass.: Harvard University Press, 1996.

Welfare Council of New York City. *An Impressionistic View of the Winter of 1930–31 in New York City.* New York: Welfare Council of New York City, 1932.

Welfare Council of New York City. Committee on Puerto Ricans in New York City. *Puerto Ricans in New York City: The Report of the Committee on Puerto Ricans in New York City of the Welfare Council of New York City,* 1948; reprint, New York: Arno Press, 1975.

Welfare Council of New York City. Central Harlem Street Clubs Project. *Working with Teen-Age Gangs: A Report on the Central Harlem Street Clubs Project.* New York: Welfare Council, 1950.

Wilson, Sherrill D. *New York City's African Slaveowners: A Social and Material Culture History.* New York: Garland, 1994.

Windhoff-Heritier, Adrienne. *City of the Poor, City of the Rich: Politics and Policy in New York City.* Berlin: de Gruyter, 1992.

The WPA Guide to New York City. Originally published 1939; reprint, New York: Pantheon, 1982.

Los Angeles

Abelmann, Nancy, and John Lie. *Blue Dreams: Korean Americans and the Los Angeles Riots.* Cambridge, Mass.: Harvard University Press, 1995.

Abrams, Charles. "Rats among the Palm Trees." *Nation,* February 25, 1970.

Abudu, Margaret J. G., et al. *Black Ghetto Violence: A Case Study Inquiry into the Spatial Pattern of Four Los Angeles Riot Event-Types.* Long Beach, Calif., 1972.

Acuna, Rodolpho. *A Community under Siege: A Chronicle of Chicanos East of the Los Angeles River, 1945–1975.* Los Angeles: Monograph 11, UCLA; Chicano Studies Research Center, 1984.

Aguilar-San Juan, Karin, ed. *The State of Asian America: Activism and Resistance in the 1990s.* Boston: South End Press, 1994.

Allen, J. P., and E. Turner. "The Most Ethnically Diverse Urban Places in the United States." *Urban Geography* 10 (1989): 523–39.

Almaguer, Tomás. *Racial Fault Lines: The Historical Origins of White Supremacy in California.* Berkeley: University of California Press, 1994.

American Civil Liberties Union. Southern California Branch. *Day of Protest, Night of Violence, the Century City Peace March: A Report.* Los Angeles: Sawyer Press, 1967.

Anderson, Stuart, et al. *An Atlas of South-Central Los Angeles.* Claremont, Calif.: Rose Institute of State and Local Government, Claremont McKenna College, 1992.

Baldassare, Mark, ed. *The Los Angeles Riots: Lessons for the Urban Future.* Boulder, Colo.: Westview Press, 1994.

Bergesen, Albert, and Max A. Herman. "Immigration, Race and Riot: The 1992 Los Angeles Uprising." *American Sociological Review* 63, no. 1 (February 1998): 39–54.

Bobo, Lawrence D., et al. "Public Opinion before and after a Spring of Discontent." Occasional working paper series, vol. 3. Los Angeles: Center for Studies of Urban Poverty, UCLA, 1992.

Bobo, Lawrence D., Camille L. Zubrinsky, James Johnson, Jr., and Melvin Oliver. "Public Opinion before and after a Spring of Discontent." In Baldassare, *The Los Angeles Riots,* 103–33.

Bobo, Lawrence D., Melvin Oliver, James Johnson Jr., and Abel Valenzuela, Jr. *Prismatic Metropolis: Inequality in Los Angeles*. New York: Russell Sage Foundation, 2000.

Bond, Max J. "The Negro in Los Angeles." Ph.D diss., University of Southern California, 1936. Later published as *The Negro in Los Angeles*, San Francisco, Calif: R and E Research Associates, 1972.

Broder, John M. "A Black-Latino Coalition Emerges in Los Angeles." *New York Times*, April 24, 2005, pp. 24, 32.

Bruck, Connie. "Fault Lines" [A profile of Mayor Antonio Villaraigosa]. *The New Yorker*. May 21, 2007: 44–55.

Bullock, Paul. *Watts: The Aftermath; An Inside View of the Ghetto, by the People of Watts*. New York: Grove Press, 1969.

California Citizens Committee on Civil Disturbances in Los Angeles. *Report and Recommendations of Citizens Committee*. Los Angeles: California Citizens Committee on Civil Disturbances in Los Angeles, 1943.

California Department of Industrial Relations, Division of Labor Statistics and Research. *Negroes and Mexican Americans in South and East Los Angeles: Changes between 1960 and 1965 in Population, Employment, Income and Family Status*. Microform. San Francisco: State of California, Division of Fair Employment Practices, 1966.

California Governor's Commission on the Los Angeles Riots. *Staff Report of Actions Taken to Implement the Recommendations in the Commission's Report: Status Report 2*. Los Angeles: California Governor's Commission on the Los Angeles Riots, 1967.

Cannon, Lou. *Official Negligence: How Rodney King and the Riots Changed Los Angeles and the LAPD*. New York: Times Books, 1997.

CBS News. "CBS Reports; Watts: Riot or Revolt?" Television broadcast, December 7, 1965.

Cohen, Nathan, ed. *The Los Angeles Riots: A Socio-Psychological Study*. Published in cooperation with the Institute of Government and Public Affairs, UCLA. New York: Praeger, 1970.

Cohen, Nathan. "The Context of the Curfew Area." In Cohen, *The Los Angeles Riots*, chap. 1.

Collins, Keith. *Black Los Angeles: The Maturing of a Ghetto*. Saratoga, Calif.: Century Twenty One, 1980.

Conot, Robert. *Rivers of Blood, Years of Darkness*. New York: Bantam Books, 1967. Reprint, 1973. Page references are to the 1973 reprint.

Crigler, William Robert. "The Employment Status of Blacks in Los Angeles: Ten Years after the Kerner Commission Report." Ph.D. diss., Claremont Graduate School, 1979.

Crump, Spencer. *Black Riot in Los Angeles: The Story of the Watts Tragedy*. Los Angeles: Trans-Anglo Books, 1966.

Davis, Mike. *City of Quartz: Excavating the Future in Los Angeles*. New York: Vintage Books, 1992.

Davis, Mike. "Fortress LA: The Militarization of Urban Space." In *Variations on a Theme Park*, edited by Michael Sorkin. New York: Noonday Press, 1992, pp. 154–80.

Davis, Mike. "Who Killed LA? A Political Autopsy." *New Left Review* 197 (January/February 1993).

Davis, Mike. *The Ecology of Fear: Los Angeles and the Imagination of Disaster*. New York: Holt, 1998.

De Graaf, Lawrence Brooks. "The City of Black Angels: Emergence of the Los Angeles Ghetto, 1890–1930." *Pacific Historical Review* 39 (1970): 323–52.

Erie, Steven. "The Local State and Economic Growth in Los Angeles, 1880–1932." *Urban Affairs Quarterly* 27, no. 4 (1992): 519–54.

Fogelson, Robert. *The Fragmented Metropolis.* Cambridge, Mass.: Harvard University Press, 1967.

Fogelson, Robert. *White on Black: A Critique of the McCone Commission Report on the Los Angeles Riots.* Privately printed, n.d, n.p.

Ford, Richard T. "Urban Spaces and the Color Line: The Consequences of Demarcation and Disorientation in the Postmodern Metropolis." *Harvard Black Law Journal* 9 (spring 1992): 117–47.

Freer, Regina. "Black-Korean Conflict." In Baldassare, *The Los Angeles Riots,* pp. 175–203.

Fukurai, Hiroshi, Richard Krooth, and Edgar W. Butler. "The Rodney King Beating Verdicts." In Baldassare, *The Los Angeles Riots,* pp. 73–102.

Georges, Kathi, and Jennifer Joseph, eds. *The Verdict Is In.* San Francisco: Manic D. Press, 1992.

Gooding-Williams, Robert, ed. *Reading Rodney King/Reading Urban Uprising.* New York: Routledge, 1993.

Hazen, Don, ed. *Inside the L.A. Riots: What Really Happened, and Why It Will Happen Again.* New York: Institute for Alternative Journalism, 1992.

Hoffman, Abraham. *Unwanted Mexican Americans in the Great Depression: Repatriation Pressures, 1929–1939.* Tucson: University of Arizona Press, 1974.

Horne, Gerald. *Fire This Time: The Watts Uprising and the 1960s.* Charlottesville, Va.: University Press of Virginia, 1975; reprint with epilogue, New York: Da Capo Press, 1997.

Hubler, Shawn. "South L.A.'s Poverty Rate Worse Than '65." *Los Angeles Times,* May 11, 1992, pp. A1, A22.

Hunt, Darnell M. *Screening the Los Angeles "Riots": Race, Seeing and Resistance.* Cambridge: Cambridge University Press, 1966.

Jackson, Maria-Rosario, James Johnson, Jr., and Walter C. Farrell, Jr. "After the Smoke Has Cleared: An Analysis of Selected Responses to the Los Angeles Civil Unrest of 1992." *Contention* series (mimeograph), June 1993.

Johnson, J. H., Jr., and W. C. Farrell, Jr. "The Fire This Time: The Genesis of the Los Angeles Rebellion of 1992." *North Carolina Law Review* 71 (1993): 1403–20.

Johnson, J. H., Jr., W. C. Farrell, Jr., and M. L. Oliver. "Seeds of the Los Angeles Rebellion of 1992." *International Journal of Urban and Regional Research* 17 (1993): 115–19.

Johnson, J. H., Jr., and M. L. Oliver. "Inter-ethnic Minority Conflict in Urban America: The Effects of Economic and Social Dislocations." *Urban Geography* 10 (1989): 449–64.

Johnson, J. H., Jr., and Melvin Oliver. "Economic Restructuring and Black Male Joblessness: A Reassessment." In *Urban Labor Markets and Job Opportunity,* edited by G. Peterson and W. Vroman. Washington, D.C.: Urban Institute Press, 1992.

Johnson, J. H., Jr., et al. "The Los Angeles Rebellion of 1992: A Retrospective View." *Economic Development Quarterly* 6 (1992): 356–72.

Johnson, J. H., Jr., et al. *First Status Report on the Center for the Study of Urban Poverty's Evaluation of Responses to the Los Angeles Civil Unrest of 1992.* Los Angeles: Center for the Study of Urban Poverty, UCLA, 1993.

Johnson, James H., Jr., Walter C. Farrell, Jr., and Jennifer A. Stoloff. "African American Males in Decline: A Los Angeles Case Study." In Bobo et al., *Prismatic Metropolis*, pp. 315–37.

Katz, Cindi, and Neil Smith. "L.A. Intifada: Interview with Mike Davis." *Social Text* 33 (1992): 19–33.

Kennedy, J. Michael. "Overview." In *Images of the 1994 Los Angeles Earthquake by the Staff of the Los Angeles Times*. Los Angeles: Times Mirror, 1994.

Kotkin, J., and D. Friedman. *The Los Angeles Riots: Causes, Myths and Solutions*. Washington, D.C.: Progressive Policy Institute, 1993.

LA Is Burning: Five Reports from a Divided City. Television broadcast, WGBH Educational Foundation, PBS, 1993. (Video disc available from PBS.)

Lichter, Michael, and Melvin Oliver. "Racial Differences in Labor Force Participation and Long-Term Joblessness among Less-Educated Men." In Bobo et al., *Prismatic Metropolis*, pp. 240–48.

Los Angeles City Planning Department, Research Section. *Race/Ethnicity in the City of Los Angeles as of April 1990: A Report*. Los Angeles: Los Angeles City Planning Department, 1991.

Los Angeles County, Commission on Human Relations, and Los Angeles City, Human Relations Commission, Joint Commissions on the Public Hearings. *McCone Revisited: A Focus on Solutions to Continuing Problems in South Central Los Angeles*. Mimeograph report, Los Angeles, 1985.

Los Angeles Times. *Understanding the Riots: Los Angeles before and after the Rodney King Case*. Los Angeles: Los Angeles Times, 1992.

Los Angeles Weekly. Special issue, May 8–14, 1992, devoted to the riot.

Madhubuti, Haki R., ed. *Why L.A. Happened: Implications of the '92 Los Angeles Rebellion*. Chicago: Third World Press, 1993.

Maharidge, Dale. *The Coming White Minority: California's Eruptions and the Nation's Future*. New York: Times Books, 1996.

Marin, Marguerite V. *Social Protest in an Urban Barrio: A Study of the Chicano Movement, 1966–1974*. Lanham, Md.: University Presses of America, 1991.

Marks, Mara A., Matt A. Barreto, and Nathan D. Woods. "Race and Racial Attitudes a Decade after the 1992 Los Angeles Riots." *Urban Affairs Review* 40, no. 1 (2004): 3–18.

Massey, Douglas, and B. Mullan. "Processes of Hispanic and Black Spatial Assimilation." *American Journal of Sociology* 89 (1984): 836–73.

Matheson, Victor, and Robert Baade. "Race Riots: A Note on the Economic Impact of the Rodney King Riots." *Urban Studies* 41, no. 13 (December 2004): 2691–96.

Mazon, Mauricio. *The Zoot-Suit Riots: The Psychology of Symbolic Annihilation*. Austin: University of Texas Press, 1984.

McWilliams, Carey. *Southern California Country: An Island on the Land*. New York: Duell, Sloan and Pearce, 1946. Reprint, *Southern California: An Island on the Land*, Salt Lake City: Peregrine Smith, 1990.

McWilliams, Carey. "Getting Rid of the Mexican." *American Mercury* 28 (March 1933).

Morales, Armando. *Ando Sangrando! (I am Bleeding): A Study of Mexican American–Police Conflict*. Distributed by the Congress of Mexican American Unity, Task Force on Police-Community Relations, 1971. La Puente, Calif.: Perspectiva, 1972.

Morrison, Peter A., and Ira S. Lowry. "A Riot of Color: The Demographic Setting." In Baldassare, *The Los Angeles Riots*, pp. 19–46.

Morriss, Richard T., and Vincent Jeffries. "The White Reaction Study." In Cohen, *The Los Angeles Riots*, pp. 480–560, 601.

Murphy, Raymond J., and James W. Watson. "The Structure of Discontent: Relationship between Social Structure, Grievance and Riot Support." In Cohen, *The Los Angeles Riots*, pp. 140–257.

Nelson, Howard, and William Clark. *Los Angeles: The Metropolitan Experience*. Cambridge, Mass.: Ballinger 1976.

Nelson, Howard. *The Los Angeles Metropolis*. Dubuque, Iowa: Kendall Hunt, 1983.

Oberschall, Anthony. "The Los Angeles Riot of August, 1965." *Social Problems* 15 (winter 1968): 322–41.

Oliver, Melvin L., and James H. Johnson, Jr. "Inter-ethnic Conflict in an Urban Ghetto: The Case of Blacks and Latinos in Los Angeles." *Research in Social Movements, Conflict and Change* 6 (1984): 57–94.

Oliver, Melvin, James Johnson, Jr., and Walter Farrell, Jr. "Anatomy of a Rebellion: A Political-Economic Analysis." In Gooding-Williams, *Reading Rodney King/Reading Urban Uprising*, pp. 117–39.

Ong, Paul, and Suzanne Hee. *Losses in the Los Angeles Civil Unrest, April 29–May 1, 1992: Lists of Damaged Properties and the L.A. Riot/Rebellion and Korean Merchants*. Los Angeles: UCLA, Center for Pacific Rim Studies, 1993.

Parson, Donald Craig. "The Development of Redevelopment: Housing and Urban Renewal in Los Angeles." *International Journal of Urban and Regional Research* 6 (1982): 393–413.

Parson, Donald Craig. "Urban Politics during the Cold War: Public Housing, Urban Renewal and Suburbanization in Los Angeles." Ph.D. diss., University of California at Los Angeles, 1985.

Price, Kendall O., et al. *A Critique of the Governor's Commission on the Los Angeles Riot*. Inglewood, Calif.: Public Executive Development and Research, 1967.

Rabinowitz, Francine. "Minorities in the Suburbs: The Los Angeles Experience." Working paper no. 31. Cambridge, Mass.: MIT Harvard Joint Center for Urban Studies, 1975.

Raine, Walter J. *Los Angeles Riot Study: The Perception of Police Brutality in South Central Los Angeles*. Los Angeles: Institute of Government and Public Affairs, UCLA, 1967.

Ransford, H. Edward. "Isolation, Powerlessness and Violence: A Study of Attitudes and Participation in the Watts Riot." *American Journal of Sociology* 73 (March 1968): 581–91.

Ridenour, Ron, Anne Leslie, and Victor Oliver. *The Fire This Time: The W. E. B. Du Bois Clubs View of the Explosion in South Los Angeles*. Los Angeles, Calif.: W. E. B. Du Bois Clubs, 1965.

Romo, Richard. *East Los Angeles: History of a Barrio*. Austin: University of Texas Press, 1983.

Rossa, Della. *Why Watts Exploded: How the Ghetto Fought Back*. New York: Merrit, 1969.

Salak, John. *The Los Angeles Riots: American Cities in Crisis*. Brookfield, Conn.: Millbrook Press, 1993.

Sanchez, George J. *Becoming Mexican American: Ethnicity, Culture and Identity in Chicano Los Angeles, 1900–1943*. New York: Oxford University Press, 1993.

Sears, David O. "Black-White Conflict: A Model for the Future of Ethnic Politics in Los Angeles." In Halle, *New York and Los Angeles*, pp. 367–89.

Sears, David O., and John B. McConahay. *The Politics of Violence: The New Urban Blacks and the Watts Riot*. Boston: Houghton Mifflin, 1973.

Sears, David O., and T. M. Tomlinson. "Riot Ideology in Los Angeles: A Study of Negro Attitudes." *Social Science Quarterly* 49 (December 1968): 485–503.

Skerry, Peter. *Mexican Americans: The Ambivalent Minority*. Cambridge, Mass.: Harvard University Press, 1993.

Smith, Anna Deavere. *Twilight Los Angeles*. Available on videocassette. New York: Twilight 1999. Distributed by PBS Home Video, Alexandria, Va.

Sonenshein, Raphael J. *Politics in Black and White: Race and Power in Los Angeles*. Princeton, N.J.: Princeton University Press, 1993.

Starr, Kevin. *Material Dreams: Southern California through the 1920s*. New York: Oxford University Press, 1990.

Stern, James. "What Is Made of Broken Promises." *New York Times*, October 13, 1996, sec. 4, pp. 1, 5.

Tomlinson, T. M., and Diana L. Tenllouten. "Methods and Sampling." In Cohen, *The Los Angeles Riots*, pp. 127–39.

Tucker, M. Belinda, et al. *Ethnic Groups in Los Angeles: Quality of Life Indicators*. Los Angeles: Ethnic Studies Center, UCLA, 1987.

Turner, Eugene, and James Allen. *An Atlas of Population Patterns in the Metropolitan Los Angeles and Orange Counties 1990*. Northridge, Calif.: Department of Geography, California State University, 1991.

Tyler, Bruce M. "The Watts Riot and the Watts Summer Festival." *Journal of Kentucky Studies* (September 1968): 76–95.

U.S. Department of Commerce, Bureau of Census. *Special Census Survey of the South and East Los Angeles Areas, November 1965*. Washington, D.C.: Government Printing Office, 1965.

Useem, Burt. "The State and Collective Disorders: The Los Angeles Riot/Protest of April 1992." *Social Forces* 76 (1997): 357–77.

Vigil, James Diego. *Barrio Gangs: Street Life and Identity in Southern California*. Austin: University of Texas Press, 1988.

Waldinger, Roger, and Mehdi Bozorgmehr, eds. *Ethnic Los Angeles*. New York: Russell Sage Foundation Press, 1997.

Watts, 1980—Fifteen Years after the Riot: A Series of Articles Reprinted from the Los Angeles Times. Los Angeles: Los Angeles Times, 1980.

Williams, Dorothy S. "Ecology of Negro Communities in Los Angeles County: 1940–1959." Ph.D. diss., University of California at Berkeley, 1961.

Yu, Eui-Young, Earl H. Phillips, and Eun Sik Yang, eds. *Koreans in Los Angeles: Prospects and Promises*. Los Angeles: Center for Korean-American and Korean Studies, California State University, 1982.